EVANGELICALS
IN THE
CHURCH OF
ENGLAND

1734 ~ 1984

EVANGELICALS
IN THE
CHURCH OF
ENGLAND

—

1734~1984

Kenneth Hylson-Smith

—

T. & T. Clark
Edinburgh

Copyright © T. & T. Clark Ltd, 1988

Typeset by Bookworm Typesetting Ltd, Edinburgh
Printed and bound by Billings & Sons Ltd, Worcester

for

T. & T. CLARK LTD
59 George Street, Edinburgh EH2 2LQ

First printed in 1989

British Library Cataloguing in Publication Data
Hylson-Smith, Kenneth
Evangelicals in the Church of England 1734–1984
1. Church of England, Evangelicalism, 1734–1984
I. Title
283'.42

ISBN 0-567-09454-5 (cased)
ISBN 0-567-29161-8 (paperback)

Contents

Preface

Evangelicalism in the Church of England is an integral and important element in the English heritage. It is intricately woven into the fabric of the country's history. It has been the faith of countless men and women, many of whom have exercised a great and lasting influence in various ways; and it has been of crucial significance as a factor in determining the distinctive English character. Without an appreciation and understanding of the nature and history of Evangelicalism in the Church of England much of English church history will be misunderstood.

Although the Evangelicals may trace their history back to the Puritans, the Reformers and the Lollards, in its modern phase the story begins in the eighteenth century. It is only necessary to recall some of the movements since then which owe their existence, development and effectiveness entirely or largely to Evangelicals to realize the richness of the Evangelical inheritance. These include the revival of the eighteenth century; the outstanding achievements of the 'Clapham Sect' and the early nineteenth century 'saints in politics'; the establishment and subsequent heroic history of the Church Missionary Society and the Church Pastoral-Aid Society; the prolonged and valiant endeavours of the seventh earl of Shaftesbury in his campaign for social justice; the innumerable works of charity and acts of mercy undertaken by numerous Evangelical societies in the nineteenth century; and the varied forms of Evangelical resurgence in the post-Second World war era. Additionally, Evangelicals were at the centre of the stage in modern church history, as combatants or in important supporting roles when the Oxford movement dominated public attention; at the time of the mid-nineteenth century debates over 'liberal' theology and evolution; in the Anglican/Methodist conversations of the nineteen sixties and seventies, and on many other occasions.

Nonetheless, despite the central importance of Evangelicalism, the history of the Evangelicals in the Church of England during the last two hundred and fifty years has been the subject of but one comprehensive study and analysis. Scour bookshops new and secondhand, scan the shelves of libraries private and public, and occasionally a copy will be found of that sole work: *A History of the Evangelical Party in the Church of England* (London, 1908), by G.R. Balleine. This excellent book takes the story up to 1900 (with a brief appendix in the 1951 edition to cover the period 1900–1950), but much subsequent research has greatly enriched, and in certain respects transformed or modified, our understanding of the subject, and we are bereft of any similar history of the post-1900 period. Also, new disciplines, such as sociology and the social sciences in general, have enlarged our knowledge of movements and periods of history which Balleine approached with the inevitably more restricted, perspectives of his day. The present volume attempts to provide a replacement and updating of Balleine.

A recent book, *From Controversy to Cooperation* by Randle Manwaring, traces the history and theology of Evangelicals in the Church of England from the First World War to the appearance of the Alternative Service Book in 1980. Manwaring was breaking new ground and, perhaps inevitably, left many loose ends, and provoked many questions. The present work is able to address itself to a range of issues either not covered by Manwaring or only partially examined by him. In so doing, it incorporates much that is essential to a full understanding of twentieth century Evangelicalism.

In undertaking such a history there is a particular danger of undue partiality and even partisanship. This could result in distortion and misrepresentation: a biased view of history. It is questionable if true objectivity is either attainable or desirable, whether the study be modern religion or ancient political structures. Debate and even passion are not unknown among historians, and such 'subjectivity' may well add spice and interest to a work without detracting from its historical value. A total lack of bias is not claimed for this study of Evangelicalism. The writer has been an Evangelical for many years, and has been actively engaged in the affairs of the Church of England Evangelicals for three decades and more. But to be conscious of the possibility of partiality in one's self is to enhance the probability of a reasonable measure of detachment and fairness in the selection and interpretation of the historical data under investigation. Indeed, the worth of the work can be strengthened when it gains from the perceptions, sensitivity to nuances, and appreciation of meaning, which are so much greater for an active participant, provided that this approach is balanced by a determination to maximize the extent of historical objectivity. In this present work an effort is made to achieve such a creative blend.

It is only when an author sits down quietly and considers those who have helped in the writing of a book that the full extent of his indebtedness becomes apparent. So it is with the present work. There are countless individuals who have contributed insights and information without being aware of the help they have given. I am most grateful for this unsolicited assistance.

Naming particular people can be invidious. Nevertheless I want to express my appreciation to Dr P.R. McKenzie, formerly of Leicester University, and Professor Stuart Hall of King's College, London for the sensitive way they supervised my research; Dr John C. Bowmer for assistance in the use of the Methodist Archives, and for his unfailing kindness and willingness to share his intimate knowledge of Methodist history; Mr G.R. Sayer, the late Librarian of the Evangelical Library, and his staff for their friendliness; Bishop Colin Buchanan, Canon Michael Hennell, Dr Harold Rowdon and Dr Peter Toon for their valuable criticism and advice; the authors of many unpublished theses, who are acknowleged in the notes; Professor K. Alan-Smith and Hector G. Jelf of the Polytechnic of Central London for granting a few weeks' leave during a hectic administrative career in which to write up research; Dr Philip Hillyer and the Rev Norman Hillyer for their most thorough and helpful work in copyediting and indexing; and Dr Geoffrey Green of T. & T. Clark, for the sympathetic and considerate way he helped to give birth to the author's first book.

Finally, I willingly make reference to our daughter Clare who painstakingly but cheerfully typed the draft manuscript (and thereby also helped to 'pay her way through college'), and the rest of the family, Gillian, Simon and Luke, who, with a good measure of equanimity, endured the inevitable consequences of my writing this work in the all too few spare moments of a busy life: I dedicate the book to them.

Introduction

The age of the first two Georges was an oasis of comparative tranquillity set between two periods of activity and agitation.[1] From 1714 to 1760 there was relative stability in politics, in social observances, in literature and in the life of the established church. It was an age which seems to have concentrated in itself 'all the faults and merits that we are apt to think of as specially characteristic of the whole eighteenth century'. Common sense was seen as the highest virtue, enthusiasm was distrusted; individual enterprise was encouraged but communal effort neglected; the boundaries between the different classes in society were well marked and not easily overstepped; and there was a prevailing and pervasive aura of complacency and self-satisfaction. Yet with all its composure it was not inert. Under cover of its orderliness, 'ideas and movements were originated that found fuller expression in later years'.[2]

---

[1] For the general history of the eighteenth century see W.E.H. Lecky, *A History of England in the Eighteenth Century*, 7 vols. (London, 1892); Dorothy Marshall, *Eighteenth Century England* (London, 1968); J.H. Plumb, *England in the Eighteenth Century* (Harmondsworth, 1969); Charles Grant Robertson, *England Under the Hanoverians* (London, 1911); Norman Sykes, *Church and State in England in the Eighteenth Century* (Cambridge, 1934); J. Steven Watson, *The Reign of George III 1760-1815* (Oxford, 1960); and Basil Wiliams, *The Whig Supremacy 1714-1760* (Oxford, 1962).
[2] Williams, *op.cit.*, p.1.

1

In 1714, when George I ascended the throne, everyone knew that the future belonged to the Whigs; a party which was averse to all manifestations of unusual activity.[3] Under Robert Walpole the priority at home and abroad was identical: peace and stability. After a time of war and domestic disturbance he enabled the country to settle down. He restored a measure of normality, made the Hanoverian succession secure, and helped to establish a routine of government. Safety was the order of the day. Lingering Jacobite sympathy made persistent vigilance the price to be paid for civil rest. Excessive vitality and any form of 'fanaticism' was discountenanced either in the political arena or in matters ecclesiastical.

But despite the dominant conservative mood, there was an unfolding political consciousness in the country at large. Newsletters, which had exercised a considerable influence in the seventeenth century, and the printed newspaper, became effective means of communication.[4] In the first half of the eighteenth century brilliant opposition writers used such means to provoke extra-parliamentary opinion against the government, and effective petitions were organized. Public opinion was seen to be important in the Sacheverell trial in 1710, during the controversy over the Excise Bill in 1733 and in the popularity which the elder Pitt acquired.

This heightened political awareness also contributed to a growing process of secularization. The Civil War, Commonwealth and Restoration and the upheaval of the events leading to the Glorious Revolution had profoundly modified the ancient alliance between church and state. Hitherto the ideal had been the state as a politico-ecclesiastical society, in which political and economic activity were governed and checked by Christian ethics. With the increasing influence of rationalistic philosophies, the emergence of deism, a greater degree of toleration and more widespread religious indifference, there was a move towards the idea of a secular society, with religion as a personal and voluntary affair. No longer was the monarch almost universally acknowledged as the divinely ordained governor of the kingdom. Neither was the government readily accepted as the handmaiden of the church.

The element of stabilty, so prominent in the political life of England in the period 1714 to 1760, was also a major feature in the demographic and

[3] There was not unity or uniformity in the party but there was a dominant trend. See, for example, the assessment of Rupert E. Davies and Gordon Rupp (Eds.), *A History of the Methodist Church in Great Britain*, 3 vols, (London, 1965), Vol. I, pp.19, 20 and the older but full analysis in Lecky, *op.cit.*

[4] The first daily newspaper was produced in 1702.

social structure of the country.[5] In the second decade of the century England was a land of rural settlement: towns, other than London, were small and mainly located on the coast. The countryside was studded with widely dispersed homesteads, mansions or hamlets, and villages in which compact groups of dwellings almost invariably found their focus in the parish church. The total population was probably not more than five and a half million, and for some time it had been static.[6] Of the towns few had over ten thousand inhabitants. London had more than half a million; a disproportionate size and concentration of population which helped to give it a remarkably dominant role in national life. Manchester, Liverpool, Sheffield, Leeds, Halifax, Birmingham and Coventry had all ceased to be the sprawling villages they had been half a century earlier, but none of them had reached a population of 50,000 by the second quarter of the eighteenth century and there were no industrial conurbations.

Although the towns were small, in the first part of the century there began that process of urbanization which was later to assume such gigantic proportions. Already towns were beginning to absorb men, women and children who migrated from the countryside, and urban conditions deteriorated. There were no sanitary systems, and the stench was great. The poor used every nook and cranny as a public convenience, and open cesspools were common. The unpaved streets were narrow, and the dwellings of the poor were one or two room hovels, 'ramshackle warrens of filth, squalor and disease'.[7] Houses and cellars were desperately overcrowded, the cellars often being inhabited not only by people but also by their pigs, fowls, and even their horses and cattle. Drinking, gambling and violence abounded. Disease was prevalent, and infant mortality high.

The lack of efficient transport, and the generally low standard of roads and highways also helped to ensure that different parts of England were largely disconnected and locked in a narrow local existence. Every

---

[5] For the demographic, economic and social history of the eighteenth century, in addition to the works already cited, see T.S. Ashton, *An Economic History of England: The Eighteenth Century* (London 1955); J. Wesley Bready, *England Before and After Wesley* (London, 1939); Paul Mantoux, *The Industrial Revolution in the Eighteenth Century* (London, 1928); E.P. Thompson, *The Making of the English Working Class* (Harmondsworth, 1968); G.M. Trevelyan, *English Social History* (London, 1948); and A.S. Turberville (Ed.), *Johnson's England* (Oxford, 1933).

[6] It is widely accepted that England and Wales had a population of about 5.5 million at the end of the seventeenth century, and a census of 1801 shows it to have been approximately 9 million. The increase was not steady. There may have been an absolute check between 1720 and 1740, when there was much smallpox and a series of influenza epidemics, and there was no rapid increase until the latter part of the century (see Marshall, *op.cit.*, p.7, note 1).

[7] Plumb, *op.cit.*, pp.11 f.

community was to a great extent isolated from its neighbour. Villages had a high level of self-containment, and there was a separation of town and country sufficient to give each its own distinctive tastes and preoccupations. By the fourth decade of the century, when our history begins, there were still only faint, albeit telling, evidences of the impending demographic revolution.

As with demography and social structure, so it was with economic change: the pace was quite slow at first but gradually increased. The foundations for future prosperity had been laid by the end of the previous century, and new techniques allowed for some growth in industry and agriculture, but until about 1760 most Englishmen were engaged in primary production. They were husbandmen, graziers, shepherds, fishermen, miners or quarrymen; while each country town had its miller, maltster, brewer, tanner and sawyer, and each village its baker, blacksmith and cobbler. Over a third of the population undertook work connected with agriculture. The great age of inventions and the exploitation of coal and iron had not yet dawned, although a start had been made.

In 1733 the rapidity of weaving was enormously increased by John Kay's invention of the flying shuttle. But it was not brought into general use in either Yorkshire or Lancashire until after 1760, and the weavers had to wait until the seventeen-sixties for James Hargreaves' invention of the spinning jenny to speed up the process of spinning wool enough to match the flying shuttle. Likewise with the production of iron. It appears that Abraham Darbyshire was developing the use of coal for the smelting of iron around 1708-9, but it was not until the last two decades of the century that monumental changes took place.

As in industry, so in agriculture. The agricultural revolution began as early as 1740, but it did not assume radical proportions until towards the end of the eighteenth and the beginning of the nineteenth century. By 1760 half the country still retained the open-field system.[8]

The industrial and agricultural revolutions were accompanied by a political radicalism which questioned the social class system, but this was not much in evidence by 1760. Until the latter part of the century the rigid hierarchy of classes was generally accepted as part of the natural order of things, even by members of the lowest strata of society, such as the urban poor, the somewhat riotous Cornish tin-miners and the rough Kingswood colliers. The contrast between the lower and the upper ranks

---

[8] The pace of enclosure is shown by the number of Enclosure Acts, see Plumb, op.cit., p.82.

of society was immense. The landowning nobility displayed a magnificence with their coloured costumes, their wigs and sedan chairs and the grace or the artifice of their formal behaviour which was matched by the splendour of their houses. At the head of urban society were the merchant princes who bought up great estates and vied for places among the aristocracy; and below them the middling people who were mildly prosperous because of their industry and thrift, with a distinctive ethos which reflected this. Craftsmen and artisans were the bridge between the rich and poor; while in rural England the traditional, stable pattern of social class relations largely persisted.

Religion

Among the upper echelons of society there was much vague scepticism and avowed scorn of religion.[9] In the rest of the population there was ignorance and carelessness, rather than infidelity. Prevailing attitudes were distinctly unfavourable to the growth of religion. Contemporary witnesses commented on what appeared to them a lamentable state of affairs. In 1738, the year in which John and Charles Wesley were converted, George Berkeley, Bishop of Cloyne, declared that morality and religion in Britain had collapsed 'to a degree that has never been known in any Christian country'. 'Our prospect', he wrote, 'is very terrible and the symptoms grow worse from day to day'.[10] In the same year Thomas Secker, Bishop of Oxford, in an episcopal charge, added to the lamentation. He declared:

> In this we cannot be mistaken, that an open and professed disregard of religion is become, through a variety of unhappy causes, the distinguishing character of the age. Such are the dissoluteness and contempt of principle in the world, and the profligacy, intemperance, and fearlessness of committing crimes in the lower part, as must, if the torrent of impiety stop not, become

---

[9] For the history of the Church of England in the eighteenth century, in addition to the works already cited, see Charles J. Abbey and John H. Overton, *The English Church in the Eighteenth Century*, 2 vols. (London, 1878); S.C. Carpenter, *Eighteenth Century Church and People* (London, 1959); W.K. Lowther Clarke, *Eighteenth Century Piety* (London, 1944); Gerald R. Cragg, *The Church and the Age of Reason* (Harmondsworth, 1966); E. Elliott-Binns, *The Early Evangelicals: A Religious and Social Study* (London, 1953); John H. Overton and Frederic Relton, *The History of the English Church from the Accession of George I to the End of the Eighteenth Century, 1714-1800* (London, 1906); J. Walsh, 'Origins of the Evangelical Revival' in G.D. Bennet and J.D Walsh (Eds.), *Essays in Modern Church History* (London, 1966); Robert F. Wearmouth, *Methodism and the Common People of the Eighteenth Century* (London, 1945); and A. Skevington Wood, *The Inextinguishable Blaze* (Exeter, 1960).

[10] George Berkeley, *Discourse Addressed to Magistrates and Men in Authority*, pp.41 ff, quoted in Wood, *op.cit.*, p.15, and Bready, *op.cit.*, p.19.

absolutely fatal. Christianity is ridiculed and railed at with very little reserve; and the teachers of it without any at all.[11]

Although the value of many such testimonies is lessened by the fact that the commentators were High Church clergymen, not averse to discovering evidence of deterioration which they attributed to the neglect of their principles, and other observers were Roman Catholics perhaps similarly motivated, they should not be ignored. Likewise, the comment of Montesquieu that in England there was 'no religion and the subject, if mentioned, excites nothing but laughter',[12] is a reflection of the opinion current in the circles in which he moved, and does not apply to the population as a whole; but it is useful supporting evidence. More impressive are the comments of Bishop Butler. Writing in 1736 he bemoaned a general decay and disregard of religion:

> It is come, I know not how, to be taken for granted, by many persons, that Christianity is not so much a subject of inquiry; but that it is, now at length, discovered to be fictitious And accordingly they treat it as if, in the present age, this were an agreed point among all people of discernment; and nothing remained, but to set it up as a principal subject of mirth and ridicule, as it were by way of reprisals for its having so long interrupted the pleasures of the world.[13]

The revival preachers could assume that there was a widespread belief in God, but they went to people who were unreached by the church, or who, if reached, had only heard a rather undynamic, rationalistic and moralistic message. Indeed, the Church of England was ill-equipped to serve any of the social groups we have identified, and especially those in the towns. In its ministry and leadership it still suffered from the loss of a significant proportion of its most able clergy as a consequence of the anti-Puritan Code of Persecution of 1661-1665; the departure or alienation of a further body of high-minded ministers as a result of the expulsion of the Non-jurors in 1689 and 1690; and the prorogation of the Convocation from 1717 onwards. The church did not lack good and even great men at every level of its life, nor did it lack ideals of pastoral care. If it had ceased to merit the description of 'church militant', this was perhaps in large measure because of its structure and its preoccupations.

---

[11] B. Porteous and G. Stinton (Eds.), *The Works of Thomas Secker*, Vol.V, p.29, quoted in Wood, *op.cit.*, p.16, Davies and Rupp, *op.cit.*, p.xxii.

[12] See *Lettres persones*

[13] See S. Hallifax (Ed.), *The Works of Joseph Butler*, Vol.II, pp.lxxv, lxxvi, quoted in Wood, *op.cit.*, p.15.

'The very shape of the Church was antiquated'. Some of the sees like York and Lincoln were cumbrous, and the thousand or so parishes constituted a system which had 'its roots in the Heptarchy'.[14] There was not the flexibility which might have facilitated easy adjustment to a shifting, and later rapidly growing, population; and the plurality of livings made havoc of any attempts at achieving orderly administration. The appropriation of patronage to serve the ends of party politics, and the prevalence of polite touting or blatant subterfuge and intrigue in the strife for preferment only helped to contaminate and confound the work of the church. Great too were the disparities of wealth and income within the church. At one extreme there were rich bishoprics like Durham and Winchester, and at the other there were perpetual curates eking out precarious livings in uncertain tenures. With all its ills and abuses the wonder is not that the administration of the church worked badly, but that it worked at all. At every level there were holders of office who laboured faithfully and would have adorned any century in the history of the church. But they were locked within a structure which was not appropriate for the age in which they lived, and even less so for the times to come.

Meanwhile many of the most able leaders of the Church of England were engaged in a scholarly, reasoned defence of orthodoxy against deism. It is perhaps impossible to give an exact account of the views held by deists. Like gnosticism in the early church deism was a tendency rather than a body of definable belief. Two tenets, however, stand out: God was seen as the transcendent and beneficent creator of the world who had then retired from the scene; and natural religion was given supreme importance to the exclusion of divine revelation, which was regarded as superfluous. The duty of man was to lead a good life, and to acknowledge, admire and reverence the works of God in creation.

Ranged against the deists were such eminent divines as Butler, Conyers, Middleton, Warburton, Paley, Sherlock, Waterland and Chandler. Pride of place must go to Joseph Butler. In his *Analogy of Religion Natural and Revealed to the Constitution and Course of Nature* (1736) he dealt the deists a death blow. He demonstrated that 'natural religion' was open to the same objections as revealed religion; it was far removed from being the clear and universal thing which its advocates imagined. Deism had never attracted wide influence but its collapse served to highlight the limitations of reason alone as a basis for religion.

[14] Davies and Rupp, *op.cit.*, p.xxii.

Nevertheless, within the Church of England itself the Cambridge Platonists and their successors, the Latitudinarian divines, elevated reason to such an extent that they gave rise to a new theological temper. They allowed a great freedom both in philosophy and divinity. The men of latitude enjoyed considerable popularity and their theology helped significantly in moulding the religious belief and practice of the Georgian church. They shunned speculative supernaturalism and their doctrines were marked by plainness and directness. At the centre of what they proclaimed was the Fatherhood of God and man's duty to show benevolence. Worship of God should inculcate a right attitude and the right discharge of duties in society. Further, the demands of Christianity should not be burdensome. This theme was especially developed by Archbishop Tillotson. He stressed that in all matters of religion there must be an appeal to reason. The laws of God are reasonable, suitable to our nature, advantageous to our interest and within our power to perform. He taught that the claims of spiritual intuition are to be distrusted. Latitudinarianism was essentially a practical faith in which conduct and works were of supreme importance.

The predominant tone of the church during the reigns of the first two Hanoverian kings was one of moderation. The content of sermons tended to be rational and ethical rather than emotional, dogmatic or mystical. 'The absence indeed from the texture of representative Georgian divinity of a mystical element was an outstanding characteristic of the theology of an age, whose temper was hostile and alien to the notion of a *mysterium tremendum et fascinans*.'[15] The church was seen not so much as the custodian of the keys of heaven and hell, and the proclaimer of the gospel of salvation, as the religious counterpart of civil society, wherein churchmanship was complementary to citizenship.

Evangelical Revival

In many ways the political, social and religious situation in the second quarter of the century, which we have all too briefly surveyed, augured well for the success of a movement which offered a vibrant, easily understood, emotionally dynamic, experientially transforming, living and inspiring personal faith. But there were also more specific and immediate circumstances and developments which were conducive to the birth of the revival.

---

[15] Sykes, *op.cit.*, p.283.

There was the remarkable interest taken in the two devotional works of William Law, *A Practical Treatise upon Christian Perfection* (1726), and *A Serious Call to a Devout and Holy Life* (1728). They had a revolutionary effect on the lives of a not inconsiderable number of Evangelicals.

Then there was the Oxford Holy Club. Although the origins of neither Methodism nor Church of England Evangelicalism should be sought in this rigorous society, it was a preparatory influence on the ensuing revival.

The same may be said of the revivals in America and Wales.[16] The stirring in America does not appear to have immediately precipitated the revival in England, but account must be taken of the transatlantic influence, and especially of Jonathan Edwards, whose classic work on the *Freedom of the Will* became a text-book for the Calvinistic wing of the English revival. The stirring in Wales seems to have exercised a more direct influence. The movement in the Principality was associated with Griffith Jones, known as 'the morning star of the revival', Howel Harris and Daniel Rowlands. It occurred almost simultaneously in Talgarth, Brecon and Llangeitho.

Of closer connection still with the revival in England were the Moravians and the Church of England religious societies. The Moravians had been revivified by a pietistic movement in Germany, and they appeared in England in 1728. The strictness of their conduct prevented them gaining many adherents, but they played a vital part in the life of both John and Charles Wesley and certain other key leaders in the English revival.

Lastly, the religious societies, especially in London, had for many decades helped to keep alive a concern within the established church for vital personal faith and a relating of that faith to the social needs of the time. The London societies were founded in 1678. In regular weekly meetings the members applied themselves to 'good discourses, and things wherein they might edifie one another'.[17] They remained staunchly Church of England gatherings. The members assiduously guarded against any form of schism or faction by adhering to monthly Church of England communions, by attendance at public prayers and by obtaining the

---

[16] For the American and Welsh revivals see especially Jonathan Edwards, *A Narrative of the Revival of Religion in New England: with Thoughts on that Revival* (Glasgow, 1829), John Gillies, *Historical Collections Relating to Remarkable Periods of the Success of the Gospel* (Kelso, 1845), George Godwin, *The Great Revivalists* (London, 1951), Henry Johnson, *Stories of Great Revivals* (1906), Ronald A. Knox, *Enthusiasm: A Chapter in the History of Religion with Special Reference to the XVII and XVIII Centuries* (Oxford, 1950), James Robe, *Narrative: Revival of Religion* (Glasgow, 1840), Max Warren, *Revival: An Enquiry* (London, 1954); and Wood, *op.cit.*

[17] Josiah Woodward, *An Account of the Rise and Progress of the Religious Societies in the City of London* (London, 1701), p.23.

explicit approval of their superintendent Church of England clergymen for the introduction of any rule, prayer or practice. The societies represented a continuing possibility within the established church of a more profound and intense religious awareness and personal religious experience than was generally to be attained through the regular parish ministry. With the coming of Whitefield and the Wesleys, the religious societies became a 'channel through which the revival flowed until the stream became a torrent and burst the banks of the Establishment which had contained it'.[18]

Such a revival broke out in England in the fourth decade of the century, and in the course of the next fifty years developed into three strands. The most numerous and best marshalled of the groups were the Arminian Methodists, the followers of John Wesley. Then there were the Calvinistic Methodists who, in England, looked to George Whitefield and the Countess of Huntingdon for leadership. And finally, there were the Evangelicals within the Church of England who, after some initial co-operation in some cases with the two Methodist groupings, increasingly kept clear of any commitments beyond the framework of the Church of England and concentrated upon parish work. The three movements interacted and influenced each other, and at times in certain places they were indistinguishable, but Evangelicalism needs to be recognized as largely separate in origin, in character and in outcome.

Anglican Evangelicalism

Evangelicalism in the Church of England was largely distinct in origin from the two forms of Methodism just mentioned. The majority of those who were recognized as leaders of the Evangelical movement in the Church of England in its early phases arrived at their opinions quite apart from Whitefield or the Wesleys or the revival movement with which those three were associated.

All over England men and women, and most importantly Anglican clergy, underwent the same conversion experience and came, often independently, to preach the same gospel as their more famed contemporaries. John Wesley himself gladly acknowledged the fact. 'Many have I found in various parts of both Great Britain and Ireland', he wrote, 'who enjoyed that immediate witness (of the Spirit) before they had any sort of connection with the Methodists or any knowledge either of their persons

---

[18] D. Pyke, 'Religious Societies', *Wesley Historical Society Journal*, XXV, p.16.

or writings'.[19] Among these were such stalwarts of early Evangelicalism as Walker of Truro, Grimshaw of Haworth, Adam of Wintringham, and William Romaine of London, as well as such later converts as Henry Venn of Huddersfield, John Newton and William Cowper. We will be introduced to them, and to others, later and see something of their outstanding characters and achievements.

Among the few Evangelical clergy who were 'awakened' as a result of the direct or indirect influence of the Methodists were John Fletcher of Madeley who was drawn into Evangelicalism through hearing a description of the life and activities of the Methodists, and Martin Madan who traced the source of his Evangelicalism to a sermon of John Wesley. Thus, contrary to a widely held view, the Evangelical movement in the Church of England was not derived directly from Methodism. It certainly owed much to that more prominent and initially more powerful and influential movement, and the second generation of Evangelicals were inclined to minimize this and over-emphasize the independence of the movements. But, in origin, although they may be viewed as part of one movement of the Spirit of God, their essential separateness is at least as evident as their interdependence and interaction.

From an early date Evangelicalism in the Church of England also had distinctive characteristics.[20] Although the term 'Methodist', or one of its derivatives, was applied indiscriminately for much of the eighteenth century to any Christian displaying any signs or tendencies towards 'enthusiasm', Evangelicalism and Methodism need to be distinguished. More and more, as the years passed, Evangelicalism (which, from now onwards, we will use in the accepted way as a shorthand for Evangelicalism in the Church of England) became a more clearly identifiable movement in its own right, with its own recognizable features. Both the Methodists and the Evangelicals set before themselves the task of quickening and revitalizing the church, but they had their own special marks. What were these, and in what ways did the two movements differ?

First, we note the clericalism of the Evangelical movement. In contrast, Methodism increasingly became a lay movement with lay preachers as its chief agents. John Wesley rued this trend and tried to reverse it by organizing an association of Evangelical clergy. But he failed, and Methodist dependence on lay leadership grew as the century progressed.

---

[19] J. Telford (Ed.), *John Wesley, Letters*, Vol.5, p.21.
[20] The brief discussion of the distinctive characteristics of Evangelicalism owes much to Elliott-Binns, *op.cit.*

Secondly, Evangelicals were strict churchmen. In general they were chary of any co-operation with dissenters. Although John Wesley shared this intense loyalty to the Church of England, the position of Methodists, before separation definitely placed them in the category of dissenters, was equivocal.

Thirdly, the Evangelicals were unhappy about certain aspects of the theology and general ethos of Methodism. This is not to say that the Evangelicals were uniformly Calvinistic: that is an over-simplification, for the Calvinist-Arminian divide cut right across the Methodist-Evangelical distinction. Doctrinally it can be argued that the Evangelicals collectively may best be regarded as moderate Calvinists. The Evangelical apprehension was rather over Methodist teaching on such matters as Christian perfection, and what was perceived as a Methodist over-reliance on the emotions.

Fourthly, it has been argued that John Wesley had a particular regard for the primitive church, and based many of his innovations on what he considered to be primitive practice, whereas the Evangelicals, especially in their more formative years, looked more to the Reformation and the Puritan tradition. The Methodists, of course, valued the Puritans, but not perhaps to the same extent as the Evangelicals.

Finally, and most crucially, was the problem of church order. This was the root cause of the divergence between the two movements. The Evangelicals, with varying degrees of emphasis, sought to carry out the revival strictly within the context of existing ecclesiastical structures and practices. The Methodists broke through such restraints, at first in a cautious and tentative way, but later boldly and blatantly. Even at an early stage many Evangelicals were suspicious of some of the practices adopted by the Methodists, not because they were innovations or necessarily objectionable in themselves, but because of their inherent potential danger.

This was true with prayer meetings, where unregulated lay leadership was considered a source of potential dissatisfaction with the church and the role of the clergy. Indeed, it was the general prominence of lay leadership, and more particularly of itinerant preaching by lay as well as ordained men, which was seen as the greatest threat to church order, and which most alarmed and alienated a number of the Evangelicals. Lay leadership in anything but a very clerically controlled form was resisted by some of the most ardent Evangelical clergy. Itinerant preaching was undertaken by a few Evangelicals, but stringently avoided by others such as Samuel Walker of Truro and Thomas Adam of Wintringham.

As the century advanced, and as Methodism became more clearly delineated as a body separate from the Church of England, so those who remained loyal to the order and practice of the Church of England, while retaining their evangelical theology, became more distinguishable as a group. Strict adherence to parochial discipline became a more pronounced hallmark of Evangelicalism, and such 'irregular' activity as itinerant preaching declined.

To a great extent separate in origin and in character, the three movements constituting the revival were also distinctive in outcome. Arminian Methodism emerged as a fully-fledged denomination with its own history of phenomenal growth, fragmentation and coalescence, and the later exploration of possible union with the Church in whose fellowship it had originated. The Calvinistic followers of Whitefield found their home and future in the Countess of Huntingdon's Connection. The varied fortunes and the destiny of the third strand, the Evangelicals, will now be traced.[21]

---

[21] In his thesis 'The Yorkshire Evangelicals in the Eighteenth Century with special reference to Methodism' (Cambridge University Ph.D., 1956), J.D. Walsh identified these three strands. His research also drew attention to the fact that the Evangelical movement in the Church of England was largely parallel to that of Whitefield and the Wesleys, and separate from it in origin and atmosphere. He emphasized that it was not just an offshoot of the Methodist revival. He demonstrated how the Evangelical clergy, who were at first little more than a scattered group of individuals, by correspondence, personal contact and growth in numbers became a closely-knit fraternity which by the end of the century was practically unanimous on major questions of faith and order. He pointed out that at first the isolation of 'serious' men of all shades of evangelical opinion drew the three groups together and smudged the lines that delimited them. He proceeded to show how the latent differences between the Evangelical bodies became so accentuated that by 1800 co-operation between the Church of England Evangelicals and Methodists was not so evident as suspicion between them. These are themes which have been alluded to in this Introduction and which will be explored more fully, especially in Part 1 of the present work.

Part 1 1734-1789

1

The Birth of a Movement

When George Whitefield and the brothers John and Charles Wesley proclaimed their new-found faith they startled the moribund Hanoverian church and shook the society of their day. Of the three, it was George Whitefield who first ushered in the new era of revival. Delayed in his intention to minister in the New World, in Georgia, he spent the twelve months from August 1736 in an almost unbroken succession of preaching engagements, mostly in London or the surrounding counties. It was a novelty to hear such eloquent extempore preaching of an evangelical gospel by a man with most uncommon gifts of voice and manner. From the outset the effect was sensational. He was heard in wonder, and his fame spread with astonishing rapidity. Crowds numbered in thousands attended the nine or so occasions each week when he preached. Long before daybreak on Sundays people thronged the streets, lanterns in hand, on their way to church, and not infrequently hundreds were turned away from the most spacious churches for want of room.[1]

In May 1738, first Charles Wesley and then his brother John were converted and immediately began to preach salvation by faith to individuals and groups, in houses, in religious societies, and in the few churches which had not closed their doors to such preaching and

[1] See *George Whitefield's Journals* (Edinburgh, 1965), pp.77, 87-89.

17

preachers. On his return from Georgia Whitefield rejoined them in what was rapidly to become a national crusade. Excluded from most pulpits and with a passion to make the gospel known to the multitudes outside the established church, the three evangelists took the world as their parish. They turned away from the debarred pulpits of Bristol and London and resorted to the open air as field preachers. From Cornwall to Newcastle, and from the West Country to East Anglia, they rode back and forth speaking to the people in church or market-place, meadow or quarry, or wherever they could gather an audience.

Masses assembled to hear them. A countless number responded and joined themselves together in special societies. Faced with evangelistic and pastoral responsibilities which could not be realised by the unaided efforts of three men, lay preachers and leaders were appointed. Growth in numbers and increasing hostility impressed upon the revival converts a deep sense of their corporate identity. Sharp and often bitter divisions were later to appear in their ranks, but these did not lessen the sense of independence from the Church of England. Stage by stage, in what appears with the wisdom of hindsight to be an inexorable process, that which began as a movement of renewal within the Church of England progressively assumed the characteristics of separation. This trend was reinforced by the consolidation of the societies as separate worshipping communities; the enforced registration of the newly created preaching houses as dissenting chapels; and finally the consecration by John Wesley of men for ministry in America.

George Whitefield, who in the estimation of J.C. Ryle was 'the greatest preacher of the gospel England has ever seen',[2] spent his entire ministry, from 1736 to his death in 1770, in an uninterrupted proclamation of the good news as he understood it. In these thirty-four years it is reckoned that he preached publicly eighteen thousand times, and always with immense effect. In one single Whitsuntide week, after preaching in Moorfields, he received about one thousand letters from people with various concerns. During the middle years of the century he was a power in the land.[3]

John Wesley persevered in his ministry for fifty-three years, from 1738 to 1791; always active, never swerving from his almost ceaseless travelling, preaching, organising, conferring, writing, debating,

[2] J.C. Ryle, *Christian Leaders of the Eighteenth Century* (Reprinted, Edinburgh, 1978), p.31.
[3] For the life and work of George Whitefield, see Arnold A. Dallimore, *George Whitefied*, 2 vols. (Edinburgh, 1970, 1980); Marcus L. Loane, *Oxford and the Evangelical Succession* (London, 1951); J.C. Ryle, *Christian Leaders of the Eighteenth Century* (Reprinted, Edinburgh, 1978); Luke Tyerman, *The Life and Times of George Whitefield*, 2 vols. (London, 1890); *George Whitefield's Journals* (Edinburgh, 1965).

counselling and leading an ever-expanding body of revival converts. The work accomplished was outstanding. At the time of his death there were in excess of 500 Methodist preachers in the British dominions and the United States of America, and over 130,000 Methodist members.[4]

For fifty years, from his conversion in 1738 to his death in 1788, and most creatively and productively in the years immediately following his conversion, Charles Wesley poured forth a prodigious volume of superlative hymns which inspired and animated those who responded to the revival message. By his preaching and his counsel, but supremely by his hymnody, he made a significant contribution to the history of the period.[5]

This outstanding triumvirate spearheaded a revival which was pre-eminent in the eighteenth century history of the church in England. It is a movement which has been well documented, researched and analysed.[6]

By contrast, the story we are about to unravel has received little attention.[7] The modern Evangelical movement in the Church of England did not have the same easily identifiable and dramatic origins as Methodism. It began tenuously in the unheralded and often obscure ministries of a few devout and energetic clergymen, and it continued throughout much of the eighteenth century to consist of little more than a scattered group of individuals. It was regarded by John Wesley as 'a rope of sand'. It was made heroic, not by the might and magnificence of its onward surge, but by the sacrificial, dedicated lives of a small dispersed band of men who preached Christ to the best of their ability. Only as they

[4] For the life and work of John Wesley, see Frank Baker, *John Wesley and the Church of England* (London, 1970); Ryle, *op.cit.*; John S. Simon, *John Wesley and the Religious Societies* (London, 1921), and *John Wesley and the Methodist Societies* (London, 1937); Luke Tyerman, *The Life and Times of the Rev. John Wesley*, 3 vols. (London, 1870); John Wesley, *The Journal of the Reverend John Wesley*, Ed. Nehemiah Curnock, 8 vols. (London, 1938); and A. Skevington Wood, *The Burning Heart: John Wesley Evangelist* (Exeter, 1967).

[5] For the life and work of Charles Wesley, see Thomas Jackson, *The Life of Rev. Charles Wesley* (London, 1841); Charles Wesley, *The Journal of the Rev. Charles Wesley*, 2 vols. (London, 1849).

[6] In addition to the works cited in notes 1 and 9 in the Introduction, other works include Leslie F. Church, *The Early Methodist People* (London, 1949), and *More About the Early Methodist People* (London, 1949); Ronald Knox, *Enthusiasm: A Chapter in the History of Religion, with special reference to the XVIIth and XVIIIth Centuries* (Oxford, 1950); Loane, *op.cit.* and *Cambridge and the Evangelical Succession* (London, 1952); Simon *op.cit.*; and John Telford (Ed.), *Wesley's Veterans: Lives of the Methodist Preachers Told by Themselves*, 7 vols. (London, vols. 1-3 undated, vols. 4-7 1913, 14)

[7] The main secondary works in addition to the works cited under notes 1 and 9 of the Introduction, note 6 above, and individual or collective biographies are G.R. Balleine, *A History of the Evangelical Party in the Church of England* (London, 1908); H.C.G. Moule, *The Evangelical School in the Church of England* (London, 1901); and G.W.E. Russell, *A Short History of the Evangelical Movement*.

corresponded, as personal contact increased, as they united in clerical societies and as they grew in numbers did they become a cohesive fraternity which by the end of the century was almost unanimous on major questions of faith and order. It has rightly been said that 'the history of the Evangelical Revival is essentially a history of personalities rather than of opinions',[8] and this applies especially to the Evangelicals in the Church of England.

The early phase of Evangelicalism is therefore best illustrated and understood by means of brief accounts of the lives and achievements of some of the more prominent of the fathers of the movement. We will take as our primary examples Samuel Walker of Truro, who adroitly combined innovation and adherence to church order in his ministry; the dynamic, somewhat eccentric William Grimshaw, who laboured for twenty-one years in the bleak and windswept isolation of Haworth and its surrounding moors; and scholarly, circumspect and grave William Romaine, who stood almost alone as an Evangelical clergyman in London for much of his ministry.

It was in the remoteness of north Cornwall that the first stirrings of revival in the Church of England occurred; providing one of the seedbeds of modern Evangelicalism. Two 'awakened' clergy pursued their labours, evangelical in outlook if not in name, even before the visits of the Wesleys. The more notable of these was George Thomson, vicar of St Gennys, a small, secluded village on the Atlantic seaboard. With almost no outside assistance he became increasingly convinced of those doctrines of salvation through faith alone which were learned by the Wesleys only five or six years later. His fellow labourer was the aged John Bennet, who was described by George Whitefield in 1743 as 'about eighty years of age, but not above one year old in the school of Christ'.[9] A third, more renowned figure, James Hervey, whom we will meet later as the incumbent of Weston Favell, had been an early member of Wesley's 'Holy Club' at Oxford. He was dismissed in 1743 by his rector from the curacy of Bideford for his evangelical views, but left behind a religious society which was visited by Thomson. Both Thomson and Bennet preached outside their parishes and aroused the ire of some of the neighbouring clergy by doing so. They aggravated this hostility by welcoming John Wesley in 1745 and George Whitefield in 1750, and by assisting at nonconformist places of worship. It is of little surprise that they were severely reprimanded for their behaviour by Bishop Lavington.[10]

---

[8] Charles H. Smith, *Simeon and Church Order* (Cambridge, 1940), p.6.
[9] *Letters of G. Whitefield*, Vol.II, p.44.
[10] For details of the Evangelicals in Cornwall, see G.C.B. Davies, *The Early Cornish Evangelicals 1735-1760: A Study of Walker of Truro and Others* (London, 1951).

By 1747 the Cornish Evangelicals were joined by a clergyman who was to become their leader and a man of stature to stand comparison with the leading Evangelicals of the time: Samuel Walker. His life was not very eventful, but there were few places in England where the conscientious and methodical ministry of one man produced such singular success and striking results.

Samuel Walker (1714–61)

Walker was born at Exeter in 1714 and died at the early age of forty-seven. He entered the ministry in 1737 and became the stipendiary curate of Truro in 1746; an office he held until his death. He later acknowledged that for ten years after his ordination, although he was well thought of and even esteemed beyond most other clergymen for the regularity and diligence of his ministry, he was mainly concerned to enhance his reputation and gratify his considerable appetite for pleasure. He had not experienced the evangelical conversion of which Thomson, Bennet and Hervey could speak.

All this changed in 1749. In that year, largely as a result of the friendship of George Conon, headmaster of Truro grammar school, there occurred the spiritual turning-point of his life. It was not easy for him to cast off former habits. He had been a leading figure associated with the town's pleasures and amusements and the new focus of his attention and energies meant his withdrawal from previous activities. He found the ostracism and strictures of his erstwhile friends particularly hard to bear. But his earnestness and sincerity, the evident change in his life, and his new style of preaching produced a deep effect. He aroused widespread interest in the town. His church became crowded. Indeed, so great were the numbers attending his ministry that the thoroughfares of the town seemed to be deserted during the hours of service. It was said, that you might fire a cannon down every street of Truro during a church service, without a chance of killing a single human being.

The transformation in the life style and the preaching of Walker provoked much hatred, opposition and persecution. His enemies first tried complaining to the bishop of the diocese, but to no avail. The rector of Truro then agreed to go to his curate and give him notice of dismissal from his charge. Walker received him twice with such elegance and dignity that he was overwhelmed with confusion and left without a word on the intended subject. A short time later, during a period of illness, the rector sent for Walker, entreated his prayers, conceded the rightness of his conduct, and promised him hearty support if he recovered. From that time onwards, although there was resistance to Walker, he went on his way without undue hindrance.

The direct effect of his ministry was remarkable. Two examples will demonstrate this. In 1754, only seven years after his preaching as an Evangelical began, he recorded that no less than eight hundred persons had enquired of him how they might experience the new spiritual life of which he spoke. In a parish of sixteen hundred inhabitants, even allowing that many of the enquiries came from the surrounding area, this indicates a staggering effectiveness.

A regiment of soldiers was quartered in Truro for about nine months in 1756. Walker preached a sermon for their benefit on Sunday afternoons. The attendance was very large, and an estimated two hundred and fifty men came to him for private instruction, despite the public order of their commander not to do so. Conduct and behaviour in the regiment showed a marked improvement, and before departing from Truro the regimental officers went as a body to thank Walker for the reformation he had produced in their ranks.[11]

No better testimony to the fruitfulness of Walker's parochial ministry can be found than that of John Wesley. Conversions were the aim and object of Wesley's preaching, and it was the lack of these which he considered most condemnatory both of the clergy of the Church of England and the parochial system; and this include the Evangelicals. 'We know Mr Piers, Perronet, Manning, and several regular clergymen who do preach the genuine gospel', he wrote, 'but to no effect at all. There is one exception in England – Mr Walker of Truro'.[12] Others, by extra-parochial means, were effective evangelists, but only Walker, in Wesley's opinion, out of all the clergy in England, fulfilled this essential evangelistic task working through the normal channels of the parochial system.

And it was Walker who, as much as almost anyone else in England, championed strict compliance with the demands of church order. He corresponded at length with John Wesley on the matter. He particularly objected to the system of itinerant lay preachers adopted by Wesley, saying that all such who were fit for, and could procure ordination, should be ordained; that those who remained should not be allowed to preach, but should be set as inspectors over societies, and assistants to them; that they should not be moved from place to place, but rather become personally acquainted with all the members of their society; and that they should pay particular attention to the moral conduct of the societies under their care, so that the standard of membership remained appropriately high.[13] He

---

[11] See Ryle, op.cit., pp.316-318 for these two anecdotes.

[12] Letters, Vol.III, p.152.

[13] See letter from Walker to Charles Wesley, quoted in Edwin Sidney, Life and Ministry of the Rev. Samuel Walker (2nd Ed., 1838), pp.210, 211.

was acutely aware of the paucity of evangelism, and other shortcomings in
the Church of England, but he consistently and persistently opposed
itinerant preaching and argued against separation on grounds of
expediency. Even when William Romaine faced the possibility of not
being able to find employment in the established church, Walker advised
him not to seek an alternative fellowship and field of labour.[14]

Walker's loyalty to the Church of England did not detract from a
breadth of vision which was rare among church members of those days.
He had a deep appreciation of the work of others, and especially of the
value of Wesley's ministry:

> In this day of darkness and licentiousness it becomes all the friends of the
> Gospel to bear with one another; and while they differ in opinion and
> denomination, to unite together in heart and endeavour for the support of
> the common cause. It is my great comfort there are good men of all
> persuasions, who are content to leave each other liberty of private
> judgement in lesser things, and are heartily disposed to unite their efforts for
> the maintaining and enlarging of Christ's kingdom. This I take to be the
> most promising symptom of our day, and I am hoping great things from
> this spirit of moderation and peace.[15]

One practice adopted by Walker had its parallel among the followers of
John Wesley. The private meetings for the members of his congregation,
whereby they could share their faith, problems and opportunities,
encourage one another and help promote the faith in the neighbourhood,
were similar to those of the Wesleyan class system. Walker's societies were
formed into two divisions, one composed entirely of men, and the other of
married men, their wives, and unmarried women. Each group was kept
small: between five and eight members. The rules drawn up for the
management of meetings dealt in detail with the requirements and
procedures for the admission of members, the hours to be kept, the mode
of proceeding, the things to be habitually avoided by members and the
authority of the clergyman in all the affairs of the society. It was this last
issue which caused very considerable aggravation, as some of the lay
leaders fought for increased authority and independence and Walker
resolutely asserted the need for clerical control.

Walker looked beyond his parish, and many Evangelicals looked to him
for advice and leadership. In his immediate locality he was the prime
mover in the establishment of a clerical club for Cornish clergy, which met
regularly probably from 1750 onwards. Its purpose was to increase the
efficiency and usefulness of each of the members within their own parishes

[14] See Sidney, *op.cit.*, pp.489, 490.
[15] Quoted in Davies, *op.cit.*, p.71.

as a consequence of the mutual exchange of ideas and opinions. This was part of Walker's efforts to stimulate devotedness within the framework of the parochial system. It was not unique, but it may have been the first society of its kind in the country which was specifically for Evangelical clergy.[16]

William Grimshaw (1708-63)

Almost three hundred miles away from Truro, and based on a rectory which was to be given worldwide renown by the Brontë family, William Grimshaw was exercising an outstanding and extraordinary ministry. Born in 1708, Grimshaw was ordained in 1731, and served two curacies before he went as an Evangelical to Haworth in 1742, having had a conversion experience perhaps only a few months before. The place in which he was to minister for twenty-one years, until his death in 1763, was an obscure, straggling grey village which stood amid the desolate moors of northern Yorkshire. The character of the people harmonised with the surroundings, for the inhabitants were sullen, rough, superstitious, unsympathetic to the Christian message and suspicious of strangers. The situation demanded courage, a plain unambiguous declaration of a simple message, and a concern for people which would be exhibited in a forthright yet compassionate manner. And William Grimshaw brought these qualities to the task before him, adding to them an earnestness and persistence which demanded attention and response from his parishioners.

Grimshaw began as he intended to continue. He preached fervently and took drastic steps to remedy what he thought to be unacceptable social and personal behaviour. A few anecdotes will best convey something of his bizarre but effective methods. John Newton tells us, for example, that it was Grimshaw's frequent custom to leave the church at Haworth while the psalm before the sermon was being sung to see if any were absent from worship and idling their time in the churchyard, the street, or the ale-houses; and many of those whom he found he would drive before him into church. Newton then tells of a friend of his who was passing a public house in Haworth on a Sunday morning and saw several people making their escape out of it, some jumping out of the lower windows, and some over a low wall. Newton's friend feared that the house was on fire; but on enquiring he was told that the fleeing occupants had seen the parson

---

[16] For the life and work of Walker see especially Davies, *op.cit.*; Elliott-Binns, *op.cit.*; Ryle, *op.cit.*; Sidney, *op.cit.*

coming. They were more afraid of the parson than of a justice of the peace.

Early on in his Haworth ministry Grimshaw was determined to stop the various kinds of rough and objectionable horse-play indulged in by young people who met together on Sundays. In order to do this he disguised himself as an old woman so that he might discover who they were. Throwing off his disguise, he charged them not to move, took down their names and ordered them to meet him at an appointed time, which they did punctually as if they had been served with a warrant. He made them kneel down, prayed for them, and gave them a lecture. It is said that the reprimand was heeded, and he never had to repeat it.

Another well-authenticated anecdote relates to the Haworth races. This was an annual festival organised by the innkeepers, and seemingly a great occasion for drunkenness, riot and wild behaviour. Unable to stop the races, Grimshaw made the matter a subject of earnest prayer: that God would interfere and bring them to an end in his own way. The race-time came and the people assembled; but before the races could begin heavy rain fell and continued incessantly during the three days appointed for the races. Apparently it became a sort of proverbial saying among the people of Haworth that old Grimshaw put a stop to the races by his prayers and, says Newton, there were no more races at Haworth.[17]

Grimshaw's ministry was not confined to the parish church or to Haworth. He toured his parish, conducting meetings in cottages, and then extended this practice widely in Yorkshire, Lancashire, Cheshire and north Derbyshire. He seldom preached less than twenty, and not infrequently thirty times a week. In doing so he would constantly travel scores of miles, declaring his faith in plain and forceful language. Not long before his death, while standing on a hill near Haworth, he said that when he first came into the area he might have gone half a day's journey on horseback toward the east, west, north and south without meeting one person whom he described as 'truly serious', or indeed without even hearing of one. But by the time he spoke, he could tell of several hundred people who attended his ministry and were devout communicants.[18] He justified his itinerancy as a response to pluralism and non-residence, and the inadequate evangelistic and pastoral ministry of the church in hundreds of parishes in the north of England.

[17] For these and other anecdotes, and for accounts of the life and work of Grimshaw, see especially Balleine, *op. cit.*, Elliott-Binns, *op. cit.*; R. Spence Hardy, *Life of Grimshaw*; Erasmus Middleton, *Biographia Ecclesiastica*, Vol.IV (London, 1816); John Wesley, *Journal*, *op. cit.*, Vol.IV.
[18] Cited in Ryle, *op. cit.*, p. 119.

Indeed, Grimshaw not only preached beyond his parish, but he co-operated fully with the Methodists. He acted as an 'assistant' to John Wesley, who spoke of Mr Grimshaw's circuit.[19] He visited Methodist classes, gave out tickets and held love-feasts. He made his parsonage a centre for Methodist preachers, training and encouraging them. He finally built a meeting-house in Haworth in order to help safeguard the future of evangelical Christianity in the village. Nonetheless he was a strong churchman, believing the Church of England 'to be the soundest, purest most apostolic Christian Church in the world'. He added that he could therefore in good conscience live and die in such a church.[20] In another age and in another place he may have restricted himself to a parochial ministry. He judged that the state of the country needed exceptional action. Regularity, he considered, was of secondary importance to the demands of the hour.

The forthright preaching in other parishes of a message which often attracted considerable crowds, understandably provoked opposition, especially from the incumbents of the parishes concerned. The most violent opponent was the Rev. George White, perpetual curate of Colne and Marsden in Lancashire. In a published sermon in 1748 he attacked Grimshaw and all his fellow labourers. He additionally proceeded to stir up a mob to stop the preaching by force. He issued a proclamation:

> If any men be mindful to enlist under the command of the Rev. George White . . . for the defence of the Church of England . . . let them now repair to the cross, when each man shall have a pint of ale for advance, and other proper encouragements.

When Grimshaw and John Wesley went to Colne to preach on 24 August 1748, they were assaulted by the drunken mob which was armed with clubs. They were dragged before White like criminals and as soon as they left his presence and went outside the mob closed in on them, tossed them about with great violence and covered them with mud. The people assembled to hear Grimshaw and Wesley preach had to run for their lives amid showers of dirt and stones. Some were trampled in the mud, others dragged by the hair, and many unmercifully beaten with clubs. Not long afterwards Grimshaw went to Colne again, and once more received similar treatment.[21]

On at least two occasions complaint was made to the Archbishop about this extra-parochial preaching. The outcome of each gives us some insight into the fruit of Grimshaw's ministry and the effect produced by his

[19] See John Wesley, *Works*, Vol. XII, p.355.
[20] Letter from Walker to Charles Wesley, cited in Ryle, *op.cit.*, p.130.
[21] Cited in Ryle, *op.cit.*, pp.124-126

preaching. 'How many communicants had you when you first came to Haworth?' the Archbishop enquired of him on receiving the first complaint. Grimshaw answered, 'Twelve, my lord'. 'How many have you now?' was the next question. To which the reply was, 'In the winter, from three to four hundred; and in the summer, near twelve hundred'. On hearing this the Archbishop said, 'We cannot find fault with Mr Grimshaw when he is instrumental in bringing so many persons to the Lord's Table'.[22]

On the second occasion the Archbishop visited Haworth church for a confirmation service, and at very short notice Grimshaw was required to preach the sermon. After the service, in the midst of all the assembled clergy, the Archbishop took Grimshaw by the hand and said, 'I would to God that all the clergy in my diocese were like this good man'.[23]

William Romaine (1714-95)

We travel south again for our third example of early Evangelicalism, to London. Here we encounter a man equal in zeal to Walker and Grimshaw, but different from both in character, career and method. William Romaine was born in 1714, ordained deacon in 1736 and priest in 1738. His ministerial life covered nearly sixty years, and he experienced many hardships. He was a man of some erudition, particularly known for his criticism of Bishop Warburton's *Divine Legation of Moses*, and his new edition of the *Hebrew Concordance and Lexicon* of di Calasio.

For long the Evangelicals did not have a single church in London, and there were only a few unbeneficed Evangelical clergy. During these lean years Romaine was their leader, having joined their despised ranks soon after his arrival in the capital. For sixteen years he was not offered a living. His first appointment, in 1748, was as lecturer at St Botolph's, Billingsgate. In the following year he was chosen lecturer of St Dunstan's in the West, the famous old church in Fleet Street. The rector disputed his right to the pulpit. The matter was taken to the Court of King's Bench. Romaine was deprived of one of the two lectureships involved, but confirmed in the other.

The troubles of the lectureship did not end with this decision. The churchwardens vigorously resisted him. They kept the church closed until the exact hour of the lecture, and refused to light it when it was necessary. Romaine frequently read prayers and preached by the light of a single candle held in his own hand. The crowds attending the lectures had to wait

[22] Hardy, *op.cit.*, p.232.
[23] Cited in Ryle, *op.cit.*, pp.127, 138.

outside. Observing this when passing along Fleet Street, the Bishop of London discovered the cause and promptly arranged for an earlier lecture, and for the church to be opened and lighted well in time. From then to the end of his life Romaine continued in the quiet exercise of this ministry, without disturbance. He held the lectureship for forty-six years, although it was only worth eighteen pounds a year.

For five years from 1750 he was also assistant morning preacher at St George's, Hanover Square. This was the most important pulpit he occupied, St George's being well known as the mother church of the most fashionable quarter of the metropolis. His preaching attracted such crowds that the regular seat-holders took offence and complained that they were put to inconvenience. Strong pressure was brought to bear upon the rector, and he gave Romaine notice to terminate his engagement. Thus he was dismissed for drawing too many people to church.

After a curacy at St Olave's, Southwark which ended in 1759, Romaine's career continued to be insecure, and he seriously wondered whether employment in the Church of England might not be impossible for him. He was encouraged by Samuel Walker to remain loyal and not to secede; and he declined an offer by some of his admirers to build a chapel where he might carry on as an independent preacher. Then at length he was offered the parish of St Andrew-by-the-Wardrobe with St Anne, Blackfriars. But he was once more dogged by opposition. There was an appeal to the Court of Chancery against his election which took over a year to be decided in his favour. He was instituted to the incumbency in February 1766, held it until his death in 1795, and made the church an Evangelical rallying-point in London.

Romaine was a central figure in the eighteenth century revival and has been described as 'all in all . . . the strongest man connected with the Evangelical branch of the Movement'.[24] But although his influence was undoubtedly great, it was lessened by defects in his temperament. He was zealous to promote the spiritual welfare of all to whom he preached or who were under his care; he was energetic and diligent in the service he rendered; and he was persevering in the face of extended and often severe opposition or neglect. But he was shy and reserved, severe in manner and somewhat unapproachable; and he often gave the impression of being pedantic, morose and lacking in warmth or pastoral sensitivity. His contribution to Evangelicalism was more through his public ministry than his personal contacts, and through his published works, which included *The Life of Faith* (1763), *The Walk of Faith* (1771) and *The Triumph of Faith* (1795).[25]

[24] Overton, *op.cit.*, p.68.
[25] For the life and work of Romaine, see especially W.B. Cadogan;, *The Life of the Rev. William Romaine* (1821); Elliott-Binns, *op.cit.*; T. Haweis, *The Life of William Romaine* (1797); Loane, *op.cit.*; Ryle, *op.cit.*

These three examples, of Walker, Grimshaw and Romaine, portray something of the variety of character and ministry in early Evangelicalism, the distinctive contributions made by the Evangelicals to the eighteenth century revival and to the church in general, and the reactions they evoked. Three much briefer sketches of James Hervey, Thomas Adam and Martin Madan, and a fleeting reference to some lesser-known Evangelicals, will further indicate the diversity of gifts and yet unity of fundamental purpose which characterised these pioneers.

James Hervey (1714-58)

James Hervey was one of the small circle of members of the Holy Club at Oxford. After his ordination in 1736 he held curacies at his father's church in Northamptonshire, in Hampshire and in north Devonshire, before he returned to rejoin his father at Weston Favell in 1743. This was his final move. On the death of his father in 1752, he succeeded as rector, but died six years later. There was nothing distinguished in his quiet, unobtrusive country ministry, but hundreds were reached by his writings. Charles Wesley once dubbed him the Isocrates of the movement, and the parallel was apt, for like Isocrates he owed his influence not to his oratory but to his writings.

Hervey's principal literary works were *Meditations among the Tombs*, which appeared in 1746, and *Theron and Aspasio*, which was published in 1755. The style of both is florid, bombastic and stilted, but it was suited to the manner of the time. The *Meditations* ran through twenty editions in a very short time, and *Theron and Aspasio* attracted immediate and very wide interest. Countless Evangelicals, as well as others, were immensely helped by these writings, although their theology was contentious. *Theron and Aspasio* aroused a small war of pamphlets, and John Wesley openly assaulted Hervey's view of imputed righteousness. Nevertheless, by his writings he gained the attention of certain sophisticated sections of society. He regretted the hostility his works engendered, but he rejoiced that they penetrated social strata not readily accessible to the Evangelical message.[26]

Thomas Adam (1701-84)

Starting in 1725, Thomas Adam ministered for fifty-eight years at

---

[26] For the life and work of Hervey, see especially Elliott-Binns, *op.cit.*; Luke Tyerman, *The Oxford Methodists* (London, 1873).

Wintringham in Lincolnshire, although it was not until about 1746 that he underwent an experience of spiritual liberation whereby he was able to identify himself with the Evangelicals. Although his subsequent preaching attracted a large congregation, not only from his own parish but from adjacent areas, there appears to have been little evidence of fruitfulness at the end of his thirty years' Evangelical ministry, according to John Wesley and Henry Venn.[27] The majority of his parishioner appear to have retained their rough ways, and his message went largely unheeded, though a few were helped by a school which he started. The results achieved by the preaching of Walker, Grimshaw and Romaine were not forthcoming in Wintringham. If, however, Adam was not very successful in his own parish, he had a widespread and weighty influence on the Evangelical movement as a whole, especially after the publication in 1753 of his *Lectures on the Church Catechism*. He was sought out by many Evangelicals for advice. Samuel Walker found his counsel of great value; and Henry Venn, when engaged in writing his *Complete Duty of Man*, said that but for Adam's encouragement and approval he would have given up.

Adam was distinguished by his strong churchmanship. He insisted on the need for a resolute and unwavering resistance to the irregularities of Methodism, as we see in his letter to Walker in 1756. 'Methodism', he wrote, 'as to its external form, is such a deviation from the rule and constitution of the Church of England, that all attempts to render them consistent must be in vain'.[28] Some Evangelicals went beyond the limits of rigid church order, but not Adam, and his tenaciousness conveyed itself to others.[29]

Martin Madan (1726–90)

Martin Madan was in certain respects a remarkable man. He was born in 1726, educated at Westminster and Christ Church, Oxford and called to the bar in 1748. In the midst of a somewhat undisciplined life he came to an Evangelical faith in an unusual way. He was challenged by his coffee-house companions to hear Wesley preach in order that he might return and burlesque the sermon for their amusement. The effect of the preaching on him was such that when he returned to the coffee house and was asked if he had taken off the Methodist he replied, 'No, gentlemen, but he has taken me off'. He promptly severed himself from his former associates and took holy orders, apparently on the suggestion of Lady Huntingdon, but with the encouragement of Romaine and other Evangelicals.

[27] See John Wesley, *Journal*, Vol.V, p.480.
[28] Quoted in Sidney, *op.cit.*, p.224.
[29] For the life and work of Adam, see especially Elliott-Binns, *op.cit.*; James Stillingfleet, *Life of Thomas Adam* prefaced to his *Posthumous Works*.

Madan was a man of some learning: not only was he a barrister, but he knew the scriptures in the original and had considerable musical talent. From 1750 to 1780 he was chaplain to the Lock hospital and made its chapel a stronghold of Evangelicalism in London. Musically he was far beyond the ordinary, and also an innovator. In 1760 he published a collection of psalms and hymns for the Lock chapel which reached a high literary standard and was characterised by a bright and joyous spirit: it was subsequently used in a number of Evangelical churches. Besides this, every year he produced an oratorio in the chapel: a novelty which attracted some criticism.

The most controversial and eccentric episode in the life of Madan was his publication of *Thelyphthora, or a Treatise on Female Ruin* (1780), in which polygamy was advocated as a remedy for prostitution, the evils of which he regularly encountered in his daily work at the Lock hospital. The work, which was of immense length, appealed to scripture, but it horrified many Evangelicals. In response to their concern Madan retired and occupied himself with a *New and Literal Translation of Juvenal and Persius*.

During part of the time that Madan ministered in London he had a valuable ally in Thomas Jones. As junior chaplain of St Saviour's, South-wark from 1753 to 1762, Jones had to endure many trials and bitter opposition; his teaching was denounced, his sermons were caricatured, and his character vilified in a stream of controversial tracts. For some years he was the only beneficed Evangelical in the whole London area. He died prematurely in 1762 at the age of thirty-three.

In Kent there were two Evangelical clergy of some note, both of whom identified themselves with John Wesley and the Methodists. Henry Piers was converted largely through the influence of Charles Wesley in 1738. He was an original member of the Fetter Lane society and a close friend of the Wesleys. For many years he was vicar of Bexley. He died in 1770.

Vincent Perronet was vicar of Shoreham from 1728 to 1785. At first he was prejudiced against the Methodists, but he co-operated with them after he had met John Wesley in 1744. He was gentle, generous and studious. He was one of the few men able to curb the strong will of Wesley, and in the early days of the Methodist movement Wesley often consulted him. By some he received the appellation, Archbishop of Methodism. Perhaps he should be reckoned as more Methodist than Evangelical.

Other Evangelical clergy deserve a mention. In the university towns Joseph Jane made St Mary Magdalene the focus of Evangelicalism in Oxford. Richard Symes provided a centre for Evangelicalism in Bristol, as rector of St Werburgh's. John Baddiley was a champion of Evangelicalism in Derbyshire during his incumbency of Hayfield. Yorkshire was a stronghold of Evangelicalism. There was James Stillingfleet at Hotham;

William Richardson, for fifteen years vicar of the largest church in York; Henry Crooke, who made Leeds a nodal point of Evangelical activity when he began to preach an Evangelical message in 1754; Richard Conyers at Helmsley in the North Riding, who was converted to an Evangelical ministry in 1758; John Crosse, the blind vicar of Bradford; Miles Atkinson at Leeds, who received great support from William Hey, the famous surgeon; a succession of Evangelical clergy at Slaithwaite, including S. Furly, Matthew Powley and Thomas Wilson; and Henry Coulthurst, vicar of Halifax. Thomas Vivian of Cornwood, J. Vowler of St Agnes and Thomas Michell of Veryan contributed to an Evangelicalism which was probably more flourishing in Cornwall in these early years than in any other part of England.[30]

---

[30] For the life and work of Martin Madan, Thomas Jones, Henry Piers, Vincent Perronet, Joseph Jane, Richard Symes, John Baddiley, Thomas Vivian, J. Vowler and Thomas Michell, see Balleine, *op. cit.*, Elliott-Binns, *op. cit.*; John S. Reynolds, *The Evangelicals at Oxford 1735-1871* (Oxford, 1953); the *Dictionary of National Biography*.

2

Towards a National Crusade

Throughout the half century up to 1789, and indeed for many years
beyond that epoch-making date, the Evangelicals had to struggle for a
foothold in the church. They were generally despised by the bishops; it
was sometimes difficult for known Evangelicals to secure ordination, and
even more difficult for them to obtain preferment; the Evangelical clergy
were widely dispersed, without a recognized leader and with no structure
to promote national unity among themselves; and there were few
Evangelical laymen of note or national standing. Nevertheless, as the age
of revolution approached there was a significant increase in the cohesion,
momentum and comprehensiveness of the movement.

The Evangelical network was strengthened in the first instance by an
almost unintended consequence of personal correspondence and
interaction. We have seen how Samuel Walker and Robert Adam
consulted with each other; how William Romaine took counsel with
Walker; and how Henry Venn sought advice from Adam. The diaries,
journals and voluminous correspondence of later Evangelicals such as
John Newton and Henry Venn indicate that such intercourse increased and
intensified as the century progressed. The sense of common theological
purpose was further enhanced by the writings of the Evangelicals. They
were widely read and reinforced the Evangelical awareness of separate
identity. To those works already mentioned were added such publications
as John Fletcher's *Checks to Antinomianism*; John Newton's *Authentic*

Narrative (1764), *Cardiphonia* (1780), *Review of Ecclesiastical History* (1769) and, in co-operation with William Cowper, the *Olney Hymns* (1779); Joseph Milner's *History of the Church of Christ*, Erasmus Middleton's *Biographia Evangelica* (1779-1786); Thomas Scott's *Force of Truth* (1778); and the early letters and poems of William Cowper, including *The Task* (1785).

Locally rather than nationally, Evangelical unity was further promoted by the establishment of clerical associations.[1] These instilled into the younger clergy a sense of corporate identity, which was lacking in some of their predecessors who frequently had a desperate sense of isolation from official Anglicanism. The societies were for mutual encouragement and exchange of views, and for making suggestions about pastoral duties and problems. As previously mentioned, perhaps the first in the country specifically for Evangelical clergy was that founded by Samuel Walker in Truro. The most renowned were the Elland Society in Yorkshire, the Eclectic Society in London, and the societies in Bristol, Creaton and Rauceby. But there were others dotted all over the country, providing in each case an Evangelical focus and cell of activity.

The Eclectic Society was especially significant. It was destined to play a prominent part in the life of Evangelicalism not only in London but nationwide, as a forum for much constructive Evangelical debate. It was established in 1783 and almost all the London Evangelical clergy were members, together with a few Evangelical laymen. It met fortnightly in the vestry of St John's Church, Bedford Row. Some of the most important initiatives in the history of Evangelicalism originated in the debates of this little society, as we will see in a later chapter. The ideas which came to fruition in the Church Missionary Society germinated in the Eclectic Society, and discussions on the whole issue of Christian communication were instrumental in the founding of the *Christian Observer*.

Evangelicalism was also advanced by the practice of selective patronage.[2] Aristocratic patrons were important. Lord Dartmouth moved Henry Venn to Huddersfield, Matthew Powley to Dewsbury and James Stillingfleet to Hotham; Lord Smythe offered Yelling to Henry

---

[1] See G.R. Balleine, *A History of the Evangelical Party in the Church Of England* (London, 1908); G.C.B. Davies, *The Early Cornish Evangelicals 1735-1760* (London, 1951); L.E. Elliott-Binns, *The Early Evangelicals* (London, 1953); John S. Simon, *John Wesley and the Religious Societies* (London, 1921); J. Walsh, 'Origins of the Evangelical Revival' in G.V. Bennett and J.D. Walsh (Eds.), *Essays in Modern Church History* (1966); Josiah Woodward, *An Account of the Rise and Progress of the Societies in the City of London* (Third edition, London, 1701).

[2] See J.D. Walsh, 'The Yorkshire Evangelicals in the Eighteenth Century, with special reference to Methodism' (Cambridge University Ph.D., 1956).

Venn; and Lady Huntingdon, in addition to those Evangelicals she employed as her private chaplains, placed Walter Sellon at Ledsham, probably much to her regret as he became a decided Arminian and she was a convinced Calvinist. Other humbler patrons included Richard Richardson of Bierley Hall, who had the presentation to Whitechapel; Thomas Robinson patron of Middleton; William Wilberforce, whose political popularity helped him to secure Hull vicarage for Joseph Milner, and St Crux, York, for John Overton; and John Thornton, who bought the advowson of St Mary's Hull, and inaugurated the Evangelical patronage trusts.

Later in the century proprietary chapels played an increasingly important role, especially in London, but also in Yorkshire and other areas of the country. But perhaps the most useful source of patronage lay in the control by Evangelicals, or their sympathizers, of the chapelries of ease in great rambling parishes such as Halifax, Bradford and Dewsbury, whereby a quite extensive region could be deliberately planted with Evangelical clergy.

Evangelical cohesion was further fortified by a growing sense of independent identity. As the awareness of alienation from the followers of John Wesley and the other groupings within the revival movement became more pronounced, so the distinctiveness of Evangelicalism became more evident.[3]

John Wesley had increasingly come to believe that a revived Church of England depended upon the co-operation of the Evangelical clergy. He dreamed of a national union of such clergy who would keep in touch with each other by correspondence and occasional itinerant preaching, and who would both serve Methodism and be served by it. Such a scheme would, he thought, ensure a continuing evangelical witness within the established church. It seems that he first explained the concept at the Methodist Conference in 1757. In 1760 he faced nearly disastrous separatist pressures from his followers but resisted them. He invited several Evangelical clergy to his Conferences in 1761 and 1762. At Leeds in 1762 these included Madan, Romaine and Venn, as well as Whitefield and the Countess of Huntingdon. Wesley yearned for a united front, but he was becoming more and more disillusioned about the co-operation for which he strove.

In 1766 he mailed a four-page quarto circular and a covering letter to forty or fifty sympathetic Evangelical clergy. In it he said that union required the acceptance of three essentials: the doctrines of original sin and justification by faith, and the need for holiness of heart and life.

---

[3] For the details of this process of alienation see particularly Elliott- Binns, *op.cit*; John Wesley, *The Journal of the Rev. John Wesley*, Ed. Nehemiah Curnock, 8 vols. (London, 1938).

He did not seek concord on all theological issues: it was not necessary to agree on such matters as absolute decrees or perfection – two of the contemporary contentious doctrines. He was not searching for union in expressions: some would continue to speak of 'imputed righteousness' and others of 'the merits of Christ', although both of these terms were very controversial at the time. And he was not striving after union with regard to outward order: some would still remain quite regular, some quite irregular, and some would be partly regular and partly irregular. There would not be an attempt to alter such outward behaviour: the union would, according to Wesley, be one of spirit, of sympathy, of understanding and of hopeful love, both in thought and conduct. All would speak respectfully, honourably and kindly of each other and give what help was possible to each other.

Wesley received only three replies to his letter and circular: one from his former Kingswood colleague Walter Sellon, one from his long-standing friend Vincent Perronet of Shoreham, and another from the faithful Richard Hart of Bristol. After such a poor response he almost gave up hope of union. At the Conference in 1768 he again urged loyalty to the establishment, but he was fast becoming convinced that the search for a working partnership between the Methodist societies and the Evangelical clergy was futile. He therefore turned his full attention to securing the future of Methodism within a connexional organization co-ordinated by an itinerant ministry.

Why did the Evangelicals not respond to these overtures from Wesley? Were they being obtuse, unnecessarily inflexible, or restrictive and literally too parochial? Did they miss an historic opportunity to avoid a major separation from the Church of England?

In retrospect it can be seen that the differences between the Evangelicals and the Methodists which we have noted in the Introduction, although present from the early years, became more acute as the revival evolved. In the first place, the Evangelical movement retained its clericalism despite the prominence of many laymen, while Methodism became an increasingly lay movement, with lay leadership. The climax was reached in 1784 when Wesley ordained two lay preachers, and set apart Dr Coke as superintendent for Methodist work in America. This was an affront to many Evangelicals, and there was an outcry from them. Not only were lay leaders by this action being given the authority and functions reserved for duly ordained clergy, but ordination itself was thereby demoted.

Evangelicals also remained strict churchmen, while the situation of Methodism became more and more ambiguous. First meeting-houses were erected. Then, in order to avoid prosecution for unlawful assembly, they had to be registered, making the whole position manifestly anomalous. It was also in the decisive year 1784 that Wesley's Deed of

Declaration gave the Conference legal standing and, in effect, set up a new form of church government. Two years later, this authoritative Conference relaxed the rule about not holding services during church hours. It was made permissible to do so if the minister was notoriously wicked, or preached Arian or other pernicious doctrines; if the churches in a town were not sufficient to contain half the people; or if there was no church within two or three miles. In 1787 Wesley decided that all chapels and all itinerant preachers should be licensed, not as dissenters, but simply as preachers of the gospel. He also issued his revised prayer book for use by his societies in England.

Wesley continued to be concerned to avoid separation, but the movement of which he was the undisputed leader was almost irretrievably set on the path of schism. The breach became absolute in 1791 and 1795. In the former year the circuit system was set up to cover the United Kingdom, effectively providing an alternative to the parishes; and in the latter year permission was given to the preachers to celebrate the holy communion. All these moves were anathema to the Evangelicals. For, while Methodism was assuming the features of a sect or denomination, Evangelicals were characterized by a more pronounced loyalty to the Church of England. As the century wore on irregularity among Evangelicals diminished and, as a body, their conformity to Church order became more definite. In this respect, as in others, the divide between Evangelicalism and Methodism widened.

During these years, when the secession of the Wesleyans was becoming ever more inevitable, the impact of the Evangelicals was growing markedly. The movement was strengthened by the addition of several outstanding characters, and a number of less talented or prominent men who nevertheless made their vital contributions. As for the early years of Evangelicalism, so now in the second phase, the story is still to a great extent that of individual lives and ministries. In the biographies of these leaders the life, colour and character of this still young and vigorous movement is illuminated in an especially poignant way.

John Newton (1725-1807)

John Newton was not only one of the most remarkable of the Evangelical leaders, but arguably one of the most remarkable men in the whole history of the Church of England.[4] It was his personal history prior to his

---

[4] For the life and work of Newton see especially Marcus L. Loane, *Oxford and the Evangelical Succession* (London, 1951); John Newton, *An Authentic Narrative* (1764) and *Cardiphonia* (1780); J.C. Ryle, *Christian Leaders of the Eighteenth Century* (1885, reprinted Edinburgh, 1978).

ordination which was so unusual, for it reads like an adventure story from
the pages of fiction. He was born in 1725. His mother died in 1732, and at
the age of eleven he went to sea with his father. He was away from
England five times in the next six years, including a few months in Spain.
In 1742 he met Mary Catlett, and the love he felt for her never abated from
that moment to the end of his long life. Soon after this he was seized by a
naval press-gang and endured great hardship for a while until his father
arranged for him to be posted as a midshipman on the quarter-deck. In
1744 he deserted, was caught and returned in irons, stripped and publicly
flogged, degraded from office and boycotted by command.

There followed three years of fluctuating fortune. Newton was placed
on a ship engaged in the West African slave trade, and then put under a
master on an island known as the Plantanes. His employer was almost
completely under the thumb of his negro mistress, and she intensely
disliked Newton. She took every opportunity to crush him with scorn,
abuse and harsh treatment, beyond the lot of the meanest of her own black
slaves. In the absence of his master he was almost deprived of food and
water, and he sometimes had to be content either with scraps from her
plate or a share in the meagre pittance of the slaves. She took delight in
making a white man miserable. His master often chained him to the deck
of his ship, when he nearly starved to death. He was driven to a state of
abject misery and depression, and to the lowest depths of social
degradation and moral humiliation. It was only with a change of master
that his lot improved and he was able to return to England.

He continued to be involved in the slave trade, in the sea voyages of
slave traders. He gave himself up to extremes of blasphemy, including
parodies of the cross and the passion, and was becoming hardened in a
tough, demanding and often cruel life. But a personal spiritual crisis was
near at hand. A casual reading of Thomas à Kempis; fear of eternity
engendered by a violent storm and the real possibility of death; and
thoughts of God aroused by a serious fever in West Africa, made him
resolve to serve God.

In 1750 Newton married Mary Catlett. He rejoined slave ships first as
mate, then as captain, for as yet he saw no objection to a trade which he
was later to vehemently condemn. A series of further wild adventures
ensued; among natives on the African coastline, among mutinous crews,
and in quelling or preventing slave revolts. In 1754 he met a Captain
Clunie in the West Indies and through him came to an Evangelical
understanding of his faith. He continued to consider his calling lawful and
reasonable, but he was tired of a life which ever had to do with bolts and
chains and shackles, and he now had a Christian message which he could
commend to others with all his heart. He led his crew in Prayer Book
worship on a deck beneath which all the horrors inseparable from a slaver

were to be found.

Illness prevented further voyages and Newton was given the lucrative and not very onerous post as a Surveyor of Tides for the Port of Liverpool. He came to know Wesley, Whitefield and Grimshaw. By intense exertions he learned not only to read the New Testament in the original Greek, but also acquired some knowledge of Hebrew. He sought ordination unsuccessfully among dissenters. He applied to the Archbishop of York, who refused. Finally, on 29 April 1764, through the influence of Lord Dartmouth, he was ordained by the Bishop of Lincoln as the curate of Olney.

Newton served for fifteen years as a substitute for an absentee vicar at the lowly remuneration of £60 per annum. Olney was a country town inhabited by 2,000 poor and ragged people. Lord Dartmouth and John Thornton gave Newton funds to relieve the poor, and over the years of his ministry at Olney Thornton also gave him upwards of £3,000 as a supplement to his salary. The bluff former sea captain soon became well known to all, as he diligently and devotedly visited every quarter of his parish, most typically dressed in his blue sea jacket rather than clerical dress. People came to him in great numbers for personal counsel. He had a deep affection for his parishioners, and his own experience gave him a profound appreciation of other people's problems. This was most clearly demonstrated in his relationship with Thomas Scott. Scott was in charge of the nearby parishes of Weston Underwood and Stoke Goldington. On his own admission he was nearly a Socinian in his beliefs and did not have a very high standard of ministerial duty. By his steady but unobtrusive friendship, example and help, Newton played an important part in the progress of Scott towards an Evangelical view. Scott succeeded Newton as curate of Olney; had great and wide influence through his publications, especially his autobiographical work, *The Force of Truth* (1778) and his *Commentary on the Bible*; and was the first Secretary of the Church Missionary Society.[5]

We will meet Newton again, for he lived until 1807. He became rector of St Mary Woolnoth in London; a sole survivor among the great Evangelical leaders of his generation, and a bridge between the pioneers and the new Evangelicalism of the Napoleonic era. Indeed he exercised considerable influence upon the Evangelical leadership around the turn of

[5] Scott's time at Olney (1781–85) was beset with difficulties. He was not popular and had to face rough, somewhat aggressive people in the town as well as awkward church members. He went to London as morning preacher at the Lock chapel. His commentary on the Bible made him famous. Thirty-seven thousand complete copies were sold in his lifetime, and it was used for family prayers in almost every Evangelical home. Scott became rector of Aston Sandford in 1803 and died there in 1821. For his life and work, see Thomas Scott, *The Force of Truth* (1798); and Eugene Stock, *The History of the Church Missionary Society*, Vol.1 (London, 1899).

the century. He was largely responsible for persuading Wilberforce to stay in Parliament, with all the consequences for the pursuit of social justice overseas and at home that that decision entailed; and he was the wise friend of Hannah More whose views became Evangelical to a great extent under his influence.

Newton's published works also continued to be widely read; most notably his autobiography *An Authentic Narrative* (1764), and a volume of his letters under the title *Cardiphonia* (1780). The first was used by William Wordsworth in an early draft of *The Excursion*, and it also gave ideas to Samuel Taylor Coleridge for *The Rime of the Ancient Mariner*. But his most lasting literary product was the collection of 348 *Olney Hymns* published in 1779.

This was the joint work of Newton and his close friend in Olney, William Cowper. Cowper contributed such masterpieces of poetry and devotion as 'Hark, my soul, it is the Lord'; 'O for a closer walk with God'; 'God moves in a mysterious way'; 'There is a fountain filled with blood'; and 'Jesus, where'er Thy people meet'. Newton beautifully expressed his faith in 'Amazing grace'; 'How sweet the name of Jesus sounds'; 'Approach my soul the Mercy Seat'; 'Come my soul, thy suit prepare'; 'Great Shepherd of Thy people here'; 'Glorious things of Thee are spoken'; and 'Begone unbelief, my Saviour is near'. Hymns were still a new thing in the worship of the Church of England, and the greatest change the Evangelicals made in the church services in the eighteenth century was the introduction of congregational hymn singing. The Olney hymns were important in this development.

The co-operation of Newton and Cowper in producing the *Olney Hymns* was but one outcome of a remarkable relationship. The intimacy of friendship between the robust, self-taught ex-sea captain and the delicate, timid, scholarly ex-lawyer of exquisite taste was made possible by the religious bond which united them. Cowper was one of the foremost poets of the day, and his poetry carried the Evangelical ethos into quarters which the movement had hitherto not reached, and which Wesleyanism was never to reach. Evangelicalism was portrayed by him as a philosophy of life which could appeal to the educated and sophisticated, as well as to those of lower intellect. But he had a mental and religious history of such extreme vicissitudes and anguish that it is worthy of record, especially in view of his literary prominence.

William Cowper (1731-1800)

William Cowper was born in Berkhamsted in Hertfordshire in 1731 to a respectable middle-class family.[6] His father was an Anglican clergyman. For the first six years of his life he appears to have been happy in the security of his mother's love and affectionate attention. From her homely piety he learnt the elements of that faith which was to mean so much to him in an emotionally tortured life. Then, when he was only six, she died. It was a shattering blow.

He was miserable in his first school. He was despondent, and became convinced that he was under a curse. His time at Westminster School was happier, but he still lacked self-confidence. After leaving school, he studied law, initially under the supervision of a solicitor, then at the Middle Temple. He experienced periods of intense depression. He fell in love with a woman named Theodora, but after four years her father, for reasons which are not clear, forbade marriage. In 1756 Cowper lost his father; the last link which bound him to his happy early childhood. He became morbidly introspective. Through a family connection he was offered the posts of Reading Clerk and Clerk of Committees of the House of Commons. These appointments would have solved his quite severe financial problems and given him good, secure employment, but they entailed a public examination, and the thought of that filled him with horror. As the time of the examination approached, his fear, tension and despair intensified, and finally, in an extremity of torment, he made an unsuccessful attempt to hang himself. It was realized that he was unfit for the examination and the posts, and the offer was withdrawn. A period of brooding and deepening mental anguish ensued. He was admitted to Dr Cotton's House for Madmen at St Albans.

Dr Cotton was an Evangelical, and during his time at St Albans Cowper was drawn towards Evangelicalism. On leaving the Home in 1765 he went to live in Huntingdon, and there his Evangelicalism was bolstered and encouraged by his friendship with the Unwin family. Mr Unwin was a clergyman, but the dominant influence on Cowper was exercised by Mrs Unwin. He was accepted as part of the family and went to live with them. His affection and regard for Mrs Unwin increased. She supplied all the qualities he lacked. She provided for that need which had not been met since the death of his mother, and yet, being about the same age as Cowper, she also filled the vacuum left by the severed relationship with Theodora. Not only did she supply his needs, but he supplied hers. Her husband was much older than her, her family was grown up, and Cowper was more committed to the Evangelical faith than her husband. In about 1767 Mr Unwin died after a riding accident. Neither Mrs Unwin nor Cowper considered themselves in love, but they longed to retain their

[6] For the life and work of Cowper, see especially Lord David Cecil, *The Stricken Deer* (1929); Robert Southey, *The Life and Works of William Cowper*, 8 vols. (London, 1854).

intimate friendship and yearned to live in the neighbourhood of an Evangelical incumbent. At this juncture they met John Newton, and he arranged for them to move to Olney.

At Olney life was dominated by the energetic, forceful and colourful character of Newton. Cowper spent many hours each day in his company: praying with him, attending the sick and dying and accompanying him when he preached in nearby villages. He also visited the poor himself and taught in the Sunday school. It was a pattern of life which was in many ways therapeutic, and he was outwardly calmer. But inwardly his former disturbances returned; he became lethargic and his faith was sorely tested. In all this Mrs Unwin's placid firmness and loyalty were unshakeable. His distraught state reached a new peak in 1773. Blackness descended on him, lit by flashes of light. He even imagined that Mary Unwin and Newton were trying to poison him. Nevertheless, he again recovered.

In 1779 Newton left Olney to take up his new work in London, but Cowper remained. His life was largely circumscribed by the local activities and surroundings of the small town: the view of local tradesmen from the sash window of his parlour, idyllic walks in Weston Park, a country estate about a mile from Olney owned by Mr Throckmorton, and many contemplative hours spent in the garden. Cowper's routine was interrupted by an amorous relationship with a widow, Lady Austen, whom he met in Olney, and by a renewed friendship with his cousin, Lady Hesketh, but his outward circumstances were generally uneventful.

In 1786 he moved to the delightful neighbouring village of Weston, but the change of residence did not prevent a further decline in his mental condition. Old symptoms reappeared. In his sleep he was troubled by dreams, and awake he was disturbed by accusing voices. With this change of environment he desperately sought to recover his faith, which had suffered greatly by his questionings and his mental illness. During all this time Mary Unwin tenderly cared for him. Then, to his utter horror, Mary had a stroke and was seriously ill. The final devastating blow came when she died.

Cowper dragged out his last weary years in sorrow. In 1799, the year before his death, he heard the story of a sailor who had fallen overboard in the Atlantic and had succumbed after his companions had vainly attempted to save him. He saw an analogy with his own life. 'Had he not fallen early in life from the ship which carried normal mankind from the cradle to the grave? Had not his friends tried to save him in vain? And now, after a lifetime of struggling, was he not sinking exhausted to death? He, too, was a castaway, the castaway of humanity'.[7] As he reviewed the accumulated anguish of his life Cowper turned his thoughts into a last

[7] Cecil, *op.cit.*, pp.295, 296.

burst of poetry, in which he graphically described the pitiful state of the castaway, and concluded with a sombre reflection on his own sad story:

I therefore purpose not, or dream,
Descanting on his fate,
To give the melancholy theme
A more enduring date:
But misery still delights to trace
Its 'semblance in another's case.

No voice divine the storm allay'd,
No light propitious shone;
When, snatch'd from all effectual aid,
We perish'd, each alone:
But I beneath a rougher sea,
And whelm'd in deeper gulphs than he.

John Berridge (1716-93)

Not many miles from Olney, in the adjoining county of Bedfordshire, John Berridge was vicar of Everton.[8] Although he was born in 1716 he did not become committed to Evangelicalism until rather late in life. He entered Clare Hall, Cambridge, in 1734 and was elected to a fellowship in 1742. In 1749 he combined the curacy of Stapleford with his duties in college. In 1755 he was presented by his college to the living of Everton with Tetworth. Here, as at Stapleford, his labours seemed to be unavailing. He thought this might have been due to a shortcoming in himself. He undertook a close study of the scriptures and became convinced that the doctrine of justification by faith, which he had formerly considered foolish and harmful, was true. At once he destroyed all his old sermons and began preaching in a totally new manner, often extempore. The effect was almost startling. The church became crowded and many people came to an evangelical faith.

In 1758 he began to preach outside his own parish, and in the following year commenced preaching out of doors. He became acquainted with Lady Huntingdon, John Thornton, John Wesley, John Fletcher and John Newton as well as other eminent Evangelicals of his day. In his extra-parochial preaching Berridge covered most of Bedfordshire, Cambridgeshire and Huntingdonshire, and many parts of Hertfordshire, Essex and Suffolk. He would not infrequently preach twelve times and

[8] For the life and work of Berridge, see particularly J. Berridge, *Works*, Ed. R. Whittingham (1838); Elliott-Binns, *op.cit*; Marcus L. Loane, *Cambridge and the Evangelical Succession* (London, 1952); Ryle, *op.cit.*; A. Skevington Wood, *The Inextinguishable Blaze* (Exeter, 1960).

ride a hundred miles a week. In order to care for those who were aroused by his sermons he arranged for lay evangelists to look after them when he left the area. Some of the evangelists appear to have been humble labouring men, for whose maintenance Berridge had to provide out of his own pocket. John Thornton, the rich Evangelical London merchant, also gave financial assistance.

J.C. Ryle judged that 'of all the English evangelists of the eighteenth century' Berridge was 'undeniably the most quaint and eccentric'.[9] The vicar of Everton even outdid Grimshaw in the extremity of some of his behaviour and in the results he produced. He was continually saying odd things and he employed bizarre illustrations to convey his meaning. He was aware of infirmities in his character but pleaded that he was born with a fool's cap on, and that a fool's cap was not so easily put off as a night-cap. Perhaps he had little desire to put it off, but he was not a buffoon. His outline sermons and the surviving examples of his preaching show no signs of the absurd. They are not very deep or profound but with all their simplicity they are based on the Bible and true to the Evangelical gospel. His somewhat outlandish utterances were probably confined to the extemporaneous parts of his sermons, and to the illustrations which he used on the spur of the moment.

Berridge's preaching at certain periods of his ministry undoubtedly produced curious physical effects on some of those who were aroused. Certain of his hearers cried out loudly and hysterically, some were thrown into strong convulsions, and others fell into a kind of trance or catalepsy which often lasted a long time. Berridge never encouraged such demonstrations and did not regard them as a necessary mark of conversion. He was at times perplexed by them, and initially may have attached more value to them than they deserved. Nevertheless, the whole subject of ecstatic response, like demon possession, is a deep and mysterious one, and too much emphasis should not be placed on such a phenomenon. They were essentially peripheral to the work he accomplished. He was a gifted man of real humility, constant self-denial and self-discipline, abundantly kind and utterly devoted to his calling.

John William Fletcher (1729-85)

John William Fletcher was born at Nyon in Switzerland in 1729, his original name being Jean Guilleaume de la Fléchière.[10] He had been

[9] Ryle, op.cit., p.216.
[10] For the life and work of John Fletcher see especially Frank J. Benson, *The Life of the Rev. John William de la Fléchière* (London, 1817); Elliott-Binns, op.cit.; Loane, *Cambridge and the Evangelical Succession*; Ryle, op.cit.; and Luke Tyerman, *Wesley's Designated Successor* (1882).

intended for the Calvinist ministry but he was revolted by the doctrine of election and withdrew. On coming to England he taught in a school, where he managed to make himself proficient in English, and he then became tutor to the children of Thomas Hill of Tern Hall near Shrewsbury. Fletcher became acquainted with the Methodists, and in the course of about two years or more he discovered a faith which satisfied his intellectual as well as his spiritual needs. On 8 March 1757 he was ordained deacon, and on the same day assisted Wesley in one of his services. For three years he had no appointment in the Church of England. He retained his position as tutor in Mr Hill's family, and continued to help the Methodists.

The turning-point of Fletcher's ministerial career was his induction as vicar of Madeley in October 1760. He had previously refused the valuable living of Dunham in Cheshire, a small parish in fine sporting country, as he thought that there was too much money and too little work. Dunham was then given to the vicar of Madeley so that Fletcher should have Madeley, an industrial town near Wellington in Shropshire. Its inhabitants were mainly colliers or iron-workers whose dominant characteristics were ignorance and brutality. No other clergyman in the county sympathized with the Evangelical views of Fletcher. The surroundings were utterly uncongenial to his sensitive, delicate nature but, refusing all offers of preferment, he insisted on remaining in Madeley. After two rough and stormy years of opposition in which he achieved little success, there followed comparative calm. For twenty-five years Fletcher did the work of an evangelist and pastor, mainly in his own parish, although he undertook some itinerant preaching. He worked conscientiously and intensely until he became gravely ill with consumption in 1776. After an extended period of treatment he returned to his duties in 1782, having been married in the previous year. He died in 1785 from a fever caught when visiting a parishioner.

Fletcher was one of the few Evangelical clergy who kept in close and sympathetic touch with Wesley and the Methodist movement. He thought it was 'shameful that no clergyman should join John Wesley to keep in the Church the work which God had enabled him to carry on therein'.[11] Not only did he minister in Methodist services, but his kitchen was in regular use by Methodist preachers and he vigorously and ably defended John Wesley's doctrinal views, primarily in a series of published *Checks to Antinomianism*. Wesley thought that Fletcher was more qualified than Whitefield to 'sound an alarm through all the nation' and expressed the hope that he would succeed him as the leader of the Methodist movement. Fletcher utterly refused to accept such a plan, though he

[11] Quoted in Elliott-Binns, *op.cit.*, p.210.

promised that if he outlived Wesley he would co-operate with Charles Wesley in keeping the Methodists together. In the event, Wesley outlived his younger friend. The high regard of Wesley for his designated successor is evident in the funeral sermon he delivered. 'In four-score years', Wesley said, 'I have known many exemplary men, holy in heart and life, but one equal to him I have not known, one so inwardly and outwardly devoted to God'.[12]

The Countess of Huntingdon also held Fletcher in great esteem, and about 1765 he was appointed President of her new college at Trevecca in Wales. He only accepted the post on the distinct understanding that he was not to be generally resident in the college as his parochial responsibilities were paramount. For three years he gave advice on the appointment of masters and the admission or exclusion of students; provided oversight of the studies and conduct of the students, and judged their fitness for the work of ministry. In 1771 his connection with the college ended. This may in large measure have been because of his strong determination to stand by John Wesley in the doctrinal controversy which came to a head within the ranks of the revival at that time. But there was also the strain of retaining his two spheres of activity, and he may well have welcomed an opportunity of relinquishing the one.

Henry Venn (1725-97)

Henry Venn was faced with a similar task to Fletcher when he went to Huddersfield as vicar in 1759.[13] Venn came of a family with long clerical traditions. He was born on 2 March 1725. He went in June 1742 to St John's College Cambridge, transferred to Jesus College, and in 1749 was elected to a fellowship at Queens' College. He was ordained in 1747. After two years of combining clerical work in the neighbourhood with his college duties, he served as a curate in West Horsley before going as curate to Clapham in 1754. About 1758 he was 'brought to believe for himself', and in the following year he began his ministry in Huddersfield. The parish covered a wide area and a population of about five thousand. Huddersfield itself was growing from a small village to a town, and was surrounded by a large country district with outlying hamlets. The situation was daunting. The inhabitants were not unlike those of Madeley. 'A wilder people I never saw in England', wrote the much travelled Wesley in 1757. They were largely hardened weavers and farmers living in the remote and somewhat barren environment of the Yorkshire dales.

[12] Quoted in Elliott-Binns, op.cit., p.300.

[13] For the life and work of Henry Venn see particularly Elliott-Binns, op.cit.; Loane, *Cambridge and the Evangelical Succession; Ryle, op.cit.*; John Venn, *Memoir of the Rev. Henry Venn* (1834)

In common with other Evangelicals we have considered, Venn soon drew congregations which exceeded the capacity of the church. He also made preaching excursions to various parts of England. He was often at Lady Huntingdon's chapel at Oathall near Brighton, and at Bath; he preached at Trevecca college, at Bristol, Cheltenham, Gloucester, Worcester and London. He was a close friend of the leading Evangelicals of the day and Wesley, Whitefield, Grimshaw and Romaine all preached in his church. Nonetheless, he experienced varied, and sometimes somewhat discordant relations with Methodism. An unfortunate clash occurred when Venn arrived in Huddersfield and found an active Methodist society in his parish. He asked that it should be placed under his control, but the members insisted on having their own preachers. Wesley claimed that this was not in opposition to Venn, whom the society members loved and esteemed, and whose church they constantly attended, but in order to supplement his preaching. Where there was a 'gospel ministry' Wesley declared that there was no desire to preach but if, as in the case of Huddersfield, a society had previously existed, it was questionable if the Methodist preaching should be curtailed. A compromise was reached whereby the visit of such Methodist preachers was limited to one a month. Charles Wesley confessed that if he had a parish he would not allow Methodist preachers to enter it. The main Methodist argument in favour of such a practice was the need to guarantee continuity of Evangelical preaching in a particular parish.

Venn was not parochial in outlook: he was concerned about the Church of England as a whole. He was closely associated with the Elland Society which (like the later Bristol Education Aid Society and the London Clerical Education Aid Society) provided funds for young Evangelical candidates to go to Oxford and Cambridge: it was an ordination fund. From his own ministry in Huddersfield came twenty-two ordinands with working-class backgrounds, but because they were not able to gain admittance to university they went to dissenting academies and were lost to the Church of England.

By 1771 Venn was exhausted with his parochial and other duties, and he accepted the living of Yelling. He was devoted to the work at Huddersfield but his health was deteriorating, and he went to Yelling 'as a dying man'.[14] The demands of the new parish were not great but he met with suspicion and hostility from the local clergy and suffered the withdrawal of families from his own congregation. The most fruitful and rewarding aspect of his new ministry was the beneficial influence he exercised upon students and staff of nearby Cambridge, among whom were William Farish, Thomas Robinson, John Flavel, Charles Jerram and,

---

[14] Elliott-Binns, op.cit., p.323.

most significantly, Charles Simeon. Indeed Simeon in his Evangelical isolation during his earlier years in Cambridge depended greatly on Venn: when he had time to spare he eagerly rode the twelve miles to Yelling over the open countryside. His gratitude for the friendship and advice he received is evident: 'In this aged minister', he said, 'I found a father, an instructor and a most bright example'.

In 1761 Venn had published one of the most popular Christian handbooks of the century, *The Complete Duty of Man*. *The Whole Duty of Man* had been anonymously printed in 1657 and had such a vogue after the Restoration that it ranked next after the Bible and the Prayer Book in the estimation of many churchmen; but Evangelicals were unhappy about it. They thought it made eternal life regrettably dependent on works and duty. Venn's book became popular with Evangelicals, but it failed to displace the earlier work, probably because of its prosaic style and lack of literary grace.

Thomas Haweis (1734-1820)

The last example we will take of Evangelicalism in this era is Thomas Haweis,[15] a man who distinguished himself in a number of ways. While an undergraduate at Oxford he gathered together those who, like himself, were preparing themselves for the ministry of the church, and who felt the need for fellowship. Tyerman did not hesitate to call it a second Holy Club.[16] In 1757 he became a curate of St Mary Magdalene, Oxford and by his activities caused a stir in the town and attracted a large congregation. He aroused the opposition of the Vice-Chancellor and the Bishop, and in 1762 he was dismissed from his curacy, apparently without any charge being preferred.

Haweis went to London as an assistant to Martin Madan in the chaplaincy of the Lock hospital, and in 1764 he was inducted to the living of Aldwincle in Northamptonshire. From 1774 he gave part of each year to itinerant preaching as a chaplain to the Countess of Huntingdon. Towards the end of his life, in 1795, he was one of the three most influential men in the formation of the London Missionary Society, and the one most responsible for the mission of that Society to Tahiti and the South Seas. He was among the earliest instigators of the modern missionary movement. And in his missionary endeavours he also anticipated a future trend among Evangelicals by co-operating enthusiastically with dissenters.

[15] For the life and work of Thomas Haweis see especially A. Skevington Wood, *Thomas Haweis* (1957).
[16] Luke Tyerman, *Life of Whitefield*, Vol. II, p.375.

Haweis demonstrates something of the often ambivalent relationship between the Evangelicals and the Countess of Huntingdon. He remained a staunch churchman but, in common with other Church of England chaplains of the Countess, upheld her right to employ her own chaplains in her own chapels. In 1780, as the result of a ruling by the ecclesiastical courts, she was faced with a stark choice. Either she must come under the discipline of the Church of England and accept supervision within the parochial system, or she must shelter under the Toleration Act, and register her chapels as dissenting places of worship. She chose the latter and thus, somewhat unwillingly, seceded from the established church. The first public ordination of her ministers two years later emphasized the separation. Haweis, together with Romaine, Venn, and all her other chaplains, withdrew from the connection: although he resumed his itinerant preaching under its aegis in 1789, and was appointed a trustee and executor for the Countess at her death.

In spite of this final schism, Lady Huntingdon had been a good friend to the Evangelical movement.[17] She had encouraged and supported a number of clergy. Her chapels had given Evangelicals opportunities for preaching when such were all too few. She had given an entrée into aristocratic circles for a handful of selected preachers. She had united Evangelicals in a way which Wesley, owing to his different views, could never have done.

These few men whose lives we have all too scantily reviewed, were the leaders among a steadily increasing band of Evangelical clergy. Of the others, Thomas Robinson at Leicester and the Hon. W.B. Cadogan deserve special mention for their powerful and influential ministries. Most portentously, Charles Simeon had been appointed to Holy Trinity, Cambridge in 1783. The Evangelicals had suffered long from the absence of a nationally recognized leader to whom they could look for guidance and direction. Simeon was soon to bring to Evangelicalism a statesman-like mind and organizing ability which had previously been wanting. Significantly, he was born in the same year as William Wilberforce (1759), and they were to die within three years of each other. For as Simeon and Cambridge were about to provide a focus for Evangelicalism, so the day was fast approaching when Wilberforce and Clapham were to be the focal points for monumental Evangelical political, philanthropic and missionary endeavours, as we shall see in later chapters. But we must first assess the achievements of Evangelicalism up to 1789.

---

[17] For the life and work of the Countess of Huntingdon, see especially *Life and Times of Selina, Countess of Huntingdon*, Member of the House of Shirley and Hastings, 2 vols. (1839); Luke Tyerman, *The Life and Times of the Rev. John Wesley* (London, 1870), and Luke Tyerman, *The Life of the Rev. George Whitefield* (London, 1890).

3

The Evangelical Achievement

Until well into the nineteenth century Evangelicals continued to be a despised minority within the church. More pulpits were opened to them, and there was not so much of the violent opposition which the early Evangelicals had to endure, but the favour of church and state was still withheld from them. No Evangelical clergyman other than Dean Milner and Archdeacon Bassett received high preferment. On the bench of bishops Beilby Porteus of London sympathized in a guarded way with them, Dr Shute Barrington, Bishop of Durham, gave qualified support, and Bishop Burgess, first of St David's then of Salisbury, favoured some of the objectives most dear to them but did not completely identify himself with them. It was not until the Hon. Henry Ryder[1] was promoted to the see of Gloucester in 1815 that a recognized Evangelical was elevated to the episcopate. Nonetheless, even though they were a small group with little ecclesiastical status, the foundation for the Evangelical upsurge in the late eighteenth and early nineteenth century had been well laid in the previous pioneering period. Despite many failings and shortcomings the Evangelical achievement had been considerable.

By their example and by their teaching the few scattered Evangelical clergy had, according to Lecky, 'gradually changed the whole spirit of the

[1] See G.C.B. Davies, *The First Evangelical Bishop* (1958); and the *Dictionary of National Biography* (to which the account in this chapter is especially indebted).

English Church. They infused into it a new fire and passion of devotion, kindled a spirit of fervent philanthropy, raised the standard of clerical duty, and completely altered the whole tone and tendency of the preaching of its ministers'.[2] Sir James Stephen described the Evangelical fathers as 'the second founders of the Church of England'.[3] In the view of Gladstone, the Evangelical clergy were 'the heralds of a real and profound revival, the revival of spiritual life'.[4] Thomas Grenville (1750-1842) said: 'I have seen no change in my long life equal to the change in habits and manners of the clergy.'[5] It appears that the example of the early Evangelicals contributed significantly to this improvement in clerical standards which followed the rise of the movement. We recall that it was the conscientious discharge of his ministerial duties by John Newton which first aroused Thomas Scott to an awareness of his own deficiencies.

Such commendable patterns of ministry did not consist only of preaching, evangelism and pastoral concern. Evangelicals repeatedly emphasized the value of the sacraments and helped to reinstate them to a central place in the life of the church. Typically the number of baptisms, and attendance at holy communion increased, sometimes dramatically, as a result of an Evangelical ministry.

Nonetheless, preaching was given pride of place in the worship and witness of Evangelicals. Their sermons, as we have them in printed form, are not particularly impressive; but they were powerful and effective when preached by men of intense conviction, in an often distinctive and attention-riveting manner. As a rule the sermons were simple, and not intended to arouse the admiration of their hearers. The preachers had an unambiguous purpose: they wanted to communicate an essentially straightforward message of salvation in direct, uncomplicated language, using homely and telling illustrations. They were intense and earnest, and they delivered their message with urgency and zeal. Their sermons were carefully prepared and drew upon the personal experience of the preacher. For the Evangelicals as well as for the Methodists, the intention was 'To invite. To convince. To offer Christ. To build up'.[6]

The centrality of preaching in the Evangelical régime inevitably gave special prominence to the preacher, and this sometimes tended to make the Evangelical clergy somewhat egotistical, dictatorial and pietistic. Henry Martyn noted the proclivity: 'I find that in whatever manner the most holy

[2] W.E.H. Lecky, op.cit., Vol. II, p.627, quoted in A. Skevington Wood, op.cit., p.237.

[3] James Stephen, Essays in Ecclesiastical Biography (London, 1883), p.445, quoted in A. Skevington Wood, op.cit., p.237.

[4] Quoted in E. Elliott-Binns, The Early Evangelicals, p.418.

[5] Quoted in Elliott-Binns, op.cit., p.419.

[6] Methodist Conference, 1744.

ministers speak of their success, I am very apt to be disgusted at the prominent character of the instrument'.[7] John Thornton may well have had this in mind when he advised Charles Simeon that the three lessons a minister has to learn are one, humility, two, humility, three, humility.[8]

As the Evangelical preaching was simple, so too was the doctrine they proclaimed. Evangelical theology was artless and largely uncontroversial. Even during the frequently heated debate among the Wesleyans over predestination, election and Christian perfection, the Evangelicals (apart from Augustus Toplady and John Fletcher) tended to be spectators.

Although the great majority of the Evangelicals were Calvinists, their Calvinism was of a very moderate type, and they did not want it to be a cause of dispute. Hervey, despite his controversy with Wesley, 'never taught or held, the doctrine of unconditional election and reprobation'.[9] Venn declared that he was 'no friend to High Calvinism'. Dean Milner, who abandoned Arminianism in 1780, could still say that 'Calvin is much too systematical for me'.[10] Romaine bewailed the divisiveness of theological controversy: 'The *Foundry*, the *Tabernacle*, the *Lock*, the *Meeting*, yea *St Dunstan's*, has each its party', he complained, 'and brotherly love is almost lost in our disputes'.[11] At the height of the Calvinist-Arminian debate in 1771 Berridge advised his friend Rowland Hill to 'Keep out of all controversy, and wage no war but with the devil'.[12] After an interview with Wesley in 1787, Charles Simeon concluded that what Wesley believed was in its essentials in accord with his own Calvinism. 'It is', he said, 'in substance all that I hold, and as I hold it; and therefore if you please, instead of searching out terms and phrases to be the ground of contention between us, we will cordially unite in those things wherein we agree'.[13] When Evangelicals did join in the debate, as with Fletcher in his *Checks to Antinomianism*, and Berridge with his *Christian World Unmasked*, they did so in a restrained way. Toplady alone among the Evangelicals showed an immoderate and aggressively partisan spirit.

The Evangelicals constantly and consistently taught the sufficiency and supremacy of the Bible in its totality as the sole rule of faith and practice. They were content to hold the doctrines which they believed were enshrined in the Articles, Prayer Book and Homilies, as they thought these were in accord with the Bible.

[7] Journal, February 2 1803, quoted in Elliott-Binns, *op.cit.*, p.431.
[8] See Handley C.G. Moule, *Charles Simeon* (London, 1892), p.65.
[9] Elliott-Binns, *op.cit.*, p.196.
[10] *Ibid.*
[11] *Ibid.*
[12] *Ibid.*, p.205
[13] *Ibid.*, p.207.

On the basis of such authority they declared that the whole world lay in darkness. Human nature was fallen and in a state of total corruption, not in the sense that there was no good in man but that every aspect of human life was tainted by sin. Man would perish eternally unless he responded to Christ's death upon the cross, which was the only satisfaction for sin. Christ died as our substitute, 'the just for the unjust'. In his death Christ became a curse for us, that he might deliver us from the curse to which we were doomed. Every person needed to be justified by faith.

Once converted, the Christian must of necessity demonstrate the reality of his new-found faith by personal holiness. Appeal was constantly made to the high standards and disciplined life required of the convert. The reformation of society was considered possible only through the cumulative effect of individual lives which had been totally re-orientated as a result of conversion and subsequent consecration. This intense concern for the individual tended to encourage a neglect of the social aspects of the faith; although Evangelicals were not alone in this. The church as a whole was not conspicuous in the eighteenth century either for its contribution to social thinking or its social action. The Evangelicals were to rectify these shortcomings in a major way in the ensuing one hundred years.

The desire for holiness of life also inclined Evangelicals to excessive rigours, an undue narrowing of interests and over-censoriousness. For example, when Romaine was asked on one occasion to join a game of cards and the cards were produced, he said, 'Let us ask the blessing of God'. The surprised hostess exclaimed, 'I never heard of such a thing before a game of cards'. Romaine retorted, 'Ought we to engage in anything on which we cannot ask God's blessing?' The cards were removed.[14] The incident was indicative of the general Evangelical view. Card-playing was condemned together with the theatre, dances and worldly company.

The severity of the Evangelical personal ethic was demonstrated in an acute way in the treatment of children. Evangelicals regarded the care and nurture of their own children as a sacred charge. All kinds of restraints were imposed in order to protect them from evil. The books they read, the people they met, and the things they were allowed to see, were all carefully and comprehensively supervised. Sometimes this surveillance may have been rather excessive, as in certain of the schools to which a number of Evangelicals entrusted their boys. Such was the establishment at Hammersmith of which a certain Mr Elwell was proprietor. Its early pupils included Jowett and Cecil and later another leading Evangelical, Henry Venn Elliott. The biographer of the latter states that, 'all was

---

[14] See Ryle, *op.cit.*, p.170.

suspicion and espionage'. He quotes the effect on one of his contemporaries: 'I was', said the person concerned, 'myself so disgusted with religion when I left . . . that many years later I still never opened my Bible, or said my prayers'.[15] It was perhaps almost inevitable that a beleaguered minority, who held views on life and eternity with such vehemence, should not infrequently have been overprotective of their children.

Systematic Bible teaching and religious instruction of children were accepted by Evangelicals as a solemn responsibility for parents and the church at large. But it was not until the latter half of the century that Sunday schools were inaugurated. Although there had been previous tentative efforts, it was a wealthy layman, Robert Raikes of Gloucester, who laid the foundations of modern Sunday school work in 1780. Fletcher opened six schools at Madeley, and Thomas Wilson started one at Slaithwaite. These examples were speedily followed by Cornelius Bayley at Manchester, and by Miles Atkinson and Dr Hey at Leeds.

The communication of the Evangelical message and ethical standards, whether to adults or to children, was achieved supremely through preaching. But hymns and hymn singing were also a powerful means of expressing religious views. They were especially appropriate for the many people who were not readily able to grasp abstract doctrinal concepts when they were presented in other forms, such as the written word or a well-reasoned address. Hymns heightened sensitivity to religious ideas for people not accustomed to theological language. By the constant reiteration of certain teaching through the repeated use of popular hymns, those involved became increasingly familiar with fundamental Evangelical tenets.

A large proportion of the hymns of John and Charles Wesley were composed in the early years of the revival, and collections of them were among the first of the revival publications. The Evangelicals were comparatively late in making their contribution. They inherited a system in which the choir frequently sang psalms in the presence of an inattentive congregation, so they began to compile hymn books in an attempt to encourage intelligent congregational participation. The first to appear was Martin Madan's *Psalms and Hymns* (1760). It was a small book containing only one hundred and forty-two hymns, but owing to its liveliness and high literary standard it was rapidly adopted by many churches. In the same year Berridge produced his *Collection of Divine Songs*, a far larger but less satisfactory collection. In the following thirty-five years many Evangelicals produced collections: Conyers (1767), Romaine (1775), De

---

[15] Bateman, *Life of H. V. Elliott*, p.2, quoted in Elliott-Binns, p.375.

Courcy (1775), Toplady (1776), Simpson (1776), Newton and Cowper (1779), Joseph Milner (1780), Cadogan (1785), John Venn (1785), Cecil (1785), Robinson, (c.1790), Woodd (1794) and Simeon (1795). These collections were very varied. Romaine's was the most conservative; he did not include a single hymn but used old-established psalms. At the other extreme Robinson of Leicester excluded all such psalms. Soon one or other of these books was adopted by virtually all the Evangelical clergy. The hymns were often used in house meetings, as at Olney. Enthusiastic congregational singing soon became a marked feature of Evangelical services. Non-Evangelical clergy rigidly adhered to the two old versions, Sternhold and Hopkins's collection of metrical psalms and the more recent version by Tate and Brady. They denounced hymns as a deplorable and disloyal innovation.

Among the Evangelicals there were hymn-writers of considerable merit. In addition to John Newton and William Cowper, Augustus Toplady deserves special mention.[16] He had an enigmatic character; both poetic sensitivity and vitriolic aggression were publicly displayed in his writings. As an ardent Calvinist he attacked John Wesley in what many would consider an over-zealous manner, using most abusive language. Nonetheless, in some of his hymns he rose to noble heights, as in 'Christ whose glory fills the skies' and 'Rock of ages'.

Evangelical teaching and ethical norms were additionally reinforced by means of small groups which met regularly and supplemented the Sunday services. They were a means of maintaining and intensifying the degree of social interaction and the sense of unity and purpose of those responding to the Evangelical ministries. The formation of such groups also ensured that there was a comprehensive, concentrated and continuous opportunity for fellowship, instruction, prayer and service. New converts straightway found themselves integrated into a closely-knit company of like-minded believers, and this became a primary medium for building up and establishing their faith.

The communication of the Evangelical message to society at large was facilitated by the small size of eighteenth century towns and villages. Most of the communities in which Evangelicals ministered had populations of only a few thousand, and there was a high degree of social cohesion. Both the preaching and the subsequent influence of the converts upon their

---

[16] Augustus Montague Toplady was born in 1740 and educated at Trinity College, Dublin. He was ordained in 1762 and ministered in various country parishes in Somerset and Devon. He suffered from lung trouble, and went to London in 1775 on medical advice, where he rented the French chapel in Orange Street. He also preached in Lady Huntingdon's chapels and for a number of Evangelical clergymen. He died in 1778, at the age of thirty-eight. His writings included his learned, and in some respects brilliant work, *The Historic Proof of the Doctrinal Calvinism of the Church of England* (1774).

neighbours and their neighbourhood as a whole was open for all to hear and behold. Evangelicalism typically took root in a small town and then exercised its influence upon the surrounding area. It was a pattern which was to be repeated with great effect throughout the history of Evangelicalism both in England and worldwide.

As this Evangelical influence spread, and as the number of Evangelical clergy increased, laymen also became more prominent. In the early years of movement such lay leaders were confined in their influence to a circumscribed local area, as with George Conon in Truro. In the second half of the century a great change was to take place as laymen assumed national importance. Of particular note were the Earl of Dartmouth, James Ireland, the wealthy Bristol shipowner, William Hey, the physician, Richard Hill, and in the field of literature, Hannah More and William Cowper. As a philanthropist, John Thornton was outstanding. He was one of the wealthiest men of his day and he was remarkably generous. 'He was one of those rare men in whom the desire to relieve distress assumes the force of a master-passion'.[17] In the last decade of the century many more illustrious names were to be added, especially from among those identified with the Clapham Sect.

Thus, to a limited extent, Evangelical influence spread within society. But its extensive diffusion among the middle classes was a characteristic of a later generation. In the eighteenth century the Evangelicals had little impact upon the upper middle classes or the aristocracy.

There is evidence to indicate that both Methodism and Evangelicalism in their formative early phases were especially influential among what might appropriately be described as the lower middle classes. This was largely so with the parochial ministries of Grimshaw, Venn, Hervey, Berridge and, to varying extents, with most of the other Evangelicals we have considered, with the possible exception of Romaine and Newton in London. Only occasionally in a local area, or through the good offices of the Countess of Huntingdon, were the upper classes touched by the Evangelical message until towards the end of the century.

It was not until the Napoleonic era that Evangelicalism started to be identified with the 'respectable' classes. More especially, it was with the establishment and development of Evangelicalism in fashionable watering places in the nineteenth century, and the identification of the Evangelical ethos with the Victorian middle-class ethic, that Evangelicalism increasingly assumed a middle-class face. It was in these later phases that the socio- economic distinction between Methodism and Evangelicalism became pronounced.

The initial locus of Evangelicalism in the lower middle classes, and to a

[17] James Stephen, *Essays*, p.292.

limited extent the working classes, is underlined by its geographical spread. Haworth, Wintringham, Weston Favell, Olney, Everton, Madeley, Huddersfield and Aldwincle were all distinguished by their somewhat unrefined inhabitants living in many cases in uncongenial environments. They were either unpleasant small industrial towns or rural centres. The Evangelicals who were incumbents in such places had little opportunity to reach the higher social classes. Even where there were local middle-class populations as with Walker in Truro, Romaine at St George's, Hanover Square, London, and Charles Simeon in his early ministry at Holy Trinity, Cambridge, it was from among such that the fiercest opposition frequently originated, and it was people of a lower socio-economic order who most readily responded to the preaching. But even so, such inroads into sections of the working class must not be exaggerated. At no stage in the eighteenth century does there appear to have been an extensive, widespread turning to the Christian faith by masses of religiously alienated sections of the population as a result of Evangelicalism.

The intense antagonism Evangelicals so often experienced was provoked and sustained by their own uncompromising and fervent evangelism. The pioneer Evangelicals were consumed with the urgency of the task of saving souls at any cost: but this easily became a weakness as well as a strength. We have noted the dangers of an exclusive concentration upon the individual; and the associated lack of a social dimension in the teaching and conduct of Evangelicals. There were other kindred shortcomings. There was a narrowness of perspective and theological grasp; a restriction by some Evangelical leaders to the declaration of a few favourite topics; a deficiency in the appreciation of art, literature and aesthetics, exhibited in the barrenness of much Evangelical worship, the avoidance of ceremonial and the frequent absence of a deep sense of awe.

Attention has been drawn to the austerity of the individual Evangelical code of conduct. This not infrequently entailed an unattractive negativism in which avoidance of evil could so easily be seen as more important than doing good. The strength of Evangelical convictions often resulted in disagreement within their own ranks, backbiting and even local schism. Evangelicals could be inconsistent, and on many occasions practice was at variance with precept. They could also be somewhat outlandish in their reasoning, and their language could be as absurd and incongruous as their thought. Elderly clerics wrote to young ladies to urge them not to use rouge in a style which combined, but which did not unite, those of Jeremiah and the polite letter-writer. Middle-aged women expressed their feelings on meeting a favourite preacher in the voluptuous imagery of the Song of Solomon.[18]

----

[18] See David Cecil, op.cit., p.32.

Such a catalogue of defects and failings only makes the achievement of these Evangelicals the more remarkable: for they accomplished much. They imposed a moral order on life. Amid much that was trivial they held to a philosophy which gave integration and purpose to life. 'The merchant in the counting-house, the spinner in the factory, the old maid in the village, all felt themselves actors in the great drama of mankind's salvation'.[19] Evangelicalism provided an explanation of the mystery of existence, the omnipresence of evil and the inevitability of death. It gave an heroic proportion and eternal dimension to the life of ordinary people in their daily round. Innumerable lives were transformed.

At the level of society as a whole, its achievements were no less conspicuous. The Evangelicals were to be instrumental in purifying the morals of society, and the foundation for this was laid in the early years of the revival. The abolition of the slave trade, the reform of factory and other legislation, countless works of charity and the multifarious initiatives in hospital, educational and other spheres of social action were undertaken by the heirs of these eighteenth century forerunners.

Some of these consequences of the early Evangelical movement were intended by the Evangelicals themselves; they deliberately promoted them. Other results were not foreseen; they were what may be described as unintended consequences of intended human action. Two are especially significant. Unwittingly, the Evangelicals held a view of life which perhaps uniquely among the philosophies of its day, could satisfy the temperament of the artist. 'For it alone set a supreme value on that emotional exultation in which the greatest art is produced, it alone made the imagination the centre of its system, and not a mere decorative appendage to it'.[20] Individually, Evangelicals characteristically repudiated art and secular literature, but the movement of which they were a part helped to prepare for the Romantic Age.

The second possible unintended consequence has been much debated. It was Elie Halévy who first suggested that the evangelical revival was crucial in explaining why England avoided the kind of political and social upheaval suffered by French society. In the evangelical movement Halévy found a reason for 'the extraordinary stability which English Society was destined to enjoy throughout a period of revolutions and crises; what we may truly term the miracle of modern England, anarchist but orderly, practical and businesslike, but religious and even pietist'.[21] The Halévy thesis has subsequently been extensively discussed, reappraised and reinterpreted by sociologists and historians. But whatever the influence of

[19] *Ibid.*
[20] *Ibid.*, p.83.
[21] E. Halévy, *op.cit.*, Vol. I, p.387.

the evangelical movement may have been in avoiding a revolutionary situation, any such consequence must be seen as beyond the awareness of the Evangelicals immediately involved in it.[22]

By 1789, with five decades of honourable service behind it, Evangelicalism was just emerging from its pioneering epoch. It was growing in unity, and in the clarity of its aims and objects. 'It was, indeed, about to enter upon a second spring'.[23]

[22] For a brief discussion of what is known as the Halévy thesis see the extended note below.

[23] Elliott-Binns, op.cit., p.457.

Extended Note: the Halévy thesis

The Halévy thesis was first published in 1906 in a book entitled *A History of the English People in the Nineteenth Century – England in 1815*. Three extended quotations from the Ernest Benn Limited, 1960, edition of that work make clear the questions to which Halévy addressed himself, and the answers he suggested.

> Why was it that of all the countries of Europe England has been the most free from revolutions, violent crises, and sudden changes . . . Her political institutions were such that society might easily have lapsed into anarchy had there existed a bourgeoisie animated by the spirit of revolution. And a system of economic production that was in fact totally without organization of any kind would have plunged the kingdom into violent revolution had the working-classes found in the middle class leaders . . . a definite ideal, a creed, a practical programme. But the elite of the working class, the hard-working and capable bourgeois, had been imbued by the evangelical movement with a spirit from which the established order had nothing to fear. (pp.424, 425).
>
> The majority of leaders of the great trade union movement that would arise in England within a few years of 1815 will belong to the Nonconformist sects. They will often be local preachers . . . Their spiritual ancestors were the founders of Methodism. In the vast work of social organization which is one of the dominant characteristics of nineteenth-century England, it would be difficult to overestimate the part played by the Wesleyan revival . . . We can watch between 1792 and 1815 an uninterrupted decline of the revolutionary spirit among the sects. (p.425).
>
> We shall witness Methodism bring under its influence, first the Dissenting sects, then the Establishment, finally secular opinion. We shall attempt to find here the key to the problem whose solution has hitherto escaped us; for we shall explain by this movement the extraordinary stability which English Society was destined to enjoy throughout a period of revolutions and crises; what we may truly term the miracle of modern England, anarchist but orderly, practical and businesslike, but religious, and even pietist. (p.387).

Halévy argued that in the seventeenth and eighteenth centuries dissent in general was associated with republicanism, libertarianism and, especially after the French Revolution, with Jacobinism. Certain members of the Tory party and of the Anglican Church in particular saw in every dissenter a potential revolutionary. Wesley exerted himself to clear Methodism of these and similar charges. By his teaching, by the organizational structure adopted, by the delimiting of the power and authority of the laity, and by care not to unnecessarily provoke the Anglican Church, the Methodist Connection adopted a position intermediate between the establishment and the older nonconformist bodies. When new sects arose in turn from Wesleyanism, they occupied the space between the Connection and the original sects. Wesleyan influence spread and penetrated all the dissenting bodies; and everywhere it was a spirit of reaction against the rationalism and republicanism of the old nonconformity. The dissenting sects of rationalistic tendency were decaying. The progress of Methodism was tending to render the Protestant dissenters politically conservative.

During the early years of the nineteenth century only isolated and eccentric individuals among the nonconformists demanded either a reform of the constitution of the national church in conformity with their ideas, or disestablishment and equal rights for all denominations. The social class division between adherents of the establishment and the sects remained, and even became more rigid. What was new, and most characteristic of the new spirit of dissent, said Halévy, was its acceptance of its subordinate position. Social mobility was perceived as a real possibility, and it was recognized that upward mobility almost inevitably entailed a transition from dissent to the Church of England. The middle class nonconformist was content to be despised by members of a Church which his own family might some day enter. He compensated himself by indulging in an even deeper contempt for the common people of the fields and factories from whom his family had emerged. Nonconformists had a devotion to social order. They inculcated a middle-class morality, a want of imagination, solid virtues and a capacity for organization.

The majority of the leaders of the great post-1815 trade union movement belonged, according to Halévy, to the nonconformist sects, and they were essentially non-revolutionary. By becoming the religion of the middle classes, nonconformity largely deprived the working classes of the leaders they required to wage their intended war against the rich. Bereft of such leaders, the populace fell back into a state of incoherence, demoralization, and at last apathy.

From one point of view there was greater hostility between the lower middle class and the proletariat than between the proletariat and the upper class. For the latter the working class was a mysterious world of whose sufferings its members knew little. But they were disposed to look with indulgence on the gross pleasures of the masses, so long as they kept them contented. The member of the lower middle class, on the other hand, knew the workers only too well. He or his father had risen from their ranks. He had risen by hard work. He was twice 'saved' if, in addition, he belonged to a religious sect, saved by his faith in himself and saved by his faith in God, saved in the temporal and saved in the spiritual order. Let the others follow his example and save themselves as he had done. If not, so much the worse for them. They deserved their hell. Possessed of such opinions, it is not surprising that the nonconformist showed so little enthusiasm for the cause of the workers.

Halévy also said that Methodism had exercised a significant influence over the Church of England. The rise of Church of England Evangelicalism, and its development into a force for social reform, which is traced in the present work, provided, according to Halévy, a further reinforcement of the bridge between dissent and the Church of England.

There have been many critiques of the Halévy thesis. To do justice to any of these would involve an elaborate and full discussion which the limitations of the present work do not permit. E.P. Thompson and E.J. Hobsbawm offer a particularly valuable introduction to the whole debate (see especially E.P. Thompson, *The Making of the English Working Class* (Harmondsworth, 1968) and E.J. Hobsbawm, *The Age of Revolution* (London, 1962).

Part 2 1789-1833

4

An Age of Revolution

In the years immediately prior to 1789 it appeared that the social order was settled for ever. Society had its ranks and order. A hierarchy of subordination and authority was almost universally acknowledged and rarely called in question. There was a widespread optimism and sense of security. Confidence in the essential stability of society was not shaken by the political bitterness epitomized in the rivalry between Pitt and Fox, nor by the tensions and divisions caused by the American Revolution. Neither was it undermined to any great extent by the corrosive effect of the Industrial Revolution. The future was not feared. English society was seen as established, firm and solid. God had decreed it so.

All this changed quite rapidly after the fall of the Bastille in 1789.[1] For the next twenty-six years first the French Revolution and then the Napoleonic Wars dictated the English domestic scene to a remarkable degree. 'Everything', wrote the Whig lawyer Cockburn, 'was connected with the Revolution in France, which for twenty years was, or was made,

---

[1] Of the general and social histories covering all or part of the period 1789 to 1833 special mention may be made of Asa Briggs, *The Age of Improvement* (London, 1959); E. Halévy, *A History of the English People in the Nineteenth Century*, Vol.I *England in 1815* and Vol.II, *The Liberal Awakening* ; E. Hobsbawm, *The Age of Revolution* (1962); and the Oxford History of England volumes; J. Steven Watson, *The Reign of George III. 1760-1815* (Oxford, 1960), and E.L. Woodward, *The Age of Reform, 1815- 1870)* (Oxford, 1938).

all in all, everything: not this thing or that thing, but literally everything was soaked in this one event'.[2]

At first the revolutionary events so near at hand across the Channel were acclaimed by a large number of well-informed Englishmen.

> Bliss was it in that dawn to be alive.
> But to be young was very heaven.[3]

But as the abolition of French feudal privileges and the establishment of a new constitution was followed by the reign of terror and the dictatorship of Napoleon, euphoria was replaced by apprehension, fear and condemnation. The radicalism of Paine shocked and alarmed the establishment. In 1793 the sale of his *Rights of Man* was estimated at 200,000 copies, and ideas of reform spread with disconcerting speed. Reform associations such as the London Corresponding Society were established, and proclaimed the solidarity of English reformers with the French revolutionaries. The government instituted a policy of severe restraint which was in accord with a growing resistance to revolutionary views. 'There was not a city, no, not a town', Coleridge wrote, 'in which a man suspected of holding democratic principles could move abroad without receiving some unpleasant proof of the hatred in which his supposed opinions were held by the great majority of the people'.[4]

Until the final defeat of Napoleon in 1815 England remained committed to the cause of victory despite financial troubles, the mutiny at the Nore, domestic unrest, Irish discontent and the social problems associated with the industrial and agricultural revolutions. A common purpose and a common enemy were sufficient to hold in check those forces of rebellion which were to surface as soon as peace was declared.

The termination of war left Britain the leading country in Europe. Other countries were devastated by defeat, divisions and demoralization. One of the great periods of world exploration and exploitation was under way and Britain was at the forefront as the dominant European power and mistress of the seas. Year after year new provinces and protectorates were added to the Empire.

On the domestic front, a native wealth of coal and iron combined with long freedom from war on her own soil had made possible an industrial development in Britain on an undreamed-of scale. Visitors to the country were astonished at the affluence of the British mercantile and middle classes. The Industrial Revolution was matched by a transformation in

---

[2] *Memorials of his Time* (1856), p.80, quoted in Briggs, *op.cit.*, p.129. The brief description of English society in the introductory part of this chapter owes much to Asa Briggs.

[3] William Wordsworth, *French Revolution* (1804).

[4] Briggs, *op.cit.*, pp.136, 137.

rural economy. Enclosures and labour-saving devices and techniques changed the whole country way of life. Yet accompanying this rapid social and economic metamorphosis was savage discontent. Behind British prosperity lay a nightmare of poverty, filth, misery and the abuse of labour. Revolt, Luddite violence, and armed rebellion in Ireland provoked by recurrent famines, were the signal for repression. The relationship between various socio-economic groups was characterized by antagonism and aggression as the old order underwent a painful transformation. The demand from the new classes for more power culminated in the Reform Act of 1832, which was politically significant not so much for the limited concessions it made but because it was the precursor of a series of reforms which were to transmute the political scene.

The social and political tensions in these years were compounded by the accelerated increase in population. In the second half of the eighteenth century the population of England had grown from about five and a half million to about nine million, and most of this increase was packed into the last two decades. By 1815 it had reached about 13 million and by 1841 it was approximately 16 million. The strain in coping with such a demographic revolution was immense.

The demand for reform was not confined to the political arena; it was a feature of the religious life of the country in the post-1815 era. The old dissenters had been augmented by the various Methodist bodies, and nonconformist pressure successfully brought about the repeal in 1828 of the Test and Corporation Acts. This was almost immediately succeeded, in 1829, by the Catholic Emancipation Act. As with the Reform Act, these measures were symbolic of a new age of reform, tolerance and liberalization.

Events in France had a profound effect upon the moral and religious tone of English society.[5] The Revolution was, to quote the Hammonds, 'a warning against irreligion and the frivolities of life. The red skies of Paris sobered the English Sunday and filled the English churches'.[6] The outrages perpetrated in France seemed to demonstrate the folly of trusting in things which could so easily be destroyed, and to establish the Christian doctrine of the fallen state of man.

---

[5] General histories of religion in this period include S.C. Carpenter, *Church and People, 1789-1889: A History of the Church of England from William Wilberforce to 'Lux Mundi'* (London, 1933); Francis Warre Cornish, *The English Church in the Nineteenth Century*, 2 vols. (London, 1910); R.P. Flindall, *The Church of England 1815-1945: A Documentary History* (London, 1972); J.H. Overton and Frederic Relton, *The English Church from the Accession of George I to the End of the Eighteenth Century, 1714-1800* (London, 1906); and W.R. Ward, *Religion and Society in England 1790-1850* (London, 1972).

[6] J.L. and B. Hammond, *The Town Labourer* (London, 1917), p.235.

It was the Evangelical movement[7] which, above all other forms of religion, reaped the main benefits from the new seriousness characteristic of every social class. The Evangelicals more than any others offered an authentic alternative to the strident claims and demands which had been brought to the fore by the events in France. The Methodists and some other dissenters offered a similar message, but many dissenters were suspect as they had expressed their sympathy with the views of the revolutionaries. The struggle with France had called forth a new sense of loyalty to the nation, and that loyalty took the form of an increased attachment to the national church. The Evangelical movement had reached a point in its development where it was ready to meet the felt needs of the age, and to take new initiatives in a national crusade.

Evangelicalism

The strength of Evangelicalism in the closing years of the eighteenth century and the opening decades of the nineteenth is widely acknowledged. Eugene Stock said that it was 'indisputedly the strongest force in the country'.[8] Stoughton concluded that despite their evident imperfections, the Evangelicals at the beginning of the nineteenth century, and a long while afterwards, 'did what no other band of clergymen were doing at that time'. Few, he said, would deny that they were an 'immense power', and 'that they were the very salt of the Church of England, during a period when influences existed threatening decay and corruption'.[9] Two nineteenth century High Churchmen gave a similar judgment. Liddon declared that:

> the deepest and most fervid religion in England during the first three decades of this century was that of the Evangelicals. The world to come, with its boundless issues of life and death, the infinite value of the one Atonement, the regenerating, purifying, guiding action of God the Holy Spirit in respect of the Christian soul, were preached to our grandfathers with a force and earnestness which are beyond controversy.[10]

---

[7] In addition to general histories of the Evangelical movement already mentioned, works specifically relevant to this period include Ernest Marshall Howse, *Saints in Politics: the 'Clapham Sect' and the growth of freedom* (London, 1952); James Stephen, *Essays in Ecclesiastical Biography*, 2 vols. (1860); and many biographies to some of which reference will be made in this and the succeeding chapters.

[8] Eugene Stock, *The History of the Church Missionary Society* (London, 1899), Vol.I, p.38.

[9] John Stoughton, *Religion in England from 1800 to 1850*, 2 vols. (London, 1884), Vol. I, p.114.

[10] H.P. Liddon, *Life of E.B. Pusey*, (London, 1894), Vol.I, p.235, quoted in Carpenter, *op.cit.*, p.29.

William Gladstone, brought up among Evangelicals, said of the Evangelical clergy:

> Every Christian under their scheme had personal dealings with his God and Saviour. The inner life was again acknowledged as a reality, and substituted for that bare, bald compromise between the seen and the unseen world which reduces the share of the 'far and more exceeding and eternal' to almost nil.[11]

Lastly, to take a more recent assessment, S.C. Carpenter said that the Evangelicals:

> did not cover all the ground, because there were not very many of them, and there were some matters which their limited range did not enable them to reach, but they were in deadly earnest, and wherever their influence penetrated at all it penetrated very deep.[12]

Although their sway was undoubtedly great, Evangelicals during the period 1789 to 1833 remained a small minority within the church, held in contempt or hated by most churchmen. One bishop wrote, 'Church-Methodism is the disease of my diocese; it shall be the business of my life to extirpate it'.[13] A report that one of 'the serious clergy', as they were called, had been appointed to a parish was in many cases followed by an outcry as great as if a pestilence was coming. Trinity College, Cambridge, declined to receive the sons of Evangelicals as undergraduates. Hugh Pearson, afterwards Dean of Salisbury, narrowly escaped being refused for ordination because he spoke warmly of Wilberforce's *Practical View of Christianity*.[14] When the Bishop of London conveyed a visitor from his house to that of a leading Evangelical rector he put her down at a neighbouring public house, to avoid being seen to stop at such a clergyman's door.[15] When Henry Martyn paid a visit to his native Cornwall after his ordination, although he was Senior Wrangler for his year and a Fellow of his college, he was not allowed to preach in any church in the county except his brother-in-law's.[16] The bishops frequently uttered warnings against 'Methodists' in their charges, and were careful to explain that the 'serious clergy' were included under that

---

[11] William Ewart Gladstone, *Letters on Church and Religion* (London, 1910), Vol.I, p.8.
[12] Carpenter, *op.cit.*, p.28.
[13] Charles Hole, *The Early History of the Church Missionary Society* (London, 1896), p.53.
[14] The *Private Journal of Henry Venn the Younger*, December 1852.
[15] See the *Christian Observer*, January 1870.
[16] See A.G. Smith, *Henry Martyn* (London, 1892), p.41.

name. Not a few even cast doubt upon the loyalty of such clergy to the government and constitution. Wilberforce had difficulty in reassuring Pitt on this point.

Nevertheless, in 1833 the Evangelicals were more established in the church than they had been in 1789. Their weakness in 1789 has been indicated. There were possibly no more than forty or fifty Evangelical clergy, none above the rank of parish incumbent; by 1800 there were about ·500.[17] By 1830 they represented between one eighth and a quarter of the clergy,[18] and were more accepted. By 1835 there were a number of Evangelicals in the higher echelons of the Church of England. C.R. Sumner was Bishop of Winchester, J.B. Sumner Bishop of Chester, Henry Ryder Bishop of Lichfield and Coventry, Henry Raikes Chancellor of the Diocese of Chester, Henry Law Archdeacon and Canon of Wells Cathedral, William Dealth Chancellor of the Diocese of Winchester, C. J. Hoare Archdeacon and Canon of Winchester Cathedral, while Thomas Burgess the Bishop of Salisbury was sympathetic to Evangelicals.[19]

During the Napoleonic era Evangelicals also appear to have acquired a greater theological comprehensiveness. Evangelical leaders married the eighteenth century Evangelical emphasis upon spiritual new birth with a concern for moral duty, order and reason. Charles Simeon and others, while remaining true to their Evangelical inheritance, developed a more tolerant, broader based Evangelicalism which was founded on the scriptures and confirmed in the Articles and liturgy of the English reformers. It was influenced by the humanitarianism and 'practical' Christianity promoted by Wilberforce, Hannah More and the Clapham Sect. This mellowed Evangelicalism lay behind the launching of such projects as the *Christian Observer*. The call was for a more moderate, more inclusive Evangelicalism.[20] It was a trend which was to cause severe divisions within Evangelicalism in the third and fourth decades of the nineteenth century, as discussed in Chapter 6.

The lay social composition of Evangelicalism somewhat reflected this extension of the Evangelical clerical base, and the modification in the Evangelical theological stance. It became both theologically and socially easier to be an Evangelical. The middle and upper-middle-class convert

[17] See W. Romaine, *Christian Guardian*, 1809.

[18] See P.B. Coombs, 'A History of the Church Pastoral-Aid Society, 1836-1861 (Bristol University M.A., 1960) and A.D. Gilbert, *Religion and Society in Industrial England: Church, Chapel and Social Change 1740-1914* (London, 1976) for discussions on the numerical strength of the Evangelicals.

[19] For each of these see the *Dictionary of National Biography*. Additional bibliographical details will be given when the lives of some of these are outlined in later chapters.

[20] For an elaboration of this theme, see W.J.C. Ervine, 'Doctrine and Diplomacy: Some Aspects of the Life and Thought of Anglican Evangelical Clergy 1797-1837' (Cambridge University Ph.D., 1967).

was no longer asked to be identified with a rather socially confined, predominantly lower middle class, and somewhat sectarian movement. Although Evangelicals continued to be maligned, they were recognized and accepted to an extent unknown to their predecessors. The process of social transformation was slow, and even as late as 1810 the list of subscribers to the Church Missionary Society contained no names of peers or bishops, and no members of the universities except for Simeon's friends. But within a few years the Grosvenors, the Pelhams, the Ashleys, the Shirleys, the Vansittarts, the houses of Roden and Ducie and even a Prime Minister, Spencer Perceval, were to contribute to the strength of Evangelicalism, and it was represented in Parliament by a formidable body of advocates.

Three Evangelical leaders were pre-eminent throughout this period: Henry Ryder, Charles Simeon and William Wilberforce.

Henry Ryder (1777–1836)

Henry Ryder was born in 1777, the youngest son of the first Baron Harrowby of Sandon in Staffordshire. He was educated at St John's College, Cambridge, where he obtained his M.A. in 1798, and subsequently his D.D. in 1813. He was ordained to the curacy of Sandon, the family seat of the Harrowbys, in 1800. In 1801 he became rector of Lutterworth in Leicestershire and in 1805 vicar of the neighbouring parish of Claybrook in addition. He was regarded as a model parish priest but still found time to read the early fathers and critically study the Bible.

At this stage Ryder stood aloof from the Evangelicals and even attacked their principles as being at variance with the principles of the Church of England. Within a few years, however, he changed his views, as a result of a combination of influences of which three were particularly potent: the refusal of Thomas Robinson, a leading Evangelical, to reply in public to Ryder's attack on the Evangelicals; some deaths in the family; and the reading of John Newton's *Cardiphonia* and *Letters to a Nobleman*. Ryder now openly identified himself with the Evangelicals. He took the chair at the Bible Society meeting at Leicester in 1811, and preached Robinson's funeral sermon in 1813.

In 1808 he was made a canon of Windsor. He was as zealous as ever in performing his duties. His sermons caused quite a stir and were admired by George III. In 1812 he was promoted to the deanery of Wells. This caused dismay among the somewhat old-fashioned churchmen at Wells. The discontent was not dispelled by his forthright preaching, his introduction of an evening service into the parish church (regarded at that time as a sure sign of 'methodism'), his preaching at neighbouring churches and his part in establishing a national school, then quite a new institution, at Wells. During his time at Wells he was a neighbour of Hannah More, who was much impressed by him.

In 1818 he was offered the bishopric of Gloucester. There was much opposition to the appointment in high quarters, both civil and ecclesiastical, because of his identification with a church party. This was defeated largely through the influence of Ryder's brother Dudley, first Earl of Harrowby and an influential member of the administration. Within the diocese itself the resistance of a large number of clergy soon disappeared largely because of Ryder's winsome personality, his evident scholarship and his thorough loyalty to the Church of England. He was an energetic bishop. He rarely preached less than twice on a Sunday, and often three times, besides giving a weekly lecture in one of the Gloucester churches. On Sunday afternoons he examined and instructed children in the Gloucester National School. In 1816 he established the Gloucester Diocesan Society for the education of the poor, and he was instrumental in founding the female penitentiary.

Ryder was translated to the bishopric of Lichfield in 1824. This gave greater scope for his vigour, especially as the population was much larger than in his former see. He startled many by plunging into widespread evangelistic work. After eight years there were twenty new churches and ten under construction. With the aid of Archdeacon Hodson, he organized a Church Building Association in the diocese. Evangelicalism made particularly rapid advance in Birmingham, which was part of the diocese, and this was due very much to the leadership of Ryder and his two archdeacons, Hodson and Spooner. Ryder died in 1836.

Henry Ryder was a much respected man, and of course hailed by the Evangelicals as the first bishop chosen from their ranks. Wilberforce referred to the 'highly prized and loved Bishop Ryder' as a prelate after his own heart, 'who united to the zeal of an apostle the most amiable and endearing qualities, and the polished manners of the best society'. Charles Simeon delighted in him; and Hannah More sang his praises. A person of a very different sort, Dr Samuel Parr, said that 'there is a halo of holiness about that man'. It was Ryder's reputation for piety and energy which was most extraordinary.

Charles Simeon (1759-1836)

Charles Simeon[21] was born at Reading on 24 September 1759. At the age

---

[21] For the life of Simeon see William Carus, *Memoirs of the Life of the Rev. Charles Simeon, with a Selection of his Writings and Correspondence* (Cambridge, 1847); Marcus L. Loane, *Cambridge and the Evangelical Succession* (London, 1952); and H.C.G. Moule, *Charles Simeon* (London, 1892).

of nine he was sent to Eton. At nineteen he went up with a scholarship to King's College, Cambridge, where he succeeded in due course to a fellowship, which he held until his death. He was ordained deacon in 1782 and priest in 1783. In the former year he was made perpetual curate of Holy Trinity church in the centre of Cambridge. There he laboured for fifty-four years. He died in his rooms in King's College on 13 November 1836.

Such are the bald facts. They deceptively indicate an uneventful and rather restricted career. The more accurate assessment of his true status and standing is given by his contemporary, Macaulay. 'If you knew what his authority and influence were', said Macaulay, 'and how they extended from Cambridge to the most remote corners of England, you would allow that his real sway over the Church was far greater than that of any primate'. [22]

Simeon was converted to an Evangelical faith within a few months of becoming an undergraduate. The circumstances are perhaps best described in his own words:

> It was but the third day after my arrival that I understood I should be expected in the space of about three weeks to attend the Lord's Supper. 'What', said I, 'must I attend?' On being informed that I must, the thought rushed into my mind that Satan himself was as fit to attend as I; and that if I must attend, I must prepare for my attendance there. Without a moment's loss of time, I bought the *Whole Duty of Man*, the only religious book that I had ever heard of, and began to read it with great diligence; at the same time calling my ways to rememberance, and crying to God for mercy; and so earnest was I in these exercises that within the three weeks I made myself quite ill with reading, fasting and prayer.

He read various other books in the following three months. His concern about the iniquities in his former life mounted and he experienced a growing agitation and distress of mind. But relief was in sight:

> In Passion Week, as I was reading Bishop Wilson on the Lord's Supper, I met with an expression to this effect – 'That the Jews knew what they did, when they transferred their sin to the head of their offering'. The thought came to my mind, 'What, may I transfer all my guilt to another? Has God provided an offering for me, that I may lay my sins on His head? Then, God willing, I will not bear them on my own soul one moment longer'.[23]

It was on the Easter Sunday of that year that he experienced the forgiveness about which he had been reading.

[22] G.O. Trevelyan, *The Life and Letters of Lord Macaulay* (1876), Vol.I, p.67.
[23] Carus, *op.cit.*, pp.6-9 and Moule, *op.cit.*, pp.24-26.

The waves of the eighteenth century revival appear to have left Cambridge almost untouched, and for three years Simeon had no fellow Evangelical in the town with whom he could share his faith. After ordination as deacon in 1782, he helped at St Edward's church near King's College and, in less than seventeen Sundays, there was a full attendance at the services. He had often considered the prospect of being able to proclaim his new-found faith to the university as the minister of Holy Trinity church: and in 1782, by a combination of circumstances and amid much opposition from parishioners, he was appointed curate-in-charge. The appointment was extremely unpopular. A rival candidate was chosen as the lecturer, with the right to the pulpit every Sunday afternoon, leaving only the morning to Simeon. The man concerned, Mr Hammond, exercised the right for five years, and another clergyman, Mr Berry, followed with equal tenacity for the ensuing seven years.

On the Sunday mornings, for a long time, the church was made as inaccessible as possible to Simeon and his congregation. Most of the pew doors were locked, with the authorized occupants absent, leaving only the aisles for the congregation. On the first Sunday, when the service began, the church was almost empty; but after a while people came in increasing numbers so that after a few weeks there was scarcely enough room. Simeon set up benches in the aisles and seats in nooks and corners at his own expense; but the churchwardens removed them and threw them into the churchyard.

The belligerents in the parish persisted in their attacks for ten years, but Simeon extended his ministry. After some months he began a Sunday evening lecture, in effect a six o'clock service followed by an exposition: an almost unprecedented innovation. It was well attended, but after the first few Sundays the hostile churchwardens shut the church doors and carried off the keys while the people waited in the street. On that occasion Simeon had the doors opened by a smith, but he considered it prudent to drop the enterprise for the immediate future.

Simeon was faced with a dilemma. Great numbers of people responded to his ministry but he was restricted in the use of his own church. As a staunch churchman he was fearful that those who needed further instruction would go to the dissenting meetings. In order to meet with his congregation and give them the teaching they needed, he hired a private room. He began with a small place in his own parish, but this was soon not large enough and he had to go to a room in an adjoining parish for a satisfactory alternative venue. The use of the room was certainly an irregular practice, for the assembly was extra- parochial and could have been regarded in law as a forbidden conventicle. This caused him much agony, but he could see no other course of action, and its purpose was wholly in favour of order and cohesion. Strangely, no opposition was forthcoming over many years, although it was the one side of his ministry most vulnerable to criticism, and about which his enemies might have attacked with most effect. In fact this 'society' grew and had to be broken into six sub-societies. Each was organized with care according to sex, age, and individual need, and each met with Simeon once a month. The system had its grave drawbacks. At a time when illness made it more difficult for Simeon to retain his control, some of the leaders asserted themselves, rebelled against his authority, and were at last debarred from the groups.

Simeon took an active part for a while in the administration of his college. He held one of the three Deanships at King's from 1788 to 1790, 1792 to 1798 and 1827 to 1830; he was Vice-Provost from 1790 to 1792; and, as previously noted, he was a Fellow of the college.

From the start his ministry at Holy Trinity attracted many undergraduates. For several years it was difficult to keep order in the church, for there was much unruliness among the students, but Simeon won through. With his forthright and distinctive preaching, his careful and judicious personal and small group counselling, and his evident philanthropy, which was amply demonstrated in 1783 when there was a national dearth of bread, his influence grew. And with this came increasing reproach for both the preacher and his congregation. 'Those who worshipped at Trinity Church', Sargent said in 1798, 'were supposed to have left common sense, discretion, sobriety, attachment to the established church, and love for the liturgy, and almost whatever else is true and of good report, in the vestibule'.[24] For a long time 'a Simeonite' did not merely denote but satirized a man's religious opinions.

Initially, at least, there were few men of influence in the university who were in essential agreement with Simeon. There was Isaac Milner, Senior Wrangler of 1774, who was chosen President of Queens' College in 1788. He was at first suspicious of the new preacher, and his strong, sometimes rough character contrasted with the more restrained, sophisticated authority of Simeon. Then there was William Farish, Senior Wrangler of 1778, a gentle, courageous man who upheld his Evangelical convictions as the Jacksonian Professor. Not many others identified or associated with Simeon in any way in his early years. Nevertheless, a countless number of students were brought to firm and lasting Christian faith or inspired for service by Simeon, and these included many distinguished men. Among such were Henry Martyn, Thomas Thomason, Daniel Corrie, James Hough and Claudius Buchanan. They were the most able men to go to India at this time as chaplains. Others included: Sowerby, the Senior Wrangler of 1796; Henry Kirke White, the protégé of Robert Southey;

[24] Quoted in Moule, *op.cit.*, p.60.

James Scholefield, subsequently Regius Professor of Greek; Charles Clayton, who often preached at Holy Trinity church; Thomas Rawson Birks, second Wrangler in 1834 and later Professor of Moral Philosophy; and William Carus, who became Fellow and Dean of Trinity, Simeon's curate, biographer and first successor (1836-1851).

Simeon's influence upon undergraduates in general, and upon ordination candidates in particular, was phenomenal; it was his greatest contribution to the Church of England of his day, and to the revival which that Church was undergoing. About half the total undergraduate population had come to college with the sole purpose of qualifying for holy orders; and Simeon helped many of them to discover what the calling to the ordained ministry really meant. No special theological training of any kind was provided by either the church or the university, and the ordination examination consisted merely in construing a passage from the Greek New Testament on the day of ordination. In such a situation Simeon was indeed a beacon to numberless young men. By 1817 half his congregation were gownsmen, and through his sermons, his sermon classes and his conversation parties he provided a theological education which was probably unparalleled in the country.

He started Sunday after-church sermon classes in 1792 and continued them regularly for forty years. At them, about fifteen to twenty undergraduates received practical instruction in the techniques of preaching and sermon construction. It was not until 1813 that Simeon began his Friday evening conversation parties. They were conducted in a somewhat formal way, with Simeon acting as the focal point and attempting to answer any questions directed to him. Being open to all members of the university, they helped to furnish the church with a well-educated lay and ordained leadership.

But, as has been noted earlier, the influence of Simeon went far beyond Cambridge, and indeed beyond England. His writings, as they were published in 1832, filled twenty-one large octavo volumes under the title *Horae Homileticae*. The work consisted of many discourses and shortened versions of parochial sermons, and well-ordered outlines of expositions arranged according to the books of the Bible. These 'Skeletons' as he called them were much appreciated by preachers and others in his day and beyond.

Simeon played a central part in the new missionary initiatives of this era. He made an especially valuable and distinctive contribution in helping to open up India to Christian influence, as we will see in a later chapter.

He also made his mark upon the development of Evangelical theology. After the Arminian-Calvinist controversy of the immediate past he emphasized a new way, explaining:

Here are two extremes, Calvinism and Arminianism (for you need not be told how long Calvin and Arminius lived before St Paul). 'How do you move in reference to these, Paul? In a golden mean?' 'No' – 'To one extreme?' 'No' – 'How then?' 'To both extremes; to-day I am a strong Calvinist, tomorrow a strong Arminian'. – 'Well, well, Paul, I see thou art beside thyself; go to Aristotle, and learn the golden mean'. But I am unfortunate; I formerly read Aristotle, and liked him much; I have since read Paul, and caught somewhat of his strange notions, oscillating (not vacillating) from pole to pole. Sometimes, I am a high Calvinist, at other times a low Arminian, so that if extremes will please you, I am your man; only remember, it is not one extreme that we are to go to, but both extremes.[25]

Simeon sought to be free to follow the Bible wherever it led him, even when it appeared that one passage contradicted another. He accepted the Bible with uncritical simplicity.

In almost all that he did Simeon saw himself as serving his beloved Church of England, for he was a strong churchman. He taught ordinands to keep to their parish boundaries and to value their membership of the Church of England. He objected to dissent to a large extent because he viewed dissenters as not being tied to the *status quo* and even being a seedbed for revolution or at least reform. When young he had occasionally spoken in a non-conforming chapel, or even a barn, but he subsequently refused any invitation to continue these practices, and he did as much as any clergyman in the Church of England of his day to encourage Evangelical clergy to remain loyal to the Church of England and to abide by its discipline. He was a key figure in ensuring that Evangelicalism continued within the Church of England at a time when Methodism was becoming fragmented and the Countess of Huntingdon Connection was dwindling into a small denomination. He also urged Evangelicals to stimulate and support one another in their faith, setting an example by arranging annual summer houseparties for clergy and their wives.

It was his concern to further a true spiritual ministry within the Church of England which impelled Simeon to set up the Trust which has continued ever since. Simeon saw men like Newton, Scott and Romaine, who were among the most efficient and godly clergy in the Church, remain unbeneficed almost to the end of their days, while many unworthy men were promoted. This called in question the whole method of appointing clergy. Simeon therefore used money inherited through a brother's death to buy the patronage of some livings. Others 'purchased income', he wrote, 'I purchase spheres, wherein the prosperity of the

---

[25] See *ibid.*, pp.77, 78.

Established Church . . . may be advanced'.[26] Gradually other Evangelicals gave money for the same purpose, or handed over to him livings that were in their gift. In this way the Simeon Trust came to embrace the appointment to more than a hundred parishes, including some of the most important incumbencies in the country. These included churches in strategic centres such as Cheltenham, where he secured the parish church for £3,000; Bradford, where he acquired what is now the cathedral; Colchester, Newcastle-under-Lyme, Drypool, Darlaston, Clifton, Hereford, Northampton, Ipswich and Chichester. He and his colleagues also successfully negotiated for Bath Abbey, Bridlington Priory, Derby Parish Church and Beverley Minster.

The influence of Simeon upon the Evangelicalism of his day was so diffuse that we will meet him time and time again as we recount the history of the period.

William Wilberforce (1759-1833)

William Wilberforce,[27] like Simeon, was born in 1759. He came from a family of mercantile men who had flourished modestly until the first half of the eighteenth century when his grandfather built a great fortune in the Baltic trade. When he went down from Cambridge his inherited riches were such that he did not need to earn a penny. Indolence had characterized his university career and he dreamed of a life in politics, conducted in a somewhat amateur manner. He coaxed the electors of Hull with charm and his purse, spending nearly £8,000 on the election. He was returned and took up his seat on the opposition back benches on 31 October 1780. He was soon immersed in a convivial round of London club life, private parties, entertainment and hospitality in which he attained great popularity. He relished the small, intimate world of politics, fashion and good society which London offered.

In the Commons Wilberforce was the close friend and supporter of William Pitt, who, as Prime Minister from 1783, had to face a hostile House and opposition from the Fox-North coalition. As he was drawn more into the centre of the political arena as the ally of Pitt, Wilberforce developed considerable powers of oratory, in which the peculiar sweetness and exceptional range of his tones were united with a warmth of feeling, expressed in face and gestures as well as by voice, an ability for

[26] Letter quoted in Carus, op.cit., p.780.

[27] For the life of Wilberforce, see R. Coupland, Wilberforce: A Narrative (Oxford, 1923); Robin Furneaux, William Wilberforce (London, 1974); John Pollock, Wilberforce (Berkhamsted, 1977); and Robert Isaac and Samuel Wilberforce, The Life of William Wilberforce, 5 vols. (London, 1858).

exploring both sides of a question, great pathos and devastating sarcasm.

Wilberforce experienced various Evangelical influences in his childhood. In 1767, at the age of eight, he went to Hull Grammar School as a dayboy, and briefly met the Evangelical headmaster Joseph Milner and his brother Isaac. Next year he was sent to live with an uncle and aunt, William and Hannah Wilberforce. They were great friends of George Whitefield, and Hannah's half-brother was the rich Evangelical John Thornton. Wilberforce was also impressed by the preaching of John Newton. By means of such contacts and friendships the seeds of an Evangelical faith were sown which were later to bear such abundant fruit in various works of mercy.

The first cause to attract his attention, and the one which was most to occupy his talents, time and energies for the remainder of his life, was the movement for the abolition of the slave trade. The issue was coming to the fore around 1780 and the following years. Several people, including James Ramsay, vicar of Teston, and Captain Sir Charles Middleton, an Evangelical Member of Parliament, discussed the matter with Wilberforce. He was asked to be the spokesman in the Commons for the cause of abolition but hesitated and prevaricated. Finally, under an oak tree on the Holwood Estate, just above the steep descent into the Vale of Keston, Pitt persuaded him to give notice of a motion on the subject. Wilberforce was not unaware of the implications of such a commitment and the magnitude of the task confronting him. Neither was John Wesley. In what was possibly his last letter, written a week before he died, Wesley encouraged Wilberforce at the outset of his crusade:

My dear Sir,

Unless the Divine Power has raised you up to be an Athanasius *contra mundum* I see not how you can go through your glorious enterprise in opposing that execrable villainy which is the scandal of religion, of England, of human nature. Unless God has raised you up for this very thing, you will be worn out by the opposition of man and devils; but, if God be for you, who can be against you? Are all of them together stronger than God? Oh, be not weary in well doing. Go on, in the name of God and in the power of His might, till even American slavery, the vilest that ever saw the sun, shall vanish away before it. That He who has guided you from your youth up may continue to strengthen you in this and all things is the prayer of, Dear Sir, your affectionate servant –

John Wesley.[28]

---

[28] Quoted in Carpenter, *op.cit.*, p.30.

From 1787 onwards the life of Wilberforce and a small band of fellow Evangelicals was dedicated to this 'glorious enterprise', and to other aims of national and international importance, consistent with and expressive of their Evangelical faith. An inner circle of the band lived in the same neighbourhood and subsequently became known as the 'Clapham Sect'; a few were Members of Parliament, where they were collectively designated 'the Saints'. Such is the importance of what Wilberforce and his colleagues undertook and accomplished that it merits full consideration in the next chapter.

5

The Clapham Sect and
the Saints

The Thornton family had long been connected with Clapham. John
Thornton (1720-1790), the philanthropist, lived there. In the year of his
death his son Henry, who became the first treasurer of the Bible Society,
bought Battersea Rise House from the Lubbock family. In the spring of
1792 he suggested to Wilberforce that they should share the residence,
each paying his part of the housekeeping, and Wilberforce agreed.
Thornton built two smaller houses on the edge of his estate, one of which
Charles Grant bought and named 'Grant Glenelg'. Sir John Shore, the first
Baron Teignmouth, Granville Sharp, Zachary Macaulay and James
Stephen all settled in Clapham from overseas around the turn of the
century. For their rector Thornton secured John Venn: a clergyman who
attracted large congregations. All these outstanding leaders were
identified with the Evangelical movement. They were a company of
friends who worked together to achieve quite remarkable results; but they
were part of a much wider group of influential Evangelicals.[1]

---

[1] For an account of the 'Clapham Sect' and 'the Saints', see especially James Stephen, *Essays
in Ecclesiastical Biography*; and Ernest Marshall Howse, *Saints in Politics: The 'Clapham Sect'
and the growth of Freedom* (London, 1953). For a thorough analysis and critique, see
particularly Ian Bradley, *The Call to Seriousness: The Evangelical Impact on the Victorians*
(London, 1976); I.C. Bradley, 'The Politics of Godliness: Evangelicals in Parliament,
1784-1832' (Oxford University D.Phil., 1974); and F.K. Brown, *Fathers of the Victorians: The
Age of Wilberforce* (Cambridge, 1961). Much further light is shed on both the 'Clapham Sect'
and 'the Saints' in a number of biographies to which reference will be made later in this
chapter.

The term 'Clapham Sect' was never applied during the life of Wilberforce. Those who associated closely with him were not identified with Clapham in the public mind. The only contemporary nickname was 'the Saints': an appellation given to a group of Members of Parliament who aligned themselves with Wilberforce, and voted with him on most major issues. They went far beyond the residents of Clapham, and there were other Members of Parliament who were 'occasional Saints'.

Political and religious affiliations during these years were considerably more complex than has often been appreciated.[2] It appears that there were 112 or more Members of Parliament between 1784 and 1832 who can be reckoned as Evangelicals. This included a small group of somewhat extreme millenarianists; a larger group who, while being Evangelical in their religious beliefs, owed political allegiance to one of the two main political parties, and in the case of the majority of them to the Tory party; and the Saints proper, whose most determined and unshakeable maxim was total repudiation of all party alignment and the maintenance of absolute independence. For the latter, the individual conscience was held to be the basis of political behaviour, which of course meant that they did not always vote in the same way. Although the number of those who combined Evangelical faith with this political independence varied, there were an average of about thirty such Members during these years.

The temperament and political ideology of these three Evangelical sub-groups were widely different: in this respect, as well as in others, the Evangelicals should not be seen as homogeneous. The millenarianists who, in the latter years of the 1820s, tended to be followers of the *Record* newspaper, were inclined to be activist but reactionary. The larger grouping, who were mostly loyal to the Tories, were characteristically pessimistic, passive and conservative, sharing the views of most of the Evangelical clergy. The Saints, in contrast, were more optimistic, activist and reformist in outlook. They were the most dynamic and prominent of the Evangelicals in the House of Commons; although the first-generation Saints, with their urgent mission to redeem the nation from divine judgement, need to be distinguished from the more liberal and secular second-generation Saints of the post-Napoleonic Wars era. The Clapham Sect operated, at least on its political front, as part of this broader parliamentary coterie.

The members of the Clapham brotherhood under the leadership of Wilberforce were outstanding.

---

[2] The following comments owe much to I.C. Bradley, *op.cit.*

Henry Thornton (1760-1815)

Henry Thornton inherited an estate which was not splendid but enough to allow him to live in comfort.[3] He decided that it should never be increased by accumulation or diminished by sumptuousness, and he remained faithful to this resolve throughout his life. He gave generously to the needy. Before his marriage he gave away nearly six-sevenths of his income, and after marriage one third. He was a Member of Parliament for more than thirty years, and his estate in Clapham was shared with fellow Evangelical Members and others. He was a peaceable, tranquil man; affectionate but lacking in passion, with a fine, even fastidious, taste, but destitute of creative imagination. He brought to the group the gifts of prudence and wisdom rather than inspiration.

John Shore (1751-1834)

John Shore was born in 1751.[4] He had a meteoric career in India. Going out at the age of seventeen as a clerk in the East India Company, he rose rapidly and was soon promoted to membership of the Supreme Council. In his third period of service he was Governor-General of India, having been made a baronet on appointment to this high office. During his Governor-Generalship he was raised to the peerage as Lord Teignmouth. Soon after his return to England he settled at Clapham and sought a second career. He found it as the first President of the British and Foreign Bible Society, and as a much valued member of the Clapham fraternity in its multifarious ventures.

Granville Sharp (1735-1813)

Granville Sharp was born in 1735 and, although the son of an Archdeacon of Northumberland and grandson of an Archbishop of York, he was apprenticed at the age of fifteen to a linen-draper. Shortly after completing his seven year apprenticeship, he gave up that trade to take up a post in the Army Ordinance Department, and there he remained for eighteen years. While still in government service, he became deeply interested in the

---

[3] For the life of Henry Thornton, see Standish Meacham, *Henry Thornton of Clapham 1760-1815* (1964).

[4] For the life of John Shore, Lord Teignmouth, see Josiah Pratt, *Sketch of the life of the late Right Honourable Lord Teignmouth* (London, 1834); and Charles John Shore, *Memoir of the Life and Correspondence of John, Lord Teignmouth*, 2 vols. (London, 1843).

slavery question. He championed the cause of a number of negroes. This culminated in a trial before Lord Mansfield in 1772, and the historic verdict that no man who has put his foot on English soil can be a slave. It was a milestone in the emancipation struggle. Sharp was also chosen Chairman of the Abolition Society, which was founded in 1787, and first Chairman of the British and Foreign Bible Society.

Zachary Macaulay (1768–1838)

Zachary Macaulay's father and grandfather were both ministers of the Church of Scotland.[5] Born in 1768, he first worked for two years from the age of fourteen in a merchant's office in Glasgow. He then went to Jamaica to seek his fortune, and experienced slavery at first hand. He returned after four years, disillusioned and with no plans for the future until he met Thomas Babington, a close friend of Wilberforce and an ardent abolitionist. Babington arranged for him to visit and assist the newly-founded colony of Sierra Leone. So well did he acquit himself that he was later given an appointment as Second Minister of the Council in Sierra Leone, and success in that position led to him being elected Governor a few years later. He spent six years in West Africa, and returned to be Secretary of the Sierra Leone Company in London. He subsequently dedicated almost forty years without stint to the abolitionist movement. In addition he undertook the editorship of the *Christian Observer*, the newly-launched monthly periodical designed to represent Evangelical opinion in the Church of England.

James Stephen (1758–1832)

James Stephen spent eleven years in the West Indies and, like Macaulay, personally witnessed the slave system. It so horrified him that he returned to England in 1794 burning with indignation. He immediately threw himself into the campaign against the slave traffic led by Wilberforce. He was made Master of Chancery, but ungrudgingly gave whatever spare time and energy he could to the cause of the slaves.[6]

---

[5] For the life of Zachary Macaulay, see Vicountess Knutsford, *Life and Letters of Zachary Macaulay* (London 1900).

[6] For the life of James Stephen see Caroline Emelia Stephen, *The Right Honourable Sir James Stephen: Letters with Biographical Notes* (1906); and Leslie Stephen, *The Life of Sir James Fitzjames Stephen, Bart, KCSI, a Judge of the High Court of Justice* (London, 1895).

Charles Grant (1746-1823)

Charles Grant went to India as a youth.[7] After a while he entered the East India Company and, like John Shore, he soon achieved the highest seniority in its service. During his time in India he joined with two friends in establishing a local church, and he paid the salary of a chaplain sent out from England. The three of them also attempted to start what was named the Bengal Mission which, though unsuccessful, led indirectly to the establishment of the work of the Church Missionary Society in India. Together with other friends he prepared a scheme, details of which were sent to clergy and Members of Parliament in England, whereby missionary schoolmasters should go to Bengal and work under the East India Company. The idea was even laid before George III by the Archbishop of Canterbury, but the king objected, quoting the French Revolution as a warning against changes. Rebuffed, Grant and his friends persisted in their efforts to attract men to offer their services to India, and they succeeded after many years. Grant also had much to do with the sending of Henry Martyn to India. When he settled in Clapham in 1790 he was nearing the summit of his career with the East India Company, for he became Chairman of Directors in 1805.

John Venn (1759-1813)

From 1792 to his death in 1813, John Venn was rector of Clapham. He was a son of the distinguished Henry Venn of Huddersfield. He was a man of culture, good judgement and perseverance, who organized his parish on vigorous Evangelical lines. He was one of the first clergymen to introduce parish schools; boldly started a Sunday evening service; organized a system of district visiting; published a collection of psalms and hymns for use in the parish; and was active in the work of the Society for Bettering the Condition of the Poor at Clapham. He was a member of the Eclectic Society and combined with Simeon to draft a set of initial rules for the Society for Missions in Africa and the East (the future Church Missionary Society). Above all, he was the personal friend and spiritual guide of perhaps the most notable congregation in the whole of England in his generation.

This band of friends had a wide circle of Evangelicals from which to receive support and encouragement. There were the Saints in Parliament,

---

[7] For the life of Charles Grant, see Thomas Fisher, *A Memoir of the Late C. Grant, Esq., Member of Parliament for the Shire of Inverness* (London, 1833); and Henry Morris, *The Life of Charles Grant* (London, 1904).

including Thomas Babington, to whom Wilberforce frequently turned for advice, and who gave wholehearted support to the crusade on behalf of the slaves. Both Isaac Milner,[8] the robust President of Queens' College, Cambridge, and Charles Simeon were frequent visitors, and habitual associates. John Newton was close at hand to lend the weight of his experience, knowledge and wisdom; and others, such as Thomas Gisborne, were constantly available as much-valued sympathizers and aides. Notwithstanding, such support was often somewhat muted. Many of the foremost Evangelicals had considerable reservations about the legitimacy of Christian involvement in political matters and thought there was little that could be achieved through political activity. If there was one positive political demand in their teaching, it was for absolute submission to the government of the day. The Evangelicals during these turbulent years were predominantly conservative in their political philosophy. The reforms achieved or endorsed by the Clapham Sect and the Saints did not attract the support of the body of Evangelicals as a whole.

The members of the Clapham Sect were united by intimate friendship and commitment to each other. Their homes were open for casual and informal visits as well as for the more formal hospitality which they delighted to offer one another. Their children played together, and the families enjoyed joint holidays.

The qualities of character and the expertise of the Clapham fraternity differed greatly; what one lacked, another was often able to supply. Wilberforce was the leader, organizer, co-ordinator and orator. Henry Thornton contributed his business acumen and his careful, reasoned judgement. Lord Teignmouth and Charles Grant brought all the authority and administrative skills which stemmed from wide experience in high office. Granville Sharp combined an inflexible will with a gentle approach, and was invaluable as a collector and distiller of factual information. Macaulay worked strenuously and tirelessly, was utterly dependable, and was the right-hand man first of Wilberforce and then of Sir Thomas Fowell Buxton in forty years of unremitting labour behind the scenes:

> He was always at hand while Parliament was sitting, and would be found either in the gallery of the House of Commons or below the bar in the House of Lords, able to furnish facts or suggestions to the leaders of his party, and ready to produce any Blue-books or State-papers required for reference, or to point out some quotation apt to the subject immediately before them.[9]

[8] For the life of Isaac Milner, see Mary Milner, *The Life of Isaac Milner, Dean of Carlisle* (London, 1842).
[9] Quoted in John A. Patten, *These Remarkable Men. The Beginning of a World Enterprise* (London, 1945), p.107.

Finally, James Stephen played a distinctive part not only as a loyal adviser, but as perhaps the closest of Wilberforce's friends. Collectively they constituted a formidable consortium. They variously sacrificed money, career, reputation and in each case time, in common philanthropic or religious objectives.

The influence of the group, and the causes to which they dedicated themselves, were promoted through the columns of the *Christian Observer*. Each month the paper encouraged active involvement in public affairs, while the *Christian Guardian*, reflecting a majority Evangelical approach, was almost entirely theological and devotional in content, although it did strongly support the anti-slave trade and anti-slavery campaigns.

The Abolition of Slavery

The most notable achievement of the Saints, and more particularly the Clapham Sect, was the abolition first of the slave trade and then of slavery itself within the British Empire. This entailed a titanic struggle. Arrayed against the abolitionists was a formidable phalanx of opponents. The slave-owners, the perpetrators of the slave trade, the shipowners, the financiers and all those whose fortune was bound up in slavery, as well as the many whose fear of too much freedom was aggravated by the events in France, joined in an almost impregnable alliance.

The power of vested interests was buttressed by well-marshalled arguments. Slavery had become a long-established and accepted part of the life of the colonies. The slave trade was integral to the whole commercial relationship between the colonies and the mother country. The cry was raised that Liverpool would be ruined, the colonies lost, and that the negroes would rise up and massacre their owners. The abolitionists were viewed by many as ultra-revolutionists. Wilberforce and his Evangelical friends faced a daunting task when they declared their intention of bringing about the abolition of such an institution.

The horrors of slavery and the slave trade will perhaps never be adequately appreciated. It was a massive, iniquitous industry. In Africa it entailed sudden and brutal night raids on native villages, and the dragging of an estimated 100,000 chained men, women and children each year to the coast. In the infamous middle-passage it meant vast numbers packed in ships where chains, filth, stench and suffering abounded in a long and slow voyage across the Atlantic. In the country of destination, it consisted of a life of confinement and deprivation beneath the overseer's whip.

The struggle to abolish both the trade and then the whole practice of slavery lasted almost fifty years. The Bill for the abolition of the trade was introduced, debated and defeated eleven times before its final success in 1807. Sometimes the Commons, and later the Lords, decided to hear further evidence. Detailed information needed to be amassed, witnesses collected from all parts of the world, and opposing witnesses cross-examined to expose their false assertions. An endless succession of meetings were held and hundreds of pamphlets written in an attempt to educate public opinion. Committees had to be attended almost daily, petitions organized, deputations headed, Cabinet Ministers, newspaper editors and others interviewed and instructed. The work for such a small company of advocates was overwhelming. Others, most notably Thomas Clarkson,[10] were co-workers, but the bulk of the labour fell upon the Clapham group. At one time they agreed to sacrifice one night's rest a week in order to sift the mass of evidence that was pouring in. At last they achieved what Lecky calls one of 'the three or four perfectly virtuous acts recorded in the history of nations'.[11]

The slave trade was now illegal, but slavery still remained. Extreme cruelty was perpetrated against wretched slaves who had no redress, for the courts would not hear the evidence of a black man against a white. The slave was regarded by most owners as an animal; lazy, obstinate and dangerous but essential for the cultivation of sugar. A new champion of the oppressed slave entered the lists determined to overthrow the whole system of slavery: Thomas Fowell Buxton.[12] He took up and completed the work the Clapham men had begun.

Buxton's first resolution in the Commons in 1823 declared slavery to be repugnant to the British constitution and the Christian religion and proposed that it ought to be gradually abolished. An insipid amendment was carried which pronounced it expedient to adopt measures for ameliorating the condition of the slaves in the hope that this would produce such an improvement in their character as would prepare for the early introduction of civil rights compatible with the interests of private property. Even this mild enactment produced wild excitement in the West Indies. The planters threatened rebellion. Rumour spread among the negroes that the king had set them free. On some estates in Demerara they refused to work, and the revolt was crushed with barbarous severity.

These reactions reinforced the determination of the home government to do nothing more. Buxton responded with a vigorous ten-year appeal to the country in which facts were mustered, pamphlets issued, lectures

[10] For the life of Thomas Clarkson, see Earl Leslie Griggs, *Thomas Clarkson – The Friend of Slaves* (London, 1936).
[11] W.E.H. Lecky, *European Morals, Vol.I, p.160, quoted in G.R. Balleine, op.cit., p.119.*
[12] For the life of Thomas Fowell Buxton see Charles Buxton (Ed.), *Memoirs of Sir Thomas Fowell Buxton, Baronet, with Selections from his Correspondence* (London, 1850).

given, public meetings held. Delegates from every county met in Exeter Hall, marched to Downing Street and met the Prime Minister. Massive petitions were drawn up and presented to the Commons. Innumerable discussions and interviews were conducted. The opposition was vehement and determined, but victory for the abolitionists was achieved in 1833. A Bill was passed and given the royal assent which declared slavery unlawful in any British possession, and a sum of twenty million pounds was voted as compensation to the planters. The epic of nearly half a century was brought to a triumphant end. If for nothing else this protracted and finally successful crusade would ensure that the names of the Clapham Sect brotherhood and the Saints endured for ever.

Associated with the whole issue of slavery was the founding of Sierra Leone as a refuge for freed slaves. It was accomplished almost independently by the members of the Clapham Sect. As early as 1787 Granville Sharp had been concerned to help London's 'black poor', the freed slaves and unemployed black servants who wandered about the city. With Treasury help he shipped some of them to form a self-governing community at the abandoned trading stations of the small mountainous peninsula which formed Sierra Leone. It was to be a 'Province of Freedom' in which peaceful commerce replaced the slave trade. First Sharp and then Henry Thornton were chairmen of the company established to further this venture. Thornton and Wilberforce each contributed large shares of the capital. Macaulay served as Governor, and experienced some of the early traumas of the new settlement. The little community had to weather many trials. The capital, Granville Town, was burned to the ground by the local chieftain in revenge for an outrage by unruly settlers. The French invaded the colony, burned the houses, destroyed all they could lay hands on, robbed the colonists of their possessions and wrecked the contents of the church. There were tensions and difficulties among the members of the settlement itself. Nevertheless, the colony survived; one more testament to the unremitting endeavour of the Clapham Sect.

World Mission

Another persistent and central concern of the Clapham Sect was the establishment of Christian missions in India. It was one of the main interests of Wilberforce and those members of the Clapham circle who had worked in India. For Charles Grant it was a consuming passion. His privately founded mission in Gumalti is reckoned by Howse as the first attempt by any Protestant to reach the people of India. It was abandoned in 1790, but on his return to England Grant gave priority to the encouragement of missionary schemes.

The focus of effort was upon the East India Company's Charter. The aim was to introduce into the Charter measures for the gradual promotion of the religious and moral improvement of the inhabitants of India; more specifically to empower and require the Company to send out fit and proper persons to act as schoolmasters and missionaries. Opposition from the East India directors was forthright and decisive. The attempt to introduce such clauses into the Charter failed in 1793. It took a further twenty years of pressure and persistence before the East India Company Charter of 1813 guaranteed liberty to propagate the Christian faith. A fast-locked door was thus opened, and the Clapham Sect had achieved the victory almost completely by themselves, with their own enthusiasm and their own resources. In 1813, after the measure had been passed, Wilberforce wrote: 'I am persuaded that we have . . . laid the foundation stone of the grandest edifice that ever was raised in Asia'.[13]

In its worldwide concern the Clapham brotherhood also engaged in attempts to open up new overseas territories and improve the lot of various disadvantaged groups and societies. A few examples will illustrate this. Wilberforce was one of the early members of the African Association which was established in 1788 to send out explorers. Within less than three weeks of the passing of the 1807 Abolition Bill the men of Clapham founded the African Institution, of which the main object was to promote civilization in Africa by providing 'example to enlighten the minds of the natives, and instruction to enable them to direct their industry to proper objects'. As the slave trade did not cease with official abolition, the Institution was soon transformed into an anti-slavery society.

A further demonstration of world mission concern was the appointment in 1787, largely through the influence of Wilberforce and Henry Thornton, of a chaplain to Botany Bay, to minister to the transported convicts.

A final and most notable example of missionary interest was the engagement of almost all the Clapham fraternity in the affairs of the Society for Missions in Africa and the East, afterwards renamed the Church Missionary Society.[14] Wilberforce had discussed the possibility of such a vehicle for mission work before John Venn, the rector of Clapham, initiated an Eclectic Society debate in 1799 which led directly to the establishment of the Missionary Society. The origin, development and varied universal ministry of what was to become the largest of British denominational missionary societies will be described later. It will suffice

---

[13] *Correspondence of Wilberforce*, Vol.II, p.271, quoted in Howse, *op.cit.*, p.94.
[14] For the history of the early years of the Society, see Charles Hole, *The Early History of the Church Missionary Society* (London, 1896); and Eugene Stock, *History of the Church Missionary Society*, 4 vols. (London, 1899-1916).

to note here that some of its key posts in its formative years were held by Clapham Sect members.

Criticism and Assessment

The Clapham Sect and the Saints have been widely applauded for their abolitionist activities and their efforts to promote the good of various overseas communities, but when it comes to the domestic affairs of England, they have been accused of hypocrisy and double standards in their attitudes and actions. Ian Bradley voices such criticism:

> For all their protestations about the cruelties inflicted on the negro slaves and other groups in the far flung corners of the world, the Evangelicals generally and the Saints in particular, seemed to be singularly unconcerned with the sufferings of those at home.[15]

Bradley concedes that there was a strong humanitarian element in the Evangelical creed, but he says that it was essentially spontaneous and individualistic. The Evangelicals did not have a vision of a Christian society with mutual ties and obligations; nor did they reflect on the root causes of misery and want. Consequently they did not formulate a plan for reordering social and economic structures as the early Christian Socialists did. The basis of their response, he asserts, was emotional rather than ideological. Such an approach resulted in works of charity and relief rather than curative measures. Political action was restricted to the remedying of specific and acute suffering. On the whole, Bradley says, the Evangelicals did not evolve political campaigns to deal with the more general problems of poverty and distress. They were concerned with the fruit of social injustice without regard for the root causes.

The condemnation of critics goes beyond the Clapham Sect and the Saints. Hannah More and her sisters laboured tirelessly amid the Mendip Hills, providing schooling for about twenty thousand socially and educationally deprived children over a period of twenty-five years. Some, including the Hammonds, applaud these charitable efforts and works of mercy, but they reprimand the Mores for not reflecting on the system which produced such social deprivation. 'It never seems to have crossed the minds of these philanthropists', say the Hammonds, 'that it was desirable that men and women should have decent wages, or decent homes, or that there was something wrong with the arrangements of a society that left the mass of the people in this plight'.[16]

---

[15] I.C. Bradley, 'The Politics of Godliness', p.192.
[16] J.L. and B. Hammond, *The Town Labourer, 1760-1832* (1917), p.216.

This is a stricture echoed by Ford K. Brown:

> The Evangelicals were concerned with no reform but the reform of vice and sin and of infidelity that to their mind was the sole cause of vice and sin. Their only object was to have a nineteenth century peopled by Evangelical Christians leading moral lives of a puritanical kind.[17]

It is evident that the Clapham Sect members, the Saints and the Evangelicals in general did not, in the words of Stephen Neill, challenge the false theories 'that lay behind the industrial evils of the age'. As he says, 'They took it for granted that poverty would always exist, and that all that could be done was to mitigate the sufferings which accompanied it'.[18] In so doing they were but children of their time. It was generally taken as axiomatic that the hierarchical order of society was providential. Social mobility was possible but each man should conduct himself according to his station. Those in positions of wealth, power and influence should exercise their influence for the good of their fellow members of society who were less well endowed with this world's goods.

Thus, when Wilberforce introduced the Bill to strengthen the laws preventing the combination of workmen against their masters, which became the detested Combination Act of 1799, he did not see this as a repressive measure against 'the workers'. He saw himself as politically on the side of the working men. He regarded the Combination Act as a defence of the realm; he was saving the poor from political agitators. Also, the forcing up of wages would increase the cost of living and thus hurt the poor. His action was consistent with his social philosophy: it was fundamentally benevolent, albeit somewhat paternalistic and reactionary. Conditioned by the prevailing thought of the day, Wilberforce did not realize that the new industrial poor would need the right to combine in trade unions in order to protect their interests.[19]

Although they acquiesced in domestic legislation which would now be considered repressive, Bradley admits that 'the Saints were more liberal in their attitudes and activities than most historians have acknowledged'.[20] Not only did nearly every Evangelical Member of Parliament fully participate in the crusades against the slave trade and colonial slavery, but they 'emerge as a group of highly active and liberally inclined Christian politicians, committed to bringing about reforms on a wide variety of fronts'.[21]

---

[17] Ford K. Brown, *op.cit.*, p.5.
[18] Stephen Neill, *Anglicanism* (Harmondsworth, 1958), p.243.
[19] See for example Pollock, *op.cit.*, pp.168, 169.
[20] Bradley, 'The Politics of Godliness', *op.cit.*, p.iii.
[21] *Ibid.*, p.iv.

It is arguable that the Evangelicals were more questioning, and more willing to introduce change, than their peers in church and state. Churchmen, like public men in general, were so obsessed with opposition to any radicalism, and to Jacobinism, and so determined to uphold the rights of property, that they strongly resisted the Clapham Sect and the Saints in their campaign for the abolition of slavery. Most church leaders regarded social inequality as an essential part of the divine will, and with this went a justification of property, and what was associated with the defence of property. The Clapham Sect and the Saints not only surmounted such inclinations in their crusade against slavery, but worked unceasingly for the improvement of the human lot by means of charitable works. Such efforts can be maligned as mere palliatives; but the Evangelicals did as much as any other group in their generation to meet the promptings of their own consciences.

The Evangelicals in Parliament supported, or even initiated, a broad range of humanitarian reforms. The conditions suffered by inmates of prisons attracted their attention, as did the plight of petty criminals sentenced to savage punishment for minor offences. As early as 1786 Wilberforce carried through the Commons a small measure of penal reform and subsequently supported Romilly in his various attempts to abolish the death penalty for various offences. With the general support of the Saints, he presented a petition in the Commons against the severity of the criminal code. The Clapham Sect advocated the abolition of the press gang, improvement of conditions in asylums and madhouses, the relief of climbing boys and the regulation of factory conditions. Wilberforce united with Sir Robert Peel in launching the first Factory Act in 1802, but protested that it did not go far enough. In 1805 he took up the cause of the Yorkshire weavers; and in 1818 he supported Peel in a further extension of the Factory Act. The liberal Sir James Mackintosh judged Wilberforce to be a Tory by predilection, but by his actions 'liberal and reforming'.[22]

The Clapham Sect, the Evangelicals in Parliament and those in the country at large during the period 1789 to 1833 cannot justifiably be dismissed as repressive and reactionary, nor can they be hailed as progressive and reformist. Both claims represent an oversimplification. This is well illustrated in the varied attitudes towards Catholic emancipation and parliamentary reform shown by Evangelicals.

Most of the Evangelical clergy were strongly anti–Roman Catholic and opposed Catholic emancipation. The Saints also considered Roman Catholicism an evil, but the majority of them gradually came round to supporting emancipation. Spencer Percevel, the Evangelical who was

---

[22] *Edinburgh Review* (1838), p.167, quoted in Howse, *op.cit.*, p.131. The comments in this paragraph owe much to Howse, *op.cit.*, pp.129-131.

Prime Minister for a brief time before his assassination, opposed emancipation and sustained the opposition in Parliament of Evangelical Members who agreed with him. The support of the Saints for emancipation came about because of their generally increased liberalism, the death of Perceval, and the conversion of Wilberforce to the cause in 1813 – largely because he was persuaded that it would help in the resolution of the Irish question.

The complexity of Evangelical political views is even more clearly depicted in the matter of parliamentary reform. Wilberforce introduced into Parliament as his maiden measure a Bill in 1786 for purifying county elections. In 1809 he supported Curwen's Bill for making the sale of parliamentary seats illegal. He continued to declare himself in favour of moderate, gradual reform and told his sons that on the whole he agreed with the Reform Bill.

The Saints followed Wilberforce in advocating reform to end certain blatant electoral and other corrupt practices, but they were slow to take up the cause of franchise extension. As the threat of revolution gradually receded, several of the Saints joined the pro-reform lobby in favour of extended franchise. The arrival in Parliament of the second generation of Saints, and the general movement towards a more liberal political stance among the original members of the group after the Napoleonic Wars contributed to the furtherance of this tendency.

The divisions in the Evangelical vote over the Reform Bill followed the same lines as they did with Catholic emancipation and the repeal of the Test and Corporation Acts. On the one side were the Evangelical Tories now joined by most of the Recordite group, and on the other were the Evangelical Whigs and the Saints. Those who opposed the Bill considered the proposed reforms an inevitable prelude to social and political revolution; the 1688 settlement was permanently acceptable to them and the suggested Bill was a capitulation to radical pressure. The supporters reckoned that parliamentary reform was unavoidable in the circumstances of the time: the Bill, if enacted, would scotch a movement of revolt and disorder, for by it the leading agitators would be won over, and would uphold the existing constitution. The supporters were also convinced that those to be franchised by the Bill were the middle classes among whom lay most of the piety, good sense and right sensitivities of the country.

All the Evangelicals were united in their final analysis of cause and effect in matters political, social and economic. To them it was ultimately a question of morality and personal religion. Whatever the issue currently at stake, the most pressing need was for the country to return to Christian morality. Wilberforce and his friends stressed the need for legislation to encourage the reform of morals, or 'manners'. It was with this object in mind that he wrote his *Practical View* in 1797; and it was with an eye to such a moral reformation, especially at times of political or social disturbance, that the Saints called for national fasting and humiliation.

Because the Clapham Sect and the Saints were motivated primarily by a personal religious and moral drive, they devoted much of their money and time to charitable activities. The beneficence of Henry Thornton has already been indicated. Before he was married Wilberforce devoted a quarter of his income to charity and by his generosity seriously depleted his family resources. In one year he gave away £3,000 more than he received. At the close of his life he had no house of his own but lived with his different sons. Macaulay, at one time worth £100,000, gave away virtually all he had in his devotion to the negro slaves; he died a poor man, though wealth was within his reach. Babington ran a soup kitchen every winter for the poor of Clapham. Buxton set up a shop in the centre of Spitalfields to sell cheap food.

The Saints helped to found, finance or administer a host of charities, including the Society for the Relief of Persons Imprisoned for Small Debts; the Society for Bettering the Condition of the Poor at Clapham; the Society for the Reformation of Prison Discipline; the Indigent Blind Institution; and the Foundling Hospital. They gave support to war widows, distressed sailors, 'suffering Germans', 'Spanish patriots', French Protestants, Russian sufferers, Lascars, and foreigners in distress. This catalogue is only very partial, for many more societies and schemes are mentioned in passing reference in biographies or contemporary diaries and other sources. There was hardly a charity of their day which the Saints had not assisted at some time, or to which they had not subscribed.

By about 1833 the Clapham Sect was a brotherhood of the past, and the Saints had declined significantly as a force in the House of Commons. With all their undoubted shortcomings, they had assisted in a wide variety of reforms, they had given an example of what Christian zeal, compassion, devotion and co-operation could accomplish, and they had established the practice of politics as a true Christian vocation.

6

Fathers of the Victorians

For the Evangelicals 1789 to 1833 was a period when restlessness and some confusion and discord were co-existent with creativity. To help in the appreciation of the somewhat tangled skein of Evangelicalism in these years we will isolate four strands. The agitation and dissonance were manifested in an upsurge of millenarianism, the impact of Irvingite and Brethren teaching and a fundamental reappraisal by many Evangelicals of the faith of their fathers (our first strand). The creativity was demonstrated, in addition to the activities of the Clapham Sect and the Saints, in a pan-evangelical impulse and the establishment of new societies (our second strand), in an outpouring of Evangelical literature (our third strand), and in new forms of Evangelical debate (our fourth strand).

Doctrinal Ferment

Many Evangelicals moved into the nineteenth century convinced that the latter days were beginning and that the end of the world was not far off.[1] The French wars drove a number of them to prophetic views. Two

---

[1] See S.C. Orchard, 'English Evangelical Eschatology, 1790-1850' (Cambridge University Ph.D., 1968), to which this section owes much; R.A. Soloway, *Prelates and People: Ecclesiastical Social Thought in England, 1783-1852* (London, 1969), pp.34, 35; and W.R. Ward, *Religion and Society In England 1790-1850* (London, 1972), p.2.

men in particular were regarded as authorities on prophetic interpretation. G.S. Faber was convinced that the personal second advent of Christ would follow the millennium; a post-millennial view. J. Hatley Frere adopted the growing belief that Christ's coming would precede the millennium; a pre-millennial interpretation. Henry Drummond, a banker and Member of Parliament, gathered together a body of Evangelicals interested in prophecies. He violently shook the Evangelical fraternity by taking his money and some of his men into Irving's recently founded Catholic Apostolic Church.

Edward Irving had ministered to a small group of Scots at the Caledonian Presbyterian chapel in London. Between 1825 and 1833 he was at the zenith of his great reputation. His preaching attracted much attention and drew large congregations. Crowds from the highest classes of society thronged the modest Scottish churches in Hatton Gardens and Regent Square. De Quincey declared him to be 'by many degrees the greatest actor of our times', and Carlyle judged him 'the freest, bravest, brotherliest human soul mine ever came in contact with'.[2] Irving shared the confidence and the platforms of the Evangelicals and took a lead in the prophetic studies which were so dear to many of them. Then he strayed into heresies regarding the nature of Christ's humanity. He set forth novel views of prophecy, and hailed the speaking in tongues in his congregation as a herald of the second advent. He was excommunicated by the Church of Scotland in 1833 and established the Catholic Apostolic Church. His popularity evaporated among many of his former admirers; and Evangelicals were divided in their attitudes and responses.

The Plymouth Brethren also originated, to some extent, as a result of this resurgent millenarianism. A small group of Evangelicals in Dublin longed for a perfect church, and in 1827 they joined together to express the principle that anyone may celebrate the Lord's Supper or preach. The name was appended when the powerful Irish ex-Anglican clergyman, J.N. Darby, a leader of the new movement, went to Plymouth in 1830. Plymouth Brethrenism rapidly exerted a significant influence and drew away some Evangelicals, largely as a consequence of its thorough devotion to the intensive study of the Bible. In particular it developed distinctive futurist views of unfulfilled prophecy which caused much questioning in Evangelical circles.

This ferment of eschatological thinking contributed to a searching reassessment by many Evangelicals of their inherited traditions and beliefs. Some, including the young Hugh McNeile of Liverpool, who drew his inspiration from Edward Irving, attacked the prevalent Evangelical

---

[2] Eugene Stock, *History of the Church Missionary Society* (London, 1899), Vol. I, p.282. This section owes much to Stock as well as to Orchard.

eschatology. The Evangelicals were in the main post-millennialists, believing that the Church would usher in the future Golden Age by its own exertions. McNeile and his sympathisers regarded this as baseless and unbiblical optimism which they countered with the pre-millennial theory. They deplored what they discerned as a decline of Calvinism among Evangelicals, and the rise of an anti-doctrinal cast of mind.

A further critique was offered by Robert Haldane and his nephew Alexander. They were somewhat puritanical. They were inclined to be pessimistic about the church, and anticlerical; and they had little sympathy with Roman Catholicism. Alexander secured control of the *Record* and brought his point of view forcefully before the Evangelical public. Such was his influence that those who aligned themselves closely with him were identified as Recordites. The cement which bound the Recordites together was not merely a common theological system. They were also united by a shared political philosophy. Most Evangelicals, as has been noted, were conservative if not ultra-conservative. In the late eighteen-twenties and thirties the British constitution was assailed by liberals. At this crucial juncture the Recordites combined as the defenders of the constitution and were welcomed as such by many Evangelicals. The Recordites provided the political leadership for the Evangelicals, making them a significant force for conservatism in the country.

During the eighteen-twenties the breach between the Saints and the Recordites became severe.[3] The Saints regarded the Recordites as fanatical. The Recordites condemned the Saints for their association with dissenters and even with Socinians; and they censured them for being lax in their performance of Christian duties by an over-concentration on secular issues. The differences in ethos and theological perspective found focus in the British and Foreign Bible Society. A revolt against the alleged doctrinal indiscipline of the Bible Society resulted in the establishment of the rival Trinitarian Bible Society. Also, those Evangelicals who sought a strong and uncompromising defence of Protestantism founded the militantly anti-Catholic British Society for Promoting the Religious Principles of the Reformation (the Reformation Society).

Pan-evangelicalism

A prominent element in the religious life of England in the period 1789 to 1833 was a pan-evangelical impulse which stressed co-operation

---

[3] Much of what follows is indebted to I.C. Bradley, 'The Politics of Godliness: Evangelicals in Parliament, 1784-1832' (Oxford University D.Phil., 1974) and I.S. Rennie, 'Evangelicals and English Public Life, 1823-1850' (University of Toronto Ph.D., 1962).

between Evangelicals and dissenters.[4] Evangelicals responded in different ways. On the one hand, as previously noted, the latter part of the eighteenth century witnessed an increasingly strict churchmanship among Evangelicals. Full canonical obedience was emphasized. Itinerant preaching was shunned, partly because it tended to build up nonconformity, and Evangelicals feared that by it 'the clergymen beat the bush, and the Dissenters catch the game'.[5] By the late seventeen-eighties a revived dissent was pressing for the repeal of the Test Acts, and it began to whisper menacingly of disestablishment. There was some Evangelical anxiety that past irregularity might reap an unforeseen harvest. Evangelicals were developing a greater sense of their identity with the established church and their distinctiveness from dissenters.

On the other hand, there were forces at work which encouraged greater co-operation between Evangelicals in the Church of England and like-minded Christians in the various dissenting bodies. Certain Evangelicals, such as Thomas Haweis at Aldwincle and Rowland Hill at Surrey Chapel in London, continued to undertake extra-parochial preaching well into the nineteenth century, moving with ease between church and dissent. Also, in the years after 1780 there was a perceptible softening of doctrinal rigidity vis-à-vis the Arminian-Calvinist divide on baptism and on other issues; and with this there came a greater awareness of a common interest among evangelicals which crossed denominational barriers.

The French Revolution was at first a cause of Evangelical antagonism to dissenters. For example, John Newton, previously one of the most catholic-minded of the 'regular' Evangelicals, believed in 1793 that 'all the Dissenters, even the orthodox not excepted, are republicans and enemies to the Government'.[6] Gradually this suspicion and even animosity eased, until after about 1810 Church of England and non conformist evangelicals were drawn closer together than perhaps they had ever been.

The founding of the London Missionary Society in 1795 was the first major attempt at pan-evangelicalism on a large scale in Britain. It was mainly the work of nonconformist evangelicals. The support of Anglican Evangelicals was courted, but in general they did not respond. The Church Missionary Society, an exclusively Church of England organization, was founded in 1799. The British and Foreign Bible Society, which was started in 1804, was the first pan-evangelical institution to win the patronage of most evangelicals in the various denominations. Evangelicals

[4] The comments on pan-evangelicalism are largely based on R.H. Martin, 'The Pan-Evangelical Impulse in Britain 1798-1830; with special reference to Four London Societies' (Oxford University D.Phil., 1974).

[5] William Carus, *Memoirs of the Life of Charles Simeon* (Cambridge, 1847), p.139, quoted in Martin, *op.cit.*, p.13.

[6] Quoted in Martin, *op.cit.*, p.49.

were encouraged to participate in it because of its one, uncomplicated objective, to distribute the Bible; because it restricted the Bibles circulated to those established by public authority; and because it provided that the committee should consist of an equal number of churchmen and dissenters. Even though some Evangelicals, most notably Charles Simeon, hesitated to support it, it was not long before many subscribed to it, and it was established as the largest and most ambitious of the great pan-evangelical organizations. It was viewed as an essentially Christian business venture, solely committed to the distribution of the Bible, which did not impinge upon denominational interests or autonomy.

Nonetheless, from the start the Bible Society was ardently opposed by some High Churchmen. They saw it as a challenge to the authority of the SPCK, and they feared that unwary clergymen would be drawn into what was patently an organisation upholding evangelical interests. Co-operation with nonconformists was anathema to such churchmen, implying the abandonment of a distinctive Anglican ecclesiology. It was a denial of the concept of a single, national, established church, and a threat to church order. The confrontation was especially intense in Cambridge where an auxiliary of the Society was established despite entrenched resistance and disapproval.

By the third decade of the nineteenth century the conflict with High Churchmen was superseded by contention over the continental practice of distributing Bibles containing the Apocrypha. The Edinburgh and Glasgow auxiliaries withdrew from the Bible Society because the parent body in London, while agreeing not to circulate the Apocrypha with Society Bibles, would not withdraw all support from the continental societies which still elected to print Apocryphal Bibles at their own expense. Other Scottish auxiliaries ended their contribution to the parent society; and this sometimes heated debate spread throughout all the auxiliaries.

Just as the agitation was subsiding, the Society was further disrupted by the Socinian or Test controversy, in which some supporters demanded a test of faith which would weed out unorthodox members. Again those for and against were set fiercely in opposition to each other. The climax was reached in 1831 at Exeter Hall when the anti-test party, consisting of many Anglican Evangelicals, and virtually all the evangelical dissenters, defeated the pro-test party which was composed almost entirely of those belonging to either the English or Scottish establishments. Largely failing in their persistent attempts to assert their view, the pro-test party established a rival Trinitarian Bible Society.

Although the British and Foreign Bible Society was the first organization to achieve pan-evangelical co-operation on a grand scale, the Religious Tract Society was founded five years before it, in 1799. Its aims were to distribute Christian literature for the edification of Christians, and to act as an evangelistic agency. Together with the Bible Society, it played an important role in the evangelical domestic mission in the early part of the century. Evangelicals gave their support, and among those who agreed to have their tracts printed and circulated by the Religious Tract Society were Charles Simeon, Thomas Biddulph, Legh Richmond and Richard Cecil. Legh Richmond served as a secretary to the Society and Zachary Macaulay was a member of the first committee.

Evangelical Literature

The Religious Tract Society helped to promote the third strand in the Evangelicalism of this period: a quite sudden appearance of varied forms of literature.

The precursor of this late eighteenth century and early nineteenth century flowering of Evangelical literature was James Hervey. He was the first of a line of Evangelical authors who set out to evangelize the reading public by appealing to its literary taste. Pervading his writings was a view of nature as beautiful, but supremely as revelatory of God the Creator and Redeemer. It was a theme taken up by later Evangelical writers. His expressed or implied suspicion of amusements, and his view of life as a preparation for a holy, happy death, a peaceful departure to be with Christ, were also to figure prominently in the Evangelical writing which followed him. Even his at times excessive emotionalism was to be reflected in the work of those Victorian Evangelicals who were to surrender to the sentimental.

The writings of the Evangelicals in the half century after 1789 were almost always didactic.[7] The purpose of most Evangelical literature, whether for children or adults, was to convey Christian doctrine and inculcate Christian morals. The conversion, religious instruction or moral education of the reader was the intention of all the writers considered in this chapter. Many of the authors were women, and the tales were often written in the form of popular tracts.

By 1789 Hannah More was well known as a successful poet and playwright, and was achieving recognition as a reformer of morals. In 1788 there was published her instant bestseller, *Thoughts on the Importance of the Manners of the Great to General Society*, and in 1790 *An Estimate of the Religion of the Fashionable World*. Both works were addressed to the men of letters and upper-class people among whom she had been accustomed to

[7] The description of Evangelical literature, and the commentary on it, owes much to A.G. Newell, 'Studies in Evangelical Prose Literature: Its rise and decline' (Liverpool University Ph.D., 1976).

move during her extended visits to London. She was the friend of Garrick and Sir Joshua Reynolds, of Johnson and Horace Walpole.

In 1792 Bishop Porteus of London appealed to her to combat the spreading influence of Thomas Paine. She responded with the publication of *Village Politics by Will Chip*, which is said to have enjoyed a wide circulation among the poorer classes to whom it was addressed. She also had such readers in mind when she undertook the editing, and much of the writing, of the *Cheap Repository Tracts* (1795-98), a venture which received considerable financial assistance from the members of the Clapham Sect. The Tracts were priced to undersell all other publications. Some were ballads, some allegories, but the most successful were simple stories with a strong moral message, like *Black Giles the Poacher* and *The Shepherd of Salisbury Plain*. Their success was instantaneous. In the first year more than two million copies were sold, and for a long time to come they continued to be the chief light literature of the villages. Hannah More not only presented the need for personal faith which issues in Christian conduct. She also contributed significantly to social, political and ethical movements affecting the whole of English society, and helped to give birth to the genre of the moral tale which was to become the characteristic expression of popular Evangelicalism.

Within the Evangelical tradition of popular literature, Legh Richmond looked back to both Hervey and More. His reputation and influence rests on his *Annals of the Poor*. They were first published in the *Christian Guardian* in 1809 and 1810, and the collected stories were issued in 1810. This omnibus edition was constantly in print up to the last decade of the century, and the most popular of the stories, *The Dairyman's Daughter*, was reprinted at various times up to 1972.

Richmond, like Hervey, emphasized the beauty of nature. He also built on Hannah More's tracts for the poor and especially *The Shepherd of Salisbury Plain*, but he would not write fiction, even for evangelistic purposes. He regarded works of the imagination with suspicion and even hostility. What helped to give his book its wide popularity was the immediacy of its emotional appeal. His sincerity was evident, and he evinced a measure of literary artistry in the way he assembled and presented his material.

His avoidance of fictional matter made his work acceptable to the most rigorously ascetic Evangelical household. Its attitude to the poor harmonized with the new humanitarian and Evangelical ideas, and the religion it presented was at the time on the upsurge. The conduct it advocated and the consolations it described as a direct consequence of the reception of Evangelical faith through conversion were acclaimed by Evangelicals and many others. The idealization of the advantages enjoyed by the poor in a rural setting offered a romantic flavour.

The original readership of *Annals of the Poor* were middle-class Evangelicals, but with their separate publication in book form this readership was extended to embrace the poor themselves, and unbelievers. This was pleasing to the author, who regarded himself as an apostle and friend of the poor. The book not only appealed to contemporary taste, it was also a foretaste of what was to come. With his accounts of the rural poor and their pious deaths Richmond foreshadows later Victorian Evangelical literature in which doctrinal imprecision was combined with sentimental tales of fictitious urban converts.

Richmond secured popular attention by adhering strictly to fact. Mary Sherwood chose another way. Her fiction was dressed up as fact. She was concerned that fiction, which was generally rejected or disregarded by Evangelicals, should become a powerful stimulus to godliness. She was motivated by her Evangelical faith, but her attitude was more literary than other Evangelical writers. Her purpose was evangelistic, and there was little possibility that her message could be misconstrued, although some Evangelicals objected to what they identified as a form of universalism in her later works.

Religious education of children was the theme of her most famous work, *The Fairchild Family* (Part 1, 1813, Part 2, 1842 and Part 3, 1847), and educational principles were to the fore in *The Lady of the Manor* (1825-9) as well as in many of her other publications. She showed considerable ability in the force of her narrative, her characterization, her use of dialogue and the way she communicated ethical and religious beliefs. What she accomplished was significant. Her books may represent the high point in the Evangelical achievement in fiction and popular writing.

Most of the Evangelical writers of popular literature in the Napoleonic and post-Napoleonic era tended to dramatize sudden conversions, to some extent for the benefit of the illiterate or semi-literate. They were also inclined to sensationalism and emotionalism, perhaps for the same reason. In contrast, Evangelical clergy in general were gradually adopting a different conversion model, and a more reflective exposition of their beliefs. The coming to faith was conceived more in terms of a thoughtful process, which might be sudden but could just as well be prolonged. It was a pattern of thinking which was evident in such leaders as Simeon, Wilberforce, Edward Bickersteth, Henry Budd, C. Jerram, Thomas Scott, John Venn, Hannah More and Legh Richmond.[8]

---

[8] This more considered approach is indicated by the diversity of views among the Evangelical clergy on the matter of baptism – see Chapter 8 and the discussion of the Gorham controversy.

This more comprehensive and meditative Evangelicalism was fostered by the newly-founded Evangelical newspapers,[9] by the discussions at the various local Evangelical clerical societies and by the Islington Clerical Conference. These together constituted new forums for Evangelical debate: the fourth strand in the Evangelicalism of this period.

New Forums

Until 1802 the Evangelicals had possessed no newspaper through which they could communicate. In January 1802, largely as a result of the initiative of the Eclectic Society, the *Christian Observer* was established as a monthly review. The cheapest magazine in those days was the *British Critic* costing a half-crown, but the price of the *Observer* was boldly fixed at one shilling. It rapidly gained a large readership. In its early numbers it contained far-ranging and well informed historical articles, theological papers, lighter essays and reviews. Henry Thornton, the son of John Thornton of Clapham, found the funds, Macaulay was editor, and all the Clapham circle were constant contributors.

The *Christian Guardian* was printed and published in London from 1809. It had originally been known as *Zion's Trumpet* when it was published in 1798 by Thomas Biddulph and his colleagues of the Bristol Education Society. It was narrower in its subject matter and less influential than the *Christian Observer*. The *Record* started in January 1828 as a weekly paper, giving a moderate Evangelical comment on news about church and state. When it was taken over after a few months by a group of laymen, to rescue it from financial difficulties, it was dominated for fifty-four years by Alexander Haldane. His editorials set forth an aggressive Calvinistic Evangelicalism which was Tory in outlook, vigorously opposed to Roman Catholicism, Tractarianism, Latitudinarianism, Socialism and Chartism. It achieved a large circulation but grieved many Evangelicals by its often very forthright presentation and dogmatic, uncompromising posture.

The Islington Clerical Meeting originated in 1827 when Daniel Wilson, vicar of Islington, and later Bishop of Calcutta, invited twelve friends to his study to discuss the subject of prayer with special reference to the Bible Society controversy and the danger of a European war. So helpful did they find the gathering that it became an annual event. The January meeting gradually established itself as one of the main occasions in the Evangelical

---

[9] The following remarks on Evangelical newspapers are based on G.R. Balleine, *A History of the Evangelical Party in the Church of England* (London, 1908), p.120, and Peter Toon, *Evangelical Theology 1833-1856: A Response to Tractarianism* (London, 1979), p.7.

year. It gave Evangelicals an opportunity to share thoughts on Christian belief and practice, and to relate these to issues of the day. It was another means of strengthening Evangelicalism in this period, and of furthering its influence.

The Impact of Evangelicalism

No one doubts that Evangelicalism was powerful in the years 1789 to 1833. It is likewise widely accepted that there was a marked change in the moral tone of the country in this half century which laid the foundation for Victorian morality.[10] Nevertheless, there are differences in interpretation and assessment of the relationship between these two concurrent historical phenomena. Undoubtedly certain distinctive Victorian values and ethical norms were foreshadowed in pre-Victorian Evangelicalism; and these include moral attitudes which have been severely condemned. There was an austerity in the Evangelical régime which was abhorrent to many, and Evangelicals in these years have been accused of being world-denying. The outraged Sydney Smith, having listed such Evangelical prohibitions as the theatre, cards, dancing, dancing dogs and blind fiddlers, complained that it was not the abuse of pleasure that Evangelical Christianity attacked, but pleasure itself.[11] Macaulay seemingly had an eye to the Evangelicals of his generation in his jibe that the Puritans 'hated bearbaiting not because it gave pain to the bear, but because it gave pleasure to the spectators'.[12] There is some truth in these retorts. The Evangelicals certainly stressed the need for seriousness. They had a strong personal faith. They inherited a Christian tradition which was coloured by their status as an oppressed minority. They were accustomed to vigorous self-examination and a profound sense of the importance of redeeming time. They were sabbatarians, and forbade indulgence in a wide range of 'pleasures'. They tended to reject secular literature as unnecessary, or at least approached it with great caution, and they were almost unanimous in their denunciation of novels.

Evangelical morality was the fruit of Evangelical faith; it was a consequence of the very features which gave the movement its force and energy. The vital individual discipline and application to 'the one thing

[10] See, for example, Ian Bradley, *The Call to Seriousness: The Evangelical Impact on the Victorians* (London, 1976); Ford K. Brown, *Fathers of the Victorians: The Age of Wilberforce* (Cambridge, 1961); and J. Wesley Bready, *England: Before and After Wesley: The Evangelical Revival and Social Reform* (London, 1939).

[11] See *The Works of the Rev. Sydney Smith* (1854), Vol. I, p.209, quoted in Newell, *op.cit*, p.53.

[12] T.B. Macaulay, *History of England*, (1849), Vol. I, p.161, quoted in Newell, *op.cit.*, p.54.

that mattered' was also a cause of what may be construed as narrowness. The one was inclined to go with the other. When the Evangelicals lost some of this dynamism and concentrated purposefulness, and became more diffuse and mechanical in their faith at a later date, they ceased to exercise the influence of their forefathers. Possibly some of the pleasures they resisted were deserving of resistance. As an example, the theatre of their day had reached a low level of artistry and a high level of decadence. Also, Evangelicals did not apply a total ban, there was a measure of discrimination: some authors, such as Milton, Shakespeare to a limited extent, the eighteenth century moral essayists with certain reservations, and some poets, notably William Cowper, were approved or even popular. Likewise, some music was hesitatingly and cautiously given approval.

But in spite of these qualifications it is perhaps true that Evangelicals could generally only subjugate and not sanctify the senses; and this subjugation frequently took a religious form. As has been cogently observed, the senses which were expelled from mainstream Evangelicalism 'took up residence with a vengeance on the peripheries of the movement, in enthusiastic preaching and the excitement and drama of Irvingism, the latter a conscious reaction against the intellectualism of evangelical faith'.[13]

The extent of this Evangelical intellectualism is a matter of debate. Evangelicals have been reproached for their intellectual poverty and disregard for academic matters, and it has been said that intellectuals were unsympathetic to Evangelicalism.[14] This is a partially justifiable conclusion, but with exceptions. Among the confined circle of Evangelicals, there were some of fair or eminent academic attainment.

In 1801 **Henry Martyn** had been first prizeman and Senior Wrangler. Martyn was one of eight wranglers among Simeon's assistants at Holy Trinity, another of whom, James Scholefield, became Regius Professor of Greek. William Farish and Francis Wollaston were senior wranglers; the latter was Jacksonian Professor of Natural and Experimental Philosophy from 1792 to 1813, when he was succeeded by the former, who had previously been Professor of Chemistry. Contemporary with them were Joseph Jowett, Regius Professor of Civil Law from 1782 to 1813, and his close friend, Isaac Milner, the President of Queens' College, sometime Jacksonian Professor, Mathematical Professor and University Vice-Chancellor, whose examiners had 'starred' his degree result with the comment 'incomparabilis'. Samuel Lee was of not dissimilar stature; he

---

[13] Doreen M. Rosman, 'Evangelicals and Culture in England, 1790-1833' (Keele University Ph.D., 1978), p.198.
[14] For example see the discussion in Rosman, op.cit., pp.364-366.

was appointed in 1819 to the Chair of Arabic and in 1831 to that of Hebrew. It was in the latter year that Benjamin Synods was appointed as Warden of Wadham College, Oxford. He was the first Evangelical to become head of an Oxford collegiate society, and his career may be seen as the culmination of Evangelical influence in the university as a whole.

This increasing impact on the universities was but one more evidence of an Evangelicalism on the march. As we have seen, it was strong in this period in the political arena, in the newly emergent societies, in popular literature, in the press, the pulpit and the platform. Nevertheless, perhaps its real strength lay in the home.[15] Children were expected to respond to the gospel in essentially the same way as adults. They were generally only allowed to mix with other Evangelicals. Religious instruction in the home was often intense. Parents were characteristically patriarchal in their attitudes and behaviour towards their children, and the children frequently felt strong affection, even reverence for their parents. Most typically, family prayers and Sunday worship were accepted as part of the unquestioned fabric of family life, and gave children a secure routine.

Understandably, there were many examples of resistance and rejection. There is an impressive roll of Victorian notables who were Evangelical in their youth, through parental influence or early teaching or both, who did not remain Evangelical.[16] Among such were Charlotte, Emily and Anne Brontë, Henry Thomas Buckle, Mark Pattison, Samuel and Robert Isaac Wilberforce, Sir James Fitzjames and Sir Leslie Stephen, Lord Glenelg, Sir Gilbert Scott, Samuel Butler, Benjamin Jowett, Elizabeth Barrett, George Eliot, Kingsley, De Quincey, Ruskin, Macaulay, Peel, Gladstone, Pusey, Manning and Newman. There is also an interesting line from Clapham to Bloomsbury via Sir James Stephen and his daughter Marianne Thornton, great-aunt of E.M. Forster. Despite these examples, family discipline and cohesion appear to have been forces for the enhancement and extension of Evangelicalism; and even if some children departed in adult life from their early Evangelical nurture, they most characteristically retained a Christian faith within a different Christian tradition.

Within the family, Evangelical spirituality took a distinctive form. The extent and the depth of the spirituality of such men as Wilberforce and Shaftesbury is revealed by their diaries: they show how highly they regarded periods of prayer, Bible-reading and meditation. Such religious practices were facilitated by daily early rising. Discipline was required, but

---

[15] For many of the following comments, see C. Smyth, 'The Evangelical Discipline', in H. Grisewood (Ed.), *The Ideas of the Victorians* (London, 1966), p.103, as well as Rosman, *op.cit.*

[16] Brown, *op.cit*, p.6. See also David Newsome, *The Parting of Friends*, (London, 1966).

the fostering of the individual spiritual life in this way was considered by Evangelicals in general to be indispensable in the pilgrimage of a Christian. Family prayers were also cultivated, and were practised most frequently at breakfast or in the evening, or both, often with the servants present. Integral to this Evangelical individual and family spiritual régime was the strict observance of Sunday as a day set apart and different. Family prayers, church attendance, family meals, the reading of a carefully prescribed selection of books, and family walks were the main ingredients of a nineteenth century Evangelical family Sunday. There were those who rebelled against such a circumscribed pattern, but there were many in addition to Wilberforce and Shaftesbury who attested to its recreative and restorative power.

Much of what was accepted as the norm in the confines of the family was reproduced in the life of the local church. There were groups for the study of the Bible and for prayer, as in Simeon's parish, and, especially during the latter part of the century or during periods of revival, there were prayer meetings which gathered together people from more than one parish, and indeed across denominational boundaries. The whole Keswick movement helped to promote this trend and to intensify that stress on Evangelical spirituality which has been outlined, and which is at the very heart of the Evangelical movement.

However vigorously they attempted to further their own cause, the Evangelicals remained loyal and enthusiastic churchmen. They were inclined to be intolerant of other men's opinions, even questioning the genuineness of those pronounced as not Evangelical, and they were somewhat one-sided and restricted in their theological systems. In general they had a rather impoverished view of the church. Nonetheless they were conscientious in fulfilling their duties as servants of the church. To take one example, they forcefully emphasized the importance of holy communion. At St John's Chapel, Bedford Row, the focal point of Evangelicalism in London at the time, there were often five hundred at the communion services. When he went to Islington in 1824, Daniel Wilson introduced the then novel custom of early, eight o'clock celebrations.[17] When J. Haldane Steward first preached at Percy Chapel in London in 1812. there were twenty-six communicants; by 1817 there were two hundred. When Simeon first went to Holy Trinity in the seventeen-eighties, three were present, but by the eighteen-thirties there were a regular five hundred. The call for frequent communion was a theme in the charges of Evangelical bishops such as Henry Ryder and C.R. Sumner.

[17] See Josiah Bateman, *The Life of the Right Rev. Daniel Wilson* (London, 1860), Vol. I, p.182.

The Evangelicals did not give prominence to the holy communion in isolation from the liturgy and worship of the Church of England as a whole. They were enthusiastic advocates of the Prayer Book and of church order, and they combined this with high standards of clerical duty. In these ways they anticipated the more general mid-Victorian clerical emphasis on professionalism, rigorous parochial requirements and pastoral innovation. They were precursors of those parish ministries which were one of the glories of Victorian Evangelicalism. But the immediate future was not to be with their form of churchmanship, disciplined and demanding though this may have been; it was to be dominated by those in the Church of England whose view of the church was dictated by a different philosophical and theological perspective. For it is from 1833 that we have come to date the beginning of the Oxford or Tractarian Movement.

Part 3 1833-1901

7

The Oxford Movement

On 12 February 1833 the Whig government introduced a Bill for the radical reconstitution of the Irish church.[1] By means of amalgamation and the removal of stipends, it effectively abolished two of the four archbishoprics and eight of the bishoprics. It reduced the revenues of the two wealthiest sees, and introduced a series of measures which diminished the income of the Church of Ireland. The money released was placed in trust with a new corporation called the Ecclesiastical Commissioners, who were responsible for its disposal.

Far away on holiday in Naples, John Henry Newman heard the news with horror, and condemned the action as atrocious and sacrilegious. In Oxford, Hurrell Froude, William Palmer and John Keble were equally indignant at what they regarded as but the latest symptom of national apostasy. On 14 July 1833 Keble publicly declared such sentiments in his Assize Sermon. The four united, determined to assert the spiritual independence of the church. They were joined by others, and most significantly received the wholehearted support of Hugh James Rose of Cambridge. Rose was vicar of Hadleigh in Essex, and there, in July 1833, he met in conference with his curate R.C. Trench, Froude, Palmer and

---

[1] This section owes much to Owen Chadwick, *The Victorian Church* (London, 1966, 1970), 2 vols, Vol.1, pp.56, 57.

Arthur Perceval, a royal chaplain and cousin to the former Evangelical Prime Minister Spencer Perceval. In September 1833 the first of the *Tracts for the Times* was issued. By the end of the year the Oxford Movement was well under way.

In the Hadleigh conference, and on other occasions, those at the heart of the new movement did not find it easy to agree, but there were certain principles basic to what they undertook. First, they resolved to proclaim the doctrine of apostolic succession. This was the central theme of the first Tract and remained a pivotal dogma. It was interpreted as a line coming down from the apostles through the ordaining bishop. Authority, said Newman in the first Tract, was grounded in apostolic descent. The bishops, as the successors of the apostles, should bear the brunt of the church's battle; and Newman added that he could not wish them a more blessed termination of their course than the spoiling of their goods, and martyrdom.

The second principle asserted the sinfulness of voluntarily allowing persons or bodies not members of the church to interfere in matters spiritual. To lay hands upon the church, whether of Ireland or England, was Erastian sacrilege. The grossest Erastianism was seen as widely prevalent, especially among politicians.

Thirdly, the Tractarians were totally at one in their opposition to Liberalism, which Newman defined as the anti-dogmatic principle:

> Liberalism is the mistake of subjecting to human judgement those revealed doctrines which are in their nature beyond and independent of it, and of claiming to determine on intrinsic grounds the truth and value of propositions which rest for their reception simply on the external authority of the Divine Word.[2]

To the Tractarians, the view that theology was a matter of opinion was anathema. They were convinced that 'orthodoxy was divine truth, revealed, and received by the divine gift of faith'.[3]

Fourthly, they unitedly affirmed the supreme importance of holiness. 'They cared for holiness, and nothing else',[4] says S.C. Carpenter. They were commanded to be perfect, even as their Father in heaven was perfect, and they spent their lives in an effort not to be disobedient to that heavenly calling. They cared nothing for the world, in which most of them never attained any prominent place, nothing for popularity and nothing for

---

[2] John Henry Newman, *Apologia Pro Vita Sua: being a History of his Religious Opinions* (New edition, London, 1893), p.288.

[3] S.C. Carpenter, *Church and People, 1789-1889* (London, 1933), p.144.

[4] Carpenter, *op.cit.*, p.139.

wealth. Neither was this passion for holiness confined to themselves or to individuals. They had a profound personal devotion, but they also yearned, perhaps above all else, for the holiness of the church.

The Tractarians believed in the Catholic Church of Christ, and in the Church of England as a true part of it. They proclaimed the church to be a spiritual entity, not created by the state, and with a life independent of the state. In 1833 this was a new idea. They were divided on the question of establishment. Froude was for cutting loose. Keble thought that the existing union of church and state was sinful, and Perceval agreed with him; Palmer favoured establishment. Newman, although he wanted to avoid premature action, believed that the church was corrupted by union with the state: he was ready for disestablishment if the government committed any further tyrannical acts. They were utterly at one in their concern for a holy church, empowered and directed day by day and hour by hour from heaven. They exalted the priesthood as clothed with supernatural powers. The Lord himself stood behind the priest, gracious and forgiving, but at the same time always austere and terrible. They were not concerned about ceremonial, but believed and taught the real presence of Christ in the eucharist.

The Tracts which set forth these principles and this teaching were issued in quick succession. Their language was pithy and deliberately alarmist, designed to arouse the attention, interest and response, especially of the clergy. By the spring of 1834 twenty-five Tracts had been published. In addition, by that time two addresses had been presented to the Archbishop of Canterbury, one containing the names of seven thousand clergy, and the other those of two hundred and twenty thousand heads of families. In different ways both these addresses expressed deep care and concern for the Church of England, and made an impression even on the rather cynical press.

Initial Evangelical Reaction

Initially there was no great reaction from Evangelicals, and no serious controversy between them and the Tractarians. The *Record* was quite violent in its attacks in the first few weeks, but modified its criticism by December 1833.

The sustained proclamation by the Tractarians of the importance of apostolic succession did not arouse opposition from Evangelicals in the first three years or so. *The Record* claimed not to deny apostolic succession, but only to attach less importance to it than did some of the paper's correspondents. In September 1836 the *Christian Observer* expressed its 'full conviction of the Apostolic succession of Holy Orders in the Church the Church of England', and it added that there was no historical fact on which it more confidently relied. Evangelicals were perhaps slower than others to oppose the Tractarians.[5] During 1834-5 Evangelicals and Tractarians found a common cause in their opposition to the admission of dissenters to the university of Oxford, and the removal of subscription to the Thirty-Nine Articles at matriculation. Controversy was perhaps further delayed because Evangelicals and Tractarians found themselves united once more in the university against the appointment by the crown of Dr R.D. Hampden as Regius Professor.

Indeed, there was a fairly widespread recognition in the early eighteen-thirties that the advance of materialism and the passion for reform could be seen as a battle between church and state, and that Christians in general needed to meet the challenge in institutional terms. The zeal of the Tractarians attracted many Evangelicals. It was not evident at that stage that sacramentalism, and all that flowed from high sacramental teaching, might cause division. The Evangelicals, as we have seen, were instrumental in re-awakening churchmen to the importance of frequent communion. But it was the common pursuit of holiness which most tightly bound the Evangelicals and the Tractarians. Even when the Evangelicals developed a distaste for the teaching and principles of the High Churchmen, they could deeply appreciate the religious poetry of John Keble, and admire Newman's sermons; and they had a sense of their oneness with the Tractarians in urging the virtues and duties of holiness on a worldly generation.

Growing Opposition

A series of events helped to provoke Evangelical resistance. These included the publication of the *Remains of the late Reverend Richard Hurrell Froude*, which made evident his hatred for the principles of the Protestant Reformation and his admiration for medieval catholicism. The coming into prominence of new recruits to the Oxford Movement such as Frederick Oakeley, G.S. Faber, and W.G. Ward, who were more antipathetic to the Church of England, and more favourably inclined to Roman Catholicism than the originators of the movement. The secession to Roman Catholicism of John Biden, who claimed to have been influenced by E.B. Pusey. The publication in 1841 by Newman of Tract XC, in which he tried to show that the Thirty-Nine Articles were 'patient

[5] See H. Clegg, 'Evangelicals and Tractarians. An investigation of the connecting links between the two movements in the Church of England in the early part of the last century and a consideration of how, and how far, these links came to be broken'. (Bristol University M.A., 1965).

of a Catholic interpretation', and that the Roman doctrines of purgatory, pardons, images and the mass were not condemned by them, but only certain perversions of these doctrines. And, finally, the secession of Newman himself to Roman Catholicism in 1845.

The determination to be faithful to the Protestant Reformation, and thus to oppose Roman Catholicism or anything approximating to it, was a powerful factor in English religious life in the eighteen-thirties and forties.[6] The Protestant Association was founded in 1836 to call for legislation based on the word of God; and its organ, the *Protestant Magazine*, was started in 1839. The Parker Society, 'for the Publication of the works of the Fathers and Early Writers of our Reformed English Church', was founded in 1840 under the Presidency of Lord Ashley (subsequently the seventh Earl of Shaftesbury), and made available some of the writings of Cranmer, Latimer, Ridley and others, as well as reformed liturgies and letters of the English Protestant exiles at Zurich. The Calvin Translation Society began to publish the works of the Genevan reformer from 1843. In 1845 the British Reformation Society started a magazine, *British Protestant*, and soon after this reprinted Bishop Gibson's *Preservative Against Popery* in eighteen volumes. The anti-Maynooth Committee was established in 1845 to unite Anglicans and dissenters in opposition to government aid for the Irish Roman Catholic Maynooth College. In the next year the Evangelical Alliance was formed in part out of this Committee. Opposition to Popery and Puseyism was central in its programme.

Nevertheless, throughout all this time the leaders in the outcry against the Tractarians were not solely or even mainly Evangelicals. In Oxford itself C.P. Golightly, a High Churchman of the older school, and A.C. Tait, the Broad Church Fellow of Balliol, were the opposition pace-setters. The first really violent press attack came in April 1836, in an article in the *Edinburgh Review* entitled 'The Oxford Malignants' from the pen of Dr Thomas Arnold. Broad Churchmen, Low Churchmen and old-fashioned High Churchmen were quite as opposed to the Oxford school as any Evangelical.[7]

Formal Evangelical opposition began with the Islington clerical meeting in January 1837, when the Tracts were condemned. There was much comment in the *Christian Observer* during 1837 involving the editor, S.C. Wilks, and Newman, in which the tenets of Tractarianism

---

[6] This paragraph draws much upon Peter Toon, *Evangelical Theology 1833-1856: A response to Tractarianism* (London, 1979), pp.60, 61. The whole of the present chapter is greatly indebted to this work by Toon.

[7] The Low Churchmen and the Evangelicals were quite separate bodies. Indeed, the Evangelicals resisted the Low Church system, and the Low Churchmen were bitter opponents of the Evangelicals.

were, perhaps for the first time, attacked at length by an Evangelical.[8] From then onwards the intensity of the Evangelical opposition increased. During 1839 every issue of the *Christian Observer* and many numbers of the *Record* carried an onslaught upon the Oxford leaders as a group or as individuals. Newman, Pusey, Keble, Isaac Williams, Manning and Hook were assailed as traitors to the Church of England. By 1840 Evangelical suspicion, or even in some cases half-hearted approval, had turned to definite antagonism. As Toon observes:

> Not only the *Record* and the strong Protestant interest it represented but also the *Christian Observer* and the cultured Evangelicalism it represented were poised together to fight the same battle, the battle for the preservation of Protestantism in the Church, the battle for the Gospel.[9]

In the controversy the Evangelicals were scarcely a match for the Tractarians in their learning or literary output. Notwithstanding, they produced a few highly competent responses. Three authors made contributions of outstanding merit and weight: Edward Bickersteth, Isaac Taylor and William Goode. In the period 1833 to 1845, and in response to Tractarian teaching, Edward Bickersteth issued his work on *The Christian Fathers of the First and Second Centuries* (1838); Isaac Taylor wrote his treatise *Ancient Christianity* (1840); and William Goode published *The Divine Rule of Faith and Practice* (1842).

Bickersteth was concerned that the Tractarians gave too much deference to human authority, and especially to that of the early Fathers. He was also anxious about what appeared to him an overvaluing of the Christian ministry and sacraments, and an undervaluing of justification by faith. He claimed that the light of the apostolic age was soon on the wane. Primary importance must be given to the authority of the Bible and not to the early Fathers. Nevertheless, even if the Tractarians had given unjustifiable prominence and value to the Fathers, Bickersteth argued that we must not devalue them as if they were of no use in assisting us to a fuller understanding of the Bible.

Taylor set himself the task of revealing more clearly the moral, spiritual and ecclesiastical condition of the ancient church. He was convinced that existing knowledge of the early church was largely confined to superficialities: little was known of the underlying beliefs and practices. In such a state of ignorance it was easy to misrepresent the supposed ideals and dogma of the Christians in these formative centuries. He collected from the Fathers much evidence tending to disturb what he regarded as an

[8] See Toon, *op.cit.*, p.32.
[9] *Ibid.*, p.45.

idealistic conception of a golden, primitive age of pure faith and practice. The church which was so admired by Tractarians was seriously infected with corruptions and errors. In addition even the English reformers of the sixteenth century, who genuinely desired to reform the church by the word of God, sometimes mistakenly quoted the Fathers as supporters of doctrines which in fact they not only did not teach, but even regarded as erroneous. Taylor concluded that in matters of doctrine and church formularies, there should not be any reliance on the Fathers.

The most learned of the Evangelical treatises in these years was probably that of William Goode. It was a defence of the Bible as the sole, divine rule of faith and practice for the church. According to the author the major question was 'whether there is sufficient evidence of the divine origin of anything but scripture to entitle it to authority over the conscience as a divine revelation?' Stated in another way the question was

> whether in the testimony of the Fathers there is to be found anything which either in form or in substance we are bound to receive as the Word of God delivered to the Church by the apostles and consequently forming part of our Divinely-revealed Rule of faith and duty.[10]

Goode contended that Newman, Keble and Pusey held views on the relation of scripture and tradition which were virtually identical with those of the Roman Catholic Church. Whereas the Tractarians rested heavily on the Fathers, Goode called the Fathers themselves as witnesses in favour of the scriptures as the supreme authority in all matters of controversy. Patristic tradition is not an infallible reflection of the oral teaching of the apostles, and it is not to be received as divinely given. Goode also tried to demonstrate that the authors whom the Tractarians cited did not support the viewpoint for which they were being quoted. It was a lengthy, well presented argument, and many contemporary Evangelicals rather prematurely thought that it struck a death-blow to Tractarianism.

Despite their differences the Evangelicals and Tractarians had much in common. The areas of agreement included

> the divine inspiration of Holy Scripture, the catholic doctrines of the Holy Trinity and the Person of Christ, the need to pursue holiness both in the visible Church and in the individual life, the blessed hope of the Second Coming of Christ, the resurrection of the dead, and the life everlasting.[11]

---

[10] William Goode, *The Divine Rule of Faith* (3 vols, London, 1842 and 1853), p.36, quoted in Toon, *op.cit.*, p.117.

[11] Toon, *op.cit.*, p.203.

Yet, in the years preceding the secession of Newman in 1845, these agreements were not regarded as significant. What mattered were differences concerning the place of tradition, the doctrine of justification by faith, and the nature of the church, ministry and sacraments. In summary, the Evangelicals regarded tradition as a tool to assist the church to understand scripture; defended the sixteenth century Protestant reformers' exposition of the doctrine of justification by faith; and resisted the Tractarian doctrine of the presence of Christ in the Eucharist.

Effects on Evangelicalism

Evangelicalism itself was affected as a result of having to face such issues, and as a consequence of the whole controversy with Tractarianism. There was a certain realignment within Evangelicalism. As previously noted, division and polarization were very evident in the Evangelicalism of the eighteen-twenties.[12] The opposition to Tractarianism strengthened the arms of those who emphasized the distinctively Protestant elements of the faith and addressed themselves to the dangers of popery. Evangelicalism in the eighteen-thirties and forties was largely occupied with a defence of the faith against what was interpreted as a threat to the supremacy of scripture and the teaching of the Protestant Reformation. This helped to increase and reinforce the sense of unity among Evangelicals, and to give a further definite identity to Evangelicalism within the Church of England. The controversy also tended to identify Evangelical theology with the theology of the Reformation. The evangelical defence of the sixteenth century reformers, and the upholding by Evangelicals of Reformation theology, persuaded many Evangelicals that Reformation and Evangelical doctrine were identical. This gave a false confidence to Evangelicalism and blinded later Evangelicals to the differences between the reformers and themselves in various points of doctrine, making the renewal of Evangelical theology difficult.[13]

The Tractarian controversy also produced a generally negative attitude among Evangelicals towards the early Fathers and the usefulness of tradition; as well as a fierce antagonism towards innovation in ceremonial, ritual and architecture. Such negativism was soon increased by further Evangelical conflict. This time it was with those who apparently set aside the authority and inspiration of the Bible in the name of natural science, and those who introduced the latest German biblical criticism.

[12] See Chapter 6.
[13] Toon, op.cit., p.205.

Nonetheless, despite these negative elements, the Evangelicals did help to preserve aspects of the Church of England's Protestant heritage which could easily have been lost. They particularly held fast to the supremacy of scripture, the direct access by individuals to God by faith, salvation by grace alone, and true regeneration as the work only of the Holy Ghost. The eighteenth century Evangelicals had helped to restore these beliefs to a central place in the life of the church, and their grandchildren reasserted them.

Tractarian Assessment of Evangelicalism

Evangelicalism also profoundly influenced Tractarianism. Many of the Tractarian leaders and supporters, including the Wilberforces, W.E. Gladstone, Charles Marriott, G.S. Faber, R.W. Church, Frederick Oakeley, and H.P. Liddon, were of Evangelical parentage. Others, including John Henry Newman, H.E. Manning, W.K. Hamilton, J.R. Hope-Scott and A.H. Mackonachie, passed through Evangelical phases. The great bulk of Evangelical teaching was accepted by the Tractarians, but they considered it was inadequate and needed supplementing. The judgement of Liddon represents their standpoint:

> The Evangelical Movement, partly by virtue of its very intensity, was, in respect of its advocacy of religious truth, an imperfect and one-sided movement. It laid stress only on such doctrines of Divine Revelation as appeared to its promoters to be calculated to produce a converting or sanctifying effect upon the souls of men. Its interpretation of the New Testament – little as its leaders even suspected this – was guided by a traditional assumption as arbitrary and as groundless as any tradition which it ever denounced. The real sources of its 'Gospel' were limited to a few chapters of St Paul's epistles . . . understood in a manner which left much else in Holy Scripture out of account; and thus the Old Testament history, and even the life of our Lord Jesus Christ, as recorded by the Evangelists, were thrown comparatively into the background. The needs and salvation of the believer, rather than the whole revealed Will in Whom we believe, was the governing consideration. As a consequence, those entire departments of the Christian revelation which dealt with the corporate union of Christians with Christ in His Church and with the Sacraments, which by His appointment are the channels of His grace to the end of time, were not so much forgotten as unrecognized.[14]

[14] H.P. Liddon, *Life of E.B. Pusey* (London, 1894), Vol.I, pp.255 f, quoted in L.E. Elliott-Binns, *The Evangelical Movement in the English Church* (Methuen & Co, London, 1928), p.50.

Tractarian despair about the Evangelicals was buttressed by the events surrounding the Jerusalem bishopric. As early as 1838 Lord Ashley had written in his diary, 'Could we not erect a Protestant Bishopric at Jerusalem?'[15] In 1841 King Frederick-William IV of Prussia proposed a joint approach to Turkey by England and Prussia in an effort to secure greater freedom for the Christians in Palestine. With this in mind, he advocated the sending out of an Anglican bishop who should act as the head of the Protestant community and superintend the German congregations as well as the English missions. He offered £15,000 towards the endowment of the See, and suggested that the bishop should be nominated alternately by the crowns of England and Prussia, the Archbishop of Canterbury having power to veto any of the Prussian nominees. All Lutheran ministers in charge of congregations in Palestine would then be ordained by the bishop after signing the Thirty-Nine Articles.

The Evangelicals welcomed the scheme with enthusiasm. Lord Ashley and the Jewish Society viewed it as the revival after long centuries of the 'Diocese of St James at Jerusalem'. Gladstone and Samuel Wilberforce favoured it, hoping that it would lead to the introduction of episcopacy into Prussia. The Archbishop of Canterbury and the Bishop of London warmly accepted the proposal. Ashley used his influence with the government to gain its support and in September 1841 the Bill passed through Parliament. In November Michael Solomon Alexander, a Jew by race, a Prussian by birth, and for many years a devout and learned clergyman of the Church of England, was consecrated at Lambeth as Bishop of Jerusalem.

Many of the Tractarians were furious. Although Manning and Palmer may have been favourable, others were hostile. The scheme involved the recognition of the Prussian Protestants as fellow Christians, whereas most of the Tractarians regarded them as heretics. Newman sent a protest to the Archbishop of Canterbury, and when the scheme was adopted he declared that this was the blow which finally shattered his faith in the Anglican Church.[16]

The Tractarian movement had come at an opportune time. It is arguable that the events of the eighteen-twenties and thirties not only aroused ardent spirits to the defence of the church against what was construed as national apostasy, but that the somewhat effete Evangelicalism of the

---

[15] H. Hodder, *The Life and Work of the Seventh Earl of Shaftesbury K.G.*, 3 vols (London, 1886), Vol.I, p.235, quoted in G.R. Balleine, *A History of the Evangelical Party* (London, 1908), p.203.

[16] Newman, *op.cit.*, ch.111.

eighteen-thirties did not afford an appropriate vehicle for a new national crusade. R.W. Church considered that Evangelicalism had become too comfortable. He judged that:

> the austere spirit of Newman and Scott had, between 1820 and 1830, given way a good deal to the influence of increasing popularity; the profession of Evangelical religion had been made more than respectable by the adhesion of men of position and weight; preached in the pulpits of fashionable chapels, this religion proved to be no more exacting than its 'High and Dry' rival; claiming to be exclusively spiritual, fervent, unworldly, the sole announcer of the free grace of God amid self-righteousness and sin, it had come, in fact, to be on very easy terms with the world.[17]

Whatever the validity of this appraisal, it is an example of how some at least of the Tractarians and their followers perceived the situation. It was no longer regarded as a kind of martyrdom to be counted an Evangelical; and the young Oriel men undoubtedly had in them something of the martyr-spirit. To be persecuted for what they regarded as the one catholic and apostolic church was an honour to be coveted. Their ideals were high and their goals were lofty. They saw the old English church with its apostolic succession as being in danger: let them live for the church, or die in its defence!

[17] R.W. Church, *The Oxford Movement 1833-45* (London, 1891), p.12.

8

In Contention

The writers of the Tracts deprecated any innovations in the way of conducting services. They were opposed to elaborate ritualism, and especially the revival of disused vestments.[1] E.B. Pusey rued the arbitrariness of making changes in ritualistic practices without first winning the people to them. He lamented the revival of obsolete customs without first ascertaining the mind of the diocesan or the people. He found himself in the strange position of having his name used as a byword for ceremonial forms and conduct with which he never had any sympathy. Neither he nor any of his fellow early Tractarians were ritualists, yet ritualism was a result of the movement they set in motion; and various ramifications of ritualism caused controversy throughout the rest of the century.

By 1850 W. J. Bennett had been for ten years at St Paul's, Knightsbridge; and the daughter church of St Barnabas, which was soon to be the scene of anti-ritualist riots, had just been consecrated. J.M. Neale was at Sackville College, and various High Church ritualists including Bryan King, C. Lowder and A.H. Mackonachie were ministering in London, the Exeter diocese and other parts of the country. The founding

[1] A helpful source of information and analysis of the church in general in the mid-Victorian era, and on the Evangelicals in particular, is B.E. Hardman, 'The Evangelical Party in the Church of England, 1855-1865' (Cambridge University Ph.D., 1964), to which the present chapter is indebted.

of the Oxford Architectural Society in 1838, and the Cambridge Camden Society a year later, and the publication by the latter from 1841 onwards of a monthly magazine called the *Ecclesiologist*, aroused great interest in the historic treasures of the church, and led eventually to the widespread restoration of ancient English parish churches. Stone altars and crosses, shrouded chancels and sedilia appeared in many churches. Evangelicals saw their introduction as representative of principles and doctrines of the highest importance. Although the writers of the Tracts rejected ritualism, the Evangelicals had responded in 1837-8 with indignation and accusations of popery when Tract 8 on the Roman breviary and Tract 80 on the doctrine of reserve were published. But it was the younger men in the Oxford Movement, with their yearning for certain Roman Catholic ceremonial, who caused offence to Evangelicals and others; and after 1850 their influence increased.

Just prior to 1850, at a time of increasingly charged feelings, the Rev. W.J.E. Bennett introduced the first prominent example of modern ritualism. He had been curate-in-charge of St Paul's, Knightsbridge, but in 1846-7, with the aid of wealthy subscribers including the Prime Minister, he built the new church of St Barnabas, Pimlico. He was a devoted and able pastor who was much loved by the poor, but his ritualism was a matter of complaint by a minority of his parishioners. They especially objected to 'the eastward position of the celebrant at the eucharist; retaining hold of the chalice at the administration; allowing six of the communicants (two of them ex-Roman Catholics) to receive directly into their mouths; beginning sermons with 'In the name of the Father, and of the Son and of the Holy Ghost'; and the use of the sign of the cross'. Bishop Blomfield of London charged him with heresy for administering extreme unction to a dying lady, but Bennett denied this. The Bishop's Charge in 1850 denounced 'the continual changes of posture, the frequent genuflexions, the crossings, the peculiarities of dress, and some of the decorations of churches'.[2]

It was also in this same period that the whole Church of England was unsettled, and the relationship between Evangelical and High Churchmen was worsened by the Gorham case.[3] George Cornelius Gorham was a Fellow of Queens' College, Cambridge and vicar of St Just with Penwith in Cornwall. He was determined to resist Tractarianism, and in 1846 incurred the displeasure of his bishop, Phillpotts, by advertising for a curate who should be 'free from Tractarian error'. When Gorham applied for transfer to another living two years later Phillpotts took the

[2] Owen Chadwick, *The Victorian Church*, 2 vols (London, 1966, 1970), Vol.I, n.1, p.302.

[3] For a fuller account of the Gorham case, see S.C. Carpenter, *Church and People, 1789-1889* (London, 1933), pp.196-207, 257, 267, 397, and Chadwick, *op.cit.*, Vol.1, pp.250-271.

opportunity to examine him on his beliefs regarding baptismal regeneration. The examination lasted for thirty-eight hours on five consecutive days divided by a Sunday; followed by a further session of fourteen hours spread over three days. Phillpotts required answers to 149 questions. Finally he declared Gorham's doctrine to be unsound and declined to institute him to his new living.

Gorham asked the Court of Arches to compel the bishop to institute him. Over one year later the Court declared that, though the meaning of regeneration was imprecise the infant was regenerated at baptism. Gorham, said the Court, had maintained a doctrine contrary to that taught by the Church of England, the bishop had shown sufficient reason for his refusal, and the case must be dismissed with costs to the bishop. To many Evangelicals the decision, if upheld, was catastrophic. Gorham appealed to the judicial committee of the Privy Council, and on 9 March 1850 it delivered judgement. Not satisfied that he had contradicted the formularies of the Church of England, Gorham was allowed to continue as an Anglican priest.

The episode was a vital test case for the Evangelicals. The doctrine of baptismal regeneration had already been a cause of controversy between Evangelicals and High Churchmen in previous decades. After the publication of Pusey's *Tract on Baptism* in 1835 the topic had been exhaustively raised in pamphlets, tracts, sermons and magazines. All Evangelicals opposed the doctrine of unconditional baptismal regeneration; but they were not entirely at one in their theological understanding of the sacrament.

There were basically two lines of Evangelical interpretation. Edward Bickersteth represented a minority Evangelical view. He said that the reformers had used the word 'regenerate' in the Prayer Book baptismal service in a lower sense, implying admission to the privileges of membership of the visible church. They had justified their view by several biblical examples of the twofold use and meaning of important words. Henry Venn represented a counter view. In common with the majority of Evangelical writers, he maintained that the reformers used the word in the highest spiritual sense, but sacramentally.

For many churchmen the primary question in this whole affair was not whether Gorham was a heretic, or whether the Evangelical repudiation of baptismal regeneration as propounded by High Churchmen excluded them from the Church of England; it was, What authority possessed the right to determine whether Gorham was a heretic or not? Had the patron, whoever he be, the right to present whomsoever he liked without regard to objections from the relevant authority of the church? To what extent should ecclesiastical affairs be influenced or determined by a secular power?

The theme often recurred during the ensuing century. It was, for example, to be central in the traumatic Prayer Book controversy of 1927 and 1928. Nonetheless, for the moment, if the judgement had finally gone against Gorham, no Evangelical clergyman could have conscientiously remained in the Church of England. The verdict helped to drive Archdeacon Manning, Archdeacon Wilberforce and other Tractarians into the Roman Catholic fold, but it avoided a mass exodus, in a different direction, of many of the six thousand Evangelical clergy.

It was probably no exaggeration for the editor of the *Christian Observer* to write that 'a contrary decision would . . . have issued in driving nearly as many of her best Ministers out of the Church as in the days of Charles II'.[4] John Morley, the biographer of William Gladstone, declared that 'if Gorham had lost the day it would or might have meant the expulsion from the establishment of calvinists and evangelicals bag and baggage'.[5] Not only did the Evangelicals not leave the Church of England, but the Gorham judgement helped to replace the prevailing Evangelical doubt and hesitancy of the 1840s by a new confidence and even a spirit of self-assertion. They felt secure in their beloved establishment.

Further contention was, however, generated by developments in English Roman Catholicism. For twenty years after the granting of Catholic emancipation in 1829, Roman Catholics were confronted with unforeseen possibilities and acquired unexpected converts. The surge in their fortunes, and the new demands made upon the Roman Catholic Church, entailed problems as well as opportunities. In September 1850, Pope Pius IX issued a Bull by which England was constituted an ecclesiastical province of the Roman Catholic Church with an Archbishopric of Westminster, and twelve diocesan bishoprics based on Liverpool, Birmingham, Nottingham and other important English towns. The new Roman Catholic Archbishop, Dr Wiseman, with what many considered undue haste and inappropriately forthright language, put forth a pastoral, in which he spoke in triumphant tones of 'Catholic England' being 'restored to its orbit in the ecclesiastical firmament'. This 'Papal Aggression', as it was universally called, aroused a perfect frenzy of indignation throughout the whole country. From one end of the land to the other there rang out the cry of 'No popery'. Great meetings were convened and protests were issued against what the Prime Minister Lord John Russell described as the 'insolent and insidious' aggression.

In the eighteen-fifties, in the wake of the Gorham case and 'Papal Aggression', controversy over ritualism and associated matters came to

---

[4] *Christian Observer*, August 1857, p.568, quoted in Hardman, *op.cit.*, p.1.
[5] John Morley, *The Life of William Ewart Gladstone*, 2 vols (London, 1908), Vol.I, p.281, quoted in Hardman, *op.cit.*, p.348.

the fore. It persisted with lulls but overall with increasing acrimony until well into the twentieth century. Some of the most blatant cases of ritualism were in London. Again St Paul's Knightsbridge was the scene of fierce confrontation. In December 1853 the incumbent, Robert Liddell, was cited before the Bishop of London by Charles Westerton, one of the churchwardens, for ceremonial malpractice. Liddell made appeal first to the Court of Arches and then to the Judicial Committee of the Privy Council. The final judgement in 1857 was something of a compromise and allowed both the ritualists and their opponents to claim certain gains. It thus tended to perpetuate and inflame the antagonism. The case was the first in a series of state court actions against ritualists which continued for forty years. In that time the anti-ritualists were more often than not to achieve the advantage in the legal decisions; but it was of little value, especially when the ritualists ignored the law and were willing to suffer in defiance of it.

Of more notoriety than the Liddell case were the circumstances which gave rise to and accompanied the riots at St George's-in-the East. Bryan King, the rector, offended members of his congregation by ritualism, and many of them left the church. It was King who was one of the first, in 1856, to wear a chasuble. The ensuing gross and unseemly rioting prevailed for eighteen months.

Outside London, it was action against Archdeacon George Anthony Denison in the Exeter diocese which attracted most attention. In 1855 he was charged by a neighbouring clergyman, Joseph Ditcher, with falsely teaching that the inward reality of the sacrament was received by all, wicked as well as faithful. Behind Ditcher the Evangelical Archdeacon Henry Law vigorously assembled the evidence. Behind Law stood the Evangelical Alliance and Lord Shaftesbury. The Evangelical Archbishop of Canterbury, J.B. Sumner, having satisfied himself by a commission of inquiry that there was reason to proceed, tried the case, and judgement was finally given against Denison, with sentence of deprivation. On appeal the case was dismissed by both the Court of Arches and the Judicial Committee of the Privy Council on technical and not doctrinal grounds.

The concern in the Church of England over ritualistic excesses was widespread: it was not a particular, idiosyncratic preoccupation of the Evangelicals. In 1851, after much discussion, all the bishops, with the exception of Bath and Wells, Exeter, Hereford and Manchester, issued a pastoral to the clergy in the hope of calming some of the agitation. 'We have', they wrote, 'viewed with the deepest anxiety the troubles, suspicions, and discontents which have of late, in some parishes, accompanied the introduction of ritual observances exceeding those in common use amongst us'. Any change of usage with which the religious feelings of a congregation had become associated was in itself so likely to do harm, they said, that it was not to be introduced without the greatest caution. Any change which made it difficult for the congregation at large to join in the service was still more to be avoided. The diocesan bishop should be consulted when any potentially divisive measure was contemplated.

The bishops explicitly stated that at the Reformation, the English church not only rejected certain corruptions, but also, without in any degree severing her connections with the ancient Catholic Church, intended to establish one uniform ritual, according to which her public services should be conducted. The measure of licence in ritualistic matters for which some contended was wholly incompatible with any uniformity of worship whatsoever. It was, the bishops said, at variance with the universal practice of the Catholic Church which had never given to the officiating ministers of separate congregations any such large discretion in the selection of ritual observances.[6]

Auricular confession was another cause of ecclesiastical controversy in these years, and a matter of anxiety to most churchmen, not only Evangelicals. It was regarded as one of the most radical departures from the principles of the Reformation in the direction of Rome. In 1854 a meeting at Brighton under the chairmanship of Lord Shaftesbury severely criticized the vicar of Brighton for such practice. Three years later J. Scobell, the Evangelical rector of All Saints, Lewes, and Honorary Canon of Chichester, published a pamphlet charging J.M. Neale, the chaplain of St Margaret's Sisterhood, East Grinstead, with the use of auricular confession. Other cases followed in the next few years. The most publicized was that in which the Bishop of London, A.C. Tait, withdrew the licence of Alfred Poole, curate of St Barnabas, Pimlico.

English Church Union and Church Association

As a result of these various attacks, the practitioners of auricular confession and advanced ritualism developed an acuter sense of their distinctive churchmanship and common purpose. This was expressed in 1859 in the establishment of the English Church Union,

> to defend and maintain unimpaired the doctrine, discipline, and ritual of the Church of England against Erastianism, Rationalism, and Puritanism, and to afford counsel and protection to all persons, lay and clerical, suffering unjust aggression or hindrance in spiritual matters.[7]

[6] See George Henry Sumner, *Life of Charles Richard Sumner* (London, 1876), pp. 350-353.

[7] Quoted in Eugene Stock, *The History of the Church Missionary Society*, 3 vols (London, 1899), Vol. II, p. 348.

The general line adopted by the Union was supported by the *Church Times*, a vigorous and well-written paper which was founded in 1863. Its sympathies were clearly with the High Churchmen. The Union was in the main defensive, but in its early years it had some persecuting instincts. In 1860 it tried to prosecute the Evangelicals who held services in theatres, and in 1862 it attempted to institute legal proceedings against Waldegrave, the Evangelical Bishop of Carlisle, for heresy.

In 1865 the Church Association was started,

> to counteract the efforts now being made to pervert the teaching of the Church of England on essential points of the Christian faith, or assimilate her services to those of the Church of Rome; and to effect these objects by publicity through lectures, meetings, and the use of the press, by appeals to the Courts of Law to ascertain what the law is, and by appeals to Parliament.[8]

It attempted to unite all moderate churchmen who were prepared to stand by Reformation principles. It was not intended to be a solely Evangelical body, and efforts were made to include in the Council men who were not usually identified as Evangelicals.

During the twenty-five years after the founding of the Church Association, Evangelicals used the legal machinery of church and state in a prolonged effort to suppress what they regarded as most pernicious errors and practices.[9] Ritualism was seen as indicative of false teaching and Romeward trends. The vestments and ornaments, and the high ceremonial introduced increasingly into parish churches up and down the country, were, it was claimed, dangerous, not in themselves, but as signifying the sacrificial and sacerdotal doctrine of Christ's real presence in the consecrated elements, offered anew by the priest in holy communion for the sins of the communicants. They were dangerous too, in some more general, undefined sense, as being openly borrowed from the Church of Rome.

Anti-Catholic sentiment was strong in this mid and late Victorian period, both within and without the established church, and Evangelicals were easily roused in opposition to Romanism or anything which appeared to subvert the Reformation. The extreme ritualists agreed that their ritual was symbolic and expressive of doctrine. The battle was not so much over the symbols as over what was symbolized.

By 1869 the Church Association was well organized, with over eight thousand members and one hundred and thirty-eight branch

---

[8] Quoted in Stock, *op.cit.*, p.348.

[9] A full description and discussion of the late nineteenth century ritualist controversy is contained in A. Bentley, 'The Transformation of the Evangelical Party in the Church of England in the later Nineteenth Century' (Durham University Ph.D., 1971).

associations.[10] Tracts and pamphlets were published against ritualism, and money was collected to assist parishioners in appeals to the law courts.[11] Initially the concern was to prove, by court decisions, that ritualist doctrines and practices within the Church of England were illegal. It was not foreseen that the law, once ascertained, would not be obeyed.

One of the most notorious cases was that of A.H. Mackonachie of St Albans, Holborn. He was made the object of a long series of prosecutions lasting from 1867 to 1880. He was more than once suspended, on one occasion in 1878 for three years. He was never imprisoned, and throughout he continued to devote himself to his parish.

With the prosecution of W.J.E. Bennett, vicar of Frome, the issue clearly and explicitly moved from symbols to the doctrine symbolized. In *A Plea for Toleration in the Church of England* (1867), Bennett spoke of 'the real, actual and visible Presence of the Lord upon the altars of our churches'. He taught people to adore 'the consecrated elements', believing Christ to be in them; and he described the eucharist as a sacrifice. After various court hearings, Bennett published a revised edition of his book, changing the crucial phrases to 'the real, actual Presence of the Lord, under form of bread and wine upon the altars of our churches', and 'Christ present in the elements under the form of bread and wine'.

The final judgement of the Judicial Committee of the Privy Council was that the Church of England taught a presence of Christ in the ordinance and in the soul of the worthy recipient, but affirmed nothing as to the mode of that presence, except that the Body of Christ is received by faith, after a heavenly and spiritual manner only. It was illegal to teach that Christ's sacrifice on the cross could be repeated in an offering of Christ by the priest at the Lord's Supper. All acts of adoration were likewise declared illegal. Nevertheless, it was not clear to the Judicial Committee that Bennett had so described the real presence, or so used the word 'sacrifice' as to contradict the language of the Articles, and the judges decided to give him the benefit of the doubt on the question of adoration. There was disagreement, disunity and confusion among Evangelicals as a result of the judgement. The most extreme reaction came from Capel Molyneux, the incumbent of St Paul's, Onslow Square, London, who caused great commotion by advocating secession from the Church of England. But Evangelicals as a whole resisted this, and when Molyneux left the church almost no other Evangelical followed his example.

[10] See the Church Association *Annual Report*, 1869.
[11] See the Church Association *Annual Report*, 1867.

Litigation failed to suppress the ritualists. Mackonachie by strictly and literally complying with the ruling was able to continue his ritualistic practices and made further legal restrictions necessary. Others completely ignored the judgement. Such court action against dedicated priests tended to increase the popularity of the ritualists.

In the meantime Lord Shaftesbury sought to restrict vestments to 'a decent and comely surplice' by means of new legislation. In 1874 Bishop Tait introduced in the House of Lords a Bill for the regulation of public worship with the avowed purpose of suppressing ritualism. Amended by Shaftesbury, it became law. The efforts of the Church Association to enforce the Public Worship Regulation Act were to make the Society increasingly unpopular, the ritualists into martyrs, and the ritualism they used increasingly attractive.

The prosecution of Arthur Tooth, vicar of St James's, Hatcham, brought the conflict to a new height of intensity and bitterness. The case was heard by Lord Penzance, as Dean of Arches, in July 1876. Tooth refused to appear, or to recognize in the court any authority whatsoever, and he ignored the judgement against him. He was suspended from conducting services in the church for three months, but disregarded this. The bishop sent a curate to take charge, and he was refused entrance. Anti-ritualist mobs disturbed the services. The Dean of Arches pronounced Tooth contumacious. He was arrested and placed in Horsemonger Lane jail. Tooth and his churchwardens would not surrender the church keys, and the church was closed for two Sundays. The following week the bishop's nominee, Benjamin Dale, forced an entrance and conducted worship according to the law, but amid much disturbance. Appeal was made to Lord Penzance, and Tooth was released after one month's imprisonment. At St James's the Church Association candidate, Fry, was elected churchwarden. Shortly afterwards Tooth broke into the church and celebrated the holy communion with his usual vestments and ceremonial. Fry, in reaction, attacked the confessional box with an axe, and destroyed the cross in the centre of the church. The disorders continued through the summer. Archbishop Tait tried in vain to come to an agreement with Tooth, who was paraded as a hero by the English Church Union. Further legal wrangles ensued, and Tooth resigned his benefice to prevent a fresh prosecution.

The policy of litigation to suppress ritualism was rapidly becoming a fiasco, what with the possibility of a bishop's veto on any action, technical legal flaws and the refusal of ritualists to obey adverse decisions. Imprisonments perpetuated this sad saga; the most notorious case being that of Mr Green of Miles Platting, who remained in Lancaster jail for nearly two years. Writing in 1889, Eugene Stock said that probably no event in the history of the previous half century had done so much to foster the Romanizing movement, and to injure the Evangelical cause, as the imprisonment of Mr Green.[12]

The last of the prosecutions was against Edward King, the Bishop of Lincoln. It was an unfortunate choice and unfavourable to the accusers. King was possibly the most cautious and most respected ritualist in England. He was arguably the saintliest bishop on the bench, and he was widely loved even by some Evangelicals. The practices of which he was accused were not those mainly in controversy like incense, vestments and statues. They were little acts then hardly noticed by many: the eastward position, lighted candles on the altar, mixing water with wine, allowing *O Lamb of God* to be sung, using the sign of the cross at absolution and blessing, and cleansing the vessels during the service. King was no ritualist in any narrow sense of the word. In January 1889 he was cited to appear before the Archbishop, and the Archbishop's judgement was given in November 1890. In it he forbade the sign of the cross at the blessing and absolution, and mixing the wine with water during the service, but allowed the eastward position, provided that the manual acts were visible to the people. He acquitted the bishop on the other charges. In response to an appeal by the Church Association, in August 1892, the Judicial Committee upheld the Archbishop's judgement, with one minor exception. The whole affair was a disaster for the Evangelicals. Owen Chadwick concluded that the 'evangelical party was more damaged by the case of Read v. the Bishop of Lincoln than by any other circumstances in the entire controversy over ritual, even the imprisonment of clergymen'. He rightly pronounced this to be unjust, as almost all Evangelicals by then disapproved of the policy of prosecution. 'But the Church Association proceeded in the name of evangelical truth, and the evangelicals suffered'.[13]

Not only did the Lincoln case reinforce the unpopularity of the Evangelicals, it caused bitter division within their own ranks. Most of the Evangelicals were deeply distressed at the final judgement: three or four clergymen seceded from the church, and a few others might have followed, but for the strenuous action taken by some of their leaders. Bishop Ryle was forthright:

> I charge my brethren not to listen for a moment to those who counsel secession. I have no sympathy with the rash and impatient men who recommend such a step. So long as the Articles and Prayer Book are not altered, we occupy an impregnable position. We have an open Bible, and our pulpits are free.[14]

[12] Stock, *op.cit.*, Vol.III, p.7.
[13] Chadwick, *op.cit.*, Part II, p.354.
[14] Letter to the *Record*, 12 August 1892.

Those Evangelicals, like Ryle, who favoured a more conciliatory approach to ritualism and other issues, were labelled Neo-Evangelicals by the more militant wing of Evangelicalism.[15]

Frustrated in the law courts, the more determined Evangelicals turned to direct action. Under the leadership of John Kensit, the Secretary of the Protestant Truth Society, the agitators began to disturb and disrupt services. The campaign was denounced by most Evangelicals, but it rapidly gained in momentum. In passion and venom it came near to matching the anti-ritualism of the previous years.

---

[15] Evangelical differences of opinion over the permissible limits of toleration, and what beliefs and practices were acceptable, extended to a number of issues. Ryle was attacked because, on one occasion, when he had no gown with him, he preached in a surplice. In 1887 Handley Moule appeared in a surplice while preaching in Cambridge, and soon many Evangelicals adopted this form of clerical dress. An increasing number of Evangelicals, concerned to reach out to the unevangelized, and to deepen the spiritual life, did not hesitate to borrow further ideas from other Christian traditions. As an illustration, after the Rev. E.H. Bickersteth had urged them not to stand aloof from retreats on account of their Romish name, the practice spread among Evangelicals, though they were usually called Quiet Days. All these trends were anathema to some other Evangelicals, who firmly resisted them.

9

The Shaking of the Foundations

Within the space of three years, from 1859 to 1862, three works were published which precipitated a religious crisis. The first, in 1859, was the *Origin of Species* by Charles Darwin. Then, in 1860, there appeared a collection of papers by seven eminent liberal churchmen, with the unpretentious title *Essays and Reviews*. In the following two years John William Colenso, the Bishop of Natal, issued a *Commentary on the Epistle to the Romans* and Part I of his *Pentateuch and Book of Joshua Critically Examined*. The first of these publications was a climacteric event in the debate, or one might even say war, between Genesis and geology. With the other works the struggle between Orthodoxy and Neology reached its height.[1]

The preoccupation of the Tractarians and the Evangelicals with the affirmation of their own positions meant that neither gave much attention

---

[1] The term 'Neology' was applied to novel views in theology tending towards rationalism at least as early as 1827. Mid–nineteenth century movements of thought, and the Evangelical reactions to them, are discussed in L.E. Elliott-Binns, *Religion in the Victorian Era* (London, 1936), S.C. Carpenter, *Church and People, 1789- 1889* (London, 1933), Owen Chadwick, *The Victorian Church* (London, 1966, 1970), C.C. Gilispie, *Genesis and Geology* (Cambridge, Mass., 1951), Stephen Neill, *The Interpretation of the New Testament 1861-1961* (Oxford, 1966), B.E. Hardman, 'The Evangelical Party in the Church of England, 1853-1865' (Cambridge University Ph.D., 1964), John Kent, *The End of the Line: Developments of Theology in the Last Two Centuries* (London, 1982), Bernard M.G. Reardon, *Religious Thought in the Victorian Age: A Survey from Coleridge to Gore* (London, 1971).

to the general intellectual movement of the times. One of the main currents in this intellectual stream was the increasingly popular science of geology. As it developed to become the science of the day, it threatened some of the basic Christian presuppositions. The Church of England and · Christians generally had rested in the security of the Genesis account of creation as the final and satisfying evidence of both the fact and the manner of the divine creation of the world. The atheists who denied such beliefs, and the scientists who, like Laplace, saw no need to hypothesize the existence of God, or were contemptuous of religion, were regarded as the aberrant few. There was not much counter-argument to the biblical view of creation, and talk of such matters as evolution was occasional and apparently harmless. This somewhat comfortable, quiet and confident world of the pre-eighteen-twenties was shattered by a series of pronouncements and publications.

New Scientific Thought

In his inaugural lecture to Oxford university in 1820 the Rev. William Buckland, who held the chair of geology, declared that the words of Genesis chapter I verse 1 'in the beginning' described an immense period. The six 'days' of creation, he said, were epochs of unspecified length and not days of twenty-four hours. Ten years later, Charles Lyell administered another shock. In his *Principles of Geology* he accounted for the present condition of the earth's surface by postulating a uniform process of gradual development. He was the first to use such terms as Eocene, Meiocene and Pleiocene. It was during such vast eons of time that the chalk cliffs of Dover were formed, as the remains of marine creatures were deposited there at a rate of an inch or two a century and then raised by an upheaval: likewise the fossils of the cliffs of Lyme Regis or Whitby or elsewhere were the remains of creatures dating back to an almost incalculable antiquity. In 1836 he caused further offence by declaring Noah's flood to be a local catastrophe, sufficient only to drown all mankind who then possibly lived in the Euphrates valley, and totally insufficient to have the universal dimensions indicated by the Genesis narrative. The animals of the ark were only acceptable as domestic pets; and the notion that there were two of every species was discounted.

In 1844 the *Vestiges of the Natural History of Creation* was published anonymously. It extended the idea of evolution from earth to animal life. There was, it said, no special creation; the varieties were gradually formed in obedience to the perpetually operating divine will. The work was scorned even by serious students of evolution, and it embarrassed literate Christian geologists because it was reckoned as slipshod. Huxley was furious because he thought the author, who was later found to be Robert Chambers (a journalist and publisher of the famous encyclopedia), made truth appear ridiculous. The ridicule promoted its sale: 23,750 copies in eleven British editions alone, with four of the editions in the first six months.

Then Darwin issued the *Origin of Species*. He enlarged the whole concept of evolution in an elaboration of the process of natural selection. He was an agnostic in religion, but he never posed as a philosopher, or aspired to guide the minds of others. He simply wanted to call attention to the evidence he had collected. In the *Origin of Species* he did not draw any conclusions adverse to religious belief; regrettably others did. Educated Christians may not generally have been moved, or substantially changed their understanding of Genesis; but the world at large reacted differently. It was widely understood that geology contradicted Genesis, and that science and religion had opposed conclusions.

Biblical Criticism

The second intellectual current which reached a high point in the eighteen-sixties, and unsettled popular faith in the Bible, arose out of the work of historians who commented on the texts of the Old and New Testaments. The new geological and biological teaching relating to the early chapters of Genesis contributed to a surge of radical Old Testament criticism. The first indications of such criticism came with the publication in 1829 of Dean H.H. Milman's *History of the Jews*, in which Abraham was spoken of as 'an Arab Sheikh', and there was a tendency to rationalize some of the miracles. Dean A.P. Stanley introduced large numbers of Englishmen to a mildly critical view of the Old Testament when he published his *Lectures on the History of the Jewish Church* (Part 1, 1863, Part 2, 1865 and Part 3, 1876). He minimized the miraculous to such an extent that he was thought by some to have de-supernaturalized and secularized the Bible.

A far more serious inroad into the traditional view of the Bible came from Germany. The Tübingen School offered a radical reconstruction of the received version of early Christian history. Its distinctive teaching was confined to a small academic circle in England, until the appearance of *Leben Jesu* by Friedrich Strauss in 1835, which was translated into English by George Eliot in 1846. Strauss took the Tübingen critical results for granted and tried to explain exactly how the gospel narratives had developed. He portrayed Jesus as a Galilean teacher of pure and holy life who had come into inevitable collision with the ecclesiastical authorities, had been put to death, and had been surrounded by an increasing aura of mystery and miracle. The miraculous was introduced not out of any intention to deceive, but because the early Christians viewed Christ with Messianic expectations. For Strauss, miracles did not happen.

Essays and Reviews and the works of Colenso were attempts at restatement in the light of such rationalizing movements as these. An incident such as the dismissal of F.D. Maurice from his Professorship of King's College, London, on account of his publicized doubts regarding the eternity of future punishment, though of lesser importance, entailed the same clash between those who upheld the orthodox view of scripture and those who were far more liberal.

Essays and Reviews in its preface is described as:

> an attempt to illustrate the advantage derivable to the cause of moral and religious truth, from a free handling, in a becoming spirit, of subjects peculiarly liable to suffer by the repetition of conventional language, and from traditional methods of treatment.

The essay by Frederick Temple was orthodox and theologically uncontentious. That by Rowland Williams introduced a formidable array of critical results and conjectures: the Pentateuch was a gradual growth, the 'child' of Isaiah VII was to be born in the reign of Ahaz, chapters XL – LXVI of Isaiah were not by the prophet Isaiah, the book of Daniel was of the second century, and the Epistle to the Hebrews was not Pauline. The list was extended to include a number of other ideas novel at the time. Baden Powell was a wholehearted evolutionist, and in his essay he enthusiastically welcomed the *Origin of Species*, evidently had no place for miracles and placed the natural and the spiritual in separate compartments. A.B. Wilson called for a drastic amendment of the terms of subscription of the Church of England, and caused offence by referring to passion and error in the Bible. C.W. Goodwin thought that theologians should accept the discoveries of modern science. The essay by Mark Pattison was purely historical. The most significant contribution was by Benjamin Jowett, who asked that the Bible should be interpreted like any other book. His qualification that there were many respects in which scripture was unlike any other book was forgotten. It was supposed that when he pleaded for open enquiry he was casting Christianity away. His essay gave the impression of antagonism to the prevailing orthodox interpretation of scripture, with little offered in its place. It was marked by a clear tendency to resolve Christianity into a set of ideas and a way of moral life.

The effect on the English mind of the publication of Colenso's *Commentary on the Epistle to the Romans* and his volumes on the Pentateuch was 'startling in the extreme'.[2] Colenso displayed a low view of biblical

---

[2] Carpenter, *op.cit.*, p.504.

inspiration; made plain his disbelief in eternal punishment; judged parts of the Pentateuch unhistorical and a compilation of different sources; declared that Anglican doctrine must be broadened if it was to be acceptable to intelligent men; and asserted that the essential truth of the Bible did not depend upon the historic truth of all its narratives.

Evangelical Reaction

During the decades preceding 1860 the Evangelicals were not excessively defensive or aggressive in the face of new scientific theories: they largely accepted the relevance of scholarship. This was shown in the discussions of the relationship of geological discoveries to the truths of scripture in the eighteen-twenties and the early eighteen-thirties. J.B. Sumner and the *Christian Observer* were illustrative of an enlightened Evangelical interest in all things scientific. Some Evangelicals cautiously accepted the theory of such geologists as Baron de Cuvier, that the world had been created by a long series of geological revolutions extending many thousands of years into pre-history. Grounded as they were in eighteenth century rationality, order and first and second causes, certain Evangelical intellectuals fought hard to reconcile Genesis and geology, and to preserve the unity of truth as declared by theologians, scientists and historians.

A decided change took place with the various scientific, historical and theological developments of the eighteen-sixties. The general resistance to the new teaching stiffened, and not least among the Evangelicals.[3] They did not adopt a posture peculiar to themselves, but they were distinguished by their strong and tenacious insistence on the infallibility of the Bible. The confrontation even gave them a temporary *modus vivendi* with the High Churchmen.

After the publication of *Essays and Reviews* hardly an issue of either the *Christian Observer* or the *Record* appeared without an attack on Neology. From 1861 to 1865 at least thirty long articles appeared in the *Christian Observer*. Some were reviews of offensive or unorthodox publications, while others were direct refutations of Neology or expositions of the orthodox position. Apart from editorials, the correspondence columns were filled week by week with letters reiterating the well-established Evangelical views.

Even the more restrained and diplomatic *Church Missionary Intelligencer*, the leading quarterly and foremost missionary organ of the Evangelicals, was not averse to using strong language against the Neologists. Colenso's views on biblical inspiration were described by it as 'heaps of tedious and

---

[3] The observations which follow are based on Hardman, *op.cit.*, p.88.

worthless matter', and the truth that could be extracted from them, when balanced against the evidence which could be accumulated in support of the orthodox view of the inspiration of scripture, was reckoned to be like a molehill compared to a mountain mass.[4]

Evangelicals offered some scholarly appraisals, as when Alexander and J.B. M'Caul examined the Hebrew text and exposed the linguistic incompetence of Colenso. Thoughtful contributions on some of the debated theological topics were provided by T.R. Birks, C.H. Davis and W.H. Fremantle. But such an approach was not typical. The tenor of the Evangelical attack on Neology during this period of highly charged emotions was one of uncompromising hostility. Any Evangelical who queried the justice of the attack, or indicated that some of the Neologists had made a useful contribution, was speedily corrected. T.D. Harford-Battersby of Keswick and E.H. Bickersteth, the future Bishop of Exeter, were chided by the *Record* for showing such sympathy or appreciation.[5]

To Evangelicals as a body the implications and consequences of the new teaching were plain. They included the tendency to subvert faith; emptying the scriptures of all their force and practical efficacy by denying the historical character of the biblical narratives; sapping the authority of the Bible and thus denigrating it as the guide to life and eternity; and allowing a man to retain the orders and benefices of the church when he did not accept the full and final authority of the Bible.

The inspiration and authority of the Bible was the pivotal issue. Repeatedly the Evangelicals and others said that to invalidate any one part of the Bible was to throw discredit on the rest. Tradition was accepted as a witness to facts, but not as an independent authority for faith and practice.[6]

Nevertheless, in spite of their strong repudiation of the teaching of Colenso, the Evangelicals did not concur with a contemporary demand that he should be unfrocked. They held his beliefs to be inconsistent with his profession as a clergyman and bishop in the Church of England, and would no doubt have welcomed his resignation, but they abhorred any attempt to take action which, in their opinion, would flout the authority of the crown. Many Evangelical leaders emphasized that this was a moral issue. Robert Bickersteth of Ripon charged Colenso with moral dishonesty for retaining office in the church while striving to propagate opinions which were directly at variance with what the church professed

[4] See the *Church Missionary Intelligencer*, September 1865, pp.257 f.
[5] See the *Record*, 5 October 1860, p.4.
[6] See Peter Toon, *Evangelical Theology 1833-1856* (London, 1979), pp.128, 131.

to hold and teach. C.R. Sumner of Winchester and Hugh Stowell of Salford both took the same line.[7]

The concerted crusade by Evangelicals and High Churchmen made full use of petitions. Dozens of them were presented by clergymen and laymen to bishops, archbishops and other dignitaries. Most notable among these was the so-called *Oxford Declaration* for which Pusey and Shaftesbury collaborated. The Evangelicals and High Churchmen combined because they recognized a common enemy. It is a moot point whether there was substantial agreement between them touching the doctrine of inspiration. Certainly they were not at one regarding the authority of scripture, and for Evangelicals inspiration and authority were so complementary as to be well-nigh inseparable. The logic of the alliance was not examined too closely by either party. The charge of compromise was countered by the assertion that co-operation on one issue did not imply agreement on all issues, and that it would have been wrong to remain silent in the face of the tide of unbelief.

A large number of Evangelical books and pamphlets attacked the 'new' theology, but nothing of substantial or permanent value was produced which could compare with the works of men like Stanley, Jowett or Maurice. This is a little surprising, as ever since the turn of the century, the Evangelicals had in their midst those who were not ill-equipped to make a reasoned response to the intellectual movements of their day. For instance, there was always a solid phalanx of them among the seniors at Oxford, and their contribution to scholarship was acknowledged, as in the frequency with which they were invited to deliver the Bampton Lectures.[8] Nolan did so in 1833, E. Garbett (1842), Hurtley (1845), Shirley (1847), E.G. Marsh (1848), Riddle (1852), Waldegrave (1854), E. Garbett (1867) and Payne Smith (1869).

In addition, in the eighteen-sixties Goode, Birks, M'Caul and Davis were at hand. Birks was elected Professor of Moral Philosophy at Cambridge in 1872. He wrote a number of works in defence of what may perhaps be described as a liberal evangelical position. Of these, probably the most important was *The Bible and Modern Thought* (1861). Edward Garbett, in addition to his Bampton Lectures, gave the Boyle Lectures in 1861. In them he asserted the objective reality of revelation, which admitted of neither addition nor diminution.[9] Later, in his 1867 Bampton Lectures, he spoke of the absolute necessity of a dogmatic faith, and the

---

[7] See the *Record*, 16 March 1865, p.4, to which reference is made in Hardman, *op.cit.*, p.95.

[8] For a discussion of the Evangelicals at Oxford see J.S. Reynolds, *The Evangelicals at Oxford, 1735-1871* (Oxford, 1953).

[9] See E. Garbett, *The Bible and its Critics* (1861).

supremacy of revealed Christian truth over subjective human reasoning.[10] Payne Smith, primarily a Syriac scholar, also took some part in this theological debate.

But none of these were conversant with the primary sources from Germany, and they were perhaps not able to write in a manner acceptable to the rank and file of the clergy and intelligent laymen. The only works of substantial academic calibre from the orthodox and conservative camp were the commentaries of E.B. Pusey, who not only knew German, but had studied in Germany in his earlier days and had experienced a phase of fascination with German liberalism. By far the greater part of Evangelical apologetics was at the level of popular polemics; and very soon the attention of the polemicists was almost entirely diverted to the conflict over ritualism. There was also a growing rapport between many High Churchmen and the Neologists. The alliance between the Evangelicals and Tractarians such as Pusey came to an end: it had been short-lived.

Neither the Evangelicals nor the Christian public in general had forgotten *Essays and Reviews* when, in August 1869, Gladstone nominated Temple, the author of its introductory article, to succeed Phillpotts as Bishop of Exeter. An immediate outcry arose on all sides. Pusey pressed for a High Church–Evangelical alliance in protest, and the *Record*, which regarded the appointment as a more severe blow than Irish disestablishment, seemed to favour such a step.[11] But Shaftesbury recalled his earlier somewhat misunderstood and controversial association with Pusey and feared that the Evangelicals would oppose the union. He also reckoned that public opinion was now indifferent. He therefore refused to chair a united committee of protest, but announced his willingness to head a separate Evangelical remonstrance.[12] Other Evangelicals followed this lead. The Church Association prepared a memorial which was forwarded to Gladstone by Shaftesbury. Nonetheless, these responses were unco-ordinated and in some cases unenthusiastic. The Evangelicals, and churchmen as a whole, had shown themselves to be weak and divided, and Gladstone found no difficulty in refusing to withdraw his nomination. Temple would not dissociate himself from the other papers in *Essays and Reviews*, and both Evangelicals and High Churchmen pressed for the Dean and Chapter of Exeter to reject him. Despite all the opposition he was elected, and consecrated bishop. After that the protest soon died down.

[10] See E. Garbett, *The Dogmatic Faith* (1867).
[11] See the *Record*, 15 October 1869.
[12] See Shaftesbury's MS Diary 15, 21, 23 October 1869 and the *Record*, 20 October 1869.

In this mid-Victorian period the Evangelicals in general were quick to denounce any work which departed from traditional Christian orthodoxy. Sometimes this tended to be counter-productive. For example, in 1866 the anonymous publication *Ecce Homo* depicted Christ primarily as the founder of a morality which changed history. Shaftesbury promptly castigated it as 'the most pestilential book . . . ever vomited from the Jaws of Hell'.[13] His critique caused an uproar in the press, and made the book a bestseller. Publications which accepted many of the theories currently held by scientists, such as T.G. Bonney, *A Manual of Geology* (1876), were also attacked by Evangelicals. The refusal by Evangelicals in the main to concede anything to historical and scientific criticism weakened their ability to provide an intellectual defence of Christianity. It encouraged a depreciation of reason in matters which touched upon Christian belief; and it tended to lessen the academic credibility of Evangelicalism.

Lux Mundi

The next major landmark in theological thought entailed what H.P. Liddon regarded as a betrayal of everything for which Pusey and the Tractarians stood. For it was Charles Gore, the Principal of Pusey House, Oxford, who, in 1889, edited the volume entitled *Lux Mundi: A Series of Studies in the Religion of the Incarnation.* In the controversy which ensued, the disposition of churchmen was not clear. Some High Churchmen associated with Evangelicals in opposing what was regarded as an assault upon the fundamentals of the faith. Other High Churchmen hailed the work of Gore and his colleagues as timely and liberating.

The preface to the work made clear both its genesis and purpose. The writers found themselves together at Oxford between the years 1875 and 1885, and felt compelled for their own sakes, no less than for others, 'to attempt to put the Catholic faith into its right relation to modern intellectual and moral problems'. They wrote as 'servants of the Catholic Creed and Church', but were conscious that 'if the true meaning of the faith is to be made sufficiently conspicuous it needs disencumbering, reinterpreting, explaining'. In a time of intellectual ferment, with new points of view and new questions being asked, they were convinced of the need for a general restatement of the claim and meaning of Christian theology.

The writers saw God's revelation of himself as progressive. They were thus able to accept the methods and results of biblical criticism. The early

---

[13] See Shaftesbury's MS Diary 12 May 1866.

chapters of Genesis were regarded as folklore and poetry, and the subsequent history of Israel was seen as a slow ascent from primitive beginnings through the ethical monotheism of the prophets to the culmination in the incarnation, with its sequel in the sacramental life of the church.

The essay which received the greatest attention and gave most offence was that by the editor, Charles Gore, on 'The Holy Spirit and Inspiration'. It declared that belief in the inspiration of the Bible was compatible with the opinion that Christ was ignorant of the true authorship of the Pentateuch or Psalms. The knowledge of the incarnate Lord was limited by the conditions of the time, and his shared humanity. Gore also used the term 'myth' to denote not a falsehood, but an apprehension of faith by a child or a primitive people; a faith 'not yet distinguished into the constituent elements of poetry and history and philosophy'.[14]

There was little Evangelical reaction to *Lux Mundi*. The controversial issues raised by the book received intermittent attention in the *Record* throughout 1890.[15] The Islington Conference in January 1891 discussed the testimony of Christ to scripture; and in the *Churchman* Christ's infallibility was vigorously defended. The Evangelical response was, as in former years, complicated by the fact that a number of the older High Churchmen, such as Denison and Liddon, were as vehemently opposed to some of the teaching as some of the Evangelicals. Also, the Evangelicals were divided in their response: a few of those who were somewhat 'liberal' actually sided with the *Lux Mundi* school. Hay Aitkin, an Evangelical whose orthodoxy had caused some doubt before this, declared his belief in the doctrine of kenosis – that Christ, as man, was not infallible.[16]

Two particular points can, however, be identified in the Evangelical response to *Lux Mundi*. Christ's attitude to the Old Testament was said to be indisputable; any questioning of the reliability of the Old Testament compromised the authority of Christ, and made Christian belief impossible for many. Such questioning was therefore unacceptable. Secondly, the organic unity of the Old and New Testaments was affirmed: to surrender parts discredited the whole. Crucial to the Evangelical view was their interpretation of biblical inspiration. The Bible was regarded as the supreme authority; literally and historically true in all parts. To doubt this for one part of scripture was 'to place in jeopardy – not God's truth, which remained whatever men said – but the faith of millions'.[17]

---

[14] Owen Chadwick, *op.cit.*, Part II p.201.

[15] See the *Record*, 16 January 1891.

[16] See the *Record*, 22 January 1892.

[17] Anne Bentley, 'The Transformation of the Evangelical Party in the Church of England in the Later Nineteenth Century' (Durham University Ph.D., 1971) p.123.

10

Proclaiming the Faith

The Evangelicals have never been outstanding in disputation or apologetics, nor in their ability for academic debate. Their strength has always been in their commitment to evangelism and teaching both at home and abroad. The engagement in controversy which occupied so much of their energy and time in the age of Victoria did not divert them from what at heart they held most dear. In this and the succeeding chapters evangelism, teaching, spiritual renewal, social action and world mission will be seen as their central concerns, and the aspects of their life by means of which they made their special contribution to the life of the church in these years.

Charles Simeon provided a model for Evangelical clergy throughout the nineteenth century. He demonstrated the force and value of a rounded and sustained parochial ministry within the discipline of the Church of England. He made it clear that he 'laboured to maintain that spirit of moderation which so eminently distinguished the established church'. This pattern and spirit of ministry was copied and amply exhibited in the lives of Edward Bickersteth, Francis Close, Hugh McNeile, Hugh Stowell, William Pennefather, William Champneys and William Cadman; and in the ministries of those Evangelicals raised to the episcopate such as Charles Richard Sumner, John B. Sumner, H.M. Villiers, Edward Henry Bickersteth, C. Baring, S. Waldegrave, F. Jeune, J.C. Ryle and A.W. Thorold.

Edward Bickersteth (1786–1850)

Although Edward Bickersteth lacked a Cambridge education and never experienced membership of Simeon's classes and conversation parties, it has been argued that he stands out as Simeon's successor and as leader of the Anglican Evangelical clergy from Simeon's death in 1836 to his own in 1850.[1] He was born in 1786 into an old established Lancastrian family. After a period in London working first in the Post Office and then as an articled clerk, he married in 1812 and moved to Norwich as a junior partner to his father-in-law. As a layman he founded a CMS Association in Norwich. He was ordained deacon on 10 December 1815 and priest a few days later. On 24 January 1816, in response to a request from Josiah Pratt, the Secretary of the CMS, he embarked for Sierra Leone to undertake a special mission on behalf of the CMS. His task required much tact, firmness and wisdom as he sought successfully to correct many evils, initiate new plans and give fresh impetus to the whole Sierra Leone work. On his return he continued with the CMS, visiting CMS associations throughout the country as well as being principal of the missionary college. On the retirement of Pratt in 1824 he was CMS Secretary for six years. It was a period of rapid expansion when the number of mission stations increased from eight to fifty-six, ordained missionaries from thirteen to fifty-eight, lay missionaries from nineteen to ninety-three, native catechists from two to 457, and numbers in CMS schools from 200 to 15,791. The number of home associations doubled and the income rose from £10,000 to £40,000.

On his retirement as CMS Secretary in 1830 Bickersteth became rector of Watton near Hertford, remaining in the post until his death twenty years later. He continued to travel extensively for the CMS. The books he wrote and the hymnal he compiled during these years helped to reinforce his focal role in the Evangelicalism of his day. His enthusiastic involvement in the founding of the Evangelical Alliance was both significant and controversial. He upheld his ecumenical principles in the face of opposition from Close, McNeile and Stowell and the hostility of the *Record*. It was a bold stand in an age of increasingly rigid denominationalism.

The reign of Victoria was also an era of unprecedented urban expansion. In some of those provincial centres where such growth and change in civic status and character were most pronounced, the ministry of Evangelicals was remarkably effective. The tightly-knit and integrated political, social and religious structure of the towns and cities facilitated the type of

[1] Michael Hennell, *Sons of the Prophets* (London, 1979), p.29. This section on Edward Bickersteth is largely based on the account by Hennell.

personal influence exerted by Close. McNeile, Stowell and others.

Francis Close (1797–1882)

Francis Close was appointed curate of Holy Trinity, Cheltenham in 1824, and he continued his ministry in the town for thirty-two years. During that time the population increased from about fourteen thousand to over thirty-five thousand. Cheltenham, which had formerly been almost exclusively a spa town, was transformed into an educational centre, and the changes were largely identified with the life and labours of Close. 'His history and the history of the town are one'.[2] In these years until the middle of the century it has been said that 'the history of the town . . . was the history of a single clergyman'.[3] He ruled Cheltenham from his pulpit throne to such an extent that the wits described it as 'a Close borough'.[4] *The Times* described him as the

> Pope of Cheltenham, with pontifical prerogatives from which the temporal had not been severed. In the bosom of hundreds and thousands of households his social decrees were accepted without a thought of the possibility of opposition.[5]

Close exerted this extraordinary influence as a result of a comprehensive discharge of parochial duties. He had a high regard for the liturgy of the Church of England, for the sacraments and for preaching, and he made the church the centre of the life of the community. As the population increased, so he extended his ministry to reach them. A large proportion of the inhabitants adopted the Evangelical faith and ideals.

It was his involvement in the community which caused him to be admired by his supporters, but hated and derided by his enemies. Dissenters worked with him in areas of mutual concern: in the campaigns for scriptural centred education, sabbath observance, opposition to the local races, charitable relief to the poor, the work of the British and Foreign Bible Society, opposition to the government grant to Maynooth College and in the furtherance of missionary work. He was a man of

---

[2] Cheltenham Free Press, 23 December 1882, p.2, quoted in Alan F. Munden, 'The Church of England in Cheltenham 1826–1856 with particular reference to the Rev. Francis Close' (Birmingham University M.Litt., 1980), p.6. The following section on Francis Close owes much to this unpublished thesis.

[3] E. Humphries and E.C. Willoughby, *At Cheltenham Spa* (1928), p.198, quoted in Munden, *op.cit.*, p.6

[4] G.R. Balleine, *A History of the Evangelical Party in the Church of England* (London, 1908), p.162.

[5] Leading article, *The Times*, 19 December 1882, quoted in Balleine, *op.cit.*, p.162.

action. He fought the local magnates and stopped the races. After the theatre was burnt down in 1839 his resistance to any rebuilding helped to delay its permanent replacement until 1891. It was in large measure because of his influence that shops were closed on Sundays and Sunday trains were prevented from running between 1840 and 1846. Few if any meetings were held in the town without his permission. He received support from all levels of society, from working men and tradesmen, from the middle and the upper classes. Opposition came from a vocal minority backed by *The Cheltenham Free Press*, a radical newspaper under the leadership of free thinkers and Unitarians. In part they objected to the dominance by Close of the public life in Cheltenham, but their resistance was of little avail. By 1856 the face of the town had been changed.

Close was not parochial in his interests. He wholeheartedly supported overseas and home mission and particularly the work of the Church Missionary Society, the Jewish Mission, the Church Pastoral-Aid Society, the Religious Tract Society and the British and Foreign Bible Society. Of all his multifarious interests and activities it was probably in the sphere of education that he made his single most significant and lasting contribution both to the local community and to the national scene. In this, as in other issues, Close was no mere theorist. He helped to develop schooling at all levels and for all classes, and was the chief architect in making Cheltenham a centre for education.

Through his extensive local involvement, deputation work and publications, Close became the education spokesman nationally for the Evangelicals, who in their turn gave him their active support. He believed that an exclusively secular education system was wrong. His objective was scriptural education on the principles of the established church. He rejected the idea of entire control by the Church of England clergy, but rather sought an active partnership between church and state. Together with other Evangelicals such as Lord Ashley and Hugh McNeile, Close successfully resisted the demands from radicals for a system of universal secular education.

In Cheltenham he was intimately associated with the establishment and administration of a great number and wide range of educational institutions. He was instrumental in founding a weekday infant school at Alstone in 1826, and a second school in his Cheltenham parish in 1828. As the town developed and the population increased, further infant schools were opened. He was also actively engaged in the day-to-day administration of Cheltenham College, the first major Victorian school to be founded on new lines as a Proprietary Grammar School for the education of the middle classes. As President of the Cheltenham Diocesan Boys' School, founded in 1839, President of the Cheltenham Commercial and Classical Proprietary School, chairman of the Cheltenham Church of

England Training School for teachers, founded in 1847, and chairman of a committee for reviving the largely defunct Cheltenham Free Grammar School, Close exercised an educational influence which was almost unparalleled in the history of local civic government in the nineteenth century.

Writing in 1879, J.C. Ryle noted that outside London there were twelve centres of provincial Evangelicalism: Manchester, Liverpool, Birmingham, Sheffield, Bradford, Hull, Newcastle, Nottingham, Bath, Clifton, Plymouth and Cheltenham.[6] Close was the primary architect in the case of Cheltenham. In Liverpool the same function was fulfilled by Hugh McNeile.

Hugh McNeile (1795-1879)

Hugh McNeile was a 'big, impetuous, eloquent Irishman'.[7] He was regarded by Eugene Stock, the historian of the Church Missionary Society, as 'unquestionably the greatest Evangelical preacher and speaker in the Church of England'[8] during the nineteenth century. When he went as curate-in-charge of St Jude's in 1834 he promptly plunged into the governmental life of Liverpool. The town council had just decided that the daily routine of the corporation schools should no longer be opened with prayer; that the Bible should be banished and a book of scripture extracts substituted, taken largely from the Douay version; and that no further religious instruction should be given during school hours. McNeile led the opposition and boldly appealed for funds to open rival schools. New schools were rapidly established, and there was a mass exodus from the corporation schools.

The powerful town council conceded defeat at the hands of a newcomer to the city, and from that moment his power and authority in municipal life were prodigious. In town council debates and in the appointment of mayors, his will was sought and seldom thwarted. Through the force and persuasiveness of his oratory and the magnetism of his character he was listened to, trusted and followed. He was often unwise in his decisions, and was capable at times of blatant indiscretions, but this did not lessen the unrivalled influence he exercised in Liverpool between 1834 and 1868, when he departed to be Dean of Ripon. He left behind him a city which owed much of its strong Evangelicalism and the shape of its civic institutions to his energetic and in certain respects brilliant ministry.

[6] See *The Times*, 6 February 1879.
[7] Balleine, *op.cit.*, p.159. The following account of McNeile is much indebted to Balleine.
[8] Eugene Stock, *The History of the Church Missionary Society* (London, 1899), Vol.I, p.374.

By his writings and as a national speaker at a variety of gatherings McNeile was a formidable Evangelical protagonist beyond the confines of Liverpool. His published works also made evident his frequently reiterated loyalty, and indeed enthusiasm, for the Church of England. In his *Lectures on Church Establishment* (1840), *The Church and the Churches* and *The Church of God in Christ and the Churches of Christ Militant here on Earth* (1846) he discussed the nature of the church and defended church establishment. For McNeile, predestination was the key to the understanding of the reality of the invisible church: the one holy catholic and apostolic church of the creed was, he said, the invisible church composed of all elect believers of all times and places. The catholicity of the church was achieved by virtue of the fact that the elect came from every tribe and nation; and its apostolicity was in the doctrine of the apostles by which the elect came to their salvation.

Despite this wider influence, the supreme achievement of McNeile was his ministry in Liverpool. Indeed, Owen Chadwick considers that when he went to be Dean of Ripon, as with Close when he went to Carlisle as Dean, it was the burial of his preaching gifts.[9]

Hugh Stowell (1799–1865)

What Close did for Cheltenham, and McNeile did for Liverpool, Hugh Stowell did for Manchester.[10] He was born in 1799, educated at St Edmund Hall, Oxford, ordained in 1823, and after a curacy in Huddersfield, appointed in 1828 by a somewhat reluctant Bishop Blomfield as curate in charge of St Stephen, Salford. He came with the reputation of being an 'extemporaneous firebrand'. His oratory was even more fervent than McNeile's, though it did not have the same intellectual fibre. 'His first words were always halting, but, when he warmed to his subject, the rush of rhetoric fairly swept his hearers off their feet'.[11] His ministrations proved so acceptable, and so speedily did he win his way to the hearts of his hearers, who thronged to the church from far beyond the bounds of the parish, that they built another church to accommodate the expanded congregation, and as an inducement to him to remain. He was persuaded, and stayed until his death in 1865.

---

[9] Owen Chadwick, *The Victorian Church*, Part II (1970), p.382.
[10] The account of the life and work of Stowell which follows is based on Balleine, *op.cit.*, and Charles Bullock, *Hugh Stowell: A Life and Its Lessons* (London, 1881).
[11] Balleine, *op.cit.*, p.160.

Stowell's parochial work was noteworthy. During the first twenty-one years of his ministry, the number of communicants increased from one hundred and eighty to between five and six hundred. Parish activities and institutions included efficient schools, district visiting, adult classes, libraries, a mutual improvement society and clothing clubs. He worked through these channels to promote the temporal and spiritual welfare of his parishioners. He was renowned for his pastoral concern and care for individual members of his congregation. He had a great love for children; his enormous Sunday schools were his particular pride, and he composed special hymns for them, such as 'Jesus is our Shepherd'.

It was his love for children which initially drew him into municipal life. The Lancashire Public School Association, which had been formed to agitate for secular education, tried to persuade a town hall meeting to send a petition to Parliament. Stowell made a masterly speech of over two hours with such effect that he carried an amendment asking that no system of general education should be sanctioned of which the Christian religion was not the basis. From that time he was highly regarded by local politicans. His authority grew with the passing years, until it became comparable with that of McNeile in Liverpool, and Close in Cheltenham. None of these were political clergy in that they gave priority to their political activities. All three gave precedence to the pulpit and the parish; but they did, as Balleine rightly says, 'bring religion to bear on political and municipal life with such effect that a majority of the laity looked to them for guidance, and little was done without first asking their counsel and consent'.[12] Their ministries were representative of a curious and noteworthy chapter in nineteenth century provincial history.

Stowell was strongly attached to Evangelicalism. He believed that 'to belong to no party was to have no fixed opinions, no strong and firm convictions'.[13] At the same time he was a very definite churchman. When asked to urge the Manchester clergy to join the undenominational Evangelical Alliance, he wrote: 'We cannot identify ourselves with an Association which appears to regard all the unhappy separations from our Church as comparatively unimportant'.[14] He also had wide influence through his writings. His printed sermons entitled *Tractarianism Tested by Holy Scripture*, which was issued in two volumes in 1845-6, was considered by some as perhaps the most balanced popular critique of Tractarianism.

[12] *Ibid.*, p.161.
[13] J.B. Marsden, *Memoirs of Hugh Stowell* (London, 1868), p.451, quoted in Balleine, *op.cit.*, p.160.
[14] Marsden, *op.cit.*, p.166, quoted in Balleine, *op.cit.*, p.160.

But again, as with Close and McNeile, despite all his varied activities, Stowell's abiding legacy to the church was the model organization of his parish, in which a great burden of pastoral oversight was so divided among lay helpers that an immense work could be accomplished, and time still found for other things. Together with Close and McNeile, he illustrates provincial Evangelicalism in its most dynamic form.[15] William Pennefather, William Champneys and William Cadman are equally good representatives of London Evangelical parochial work at its best in the Victorian era.

William Pennefather (1816-73)

The ministry of William Pennefather at Christ Church, Barnet and St Jude's, Mildmay Park gave him an honourable and significant place in the Evangelicalism of his generation, and indeed in the wider life of the church.[16] The diversity and volume of the work he undertook was impressive. At Christ Church between 1852 and 1864 the conscientious discharge of his preaching, visitation and other pastoral and evangelistic duties resulted in a crowded congregation and required the enlargement of the church on two occasions.[17] A great amount of correspondence included notes of comfort to the sick, sketches of sermons sent to those unable to attend church, letters to the perplexed and hymns composed for young people. In addition to this demanding service, he was responsible for two major ventures: the establishment of a work for orphans, and the founding of what was later to become the Mildmay Conference.[18]

For some time Pennefather and his wife Catherine had cared for a few orphan children in their home when, in 1855, a general fund was opened nationally to assist the wives and children of soldiers who had died in the Crimean War, or become incapacitated by wounds and sickness. In many instances it was found best to remove the children from their former homes and place them under careful supervision and instruction. Places within reach of London were selected, where clergymen and others might be willing to provide an oversight of the children and be in every way responsible for their training and instruction. Pennefather and his wife immediately agreed to co-operate. Beginning with six, the number

[15] Other leading and influential Evangelicals in provincial cities included J.C Miller in Birmingham and Henry Venn Elliott of Brighton.
[16] For the life of William Pennefather see especially Robert Braithwaite, *The Life and Letters of Rev. William Pennefather* (1878).
[17] Braithwaite, *op.cit.*, pp.294, 295.
[18] See Braithwaite, *op.cit.*, pp.290, 297 ff.

gradually increased to four hundred, and for nine years the orphan homes and schools scattered through the town became an object of much interest in Barnet.

Pennefather was convinced that the spiritual union of Christians was so important that it should not only be an article in the creed: it should be recognized, realized and manifested by every possible means and on every possible occasion. In August 1856 he brought together one hundred and twenty Christians from various denominations in Barnet in a conference 'to promote personal holiness, brotherly love, and increased interest in the work of the Lord'.[19] It lasted four days, and included prayer, Bible readings and addresses on foreign missions, home missions, personal holiness and the second coming of the Lord. At the conclusion of the conference there was a united communion service. No intimation was given in 1856 that these meetings would be annual. Nonetheless, in the course of the following year Pennefather received so many letters entreating him to go forward, and so much encouragement from some who had in the first instance doubted, that he not only decided to make it a yearly event, but sent out the invitations more widely than before. Those who subsequently attended included members of the Church of England, Baptists, Independents, Wesleyans, Moravians, Plymouth Brethren, Church of Scotland (Established and Free) and Dutch Reformed Church members and Lutherans.[20] In later years the conferences were to achieve an international reputation and be attended by Christians from various parts of the world.

In 1864 Pennefather moved to St Jude's, Mildmay Park, and immediately found scope for an even fuller ministry. Confronted by an inadequate provision for the education of the very poor and neglected children who abounded on every side, he strenuously sought and found the necessary funds for the erection of a school where elementary instruction was given at a low cost. Meanwhile he supervised a soup kitchen for the poor, another kitchen where dinners were cooked for the sick, and clubs of various kinds. He provided facilities for the infirm and aged in a specially constructed building.

What with the growth of work among all ages of people, a Sunday school which on occasions numbered in excess of one thousand, and the annual conference which had been transferred from Barnet to Mildmay, there was need for larger buildings. As was his custom, he did not conduct any fund-raising campaign but simply made the need known and prayed about it; and the money was forthcoming. The church was enlarged. A

---

[19] Braithwaite, op.cit., p.305.
[20] See letter from Pennefather quoted in Braithwaite, op.cit., pp.314, 315.

conference hall was opened in 1870 which could seat two thousand five hundred people, with ancillary classrooms, offices, and other amenities. The work became so comprehensive that three, and later four curates were needed.

Together with his wife, Pennefather also began a work foɪ ɩhe training of women. A small deaconess house was started in 1860, as an adjunct to the Mildmay conference complex. The scheme was modelled on the Lutheran pattern of the Kaiserwerth and Strasbourg deaconesses. At first some of the clergy doubted the wisdom of the concept, but the experiment was successful, and the uniformed Mildmay deaconesses became a familiar sight in many Evangelical parishes.

Pennefather enthusiastically encouraged evangelism. In 1872 D.L. Moody, the American evangelist, went to a conference at Mildmay while on a visit to England, and his outstanding gifts were recognized by the experienced eye of Pennefather. In conjunction with Cuthbert Bainbridge, he invited Moody to return to England in the following year to conduct a series of evangelistic meetings. As we will see in the next chapter, the tour was to be a highlight in nineteenth century evangelism. By the time of the visit Pennefather was dead, but the invitation he had given was not the least of his contributions to the life of the church.

William Weldon Champneys (1807-75)

William Weldon Champneys was a forerunner of the modern urban slum parish clergyman.[21] When he went to Whitechapel in 1837 vice and crime were rampant, and the dingy old church had almost no influence on the thirty-six thousand people living round it. Church life was almost non-existent. For the previous thirty years the Low Church rector had unlocked the church door every Sunday morning, read the service and a sermon to the clerk and the charity children, and then gone home to his lunch knowing that the week's work was accomplished. Champneys energetically and courageously tackled the onerous task which faced him. With help from the recently founded Church Pastoral-Aid Society he gathered an active and earnest staff about him, and the parish was systematically visited from door to door. His indefatigable efforts, his charm and gentle goodness helped to break down opposition. Three bright and simple services were held every Sunday, and slowly but steadily the empty pews were filled. Champneys himself attributed particular importance to the evening communion, a service which was

[21] The account of William Champneys which follows is based on Balleine, *op.cit.*, and L.E. Elliott-Binns, *Religion in the Victorian Era* (London, 1936).

being tentatively introduced into some parishes in the second half of the century. He said that it enabled many to come to communion who previously were unable to do so.

His parish work was so effective that in 1851, when the church census was taken, there were over 1,500 in the morning congregation, over 800 present in the afternoon, and more than 1,600 in the evening. At the end of his first year there had been sixteen communicants. By 1854 these had increased to over three hundred and fifty. Three new churches were built and five church day schools were opened. Parish organizations included Sunday schools, mothers' meetings, a Savings Bank, a Coal Club, a Shoeblack Brigade and a Young Men's Institute; all common enough subsequently, but the first of their kind in London. In his parochial organization Champneys showed the way which countless others were to follow; an example being Robert Bickersteth during his time as rector of St Giles-in-the-Fields.

In 1851, on the recommendation of Lord John Russell, Champneys was appointed to a canonry in St Paul's, and the dean and chapter of that cathedral in 1860 gave him the living of St Pancras, a benefice at one time held by his grandfather. He was named Dean of Lichfield in 1868. He died at the deanery, Lichfield in 1875, and was buried in the cathedral yard.

Champneys was a prolific author of evangelical literature. His name is appended to upwards of fifty works, but a large number of these are either books which he edited or to which he contributed recommendatory prefaces; whilst others are single sermons and lectures which had a local circulation. His great contribution to the church, and to the unfolding story of Evangelicalism, was undoubtedly his pioneer work of inner city team ministry.

William Cadman

When William Cadman went to St George's, Southwark as rector in 1853 he was confronted with a situation as challenging as that which initially confronted Champneys.[22] He was responsible for thirty-five thousand parishioners of whom only about twenty customarily attended church. Other than the shops in the main road, the area consisted almost entirely of a concentrated population of the extremely poor, herded into courts and low-standard accommodation. Brothels, thieves' kitchens and common lodging-houses abounded.

[22] The following brief account of the life and work of William Cadman is based on Balleine, op.cit., p.189.

Cadman promptly divided the parish into six districts with a curate, Scripture-reader and schoolmaster at work in each. A building was obtained for every district which was used as a ragged-school by day and as a mission hall at night. Open-air services were held every evening, where opponents of every kind from militant atheists to the followers of Joanna Southcott could state their case and be answered. Thieves' suppers were organized, and the many dens of infamy were visited from room to room. It was not long before the church became so overcrowded that three hundred additional seats had to be provided. Two hundred voluntary workers were enrolled from among the communicants to help in this systematic attempt to meet the demands of a mid-nineteenth century urban slum parish.

In the first nineteen years of Victoria's reign, despite some outstanding parochial ministries such as those just described, no Evangelical was raised to the bench of bishops. The two Evangelicals on the bench, Charles Bird Sumner and his brother John B. Sumner, had both been elevated before Victoria ascended the throne. Neither Tories nor Whigs gave Evangelicals much thought when bishoprics and deaneries fell vacant. The Evangelicals were for the most part essentially Tory in outlook, but they could expect little from Lord Derby and Lord Aberdeen, the Tory leaders. Among the Whigs, Lord John Russell had temporarily given them hope with his explosive reaction to the 'Papal Aggression' in 1850, when he seriously considered raising the prominent Evangelical H.M. Villiers to the episcopate, but he decided against such a move. The Sumner brothers were not great theologians, nor were they gifted with qualities sufficient to provide the Evangelicals with national leadership and a focus for cohesion and co-ordination; their strength lay in the conscientiousness, efficiency and thoroughness with which they discharged their parochial or diocesan duties.

Charles Richard Sumner (1790-1874)

Charles Richard Sumner has been described as the 'first of the modern type of Bishop'.[23] While still a curate he attracted the attention of George IV and was appointed his domestic chaplain. This was no sinecure, for Sumner was determined to fulfil a genuine pastoral role, as when he withheld communion from the king, who was in a violent temper over a servant whom he had just dismissed. Sumner told the king that he must learn to restrain his passion, that it was his duty to be in charity with all

[23] Elliott-Binns, op.cit., p.67. For a full account of Sumner, see George Henry Sumner, Life of Charles Richard Sumner, D.D. (London, 1876).

men, and that he must show this by forgiving and reinstating the servant. The king concurred, and also agreed to receive communion in company with the rest of the household, including the servant at the centre of the incident.

In 1826 Sumner was appointed Bishop of Llandaff. Although he only occupied the post for one year he gave indications of what might have been attempted if he had remained longer. There was no episcopal palace at Llandaff but, as he was opposed to clerical non-residence, he rented a house and lived in his diocese, 'an almost unheard-of thing for a Welsh Bishop to do'.[24] He immediately set about the visitation of the diocese. Every incumbent was asked searching questions about the state of their parishes. It was urgently required.

> In that part of Glamorganshire which was in the Llandaff diocese, sixty-two out of one hundred and seven incumbencies were without any house of residence for the clergy, and in Monmouthshire the case was worse still, for while fifty-five incumbencies were provided with glebe-houses, seventy-two had none, and in the whole diocese, one hundred and thirty-seven out of two hundred and forty-one parishes had neither Sunday nor day-school.[25]

The church in Wales had sunk to a deplorably low condition, and Sumner earnestly and heartily tried to rouse the clergy of his diocese from a state of lethargy and indifference.

At the early age of thirty-seven, in 1828, Sumner was translated to the Bishopric of Winchester. He was to remain there for over forty years.

> It is not too much to say that, during the term of his tenure of the see, a revolution was effected in the episcopal office. Prelates with wigs, great state and corresponding haughtiness of manner gave place to real overseers of the clergy, sympathising in the pastors' struggles, cheering them in their disappointments, counselling them in their difficulties. Bishops Blomfield, Kaye, and the two Sumners were in the van of the movement. The perfunctory discharge of customary duties was felt to be no longer the ideal of perfection to be aimed at. Real hard work was the order of the day.[26]

Visitation of the diocese was again given priority. This included the clergy in Hampshire and Surrey, and also, perhaps for the first time since the Reformation by a Bishop of Winchester, those in the Channel Islands. In most cases his visits were much appreciated. Sumner initiated the division of the diocese into rural deaneries. Vigorous war was waged against

---

[24] Balleine, *op.cit.*, p.153.
[25] George Henry Sumner, *op.cit.*, p.115.
[26] *Ibid.*, p.135.

absentee incumbents. A new standard of work and efficiency was set before the clergy. A second Sunday service was insisted on in one hundred and sixty-one parishes. Neglect of church buildings was no longer tolerated. A Diocesan Board of Education was started. He also gave an impetus to church-building in the diocese. It was in the larger towns that the deficiency in church accommodation was most apparent. Since the beginning of the century the population of Hampshire had increased by in excess of thirty-eight per cent and that of Surrey by sixty-five per cent. Although a considerable number of extra churches had been provided since Sumner assumed office, he decided to take a new initiative in 1837 by establishing a Church-building Society, in an effort to raise the additional subscriptions required. The Society was warmly supported, and the zeal for church-extension, thus awakened, continued for many decades. By 1875 over two million pounds had been spent on building projects in the diocese.

Sumner was also deeply concerned about world mission. One of the first objects to which he turned his attention was the miserable support given throughout the diocese to the missionary societies of the church. In order to provoke missionary interest he was instrumental in forming district associations at Winchester, Droxford, Christchurch and Alton. In the early years of his episcopate only seventy pounds was sent from the diocese to the Society for the Propagation of the Gospel. By 1866, at the close of his episcopate, this had risen to over four thousand pounds, and in the same year Hampshire, Surrey and the Channel Islands contributed almost nine thousand pounds to the Church Missionary Society.

Sumner corresponded, debated and wrote articles on various issues which agitated the nation and the church, such as Catholic emancipation, parliamentary reform, the Gorham case, ritualism and Tractarianism. Politically he was a Tory, although his party allegiance was more pronounced in early life than in later years. In ecclesiastical matters his comments revealed his Evangelicalism, but he showed great respect and understanding for other church traditions. He was widely admired, and he was not known as either a bigot or a fanatic. Although he did not hesitate to make pronouncements on topics of public concern where it seemed appropriate and useful, this was not his forte. The main thrust of his effort was in his diocese, which was transformed during his episcopate.[27]

---

[27] This concluding summary is based on Ballcinc, *op.cit.*, pp.153, 154.

John Bird Sumner (1780-1862)

In 1828 Charles's elder brother, John Bird Sumner, was instituted as Bishop of Chester, which was then the largest and most populous diocese in England.[28] It embraced the whole of Cheshire and Lancashire, and much of Cumberland and Westmorland, as well as parts of the West Riding of Yorkshire; a region which had experienced unprecedented industrial expansion. It was a daunting diocese for which to take responsibility. He laid special stress on preaching and individual instruction, asking his clergy to arrange house meetings and cottage lectures where the exposition of the Bible could be thoroughly undertaken. He established District Visiting Societies, so that suitable lay people could be chosen and prepared as visitors under the incumbents' direction and supervision. The purpose was to explain the Christian faith to neighbours who might otherwise never hear the Christian message, and to show Christian sympathy and help as required. He did not originate this scheme, but adopted it to great effect.

Sumner was concerned that attendance at church and worship should not be inhibited by tradition. For the pew problem he had a rough and ready remedy. On visiting one parish he noticed a number of empty pews, while many of the congregation were standing in the aisles. He interrupted the service to ask for an explanation, and was told that the pews concerned were private property; the owners had shut them up. 'There can be no such thing in the House of God', he replied, 'send for a blacksmith to take off the locks. We will sing a hymn while he does it'.[29] Where church service times made it difficult for people to attend Sumner said they should be changed. It was the custom in some churches to hold evening prayer as early as 2.30 pm, and in others at 3.00 pm or 3.30 pm. Sumner recommended 5.00 pm, or at least not before 4.00 pm, to enable those living at a distance to go to both morning and evening services. So successful was this move that numbers doubled in some cases; northern deaneries reported an increase of nine per cent in communicants, and in Cheshire the increase was calculated as fourteen per cent.

Despite an unparalleled increase in population since the last decade of the eighteenth century, pastoral oversight was little more than it had been for centuries. Sumner therefore encouraged the building of new churches; in nineteen years he consecrated two hundred and thirty-two. His counsel

[28] The account of the life and work of John Bird Sumner is based on Ballcine, *op.cit.*, and E. Roy Moore, 'John Bird Sumner, Bishop of Chester' (Manchester University M.A., 1976).

[29] Quoted in Ballcine, *op.cit.*, pp.154, 155, Elliott-Binns, *op.cit.*, p.44, and Moore, *op.cit.*, p.90.

was sought in the founding of the Church Pastoral-Aid Society, and he supported every extension of its activities in the north of England. He was concerned to further the influence of the church in various spheres of community life, including education. He believed that religion should be the basis of all education. He encouraged the establishment of evening classes for the youth of the diocese; and was particularly anxious to provide infant schooling for the poor.

In 1848 he was elevated to the Archbishopric of Canterbury and remained in that high office until 1862. During this time he continued to live the same quiet, frugal life of a country clergyman which had typified him throughout his ministry. He would rise at dawn, light his fire, and deal with most of his letters before breakfast. He refused to wear an episcopal wig, or to be driven about in his state coach with outriders and armed guards. He rather wandered around in Canterbury, or walked to the House of Lords, with his umbrella under his arm. To those who complained of his lack of dignity he replied, 'I cannot imagine that any greater reproach could be cast on the Church than to suppose that it allowed its dignity to interfere with its usefulness'.[30] By his conduct and his teaching he was influential in bringing to an end the old prelatical arrogance of some of the church dignitaries, and he was a prime mover in adopting the new, more human, concept of a bishop, or archbishop, as a father in God.

In 1856 John Bird Sumner was Archbishop of Canterbury and Charles Richard Sumner was Bishop of Winchester; but the Evangelicals must have wondered if any other Evangelical would be raised to the bench in the near future. In 1855 Lord Palmerston had become Prime Minister. At first this did not seem to be a matter for Evangelical rejoicing. 'I fear', wrote Lord Shaftesbury, 'his ecclesiastical appointments will be detestable. He does not know, in theology, Moses from Adam Smith'.[31] But, knowing the limits of his own knowledge, Palmerston turned to Lord Shaftesbury for advice, and for nine years Shaftesbury was known as 'the bishop-maker'.

Shaftesbury ensured that the 'Palmerston bishops' included some leading Evangelicals, but he also recognized the claim of eligible non-Evangelicals.[32] C.T. Longley, who was appointed to Durham in 1856, York in 1860 and Canterbury in 1862, W. Thomson, who was made Bishop of Gloucester in 1857 and Archbishop of York in 1862, and E. Harold Browne, who became Bishop of Ely in 1864, were all non-party men and certainly not identified with the Evangelicals. A.C. Tait, who

[30] Quoted in Balleine, op.cit., p.155, and Elliott-Binns, op.cit., p.68.
[31] Quoted in Balleine, op.cit., p.210.
[32] See B.E. Hardman, 'The Evangelical Party in the Church of England, 1855-1865' (Cambridge University Ph.D., 1970).

was appointed Bishop of London in 1856, and elevated as Archbishop of Canterbury in 1868, and H. Philpott, who became Bishop of Worcester in 1861, were Broad Churchmen. C.J. Ellicott, who was made Bishop of Gloucester in 1863, and W. Jacobson, who was appointed Bishop of Chester in 1865, were distinctly High Churchmen of the older school. Many of the remaining sees were allotted to Evangelicals.

It is arguable that such a distribution was a fair and equitable representation of the Evangelical strength in the country, and some compensation for the way Evangelicals had been neglected in the past. Some men were passed over who might well have been promoted, but Shaftesbury did try to base his selection on merit and suitability. Hitherto, with a few notable exceptions, appointments had to a large extent been made on the basis of political affiliation and often as a result of the personal influence of a friend or relative.

Prime Ministers tended to look to the episcopal bench as one of their most important sources of support, and bishoprics had frequently been distributed among members of the governing families, quite often with the hope of winning votes in the House of Lords. Even Ryder and C.R. Sumner mainly owed their promotion to the fact that one was the brother of the Earl of Harrowby and the other was an intimate personal friend of the king. Shaftesbury was perhaps the first to attempt to apply religious instead of political criteria in choosing all bishops. Undoubtedly he was biased in favour of Evangelicals, but in later years, when patronage was in the hands of Gladstone, Lord Derby and Lord Salisbury, all of whom were High Churchmen, the balance was redressed.

Most of the new bishops were not great theologians, but they were not academic nonentities. Longley had been headmaster of Harrow, and Tait headmaster of Rugby. Philpott had been Master of St Catherine's, Cambridge; Thomson Provost of Queen's, Oxford; and F. Jeune Master of Pembroke. Elliott was formerly Hulsean Professor of Divinity, Browne Norrisian Professor, and Jacobson Regius Professor of Divinity at Oxford. C. Baring and S. Waldegrave were Oxford double-firsts and the latter was Fellow of All Souls. R. Bickersteth, H.M. Villiers and J.T. Pelham were chosen because of their distinguished service as rectors of large parishes.

The zeal and conscientiousness of Bickersteth and Baring were typical of the Evangelicals who were appointed as bishops at this time.[33] Robert Bickersteth had demonstrated his outstanding qualities as rector of St. Giles, possibly the largest and most degraded parish in London. As Bishop of Ripon he carried on his ministry in the same spirit. He toured his

[33] For the main facts in the lives of F. Jeune, J.T. Pelham, H.M. Villiers, S. Waldegrave and J.C. Wigram, see the *Dictionary of National Biography*.

diocese, preaching in the churches. When any church was too small to contain the dalesmen and others who came to hear him, he did as the old Evangelicals did, and proclaimed his message in the churchyard. He preached to colliers at the pithead, to navvies at the waterworks, and to workers in their factories. He urged the clergy to minister with the same evangelistic and pastoral zeal. If any had crowded congregations he asked them to multiply their services, or if necessary to preach in the open air; and he encouraged them to build mission-rooms.

In the neighbouring diocese of Durham, where the church had failed to keep pace with the population, another Evangelical, C.T. Baring, was striving to make the parochial machinery efficient. His church-building and church restoration achievement was impressive: one hundred and nineteen churches were constructed; one hundred and thirty existing churches were enlarged; one hundred and two new parishes formed; and the number of clergy increased by one hundred and eighty-nine.

By 1870, Villiers, Waldegrave and Wigram were dead, and the remaining Evangelical Palmerston bishops were past their best years. In the last thirty years of the century three other Evangelical bishops, J.C. Ryle, A.W. Thorold and Edward H. Bickersteth assumed national importance; two future bishops, Handley C.G. Moule and Francis J. Chavasse, were already exercising a major influence; while A.M.W. Christopher and William Hagar Barlow cannot be ignored.

J.C. Ryle (1816-1900)

It was while J.C. Ryle was the incumbent of the small, undemanding country parish of Helmingham in Suffolk from 1844 to 1861 that he came to the attention of a wide circle of people through his publications.[34] He compiled a hymn book which was published in 1849 with the title *Spiritual Songs*, and replaced in 1850 by *Hymns for the Church on Earth*. In 1854 the lives of Hugh Latimer, Richard Baxter and George Whitefield were depicted in three works, *The Bishop*, *The Pastor* and *The Preacher*. The first of his well-known *Expository Thoughts on the Gospels* appeared with the volumes on Matthew (1856), Mark (1857) and Luke (1858). Also during these years he published that for which he achieved most immediate fame, his series of tracts. They were suggested by the Oxford Tracts; but their style and purpose was new. Ryle was to write about two or three hundred

---

[34] For a full account of the life of J.C. Ryle, see Marcus L. Loane, *John Charles Ryle 1816-1900* (London, 1983), Peter Toon, *J.C. Ryle: A Self Portrait* (Swengel, PA, 1975), and Peter Toon and Michael Smout, *John Charles Ryle, Evangelical Bishop* (Cambridge, 1976).

of them. They were intended to communicate to ordinary, not necessarily very literate or erudite, people the essentials of the Christian faith, as perceived by Evangelicals. They were simply written, yet the effect was compelling. They sold for a penny and had a remarkable circulation at home and in overseas colonies.

In 1881 Ryle became vicar of the nearby parish of Stradbroke, and remained there until 1871. During this time he gave a lead to Evangelicals by his participation in the newly-instituted church congresses. The first of these was held in 1861. Speakers from all church traditions were made welcome, and the ritualists were quick to seize the chance to set forth their particular ideas. Representative Evangelicals were slow to come forward: they were reluctant to associate with men whose views they so mistrusted.

Ryle took his place on the congress platform for the first time in 1866, and was convinced by that experience that non-attendance was a mistake. He was an active participant from then onwards, and was soon joined by two fellow Evangelicals, Edward Hoare and Edward Garbett. He eloquently and trenchantly presented the case for Evangelical involvement, both in his writings, before the Church Association in 1869, and before the Islington Clerical Conference in 1872. He was hotly opposed by some Evangelicals, and even denounced as a Neo-Evangelical, but he carried the day and by the eighteen-seventies there was always a group of Evangelicals at the congress meetings.

Ryle's reputation was on the ascendant during these years. It was advanced by his appointment in 1870 as rural dean of Hoxne, and in 1872 as honorary canon of Norwich. He had 'always held that truth is most likely to be reached when men on all sides conceal nothing, but tell out all their minds',[35] and he used his enhanced influence to establish an annual diocesan conference. He also supported the move to revive Convocation. Many Evangelicals were fearful that a renewed Convocation would reverse the Gorham judgement, and threaten the future of Evangelicalism, and this drove them into active opposition. Ryle was convinced that the powers of Convocation would be revived, whether the Evangelicals approved or not, and he wanted to place his own plan for reform first in the field. He advocated the unity of Canterbury and York into a single province, recommended that there should be fewer *ex officio* and more elected members in the councils of the church, and proposed that laymen should be represented.

Ryle persistently commended organized union among Evangelicals. He recognized that in the main the Evangelicals preached the same doctrines and held the same opinions. They tended to support the same societies, go

[35] Loane, p.64.

to the same meetings, subscribe to the same charities, work their parishes in broadly the same way, go to the same booksellers' shops, read the same books, papers and magazines, and groan and sigh over the same evils in the world, but they lacked any unifying structure.

> For defending common principles, for resisting common enemies, for facing common dangers, for attaining common great objects, for harmonious conduct in circumstances of great perplexity, for decided, prompt, energetic action in great emergencies, for all this I say unhesitatingly, we have no organised union at all. Every Evangelical churchman does what is right in his own eyes and every district goes to work in its own way. We have God's truth on our side. We have numbers, strength, goodwill and desires to do what is right; but from lack of organisation, we are weak as water.[36]

His vision for a strong, united Evangelical association was never realized. The unity of Evangelicals had to rely on spiritual affinity; it was not given organizational cohesion.

Much as he espoused the visible expression of Evangelical unity, Ryle opposed the movement which sprang up in the eighteen-seventies to promote personal holiness. As will be seen in a later chapter, he was genuinely afraid that the new teaching on holiness would lead to an untenable doctrine of sinless perfection, and his concern was shared by other Evangelicals. Ryle believed that the holiness movement was seriously defective in its teaching on sin. He set out his own interpretation of the biblical view on these issues in a book entitled *Holiness* which was published in 1877, with an enlarged edition in 1879. Later his views on the movement softened, though he continued to have certain reservations about it, and he would neither appear on the platform, nor go to the meetings at Keswick.

The ministry of Ryle was being extended and diversified during these years. He spoke regularly at the Islington Clerical Conference and the Church Association. He appeared on the platform of the Church Congress meetings at Nottingham and Leeds in 1871 and 1872, at Brighton and Croydon in 1874 and 1877, at Sheffield and Swansea in 1873 and 1879, and at Leicester in 1880. He was Select Preacher for the University of Cambridge in 1873 and 1874, and for the University of Oxford in 1874, 1875, 1876, 1879 and 1880. He was closely associated with the founding of Wycliffe Hall, Oxford, in 1877, and of Ridley Hall, Cambridge, in 1879. His publications included *Knots Untied* (1874), *Old Paths*, (1877) and *Practical Religion* (1878), as well as the completion in 1873 of his *Expository Thoughts on the Gospels*. By 1880 he had become the most trusted of all the

[36] *Ibid.*, p.62.

Evangelical clergy. He was perhaps the first undisputed leader in their ranks since the days of Charles Simeon.[37] It was at that time that he was appointed the first Bishop of Liverpool.

In the new see, over which he was to preside for twenty years, there was no diocesan machinery. As Loane said, 'he had to lay essential foundations and build for the future from ground level'.[38] He appointed an archdeacon for Liverpool and another for Warrington, both Evangelicals, and twenty-four honorary canons, who were equally Evangelicals and non-Evangelicals. He increased the provision of clergy, ensuring that they were godly men of adequate academic standard. When be began his episcopate he had one hundred and seventy incumbents; by 1897 there were two hundred and five. He began with one hundred and twenty curates, and by 1897 there were two hundred and twenty. In his first year he had four thousand five hundred young people presented to him for confirmation; in 1896 he had eight thousand three hundred. Faced with a severe manpower problem he was also a precursor in the use of laymen as paid workers to complement the ministry of the clergy. He built up the work of the Scripture Readers Society in his diocese by employing their members, who were licensed to take services in mission-rooms, to conduct Sunday schools, and to visit the sick. In addition he established the Bible Women's Society, whose members worked in the poorest districts and helped where the need was greatest. At the end of Ryle's episcopate there were forty-five Scripture Readers and thirty-one Bible Women. In 1882 he also started the Voluntary Lay Helpers Association, whose members increased to about five hundred and eighty. They worked in Sunday schools and Bible classes.

The extension of clerical and lay ministry, and the outreach into the diocese, made additional churches and mission halls imperative. Ryle was concerned that the churches were perhaps used for only four or five hours on Sunday and four or five during the week. He therefore licensed mission halls and school rooms for worship in order to attract those who did not go to any place of worship. Those who shrank from entering a large parish church, and would find the Prayer Book service incomprehensible, might be willing to attend a simple, elementary service in a room or a hall. During his episcopate forty-eight mission halls were built and licensed.

When he resigned in 1900 Ryle left a diocese with a firm and wisely constructed foundation upon which his successors could build. In the wider sphere his strong personality, his writings, his utterances and his example had made him a major influence in the life of two generations of Evangelicals. But towards the end of his life he found himself increasingly

[37] *Ibid.*, p.65.
[38] *Ibid.*, p.86.

isolated from the mainstream of contemporary Evangelicalism.[39] Since before his ordination he had consistently and steadfastly held to his moderate Calvinistic theological convictions, which he thought was the religion of the Thirty-Nine Articles. His commitment to the Puritan tradition meant strong opposition to the doctrine regarding the pursuit of holiness which was taught by the founders of the Keswick Convention. As the Keswick Convention, strengthened by the support of Handley C.G. Moule, increasingly became a rallying-ground for Evangelicals, so men of Ryle's theology claimed fewer and fewer adherents.

Anthony Wilson Thorold (1825-95)

Anthony Wilson Thorold[40] did not have the same national influence as Ryle. After taxing, parochial ministries in London, at St Giles and St Pancras, he became Bishop of Rochester in 1877. Both in his parochial and diocesan work his simple Evangelical preaching, his pastoral care and his extensive visiting was very effective. At St Pancras the enthusiastic congregation filled the spacious church, and the Sunday school was the largest in London.

As Bishop of Rochester he was faced with an almost new see, because St Albans had just been founded, and in the associated rearrangements of London, Winchester and Rochester the huge mass of South London became part of Rochester. His diocese was in chaos. It was, as Balleine so graphically described it, 'a mere bundle of jarring and discordant fragments loosely tied together by an Act of Parliament'.[41] Having been a devoted parish priest, he now became an admirable bishop. The diocese contained parts of both Kent and Surrey, and so diocesan self-awareness had to be created. He resolved to make himself the centre of unity, and to this end he travelled incessantly. He promoted evangelism by establishing in the large parishes mission districts containing three to five thousand people. In each of these he planted a young clergyman, and hired for him a stable, a loft, or even a cellar. The clergyman was bidden to be diligent in visiting, teaching and praying, and to gather a group of worshippers round him. When the meeting-place became too small for the growing congregation, a mission hall would be built, and finally a new church. Thorold welcomed the various Cambridge college missions. St John's College and the Lady Margaret Mission to Walworth were the first to be

---

[39] These concluding comments are based on Toon and Smout, op.cit., pp.103-105.

[40] The following account of the life and work of Anthony Wilson Thorold is based on Balleine, op.cit., and S.C. Carpenter, *Church and People, 1789-1889* (London, 1933).

[41] Balleine, op.cit., p.222.

established; Charterhouse and Wellington followed, and then Clare, Pembroke, Corpus, Trinity and Caius.

During the early years of his episcopate Thorold was rather narrowly Evangelical, and intolerant of ritualism. He refused to visit ritualistic parishes. He remained a convinced and devoted Evangelical all his life, but in later years his sympathies were enlarged, and he laid aside his former narrowness. 'The dream of my life', he declared in 1886, 'is to make plain to all that an Evangelical Churchman can love culture, practise justice, discern differences, and respect goodness anywhere and everywhere'. [42]

Thorold was instrumental in unknowingly providing a cathedral for the future diocese of Southwark. The South-Eastern Railway were prevented from pulling down St Saviour's, Southwark. The nave was then demolished and the rebuilding of the church began. It was completed under Thorold's successor, Randall Davidson, and during the episcopate of Edward Stuart Talbot it became one of the most vigorous centres of diocesan life in the country. When Thorold became Bishop of Winchester he left behind him an integrated and united diocese. The great work he achieved was due in large measure to his leadership. He was intensely methodical and energetic, as is illustrated by the writing in 1884 of 6,258 letters in his own hand. He was no scholar, but he was devoted and faithful in the work assigned to him.

Edward Henry Bickersteth (1825-1906)

In 1885 Thorold's friend Edward Henry Bickersteth, the incumbent of Christ Church, Hampstead from 1855 to 1885, was appointed Bishop of Exeter as the successor to Frederick Temple. [43] In his parochial ministry he was 'a perpetual gentle force that made for holiness'. [44] And it was this quality which he brought to his work as a bishop. It was said of him at Exeter that whereas 'Temple pushed along, carrying work and workmen with him in an enthusiasm of labour, Bishop Bickersteth fell upon his people like dew. He came to his parishes and went his way, and those whom he visited found themselves refreshed'. [45] Temple's own verdict on the arrival of his successor was, 'That man will do; he is so transparently good'. [46] The judgement of Carpenter that he 'was not one of the great

[42] Quoted in Balleine, op.cit., p.222.
[43] The comments on Edward Henry Bickersteth are based on Carpenter, op.cit. pp.400-403.
[44] Ibid., p.401.
[45] Ibid., p.403.
[46] Quoted in Carpenter, op.cit., p.403.

bishops of the century, but he was one of the great pastors, and one of the great Christians',[47] is fair and just.

Bickersteth did many things which were of importance outside his own parish and diocese, which had effects beyond his own day and generation. He was the first Evangelical to conduct retreats and quiet days. He wrote a *Commentary on the New Testament*, and published an epic poem in twelve books entitled *Yesterday, To-Day and For Ever*. In 1870 he brought out the first edition of *The Hymnal Companion to the Book of Common Prayer*, in an attempt to ensure that the Prayer Book and the hymn book spoke with the same voice, and that no doctrine could be found in one which could not be found in the other.

'In Anglican representativeness', Julian comments, in the *Dictionary of Hymnology*, 'Bishop Bickersteth's work is at the head of all hymnals in the Church of England, and in keeping with this unique position it has also the purest texts'.[48] Such a judgement may be questioned by many, but there is little doubt about the merits of Bickersteth's hymn book, and of its significance for decades after its publication.

It would have been more widely accepted had not the date of its issue almost coincided with that of *Hymns, Ancient and Modern*, but it rapidly superseded most of the older Evangelical collections, and became the chosen book for a great number of Evangelical parishes. When Convocation took its Hymn Book Census in 1893 Bickersteth's collection was found to be in use in one thousand four hundred and seventy-eight English churches. The church also owes to Bickersteth many beautiful hymns of lasting value, including 'Peace, perfect peace' and 'For my sake and the Gospel's Go'.

Handley Carr Glyn Moule (1841-1920)

Handley Carr Glyn Moule was raised to the episcopate, as Bishop of Durham, in 1901, but for twenty years and more before this he had made a distinctive contribution to the life of the Evangelicals as a teacher, theologian, writer and leader.[49] He was successively Junior and Senior Dean of Trinity College, Cambridge from 1873 to 1877, where, in

[47] Carpenter, *op.cit.*, p.403.
[48] Quoted in Balleine, *op.cit.*, p.223.
[49] For the life and work of Handley Carr Glyn Moule, see John Battersby Harford and Frederick Charles Macdonald, *Handley Carr Glyn Moule Bishop of Durham* (London, 1922), on which the ensuing account is largely based.

addition to his required duties, he preached regularly at St Sepulchre's (the Round Church), and twice in the university pulpit in 1873. He was appointed examiner for the classical tripos in 1874 and 1875, for the theological voluntary in 1873, and for the theological tripos in 1874; and he wrote poems, which in 1873 and 1875 won him the Seatonian Prize for the fifth and sixth times. In 1880 he was made one of the examining chaplains for the diocese of Liverpool, under Bishop Ryle. In the same year he assumed responsibility as principal-elect of Ridley Hall, Cambridge. It was during his nineteen years at Ridley, his short time as Norrisian Professor of Divinity and, after 1901, as Bishop of Durham, that his impact on the church and specially upon Evangelicals was to become so great, (an account of which is given in chapters 11, 12 and 14). One aspect alone will be considered now: his prolific output as an author, which extended his sway throughout the English-speaking world, and indeed further, for several of his writings were translated into other languages.

Of his theological works, in which he specifically expounded his evangelical beliefs, none was more comprehensive than *Outlines of Christian Doctrine* (1889). He wrote it for the theological student and it embraced a wide range of Christian dogma. The bulk of Moule's theological writings, as of his writings in general, were not, however, for the theological specialist, but had the layman in view. In his *Veni Creator* (1890), for example, doctrinal teaching is made clear and definite, but expressed largely in non-technical language, and in an attractive literary style.

Such an approach also characterized his expositions and commentaries. In the Cambridge Bible for Schools series he contributed the commentaries on *The Epistle to the Romans* (1879), *The Epistle to the Ephesians* (1886), *The Epistle to the Philippians* (1889) and *The Epistle to the Colossians and Philemon* (1893). In the Expositor's Bible, he evenly balanced scholarly and devotional interests in expounding *The Epistle to the Romans* (1894), and in later years he wrote *Philippian Studies* (1897), *Colossian Studies* (1898) and *Ephesian Studies* (1900). In these volumes, instead of verse-by-verse annotation, he gave expositions of the main teaching of the epistles in sections under appropriate headings.

His other works included six volumes of sermons, and a large number of smaller devotional books, as well as over thirty tracts and papers; various poems; the biography of *Charles Simeon* (1892); *The Evangelical School in the Church of England: Its men and its work in the Nineteenth Century* (1901); and various classical and literary lectures.

In conclusion, three other Evangelicals warrant brief notice: two of them for their ministry to students, and the other for his unostentatious but important influence in determining Evangelical policy and strategy.

Francis James Chavasse (1845-1928) lacked the academic brilliance of Handley Moule, but was as committed to the Evangelical faith.[50] After parish ministries in Preston and London he returned to his alma mater (Oxford) where, for twenty-three years, first as rector of St Peter-le Bailey, and then as principal of Wycliffe Hall, from 1889 to 1900, he helped to mould the lives and thinking of scores of young people. His subsequent tenure of the Bishopric of Liverpool will be considered in a later chapter.

The life of A.M.W. Christopher (1820-1913) was dominated by his forty-six years as rector of St Aldate's, Oxford (1859-1905).[51] His influence in Oxford, especially in the world of students, was immeasurable. It was not sensational or marked by dramatic events. It was an amalgam of the consistent and sustained preaching of the distinctive Evangelical message; a much appreciated person-to-person ministry, either directly with individuals or in small groups; the regular meetings for prayer and exposition of the Bible at St Aldate's rectory every Saturday evening; and the support he gave to a wide range of Evangelical causes both locally and nationally.

His strength lay largely in his conservatism, but therein was also found his greatest limitation. He spent most of his life surrounded by seats of learning, and yet he was not a man to embark upon, or even encourage, original investigation. The Evangelical sympathies of E.A. Knox did not prevent a candid recognition of this shortcoming. 'Divagations of a literary character', he wrote, 'caused his ear-trumpet to drop lower and lower or even to be laid aside . . . he rather hindered than forwarded the work for which also the times were calling, the work of patient study of the thought and intellectual outlook of the age'.[52]

Christopher was seen by the university and city as a dedicated evangelist. In common with so many of the Evangelicals of this period, it was his personal commitment, and the quality of his character, which was the admiration of so many, and which helps to explain the impact of his ministry.

William Hagar Barlow (1833-1908) was likewise not among the great or brilliant clergymen of his day, but few rendered service with greater faithfulness.[53] As principal of the Church Missionary Society College (1875-1882), vicar of Islington and, in the years after the Victorian era, from 1901 to 1908, as Dean of Peterborough, he made a considerable

---

[50] For the life and work of Francis James Chavasse, see J.B. Lancelot, *Francis James Chavasse, Bishop of Liverpool* (London, 1929).

[51] For the life and work of A.M.W. Christopher, see J.S. Reynolds, *Canon Christopher of St Aldate's Oxford* (Abingdon, 1967).

[52] Edmund Arbuthnott Knox, *Reminiscences of an Octogenarian, 1847-1934* (London, 1934), p.109.

[53] For the life and work of William Hagar Barlow, see Margaret Barlow, *The Life of William Hagar Barlow, D.D. Late Dean of Peterborough* (London, 1910).

contribution to the life of the church. He was a key figure in Evangelicalism for a generation and more, although he mainly toiled silently behind the scenes. 'For forty years', wrote Chavasse, 'it may be confidently asserted that no new move was determined by its leaders, no fresh. step taken and no difficult questions weighed, without his judgement being asked and his counsel considered'.[54]

---

[54] Barlow, *op.cit.*, p.xiii.

11

Evangelism and Teaching

For almost the first twenty years of the Victorian age the Evangelicals were inhibited by their establishment status from using effective 'irregular' methods characteristic of Methodists and the new dissenters.[1] There was no real breakthrough until the mid-century.

During the first half of the nineteenth century the practice of open-air preaching seems to have been the almost exclusive preserve of Methodists.[2] Baptist Noel commended this method of evangelism, but it did not find favour in the *Christian Observer*, which argued that neither the British temperament nor the climate was suited to the practice.[3] Furthermore, the Irvingite use of it had denigrated the practice in the eyes of some Evangelicals. A reappraisal of open-air preaching was precipitated in part as a consequence of its successful employment by non-Christian preachers and by Mormon missionaries. Around 1850 or soon after a few clergymen in London began to preach in the open air. The Rev. William Vincent, the incumbent of Holy Trinity, Islington, was perhaps the first to

---

[1] See A.D. Gilbert, *Religion and Society in Industrial England* (London, 1976), p.136.
[2] A useful study of certain aspects of evangelism in the nineteenth century is to be found in Donald Munro Lewis, 'The Evangelical Mission to the British Working Classes: A Study of the growth of Anglican support for a pan-evangelical approach to evangelism with special reference to London, 1828-1860' (University of Oxford D.Phil., 1981).
[3] See the *Christian Observer*, April 1835.

do so systematically; he proclaimed his message from a wall at the bottom of Pulteney Street.[4]

The effective preaching in 1854 of the nineteen-year-old Charles Haddon Spurgeon to crowds of five or six thousand twice each Sunday, and his special services at the Crystal Palace drawing upwards of twenty-five thousand people, were a stimulus to evangelism.[5] Evangelists began to hold evangelistic 'missions'. These focused on a series of meetings at which there were different preachers each evening. The first was probably in the parish of J.C. Miller in Birmingham in 1856. In 1857 a week of such services was held in Ipswich, and another in Islington parish church. Increasingly Evangelical churches adopted this method of evangelism, employing such well-known Evangelical speakers as J.C. Miller, Hugh McNeile, Hugh Stowell, and J.C. Ryle as the evangelists.

Evangelicals, together with other churchmen, were made acutely aware as a result of the 1851 religious census that the Church of England had not lost, so much as never held, the allegiance of the British workman. Parish work had been well developed by Evangelicals and, as will be seen in a later chapter, social work of various kinds was increasingly undertaken. However, in the second half of the century there was more direct evangelism through special services and missions, aimed at the unconverted, in an attempt to produce a more immediate evangelistic impact than either the normal parochial ministry or soup kitchens could achieve.

Alongside parochial missions Evangelicals organized services in secular venues. These were made possible by the Religious Worship Act of 1855, which had been passed largely through the efforts of Lord Shaftesbury. It allowed the holding of services in unconsecrated buildings. In 1857 twelve Sunday evening services were held in Exeter Hall, London, arranged by a committee under the leadership of Lord Shaftesbury. The preachers included two of the new 'Palmerston Bishops', H.M. Villiers of Carlisle and Robert Bickersteth of Ripon, as well as Close, Alford, McNeile, Stowell, Miller, and Cadman. Shaftesbury was ecstatic about the new venture:

Last Sunday (May 24th) a glorious triumph for religion and the Church of England. Blessed be God! a splendid proof of the use and value of the Religious Worship Act passed two years ago! Under the powers of this Act, in Exeter Hall, an evening service was conducted by the Bishop of Carlisle in

[4] See Eugene Stock, *The History of the Church Missionary Society* (London, 1899), Vol.II, p.26.
[5] For the following comments see Lewis, *op.cit.*, and B.E. Hardman, 'The Evangelical Party in the Church of England, 1855-1865' (Cambridge University Ph.D., 1964), pp.248, 249.

full canonicals, for the benefit of all-comers who were 'not habitual church or chapel goers' – such was the advertisement. An attendance of more than three thousand – order, decency, attention, and even devotion. They sang well and lustily and repeated the responses with regularity and earnestness. Villiers preached the sermon on 'What saith the Scripture?' practical, pious, affectionate, true; delivered with dignity and power, and deeply impressive.[6]

Although the Exeter Hall services were temporary, they led to an important and long-term development in the church. Bishop Tait was encouraged by their success, and after much effort and difficulty arranged for St Paul's and Westminster Abbey to be opened for evening services. The idea of using cathedral naves for Sunday evening services had been suggested to Tait by the Evangelical Samuel Waldegrave. It was an innovation which shocked many churchmen. St Paul's was used for the first time for these new services on Advent Sunday, 1856; it was a memorable date. Initially the services were planned for only a few Sundays; but the overflowing congregations persuaded the Dean and Chapter, after a few years, to continue them indefinitely. Of particular note was the preaching of Liddon, which was undertaken with consummate authority and power.

In 1860 a further evangelistic effort was made. Theatre Services were started. These attracted a different stratum of the population than either St Paul's or Exeter Hall. Men and boys came to them in their shirt-sleeves, women without bonnets and with babies. The outcry was loud and impassioned against what many regarded as a travesty of religious worship. Even some Evangelicals did not welcome the novelty. Evangelicals had been the leading opponents of theatres and some could not reconcile themselves to the use of such buildings as a venue for Christian services.

A debate followed in the House of Lords, in which Lord Shaftesbury delivered perhaps the most eloquent of all his speeches. For three hours the House was entranced by his descriptions of the London poor and their irreligious condition. Both Archbishop Sumner and Bishop Tait gave support to this new initiative.

Lord Shaftesbury was also a prominent figure in the founding of various evangelistic agencies. Of these the one which was to last the longest as a central organization in the Church of England was the Church Pastoral-Aid Society. Shaftesbury took the chair at its foundation meeting in February 1836, and he remained president of the Society for the rest of his

---

[6] E. Hodder, *The Life and Work of the Seventh Earl of Shaftesbury K.G.*, 3 vols (London, 1886), Vol. III, p. 47.

life. His speech at its annual May meeting was always a major event in the Evangelical calendar. He was fully committed to its home mission purposes and wholeheartedly approved of the employment of lay agents. He always regarded the Society with special warmth . 'I never was called by God's mercy', he wrote, 'to so happy and blessed a work as to labour on behalf of this Society and preside at its head'.[7] He never deviated from these sentiments, but he was also active in helping to establish and maintain other evangelistic societies such as the Working Men's Educational Union, founded in 1852, the Open-Air Mission, started in 1853, and the highly successful Ranyard Bible and Domestic Mission, which was founded in 1857. Other Evangelical laymen also held key positions in these and similar organizations.

It was in the latter part of the century that individual itinerant Anglican evangelists became prominent. Hay Aitken held his first independent mission at Stroud in Gloucestershire in 1869. Within two years he was engaged in frequent missions in different parts of the country. By then it was reckoned in some areas that a greater effect could be achieved when several churches united together. In Doncaster in December 1871 services were held in all the Anglican churches of the town, as well as in the Guildhall. Canon Christopher was among the nine missioners on that occasion. A similar mission was held in Derby in November 1873, and preachers included the staunchly Evangelical Evan Hopkins and Reginald Radcliffe.[8] By 1874 the new pattern for parochial missions was established. It included careful preparation, initial gatherings of day helpers, midday services and special meetings for particular people, weekday evening services, after-meetings, celebrations of holy communion, and counselling. It was in many ways similar to the methods used by D.L. Moody in his missions and helped to prepare the way for these.

Moody and Sankey

When Dwight Lyman Moody arrived in England in 1873 he had behind him a meteoric and colourful career in America, but he was unknown in the United Kingdom.[9] In 1875 he sailed away having caused a stir in Scotland, Ireland and England, and having completed the most

[7] Geoffrey B.A.M. Finlayson, *The Seventh Earl of Shaftesbury, 1801-1885* (London, 1981), p.112.

[8] See the *Derby Mercury*, 19, 26 November 1873 to which reference is made in Anne Bentley, 'The Transformation of the Evangelical Party in the Church of England in the later Nineteenth Century' (Durham University Ph.D., 1971), p.303.

[9] For the life and work of Dwight Lyman Moody, see John Pollock, *Moody without Sankey* (London, 1963). Much of what follows is indebted to Pollock.

remarkable evangelistic campaign in England in the nineteenth century.

The mission of 1873 began haphazardly, with the minimum of preparation. In the previous year, when Moody had made a very brief visit to the United Kingdom, Henry Bewley of Dublin and Cuthbert Bainbridge, a rich Methodist layman of Newcastle upon Tyne, had promised him funds if he returned for an evangelistic tour. Also William Pennefather, who exercised wide authority, had specifically invited Moody to return. He was strongly convinced that Moody was one for whom God had prepared a great work. He wrote to Moody telling him of the wide-open door of opportunity for evangelism in London and elsewhere, and promised him a warm welcome if he would come over and help. Moody did not reply but believed that 'plans may fructify in a vacuum of unanswered correspondence'.[10] He seems to have thought that Bewley, Bainbridge and Pennefather were organizing an evangelistic tour and, without any written indication that this was so, he set out for England accompanied by his wife and children and Ira D. Sankey. On arrival at Liverpool he was informed that both Bainbridge and Pennefather had died; Bewley appears to have been unaware of the situation; and there were no engagements, no committee and no funds.

Meetings were arranged in the Corn Exchange and services held at various churches in York. Some were well attended and the response was encouraging, but the work remained scattered, the churches were not united, and the benefits were limited mainly to dissenters. One or two Anglican clergymen gave Moody verbal support, but the Church of England was only very marginally involved. There followed an evangelistic campaign in Sunderland which was a disappointment. Moody and Sankey went on to Newcastle upon Tyne, and Moody decided to remain there until prejudice died. After a few weeks the numbers attending grew; the audiences were deeply moved by impressive congregational singing, and the earnest addresses of the Yankee visitor. The effect permeated not only Newcastle itself, but the surrounding countryside. It started among the church-going middle class, and spread slowly upwards and downwards. Moody and Sankey had 'jumped from the obscurity of York to being the talk of the greatest city in the north of England'.[11]

From Newcastle Moody went to Edinburgh. Night after night all sorts of people from all parts of the city and from the countryside went to hear him. His reputation spread across Scotland. A specially raised fund of two thousand pounds provided a weekly copy of the *Christian* for each minister

[10] Pollock, *op.cit.*, pp.96, 97.
[11] *Ibid.*, p.104.

throughout the British Isles, in which reports of the mission were prominent. Those who went to the meetings came from quiet villages, from the highland glens and from lowland burghs. They returned enthused and were instrumental in promoting local evangelism, by means of which there were many converts. Invitations poured in for Moody and Sankey to go to other centres. At the age of thirty-six Moody was suddenly famous. He was 'borne on a surge'[12] as he went from Edinburgh to Dundee, Glasgow, Belfast, Dublin, Manchester, Sheffield, Birmingham, and Liverpool. Alongside Moody, Sankey was gaining an immense popularity as he sang his solos to enchanted audiences. A penny book of his musical items was distributed throughout the United Kingdom and sold at the rate of 250,000 copies per month.

In March 1875 Moody and Sankey began their mission in London. They were confronted by much criticism and abuse. Nevertheless the attendance at the Agricultural Hall rose, after more space had been arranged, to an estimated 20,000 nightly. Sunday meetings were early morning and late evening to avoid interfering with church services. Moody also preached at evangelistic services at Bow Common and at the Queen's Opera House in the Haymarket. The attendance figures were unprecedented for nightly evangelistic meetings in nineteenth century England, and were regarded at the time as fantastic. Moody was probably seen and heard by at least a million and a half people in London in 1875.

Moody and Sankey revisited the United Kingdom in 1881. They conducted a Scottish mission, and a series of shorter missions in Welsh and English provincial centres, but these were less spectacular than on the former occasions. In retrospect, the most significant meetings of this second tour, both for Moody and the church worldwide, were held in Cambridge.

At the first Cambridge meeting hoots, cheers, and cries of 'Hear, hear' and 'Encore' accompanied the preliminary prayers, comments and singing. Moody preached on Daniel in the lions' den, and his monosyllabic 'Dan'l' produced a climax of ridicule. Whenever Moody repeated the name the disorderly members of the audience called out 'Dan'l, Dan'l'. Americanisms or un-British intonations were greeted by scattered guffaws; and the unconscious click in Moody's throat before uttering certain remarks was imitated. There was also loud laughter and shouts of 'Well done'. During all this Moody remained unruffled and in good humour. He called upon any who wished to pray to remain behind for a few minutes, and about four hundred stayed.

The leader of the disruptive element was an elegant young man in the front row, Gerald Lander. On reflection he decided he had overstepped the

---

[12] *Ibid.*, p.114.

bounds of decency. He went to apologize to Moody and agreed to prove his sincerity by quietly attending the next meeting. His example and the news of what was going on spread rapidly. Attendances mounted, and on the Sunday night Moody preached to nearly two thousand university men. He asked all who had received blessing from the mission to stand up in their places while silent prayer continued. Two hundred rose. Moody looked up and murmured, 'My God, this is enough to live for'.[13] It was not only the large number of lives which were touched by the mission, but the outstanding quality and future dedication of many of them. The effect was far-ranging. Lander became a missionary bishop in China, and the going forth of the famous 'Cambridge Seven', which will be described in a later chapter, was indirectly a fruit of the mission.

Moody and Sankey came to the British Isles for a third time in 1891/92, but they attracted less attention than on their first two visits. The campaign also appears to have had less impact than formerly, although there were large gatherings at Oxford, where 5-6,000 attended the chief open-air meeting on the Sunday evening, and Manchester, where an estimated 20,000 attended during the closing day.[14]

The extent of Evangelical involvement in all these activities cannot be measured precisely, but it was considerable, after initial hesitancy. Evangelicals chaired many of the committees responsible for organizing the various missions. The leading Evangelicals identified themselves with the campaigns. Shaftesbury, despite some doubts at first, gave Moody his support; Handley Moule was intimately involved in the Cambridge mission; J.C. Ryle gave ready assistance, and Quintin Hogg was not ashamed to associate himself with Moody. Referring to 'that wonderful Mission' of 1875, Eugene Stock, who was well placed to make such an observation, said that the Church of England had little idea of what she owed to it, both in the general standard it set of reality in religion and in the men and women it influenced – scores and scores of subsequently honoured clergymen and laymen, and even bishops.[15] Whether those affected were primarily people who were already connected in some way with the church, or whether there were major inroads into the mass of the alienated working classes is open to debate, although it does seem that the influence upon complete outsiders was slight.[16]

Moody was 'rugged, delightful, compassionate, a man of total integrity, with a supreme gift for bringing Christianity before a whole

[13] Quoted in Pollock, op.cit., p.208.
[14] See The Christian, 18 August, 13 October, 24 November 1892, and Bentley, op.cit., p.380.
[15] Eugene Stock, My Recollections (London, 1909), p.187, quoted in Pollock, op.cit., p.151.
[16] See Bentley, op.cit., p.366.

range of contemporary hearers, and putting them to work for God'.[17] He endeared himself to many, even those who were biased against him. His preaching was simple and direct, as he proclaimed the new birth of a repentant sinner who trusts in Christ. Repeatedly he called it 'instant salvation'. A host of converts of all ages and social status, whose conversions endured, as with those to whom Stock made reference, were an ample testimony to the powerful impact and lasting influence of Moody and Sankey. The campaigns were also a means of reviving the individual and corporate life of church-goers, 'invigorating the machine as it were'; and indeed some would acclaim this as their chief though perhaps unintended success.[18]

Pan-evangelical Co-operation

The Moody missions were an example of Evangelical co-operation with nonconformists.[19] During the Victorian era this type of co-operation had been gradually and cautiously extended as many Evangelicals had jettisoned the traditional Simeonite self-distancing from dissent. While retaining a high regard for church order, such Evangelicals increasingly supported a pan-evangelical approach to evangelism which crossed the Anglican-nonconformist divide. As previously noted, the eighteen-twenties had seen a severe fracturing of Evangelical unity, when various factions bitterly wrangled over such issues as the Irvingites, eschatology, Catholic emancipation, the Reform Act and the balance between direct evangelism and social action. There was also disagreement between these Evangelical groupings about what should be the right attitude and relationship with nonconformists.

Following the repeal of the Test and Corporation Acts in 1828, relations between Anglican and nonconformist evangelicals rapidly deteriorated. Anglican Evangelicals were especially concerned to preserve the establishment because they considered it an important factor in the attempted conversion of England: a task which they thought that nonconformity was totally inadequate to perform. On the other hand, nonconformist evangelicals saw the establishment as a major impediment to evangelism, as it confused the sacred with the secular. The pressure for disestablishment was maintained by those who thought that the Anglican Evangelicals would eventually secede to form a voluntary episcopal church. This whole controversy did immense damage to the cause of co-operation between Anglican and nonconformist evangelicals.

[17] Pollock, op.cit., p.ix.
[18] See Bentley, op.cit., p.381.
[19] The observations in this section owe much to Lewis, op.cit.

The formation of the London City Mission in 1835 was a great boost to pan-evangelicalism. The mission was backed by many Evangelicals, and this support increased as they became aware of the inability of the newly-founded Church Pastoral-Aid Society to operate in several of London's parishes. Such support was also promoted by the growing appreciation of the value and effectiveness of lay work.

Anglican Evangelicals were further drawn towards the nonconformists as a result of the Oxford Movement. In the eighteen-forties, the *Record* underwent a noticeable change in its attitude towards dissent as it began to defend nonconformists against Tractarian charges of schism. There was a growing sense that evangelicals both Anglican and nonconformist were facing a common foe. This awareness was heightened by the Maynooth Grant. In response to an appeal from Catholic bishops in Ireland for assistance in repairing their dilapidated college for the training of priests, the Tory government under Peel passed an act to raise the annual grant to Maynooth from £9,000 to £27,000, and to give £30,000 for capital expenditure. Anglican Evangelicals and nonconformists were equally loud in their cries of protest. The no-popery campaign was reinvigorated, and it not only rocked the government but helped to unite those who had once again found a common cause. The event provided a significant if limited degree of co-operation between Anglican and dissenting evangelicals, and it was also one of the factors which led in 1846 to the formation of the Evangelical Alliance.

The founders of the Evangelical Alliance wanted an organizational expression of their shared evangelical principles.[20] Through the Alliance it was hoped that Christians would be able to cultivate brotherly love, enjoy friendly intercourse and promote other objects as they thought fit. However, it not only gave expression to the strong currents flowing in favour of pan-evangelicalism: it also helped to reveal the extent of Anglican Evangelical resistance to this trend. There was little Evangelical support for the Alliance: the majority of Evangelicals stood stiffly aloof.[21] Very severe things were said in the *Christian Observer* about those who were willing 'to fraternise with Anabaptists'.

In the eighteen-fifties there was a slight increase in pan-evangelical co-operation. The Papal Aggression of 1850 provided another opportunity for an evangelical alliance against Rome; but anti-Catholicism, despite its strength as a unifying force, did not prove to be a sustaining motive for co-operative effort. More enduring solidarity was achieved as a result of new, specialized evangelistic endeavours designed to penetrate the largely

---

[20] See John W. Ewing, *Goodly Fellowship: A Centenary Tribute to the Life and Work of the World's Evangelical Alliance 1846-1946* (London, 1946).

[21] See for example J.B. Marsden, *Memoirs of Hugh Stowell*, p.166, quoted in Balleine, *op.cit.*, p.160.

unevangelized social, economic, occupational and ethnic groupings. As the Church of England was slow to adapt to social changes, these new ventures were pioneered by the innovating and much more flexible pan-evangelical societies; although the subsequent leadership of the new organizations was dominated by Anglican Evangelical laymen. The most prominent of these societies was the highly successful Ranyard Bible Mission, founded in 1857 as the London Bible and Domestic Female Mission, which employed working-class women to evangelize their peers. The translation of Bishop Tait to the Diocese of London in 1856 also signalled a new era for interdenominational co-operation in London. He was willing to support already existing evangelistic organizations, however constituted, and he did not inhibit his clergy from co-operating with nonconformists. Finally, in this decade, pan-evangelicalism was furthered, although only to a restricted extent, by the revivals in America and Great Britain between 1856 and 1860, which will be described and discussed in the next chapter.

The Salvation Army and the Church Army

In the latter half of the century two evangelistic agencies, one non-denominational and the other within the Church of England, were to prove of lasting value: the Salvation Army and the Church Army.

The Salvation Army was the creation of a gifted married couple: William and Catherine Booth. They were originally Methodists but William left that denomination and forged ahead on his own because the Methodist Conference of 1861 refused to sanction certain of his schemes. In establishing the Salvation Army his simplicity, directness, and dedication were evident. Three things were required of his followers: belief in the possibility of instantaneous conversion, even for the most degraded; courage, and absolute obedience.

As the Salvation Army became prominent, it aroused the suspicions and even dislike of the stricter type of churchmen, and this included a number of Evangelicals. Lord Shaftesbury never liked nor trusted Booth and his methods.[22] In 1881 he was invited by Admiral Fishbourne to support the Army, but refused, and maintained strong opposition to its efforts. He told Fishbourne that this was not because he disapproved of novel and abnormal methods of organisation and evangelism. On the contrary, he had spent much of his life breaking down barriers and prejudices in his efforts to take the Christian faith to the masses. But he had always endeavoured to keep within the limits of the New Testament and primitive Christianity, and he

---

[22] Finlayson, op.cit., pp.397, 582.

could find no authority in scripture for the system and discipline of the Salvation Army. He also objected to the language and conduct of the members of the Army, which he found as offensive as any form of the wildest fanaticism. He thought there was no need for any new method of addressing the people; enough lay missions existed and a development of those was required rather than any addition to them. In common with other critics, Shaftesbury underestimated the contribution to be made to religious and social activity by the Salvation Army.

Not all Evangelicals were resistant to its methods and philosophy.[23] In 1881 Evan Hopkins began a similar work in his own parish of Holy Trinity, Richmond, with a band he called the Church Gospel Army. It had military rules and membership cards and the men wore a red cord in their button-holes. Sundays began with a drill at seven, then an open-air meeting at ten, which was followed by a church service at eleven. There was an afternoon Bible class and in the evening a band and army banner would lead a procession to the mission hall, where a gospel meeting of testimony, prayer and choruses was followed by the increasingly familiar after-meeting. Similar meetings were held in the mission hall on week-nights, culminating in a holiness meeting on the Friday night. Crowds pelted the band, and there were protests from the congregation, but the new approach brought in people who had previously been untouched by the church's activities.

Similar bands were started independently in other parishes, as in Bristol where, by October 1882, there were already two church armies.[24] The greatest testimony to the work of the Salvation Army on the part of the church, however, was the formation of a national Church Army. This was largely the work of Wilson Carlile. He had spent much of his time among the poorer classes at Holy Trinity, Richmond. He was greatly inspired by the Moody services at the Agricultural Hall, where he first helped as a deputy organist, and then as a speaker at the overflow meetings. He also gained experience by working with the Evangelisation Society. He then entered the London College of Divinity in 1878; and he was ordained deacon in 1880. He worked under Dr Carr Glyn in Kennington, but his large outdoor meetings brought complaints. He resigned his curacy to work in a slum mission. In 1882 he started to unite the various local parish armies into one large Church Army. After initial consultations with Canon Wilkinson and Hay Aitken, he decided to widen the base of the work and involve non-Evangelicals.

The Church Army attracted criticism from some Evangelicals as the Salvation Army had done. Shaftesbury was somewhat equivocal. He

[23] For this paragraph, see Bentley, *op.cit.*, p.323 and A. Smellie, *Evan Hopkins: A Memoir* (London, 1921), pp.40-44.
[24] See the *Record*, 13 October 1882, and Bentley, *op.cit.*, p.323.

approved of its Anglican context but was dubious about some of its methods. Other Evangelicals, who had pioneered the whole new strategy, continued to be influential supporters, even though the Church Army asserted its independence of sectional interests. In these early years there were further difficulties because the Church Army was identified with the doctrine of perfectionism. Although some of the membership were closely involved in the contemporary holiness movement which, as will be seen in the next chapter, was causing division of opinion among Evangelicals, Church Army supporters denied that sinless perfection was part of the Army's teaching.[25]

In spite of criticism from within the church, and opposition from without, the Church Army continued to grow and prosper. By 1891 there were 166 officer-evangelists and 44 mission nurses, and about 40,000 meetings were held each year.[26] Towards the end of the century both the Salvation Army and the Church Army introduced similar schemes for relieving social distress. In November 1889 the Church Army opened its first Labour Home in Marylebone, London, as a community providing food, shelter and employment for the poorest members of society. By the end of the century there were seven such Homes in London and twenty more in different provincial cities. Potential residents were given a three days' test followed by two weeks' steady work before being signed on for four months, mostly doing wood-chopping. After this the Army tried to find them employment. By 1895 a farm had been acquired in Surrey to which the most promising men were sent for agricultural training, and an emigration scheme was also in operation. In addition to these provisions, lodging-houses were opened for men who had found employment but needed residential accommodation. Church Army sisters were recruited in 1887. They worked largely with the destitute girls. In 1891 a Labour House for women was opened in Marylebone Road, but it proved unsuccessful and was later closed. Other ventures included market gardens and coffee houses; a sales-room for the sale of clothing and furniture to poor families at minimal prices on the presentation of chits from their vicar, and help to discharged prisoners.

Hymnody

The surge in evangelistic effort in the latter part of the century was accompanied by a revival of hymn singing and hymn writing, but not on the same scale as in the eighteenth century. The most sensational

[25] See Bentley, op.cit., pp.331, 332.
[5] See the Record, 4 May 1888, 8 May 1891, and Bentley, op.cit., p.332.

development was the phenomenal sale of the Sankey hymn book associated with the Moody and Sankey missions. But there were less dramatic changes taking place which entailed churchmen other than Evangelicals. In 1819 Reginald Heber, the future Bishop of Calcutta, had compiled a collection of hymns for his parishioners at Hodnet; but even he had certain 'High Church scruples about using it'.[27] In 1833 Edward Bickersteth published his *Christian Psalmody*, which had an immense sale. The poetry of Keble was an inspiration to many and had great power in fostering High Church tendencies. *Hymns, Ancient and Modern*, which was published in 1861, drew upon both Evangelical and High Church hymnody, and at once established itself as of prime importance. Its only rivals in high or 'via media' churches were the successive books of the SPCK. The High Church revival in the last decades of the century was deeply indebted to the influence of *Hymns, Ancient and Modern*. The Evangelicals had a large number of individual collections in their different churches, but they at length concentrated on E.H. Bickersteth's *Hymnal Companion*, which was first issued in 1870 and later revised and enlarged. By the first decade of the twentieth century *Hymns, Ancient and Modern*, *Church Hymns* published by SPCK and the *Hymnal Companion* occupied almost all the ground.

Theological Education

In the second half of the nineteenth century there was not only a renewed evangelistic effort by Evangelicals; there was also a period of revived concern for theological education.[28] In the early eighteen–fifties Evangelicals were worried by the establishment of centres of theological training outside the universities, none of which was in their control. The colleges at Wells and Chichester were High Church and even regarded by some to be under Tractarian control; and Cuddesdon College was opened in 1854. This Evangelical concern was intensified when the former Evangelical haven for undergraduates, St Edmund Hall, Oxford, fell under other influences.

There was some talk at this time of having a separate college for each diocese. This was opposed by a number of Evangelicals, led by Lord Shaftesbury. They rather envisaged building a college which would have a broad theological basis and would seek patronage and support from five or six bishops. By this arrangement Shaftesbury and like-minded Evangelicals hoped to remove the colleges from exclusive High

---

[27] Elliott-Binns, *op.cit.*, p.373.
[28] This section owes much to Bentley, *op.cit.*, and Hardman, *op.cit.*

Church influence. But there was no concerted Evangelical backing for the concept. Many thought that such an institution would never work successfully, as it would be organized and supervised by men who differed on fundamental theological issues.

At an Evangelical conference at Weston-super-Mare in 1853 chaired by Henry Law, J.C. Ryle persuasively presented the need for a distinctively Evangelical college, in addition to St Aidan's, Birkenhead, which had been founded in 1840. In the next eighteen months various correspondents to the *Record* supported the idea. In 1855 Litton Hall was founded under the auspices of Lord Shaftesbury.[29] It had little success. In no year did the number of new students exceed three, or the total rise above eight. The project was probably never given the necessary financial and moral support. It was also not limited to members of the Church of England, and this at a time when both dissenters and Evangelical churchmen remained suspicious of too close an alliance. The college closed in 1860.

In 1856 Haldane pressed for the immediate founding of a 'Protestant, Evangelical and Truly Church of England College',[30] and this proposal was repeated by T.P. Boultbee in 1860. A certain Mr Peache gave a donation of £50,000, and in 1863 Peache's College, which became known as St John's Hall of Divinity, was opened with Boultbee as the first principal. It began in a private house in Kilburn with one student. Two years later the college was transferred to St John's Hall, Highbury, and the number of students rose to fifty or sixty. Its success was assured.

Despite these developments, there was still no Evangelical theological college in a university town.[31] The need for a greater theological knowledge and awareness was emphasized by the questionings of the new biblical criticism. Yet the quality of theological education for ordination candidates was inadequate. The smallest amount of special preparation was considered necessary for graduates. Bishops only required attendance at two courses of lectures by the Divinity professors. There was no examination to show that anything had been assimilated; a certificate of attendance was sufficient. The deficiencies were partially remedied when an honours school of theology was instituted at Oxford in 1870 and a theological tripos at Cambridge in 1871. This enabled the students concerned to read a number of theological books, but it did not mean that they received training in the more definitely spiritual and pastoral aspects of their future work. Indeed it was difficult to convince men that they needed any additional training.

Evangelicals were once again provoked into action by the initiatives of

[29] See Hardman, *op.cit.*, pp.160, 161.
[30] The *Record*, 9 July 1856, p.2.-
[31] The following comments are based on J.B. Lancelot, *Francis James Chavasse, Bishop of Liverpool* (London, 1929), p.103 f.

non-Evangelical churchmen. The opening of Keble College, Oxford, in 1870 made the lack of an Evangelical college even more glaring. In 1876 Keble College Chapel was opened, as well as colleges at Ely and Leeds, and St Stephen's House at Oxford. Evangelical negligence in the matter of higher education was becoming a matter of acute Evangelical concern. A group of Evangelical clergy and laity realized the gravity of the position. The leaders among them were the retired Bishop of Melbourne, Perry, a former Senior Wrangler, a man of great ability and a true statesman; W.H. Barlow, later Dean of Peterborough; Dean R. Payne Smith, Dean W.H. Fremantle of Ripon, Canon J.C. Ryle, Edward Garbett of Surbiton, Henry Linton of Oxford, W. Carus of Winchester, Henry Wright, Honorary Secretary of the CMS, Professor Birks of Cambridge, John Deacon and F.B. Wright. They raised £53,000. In 1877 they bought a house in Oxford and started Wycliffe Hall, with the Rev. R.B. Girdlestone as principal, and just one student. Progress was slow at first. Opposition in a conservative university was considerable. In 1878 there were four Oxford men resident, four in 1879, ten in 1880, three in 1881 and twelve in 1882. By 1884 there were financial difficulties but the college continued on its way. The principal won the respect, if not the favour, of the ecclesiastical Oxford of his day. By the time he resigned in 1889, nearly 150 graduates had passed through Wycliffe Hall. Under the subsequent principal, F.J. Chavasse, the work and reputation of the college was consolidated and enhanced.

Meanwhile, in Cambridge, Ridley Hall had been founded.[32] A scheme for an Evangelical establishment had been mooted by the Rev. E.H. Carr in two articles in the *Christian Observer* in July and August 1875. He was concerned that the Evangelical clergy of the future should be equipped with solid learning in order to contend with the prevailing ritualistic and rationalistic teaching and propaganda. He discussed the matter with Handley Moule, who was then Senior Dean of Trinity College. Moule was sceptical. Nevertheless, after Wycliffe Hall was opened, the Cambridge men, whom Carr had inspired with his ideal, resolved to carry out a parallel enterprise. They raised over £20,000 and secured a site. The memorial stone of the new college, Ridley Hall, was laid on 17 October 1879, and the building officially opened on 28 January 1881. Handley Moule was selected as the principal. During the first term there were fourteen students in residence. The opposition to the college was not as great as with Wycliffe Hall, largely because of the strong Evangelical tradition in Cambridge.

[32] The fullest account of the origins of Ridley Hall is F.W.B. Bullock, *The History of Ridley Hall, Cambridge* (1941), 3 vols; but much useful information and comment is to be found in John Battersby Harford and Frederick Charles Macdonald, *Handley Carr Glyn Moule Bishop of Durham* (London, 1922), and this section owes much to that work.

The two theological Halls acted as something of a focal point for Evangelicalism within the universities. This was especially so at Cambridge, not only because of the vibrant Evangelical life of the university but because of the remarkable influence of Handley Moule. But in both cases the principals and the training given by the colleges helped to provide a much-needed guiding and restraining hand in the new Evangelical developments of the period.

Some thought that the new colleges with their Evangelical basis were too theologically narrow. The Divinity professors, perturbed by the limitations imposed, initiated a broader clergy training school, which was established at Cambridge at about the same time as Ridley Hall. It later became Westcott House.[33]

---

[33] See Bentley, *op.cit.*

12

Movements of Renewal

Revivalism is to be distinguished from evangelism, although it is sometimes difficult to determine when the one merges into the other. With a revival there is a sudden, spontaneous, noteworthy and sustained increase in the extent and intensity of the commitment of a number of individuals in a particular area to the beliefs and practices of their faith. The corporate life of those concerned is rapidly and significantly energized, and there is a renewed sense of fellowship. Accompanying this is an increased concern for the conversion of those who do not share the same faith; and a wave of conversions among both 'outsiders' and 'nominal' believers. In the Christian tradition revivals have frequently included glossolalia (speaking in tongues) and bodily manifestations of intense mental and spiritual experience. Somewhat in contrast, evangelistic campaigns, however successful, are usually pre-planned, and consist of organized activities. They have less of the spontaneous upsurge of religious renewal and revitalization which is the central feature of revivals.

Viewed globally, the most prominent, widely effective and well-attested revivals in the eighteenth century were in North America and the British Isles. It was the same in the nineteenth century. Also, as the eighteenth century Great Awakening in America and the Evangelical Revival in Great Britain originated almost concurrently, so the most notable revivals of the following century in these countries began within the same two or three years, between 1857 and 1860.

In 1857 in Hamilton, Ontario, there was suddenly what a local newspaper described as a 'Revival Extraordinary'.[1] It was reported that on the first day of the movement about twenty people professed conversion, and that this quickly increased to approximately forty-five such professions each day. The news of what was happening created an expectation of further revivals.

In parallel with the Hamilton revival, a certain Jeremiah Lanphier started a prayer meeting in Fulton Street, in a down-town area of New York. Six were present at the first gathering and forty the following week. It was decided to hold the meetings daily instead of weekly. Soon there were so many participants that three simultaneous meetings had to be held in the same building. The seats were all filled and the passages were crowded; it was difficult for people to pass in and out. Within six months about ten thousand businessmen were gathering daily in the city for prayer, in halls, churches and even theatres. Conversions were frequent.

The effect of these localized revivals was felt throughout the nation. It spread into the south as far as Texas, to the north into New England and as far as the western seaboard. Revivals were reported in such urban areas as Boston, Providence, New Haven, New Jersey and Philadelphia, and in many of the pioneer settlements. Each week hundreds or thousands of conversions were recorded. The revival continued for many months with unabated effectiveness, and lasted in total for about two years. There was no special evangelistic mission, no charismatic leader or powerful preacher: the movement had an impetus and dynamism which depended on the ordinary ministry of ordained men, and the daily witness of lay people to a faith which had transformed their lives. The total effect was considerable, and it could not be hidden. It proved to be the prelude to revival in Ireland, Scotland, Wales and, to a lesser extent, England.

In Ulster news of the American revival stimulated great interest and anticipation among the churches.[2] The particular centres in the early days of the Ulster revival were Connor in County Antrim, where a prayer meeting took place and also a number of people were converted; Ahoghill, where there was a gathering of three thousand to pray for revival; and Ballymena, where the movement was particularly dramatic. There was

---

[1] The Methodist *Christian Advocate and Journal* of New York, 5 November 1857, quoted in J. Edwin Orr, *The Light of the Nations: Evangelical Renewal and Advance in the Nineteenth Century* (1965), pp.101 f. The 1857-60 revival in North America is also described in Henry Johnson, *Stories of Great Revivals* (1906), John Kent, *Holding the Fort* (1978), William McLoughlin Jnr, *Modern Revivalism: Charles Grandison Finney to Billy Graham* (1959), and J. Edwin Orr, *The Second Evangelical Awakening in America* (1953).

[2] For the revival in Ireland, see J. Samuel Moore, *The Great Revival in Ireland 1859*, and J. Edwin Orr, *The Light of the Nations* (1965).

widespread religious excitement among the population and most of the evangelical churches in the town appear to have overflowed with enquirers. As in America, there were thousands of conversions as the revival gained momentum; but, to a greater extent than in America, there were prostrations and other bodily responses accompanying the various profound spiritual experiences. The revival spread to Coleraine, then to the towns and villages of County Derry, and to Londonderry, Armagh and other parts of the territory.

In Scotland, the news of the American movement was supplemented by tidings of the revival in nearby Ulster.[3] Again meetings for prayer were arranged, and again it was largely through these that the revival was ignited. To them came crowds of people, and within these gatherings many were converted. Aberdeen and Glasgow were two of the first centres, but the awakening was evident throughout south-western Scotland and then, via the Highlands, as far as the western islands. From the early days of 1859 the revival was intensive and extensive in north-east Scotland. In Edinburgh an additional impetus was given by the evangelistic ministry of Charles Finney. He visited the city at that time and evoked a great response, with many converts.

For more than one hundred years before the 1858-60 revival, Wales had experienced a series of spiritual awakenings.[4] There was a revival in 1735 associated with the ministries of Howel Harris, Daniel Rowlands and Howel Davies; another at Llangeitho in 1762 in which Daniel Rowlands was prominent; and possibly at least fifteen revivals between 1762 and 1862, some local, some far-reaching.

The revival of 1858-60 was distinguished from its contemporaries in America, Ulster and Scotland by its association with the labours of one man: David Morgan. In his village, in which the population did not exceed one thousand, there were two hundred adult conversions before the end of 1858. Early in 1859 he began itinerant preaching, which aroused widespread religious ardour throughout the county of Cardiganshire and resulted in nearly nine thousand converts within less than six months. The revival rapidly extended to every county of the Principality. It was characterized by an extraordinary concern to pray, a spirit of unity among the denominations and a powerful evangelistic effort. The population of Wales in 1861 was only about 1,111,000, and yet in 1860 the Rev. John Venn, Prebendary of Hereford, presented the Evangelical Alliance with

[3] The revival in Scotland is described in J. Edwin Orr, *The Light of the Nations* (1965), and *The Second Evangelical Awakening: An account of the Second Worldwide Evangelical Revival beginning in the Mid-Nineteenth Century* (1955).

[4] For the revival in Wales, see Eifion Evans, *When He is Come: An account of the 1858-60 Revival in Wales* (1959), and Kent, *op.cit.*

carefully prepared statistics which showed an increase in two years in the full membership of the various churches amounting to 90,000; and the revival had some time to run.

In England, the revival had less impact.[5] It has been argued that it was of such major proportions that it can justifiably be called a second evangelical awakening.[6] Those who deny that there was such a widespread significant movement point to the similarities between the American, Irish, Scottish and Welsh revivals of 1857–60 and the eighteenth century awakenings in New England under Jonathan Edwards and George Whitefield, and in Britain under Whitefield and the Wesleys. But they say that it is difficult to find even isolated instances, let alone a general movement of like character, in mid-nineteenth century England. It is acknowledged that there were a great number of prayer meetings to encourage a religious awakening, and there was a spate of evangelistic activity; but nothing to compare with the revivals just described.

Throughout the first twenty years of Victoria's reign, American-style revivalism was not regarded with much favour by Evangelicals. The three American revivalists who made the greatest impression in England between 1800 and 1860, Lorenzo Dow, James Caughey and Charles Grandison Finney, gained their greatest support from nonconformists. Dow and Caughey were Methodists and appealed most to their fellow denominationalists; and the association of Finney with the Congregationalist Dr John Campbell of London did nothing to allay Evangelical fears during the eighteen-forties and fifties that revivalism might be used in an effort to subvert the Anglican establishment. Finney's first preaching tour in Britain in 1849 was totally ignored by the *Christian Observer* and the *Record* despite the protracted campaign in London. The *Record* was again noticeably silent on Finney's second tour of Britain in 1858–60.

The press coverage of the 1858–60 revivals did not greatly stimulate Evangelical interest and enthusiasm. The revival in Ireland was at first sympathetically reported in *The Times*; but the extended coverage given by the Irish correspondent was quite hostile and did much to prejudice English opinion against the movement.[7] The *Record* commended the prayer meetings organized by the Evangelical Alliance, but it was not wholehearted in its advocacy of the revival. In March 1859 it published its first reports of religious stirrings in Wales and Scotland. It only wrote of a

---

[5] For the revival in England, see Kent, *op.cit.*, J. Edwin Orr, *The Second Evangelical Awakening: An account of the Second Worldwide Evangelical Revival beginning in the Mid-Nineteenth Century* (1955).

[6] J. Edwin Orr, *The Second Evangelical Awakening in Britain* (1949).

[7] See *The Times*, 17 September 1859, p.8.

few localized rumblings in Yorkshire and the West of England. The *Christian Observer* was more consistently favourable in its treatment, but it only reached a certain segment of Evangelicalism.

The Evangelicals as a whole were chary of excessive religious excitement and especially the physical manifestations which were reported. The effect of the revivals in curing drunkenness and immorality was also hotly debated. Such responses were perhaps symptomatic of a common Evangelical concern to avoid practices identified with the more extreme forms of Methodism.

The extent of Evangelical co-operation in the 1858-60 movement is difficult to gauge. Anthony Thorold at St Giles found a ready response in his area; Samuel Garratt fully supported it; and William Pennefather at Barnet experienced a notable increase in the number of prayer meetings in his parish, with crowds drawn from far afield attending special services addressed by Reginald Radcliffe and others. Radcliffe, Brownlow North and other evangelists intensified their campaigns and gained a new respectability from the interest aroused by events in Ireland.

Nonetheless, the evidence amassed so far indicates that there was nothing in England on the scale of the revival as it developed in America or the Celtic fringes of Great Britain, with its concentrated religious excitement, heightened devotion and largely spontaneous mass conversions. In after years regret was expressed that Evangelicals had not participated more fully in the revival. Samuel Garratt wrote in 1873: 'By the great majority of Evangelical clergymen that Revival was rejected'.[8] Eugene Stock commented that the movement as a whole was not taken up warmly by the Evangelical clergy, and added his appraisal that 'if our clergy had more heartily welcomed the Revival, its effects within the Church of England would have been much greater'.[9]

The link between the revival and later developments, such as the Keswick movement, is a matter of debate.[10] From the third decade of the century onwards 'a small but important Holiness Movement developed on the outskirts of nineteenth-century Protestantism'.[11] It spread from the United States to England and was associated with James Caughey, Phoebe Palmer (and her husband), Robert Pearsall Smith (and his wife) and Asa Mahan. Holiness teaching had swept through American evangelicalism in the middle third of the century, and its influence was felt in England during that time.

[8] The *Record*, 8 August 1873.
[9] Eugene Stock, *My Recollections* (1909), p.83.
[10] For an account of the Keswick movement, see J.C. Pollock, *The Keswick Story* (1964); and for a discussion of the wider holiness movement, including Keswick, see Anne Bentley, 'The Transformation of the Evangelical Party in the Church of England in the later Nineteenth Century' (Durham University Ph.D., 1971), and Kent, *op.cit.*
[11] Kent, *op.cit.*, p.295.

In 1870 Pearsall Smith, a Quaker glass manufacturer from Philadelphia, published *Holiness through Faith*. In it he expounded the doctrines which had been at the core of the holiness movement for decades. He repudiated the assertion that holiness resulted only from a slow process of change. In a 'second conversion' theory, he advocated a post-conversion experience of complete victory over all consciousness of sin. 'Holiness' was something which God gave, and gave suddenly. In 1873 Pearsall Smith toured southern England and the continent, speaking at conferences and consecration meetings. He attracted considerable support, and most significantly from Evan Hopkins, the Rev. E.W. Moore and Sholto Douglas.

As the teaching gained the ear of more Evangelicals, there was opposition from the Evangelical leadership. The doctrine of the immediate, absolute deliverance from all known sin was not acceptable to many of them. Sanctification was discussed at a number of the regular Evangelical gatherings. The frequently-reiterated orthodox view stressed the progressive nature of consecration, and the gradual, but increasing influence of the Holy Spirit in the lives of individuals. At the same time others were impressed by the new teaching, including William Cowper-Temple, Lord Shaftesbury's brother-in-law. In the summer of 1874 he and his wife offered their home, Broadlands Park, for a conference on the lines of the American camp meetings. About one hundred went for one week. They included Evan Hopkins, Stevenson Blackwood, Canon Wilberforce, William Arthur and Samuel Morley. With the agreement of Canon Christopher of St Aldate's, a convention was then arranged at Oxford 'for the Promotion of Scriptural Holiness'. It was estimated that a thousand flocked to it.

There was heated debate among Evangelicals in the next few months. At the suggestion of J.C. Ryle, a conference was called in February 1875 in London, to 'guide into a right channel' the fervour kindled at Oxford.[12] Evan Hopkins, Blackwood and H.F. Bowker represented the new teaching. The counter views were penetratingly presented by such pillars of orthodoxy as Canon Hoare and the Rev. Sir Emilius Bayley.[13] In the meantime a further holiness conference was held at Cheltenham and another, on a grand scale, at Brighton in May and June 1875. This was a key gathering for the movement. It was reckoned that about eight thousand visitors attended, with over two hundred from the continent. A large proportion were nonconformists.

The Brighton convention also represented the peak in the influence of Pearsall Smith. His eclipse was imminent. He returned to America

[12] See the *Record*, 18 November 1874.
[13] See the *Record*, 19, 22 February 1875.

ostensibly because of bad health, but in fact because he had compromised himself with a young woman. His fall from grace was swift and irreparable. It also called in question the plausibility of the new teaching, and brought the issue of Antinomianism to the fore. Nonetheless, despite this scandal, and the opposition of many Evangelicals, the conventions, which were started in various parts of the country, did seem to meet a need. Some of them became annual events, although they were usually not very large. An exception was to be the one at Keswick.

Canon Harford-Battersby, vicar of St John's Keswick, and Robert Wilson, a friend and neighbour, were two of the thousand or so people who attended the Oxford convention of the nascent holiness movement in 1874. They returned with such a vivid sense of spiritual renewal that they soon decided to hold similar meetings the following year in Keswick. At these, so many received help that it was decided to hold a second convention. The numbers at first were quite small and the gatherings received little attention, but the attendance increased. The leadership and support came largely from Church of England men, especially in the earlier years. The clergymen included H.W. Webb-Peploe, Evan H. Hopkins, C.A. Fox and E.W. Moore. H.F. Bowker was also intimately involved. Nonetheless, for a long time the leading Evangelicals held aloof and viewed the convention with undisguised suspicion.

For many years the theology of the holiness movement continued to cause consternation to some Evangelicals, and was even denounced as dangerous heresy. Ryle described the teaching of Pearsall Smith as crude, self-contradictory, one-sided and irreconcilable with scripture.[14] He expounded his view of sanctification in two books, *Holiness* (1877) and *Practical Religion* (1878), which were widely accepted as the traditional Calvinistic interpretation.

Evan Hopkins soon emerged as the leading theologian of the Keswick Convention. He had been a civil engineer before training for ordination, and he was not a profound scholar. His writings conveyed the essence of the Keswick teaching, but the movement needed to attain more balance and sophistication in what it proclaimed. This was achieved with the recruitment in 1886 of Handley C.G. Moule, a former sceptic, as a regular platform speaker. Moule was the scholarly theologian who supplied the necessary guidance. He helped to unite more Evangelicals behind the convention, and to dampen some of the criticism.

Ryle never felt able to appear at the convention, but he denounced any bitterness or coldness towards those who did not share his beliefs or practices. In 1892, on the Sunday following the convention, he entered the big tent with Moody and, before the evangelist preached, he offered a

[14] Letter to the *Record*, 28 May 1875.

prayer. It was a symbolic gesture suggesting that he wanted to live in peace with those who frequented the convention. It also demonstrated a new measure of charity which happily began to typify most of those who were divided in their opinion over this new movement of renewal, although some still questioned the theology of the convention, thought its methods strained and its terminology exaggerated. What is unquestionable is the debt owed to it by the missionary societies, and more especially the Church Missionary Society, as well as many other Christian causes. The church worldwide was aided and enriched as hundreds of convention participants responded to the challenge of Christian service. For this at least all shades of theological opinion and churchmanship could unite in uncritical gratitude.

At the same time that the Keswick Convention was profoundly assisting the work of the church, a movement was taking place in the student world which made its own incalculable contribution.[15] In 1827 five student members of Holy Trinity, Cambridge started a Sunday school in a hall in Jesus Lane. They visited all the houses in the area, inviting the children, and the response was good. Over the years the Sunday school proved to be an influential training-ground for many ordinands and future schoolmasters.

The list of undergraduate helpers is impressive. It includes J.C. Adams (Professor of Astronomy); A. Barry (principal of King's College, London); T.R. Birks (Professor of Moral Philosophy); H.M. Butler (headmaster of Harrow); W.J. Conybeare (co-author with Howsan of *The Life and Epistles of St Paul*); H. Cotterill (Bishop of Edinburgh); G.E.L. Cotton (Bishop of Calcutta); F.W. Farrar (Dean of Canterbury); A.F. Kirkpatrick (Lady Margaret Professor of Divinity); C.F. Mackenzie (Bishop of Central Africa); T. Maxwell (medical missionary in Kashmir); C.J. Vaughan (headmaster of Harrow and, later, Master of the Temple); E.O. Vidal (Bishop of Sierra Leone); and B.F. Westcott (Regius Professor of Divinity and later Bishop of Durham).

The Sunday school helpers in effect formed a small Christian Union in the university. Two of the teachers conceived the idea of the Cambridge Prayer Union; it was supported by their fellow Jesus Lane workers, and in 1862 the Daily Prayer Meeting was started. In 1877 the Cambridge Inter-Collegiate Christian Union was founded. In Oxford a Prayer Union was started in 1850 and a Daily Prayer Meeting in 1867.

---

[15] For the movement in the universities and colleges, see O.R. Barclay, *Whatever Happened to the Jesus Lane Lot?* (1977), F.D. Coggan (Ed.), *Christ and the Colleges: A History of the IVFEU* (1934), Douglas Johnson, *Contending for the Faith: A History of the Evangelical Movement in the Universities and Colleges* (1979), J.C. Pollock, *The Cambridge Movement* (1953), J.S. Reynolds, *The Evangelicals at Oxford (1735-1871)* (1953), and Tissington Tatlow, *The Story of the Student Christian Movement of Great Britain and Ireland* (1933).

In the latter part of the century an important influence was introduced from America. In the wake of the Moody campaigns, the Student Volunteer Missionary Union had been formed in Massachusetts, at Moody's first college conference in 1886. Five years later one of the leaders of the movement, Robert Wilder, came to England. In February 1892 he initiated a Cambridge Student Volunteer Missionary Union; and in April 1892 representatives from Oxford, Cambridge, London, Belfast and the Scottish universities met in Edinburgh to inaugurate the Student Volunteer Missionary Union of Great Britain and Ireland, whose main aim was to inspire students to offer themselves for missionary service. One of the Cambridge Seven, Arthur Polhill-Turner, became travelling secretary after returning from China.

By May 1893 the Union had 491 members, of whom 25 had sailed, 13 had been accepted for the mission field and 46 belonged to missionary institutions. The first student conference was held at Keswick in 1893, the week before the convention, and there the title Inter-University Christian Union was adopted. In 1894, again at Keswick, the American watchword 'the evangelization of the world in this generation' was taken as a rallying call to service. The whole student movement was invigorated, led and supported largely by Anglican Evangelicals. It thus fed the Church of England more than any other branch of the church, although its effects were not restricted either denominationally or geographically. It was one of a number of forces which helped to boost missionary endeavour in the closing years of Victoria's reign; a theme which will be taken up in a later chapter.

13

Evangelicals in Action

With some distinguished exceptions, it is in the main true that the nineteenth century Evangelicals 'are known to the world, not by their writings, which are forgotten, but by their lives, which never can be forgotten'.[1] They 'are remembered for what they did rather than for their theology'.[2] No social, economic or indeed general history of the century can with justice ignore the work of Wilberforce and his fellow Evangelicals in their fight for the freedom of the slave, or the lifelong labours of Lord Shaftesbury in the cause of factory legislation.

But the widespread social work of the Evangelicals in these years went well beyond this. 'Evangelicalism in the nineteenth century was, in its practical outworkings, a religion which functioned largely through an extensive network of societies'.[3] By means of these societies, and through voluntary charity, Evangelicals, as well as others, provided relief for the destitute and downtrodden, the uneducated, orphans, ex-prisoners, the blind, deaf and crippled, those sick in body or mind, the aged and many more necessitous groups. In addition, social and welfare work was

[1] F.W. Cornish, *History of the English Church in the Nineteenth Century* (1910), Vol.I, p.15, quoted in Kathleen Heasman, *Evangelicals in Action: An appraisal of their social work in the Victorian era* (1962), p.15.
[2] Heasman, *op.cit.*, p.15.
[3] Anne Bentley, 'The Transformation of the Evangelical Party in the Church of England in the later Nineteenth Century' (Durham University Ph.D., 1971), p.334.

undertaken by means of ragged schools, children's homes and orphanages, industrial schools, special work centres, training ships, sailors' rests and other institutions. The failings and shortcomings in the Evangelical motives and methods are manifest; but despite their imperfections, the achievements in meeting some of the clamant needs and in helping some of the casualties of an emergent industrial society are impressive.

Lord Shaftesbury (1801–85)

It is appropriate that any survey of Evangelical involvement in social work and social thinking in the Victorian era should begin with Lord Shaftesbury.[4] His contribution to social reform and social action was outstanding. The sixth Earl of Shaftesbury was married to Lady Anne Spencer, the daughter of the fourth Earl of Marlborough, in 1796. Anthony was born in 1801, their fourth child and first son. His relationship with his parents was not congenial. In his diary he referred to his mother as a 'dreadful woman' whose 'whole pleasure is in finding fault'.[5] He considered his father an honest man, who did his duty to the public, but as a parent he reckoned that he left much to be desired. 'As to friendship and affection between him and me . . . outward civility and only civility is the utmost that can be looked for'.[6] He always claimed that the only real friend of his childhood was his servant and maid to his mother, Maria Millis. She died soon after his eighth birthday, leaving him her watch and seal: and he took great pride in wearing the watch to the end of his life, saying that it had been given to him by the best friend he ever had in the world. It was Maria Millis who nurtured him in Bible reading and prayer. Shaftesbury (this title will be used throughout, although it was not until 1851 that he inherited the family name) recalled his schooldays with displeasure. He much more enjoyed Oxford, where he obtained a first in classics in 1822.

In 1826 he entered Parliament as a Tory. One of his first ventures as a Member drew him into an area of social concern, for in 1827 he served on a select committee of the House to investigate the subject of lunacy. In 1828 he seconded a motion for the introduction of Bills to amend the Lunacy

---

[4] For the life and work of Lord Shaftesbury the main secondary sources are G. Battiscombe, *Shaftesbury: A Biography of the Seventh Earl* (1974); G. Best, *Shaftesbury* (1964); E. Hodder, *The Life and Work of the Seventh Earl of Shaftesbury*, K.G, 3 vols (1886), and Geoffrey B.A.M. Finlayson, *The Seventh Earl of Shaftesbury, 1801-1885* (1981), to which the present writer is especially indebted.

[5] The National Register of Archives, London, Shaftesbury (Broadlands) MSS, SHA/PD/1, 18-23 September 1825, quoted in Finlayson, *op.cit.*, p.14.

[6] The National Register, *op.cit.*, SHA/PD/1, 1828, quoted in Finlayson, *op.cit.*, p.14.

Laws, which were severely defective and, in practice, left many persons, especially paupers, outside their scope. In 1828 he was appointed to a commissionership at the India Board of Control, which gave him responsibility for managing the affairs of the Board in the Commons. In 1833 Lord William Bentinck, an Evangelical, was made Governor-General of India. Shaftesbury's term of office at the India Board coincided with the effective beginning of a reform movement in India and, in conjunction with Lord Bentinck, he did his best to encourage it. This included the promotion of 'good government' and resistance to such practices as sutteeism – the burning of widows on the death of their husbands – which, despite strong opposition, was outlawed by Bentwick in 1829.

It was in 1833 that Shaftesbury became involved in an issue which was to remain an urgent concern for much of his life: factory reform. Popular agitation for a shorter working week had been organized in Lancashire and Yorkshire since about 1815, and became known as the Ten Hours Movement. Notable leadership was given by Richard Oastler, and in Parliament by Michael Sadler; but in 1832 Sadler was defeated at the general election. Shaftesbury accepted the offer to take on the mantle of Sadler and reintroduce the Bill for reduced factory working hours. He was little acquainted with the subject, but he was soon to be heartily committed to the cause.

Over a number of decades he experienced defeat and disillusionment, and the victories achieved were at the expense of much labour and disappointment. Opposition was both fierce and subtle. The factory owners were strongly represented in the House of Commons. Any measures which appeared to threaten or interfere with the production of wealth and the prosperity of industry were forcefully resisted by mill-owners, mine-owners and others with vested interest in the *status quo*. Obstruction and delaying tactics took various forms, including commissions of inquiry and amendments designed to displace proposed reforms by half-measures. The intensity of the opposition and the forms it took were reminiscent of the reaction to the anti-slavery campaign. The Factory Act of 1847 largely achieved that for which Shaftesbury and his fellow reformers had striven. In 1874 and 1878 further Acts consolidated previous measures. The factory legislation of the eighteen-seventies was the culmination of the process to which Shaftesbury had contributed so much.

After factory reform, the two matters of social concern to which Shaftesbury devoted most time and energy in Parliament were the reform of the laws relating to lunacy, and public health. As has been noted, the reform of the legislation on lunacy had demanded his attention within a few months of his entry to the House of Commons. Between 1828 and 1845 he served on the Metropolitan Lunacy Commission. In 1845 he successfully introduced a Bill which replaced this body by the permanent Lunacy Commission responsible to the Lord Chancellor. It consisted of five unpaid commissioners and six full-time professional commissioners, three doctors and three barristers, each paid a salary of £1,500 per annum. There was a secretary, paid £800, and two clerks. Concurrently with this, Shaftesbury introduced a Bill which made it obligatory on Justices of the Peace of a county or borough to make provision for asylums if they had not already done so. By these Bills it was anticipated that greater control and regulation would be exercised, especially for the benefit of pauper patients. Shaftesbury was to play an important part in their implementation as he had done in their initiation. At the first meeting of the new Commission he was elected permanent chairman, and he was actively engaged in the work to the end of his life.

For forty years and more Shaftesbury was heavily involved in various aspects of public health. In the eighteen-forties he worked in association with Edwin Chadwick, and their co-operation later became a prominent feature of the public health movement. In 1844 he joined with other public health enthusiasts in founding the Society for Improving the Condition of the Labouring Classes. It provided allotments for rural labourers, and aimed to improve the houses of the poor in the town and the country. As a pilot scheme it built a number of houses in the heavily populated urban area of Pentonville. It offered four per cent as a return on capital subscribed to assist its projects. Shaftesbury was chairman of the committee appointed to manage the affairs of the society. It achieved some success in the construction of two blocks of model lodging-houses in the area of the Old Pancras Road and Mile End New Town, but it did not persuade speculative builders to invest in working-class housing. Perhaps the proffered return on subscribed capital was too small.

In 1848 a Public Health Act established a central commission with considerable powers for initiating public health measures, and for introducing the machinery of local public health administration. Shaftesbury accepted the unpaid office of third commissioner. In this capacity he was parliamentary spokesman for the commission. He toiled strenuously on behalf of the commission as it faced such issues as a severe outbreak of cholera in 1848 and 1849. He had to contend with much public indifference, intense resistance from vested interests and inadequate government funding. He also continued to give support to measures designed to improve health, such as the proposal in 1853 by Lord Lyttelton to extend the practice of vaccination, the Public Health Act of 1866 which firmly established central control in certain matters where local authorities did not act, and the Artisans and Labourers Dwelling Act of 1868 which made provision for the demolition of insanitary premises. As with factory reforms, the eighteen-seventies saw a culmination of public health legislation. The Public Health Act of 1875 provided much-needed consolidation of existing sanitary legislation. The Artisans Dwelling Act of the same year was an impressive step forward in tackling the problem of working-class housing in major towns, despite many difficulties in its implementation. Shaftesbury supported it, and welcomed its boldness.

Almost at the same time as his initial active involvement with public health matters in 1844, Shaftesbury took up the cause of ragged schools for destitute children. Ragged schools had been founded in London in the first few years of the decade by Sunday school teachers associated with the London City Mission. The purpose was to teach children who were prevented by their poverty or ragged condition from attending any other place of religious instruction. In 1844 a number of teachers in London ragged schools founded the Ragged School Union and Shaftesbury accepted the presidency. He was no mere figurehead. He energetically visited slum areas and helped to found ragged schools. He took a lively interest in all the activities started under the auspices of the Union in London, such as the shoeblacks' brigades, the refuges and dormitories, which provided board and lodging for children, an emigration scheme for children and the placing of children in employment.

The range of Shaftesbury's involvement in causes for the well-being of others was so great and varied that it can only be indicated in brief. In addition to what has already been mentioned, he was intensely concerned for orphanages, homes for the crippled, and for homeless families, destitute incurables, mental after-care, the blind, cabmen, needlewomen, members of the merchant service and many others. In 1866 a dream of his became a reality when the government granted a gun frigate on the Thames, the *Chichester*, to be used for housing homeless boys and training them for trades or for naval service. Another ship, the *Arethusa*, was provided in 1874. After the death of his wife, Minny, in 1872, he set up the 'Emily Loan Fund', in order to assist the Flower and Watercress Girls' Mission. He was also Chairman, from 1884, of the London Society for the Prevention of Cruelty to Children; and, illustrative of his breadth of interest, he was closely associated with the Victoria Street Society for the Protection of Animals from Vivisection which was founded in 1875.

Despite the variety of his philanthropic interests and activities, they were all undertaken within a discernible ideological and theological framework. Shaftesbury was a Tory who opposed any undue extension of the franchise. He distrusted any major change in the political structure. His ideal was 'a stable and hierarchic society bound together by mutual obligations between rich and poor'.[7] He believed that only by showing care and concern for the poor could the rich hope to survive. This Tory

[7] Finlayson, *op.cit.*, p.76.

paternalism was in keeping with the social and, to some degree, too, the political aspects of Evangelicalism. It was consistent with such a philosophy that, with all his concern for the well-being of the labouring classes, he could write of the 'two great demons in morals and politics, Socialism and Chartism . . . stalking through the land'.[8] He was fearful that the philosophy of 'infidels' and 'democrats' would appeal to the ignorant and excitable masses and lead to social revolution. Rather, he urged the governing classes, in their own interest as well as for the good of others, to meet their responsibilities to the less fortunate.

He was concerned that social and working conditions should not be allowed to hinder or prevent people from pursuing their own moral and spiritual welfare. Social improvement, as well as being good in its own right, was a means of enabling men and women and boys and girls to become Christians. In 1840 he wrote that laws should assume the proper function of protecting the helpless; but it was more important to build churches and send forth ministers of religion. 'All hopes are groundless, all legislation weak, all conservatism nonsense', he wrote, 'without this alpha and omega of policy'.[9] This standpoint was characteristic of the Evangelicalism of the time. Evangelicals who considered it their duty to make some attempt to relieve the suffering which they saw around them and help the needy, either thought that evangelism should precede material help, since a change of heart would make a person more responsive to such help, or that social improvement could facilitate evangelism.[10] In this respect, in all his social and philanthropic work, Shaftesbury was at one with his fellow Evangelicals in having evangelism as his outstanding motive. Even so, and making allowance for a somewhat exaggerated sense of his own isolation and sensitivity to the hostility of others, he felt that he did not receive sufficient support from his co-religionists in matters of social improvement.[11]

---

[8] The *Quarterly Review*, December 1840, quoted in Finlayson, *op.cit.*, p.126.

[9] *The Quarterly Review*, (1840), LXVII, 181, quoted in Finlayson, *op.cit.*, p.127.

[10] See Heasman, *op.cit.*, p.20.

[11] See the comments of Shaftesbury in the National Register SHA/PD/2, 4 July 1840, SHA/PD/2, 16 May 1842. There were grounds for Shaftesbury's attitude. To take but one example. One of the springs of the early movement for factory reform was a small group of Yorkshire Evangelicals who had first-hand knowledge of conditions in the mills and factories. A number of Evangelical clergy gave the movement their support, but by no means all the Evangelicals in Yorkshire participated, and when the proletarian wing of the movement threatened to move into social radicalism, most of the Evangelicals quickly withdrew. During the struggles of the eighteen-forties only a few West Riding Evangelical businessmen stood with Shaftesbury and maintained their support for reform. The Evangelicals had found themselves, as in other reform movements, in alliance with groups whose objectives differed fundamentally from their own, and whose policies threatened the religious, social and political order to the defence of which they were committed. (This example is taken from I.S. Rennie, 'Evangelicalism and English Public Life, 1823-1850' (University of Toronto Ph.D., 1962), pp.370-400).

Politically, Shaftesbury's approach was not squarely within the main-stream of either of the two main parliamentary parties. In Parliament he was concerned to promote legislation to ameliorate social ills. This was a policy not ignored by either Whigs or Tories, but not given priority by them. It depended on individual initiative. Outside Parliament he mainly relied on personal acts of philanthropy to meet specific social needs. He did not identify within the Tory party either with Peelite thought and practice or with the 'Young England' group which had overtones of High Church-manship. He favoured limited state intervention when it appeared to offer the only effective remedy for a social problem and was, for example, willing to co-operate with Chadwick, despite his Benthamite assump-tions, to secure a centralized system of public health. But such government intervention should, in his view, be restricted to helping those who could not help themselves.

Both within and without Parliament, Shaftesbury's simple and over-riding belief was in 'his duty to act as a faithful steward of his God-given talents and possessions, and to use them to enlarge the area of freedom and opportunity open to the less fortunate so that they might develop their physical, moral and spiritual potential'.[12] He tried to awaken attention to the needs of the poor and the powers and duties of the rich; and to encourage remedial provisions for the poor and needy. In all these matters his contributions and achievements were outstanding. His political and social affiliations, his strong religious convictions and his inner problems of personality and temperament, to an extent imprisoned him within a quite narrow social philosophy. He also had notable inadequacies, as with the management of his own estates, where undue trust in a dishonest steward and administrative incompetence rather than indifference or disregard resulted in unfortunate financial failings and unfulfilled obligations to estate residents. Nevertheless, it is remarkable to what extent he overcame his shortcomings in order to serve the poor and the deprived of his generation. 'Dutiful service to God and to man: this was the daunting and demanding task which he set himself and which, driven by unwearying dedication, he faithfully discharged'.[13]

Evangelical Concerns

A number of upper-class families, both Anglican and non-Anglican, were associated with Shaftesbury or the Evangelicals more generally in their concern for philanthropic work and social reform. These included Lord

[12] Finlayson, op.cit., p.326.
[13] Finlayson, op.cit., p.609.

Mount-Temple, Shaftesbury's brother-in-law, the Aberdeens, the Kinnairds, the Waldegraves, Quintin Hogg and the Hon. H.T. Pelham. Several well to do middle class families were prominent, such as those of Samuel Morley, a director of the stocking-knitters firm; C.E. Tritton, E.M. Denny and the Barclays, some of whose members were partners in a banking house which managed the affairs of many evangelical charities. Among the wealthy traders who subsidized Evangelical charity were the Corys, a firm of Cardiff shipbuilders and colliery-owners, the Crossley brothers of Manchester, William Palmer the biscuit manufacturer, and a London city business magnate Francis Peek. Professional men who assisted in charitable activities included Sir Arthur Blackwood, the chief of the Post Office in the eighteen-eighties, Sir Robert Anderson of the CID, Scotland Yard, and General Gordon of Khartoum. Although Shaftesbury bemoaned the apathy of his co-religionists, these and a host of Evangelicals were active in many spheres of social work. There was a fairly close-knit group of Evangelicals responsible for a large number of enterprises, especially in the second half of the century.

Most of the actual day to day work of numberless Evangelical societies was performed by an army of middle class 'ladies', who gave a day or so each week to such activities. They had little training but frequently had the experience of managing a large Victorian household. Their interest in social work was often aroused by popular Christian literature. Mrs Sherwood's *The Fairchild Family* or Mrs Sewell's *Mother's Last Words* in the early part of the century had a middle-class household as their background, but by the mid-century the typical setting became the homes of the poor. The duty of those in better circumstances to help those not so well off was a recurring theme. The stories were in a highly emotional style with dramatic conversions and death scenes. Some of the books were immensely popular. *Jessica's First Prayer* (1866) by Hesba Stretton was a simple story of a girl waif awakened to the meaning of Christianity, and showed an extraordinarily accurate knowledge of the life of destitute children in a large city. It sold over one and a half million copies and was translated into every European language as well as some Asiatic and African ones. Other publications included *Christie's Old Organ* by Mrs O.F. Walton, which told the story of the hard life of poor old Treffy the organ-grinder; *A Peep behind the Scenes*, describing the adventures of a travelling circus family; *Saved at Sea*, the tale of a lighthouse-keeper; *Teddy's Button*, a story of village life, and *Probable Sons*, an account of the difficulties of an adopted child, both by Amy Le Feuvre. Writers such as Catherine Marsh, Mrs Ranyard, Mrs Wightman and Mrs Bayley reached a wide readership. They gave graphic accounts of their author's social work among navvies and the poor in the slums, enlivened by dramatic descriptions of the circumstances of actual people, and vivid case histories full of interesting details. Such writings not only attracted many volunteers into social work but also inspired some of the pioneers. Interest in social work was also evoked by the magazines of the larger societies, such as the *London City Mission Magazine* and the *Missing Link Magazine* of Mrs Ranyard's mission; periodicals like *Leisure Hour* and *Good Words*, which were not exclusively Evangelical but often described Evangelical social work, and the Evangelical weekly, *The Christian*.[14] The Moody-Sankey visits further stimulated Evangelical concern for social action.

The social work of Evangelicals was largely undertaken on an interdenominational or non-denominational basis. Its volume and range were bewildering and impressive.[15] There were large general city missions like the Field Lane Institution (1841) at Clerkenwell, the George Yard Mission (1854) in Whitechapel, the South London Mission in Bermondsey, the Golden Lane Mission (1862) in the City and the Tower Hamlets Mission (1870). These contrasted with small enterprises such as the Hammersmith Mission (1871) which occupied a small cottage in the area, and the East Plumstead Mission (1895) which met in a skittle saloon at the back of the Prince of Orange public house. And there were city-wide organizations like the London City Mission. For all such missions direct evangelism was a primary purpose, although many of them also widened their activities to embrace the social needs of those to whom they ministered. Some of the missions concentrated entirely upon the young, as in the case of the Juvenile Christian Mission (1875) and the Children's Mission, Camberwell (1896). Others, such as Mrs Ranyard's London Bible and Domestic Mission (1857), specifically helped women. In the cities Evangelicals were also active in providing accommodation for the homeless poor. The Metropolitan Free Dormitory Association, which was organized by Lord Shaftesbury and the Rev. William Pennefather in 1857 to cover the poorer parts of London, was the largest of these. For some of the very poor, emigration was an opportunity for a new beginning, and Evangelicals helped to facilitate this by means of bodies such as the East End Family Emigration Society (1868), and centres like the Emigrants' Home at Blackwall near London Docks, opened in 1883 to accommodate families and single people while they were waiting for departure.

Evangelicals did much to meet the needs of disadvantaged young people. The ragged-school movement, to which reference has already been made, was largely initiated and managed by Evangelicals. It offered free help and instruction to countless poor and neglected children. At the

---

[14] *The Christian* had first been published from 1859-70 as *The Revival*, to record the events and results of the 1857-60 revivals, but was continued as a paper of general Evangelical interest.

[15] See Heasman, *op.cit.*, for a fuller account of the many agencies of social work mentioned in the following brief survey.

outset such schools were located in barns, cowsheds, stables, covered-in railway arches or disused store rooms. As they grew in size, conducted regular weekday classes and became more firmly established, they rented their own premises, and occasionally owned them. The teaching was simple and it was often given amid uproar, unsavoury remarks and lewd jokes. The priority was to reclaim and civilize the children and make them useful members of the community. Much of the work had little to do with book learning. Emphasis was given to the provision of better food and clothing, lodgings for those who had no home, suitable work for those who had to support themselves, and religious services for both the children and their families.

Other societies were closely linked with the ragged schools. Thus the Destitute Children's Dinner Society (1867) was formed to give free meals to hungry children at the schools and Christian missions; shoeblack brigades were started to train the boys as shoeblacks; and the National Society for the Prevention of Cruelty to Children aimed to protect children from cruelty, and secure changes in the law to give more legal protection to children.

While the ragged-school movement catered for children from very poor and ineffective homes, Evangelicals also responded to the needs of those children of the poor who had no home at all. The Waifs and Strays Society was founded in 1881 with the renting of a house to provide for starving homeless children. Many of the homes evolved from ragged schools. One example was the National Refuges for Homeless and Destitute Children which sprang from a ragged school in a hayloft over a cowshed in Streatham Street, St Giles, and became the Shaftesbury Homes. Another was the Manchester and Salford Refuges. This originated in 1870 with a refuge in Quay Street housed in a dark ground-floor room and two cellars with hammocks in upstairs rooms. It was followed by the opening of six orphanages; and it ended as the Manchester and Salford Boys' and Girls' Welfare Society which had several organizations for the young. Evangelicals controlled most of the children's homes of the nineteenth century. They also had an important influence in determining future methods and principles of child care.

The Regent Street Polytechnic, which was later to be part of the Polytechnic of Central London, had its roots in the Evangelical concern for teenagers, and more especially in the life and work of Quintin Hogg.[16] In his Christian Institute in Long Acre technical and trade education was provided in addition to the usual Bible study and elementary teaching.

---

[16] See Heasman, op.cit., pp.121-124, and also Ethel Wood, The Polytechnic and Its Founder Quintin Hogg (1904, revised and enlarged edition, 1932).

The boys attended from 7 to 8 am for one penny a day, which included breakfast at the end of the class. They then went to their own places of work. Such was the popularity of the Institute that it soon became too small. In 1882 it was transferred to a building in Regent Street which, for over forty years, had been the Royal Polytechnic Institute.

Within twelve months there were 100 classes and about 5,000 students. Most of the courses lasted seven months and it was possible to take the City and Guilds examinations. Day as well as evening and early morning classes were introduced. The Polytechnic had a fourfold purpose: to develop the spiritual, intellectual, physical and social aspects of character. Duty to other less fortunate people was also a part of its philosophy and practice. The students organized their own mission among the very poor, ran a club for street boys and saved their pence to send the club members for short holidays. The Regent Street Polytechnic under the leadership of Quintin Hogg also played an important part in the development of technical education in England. Its example, at a time of increasing foreign trade competition, was a spur to the inclusion of technical subjects in educational plans. Technical colleges and trade schools were started and technical education gradually became a valued part of the national educational system.

Evangelicals were intensely interested in moral as well as general education. They were active in the cause of temperance, and more specifically in the Band of Hope movement. It was as a consequence of a meeting chaired by Lord Shaftesbury that the United Kingdom Band of Hope Union was formed in 1855 to unite the various separate societies. By the end of the century the union had some 26,000 bands with over three million registered members. Many of the bands were attached to churches and all held a weekly meeting in which children were asked to sign the pledge. The Hon. W.F. Cowper-Temple, Samuel Morley and F.A. Bevan also took a leading part in providing coffee houses, coffee rooms, coffee palaces or taverns in most towns as an alternative to the public house. Evangelicals were aware that all these measures had no power to influence the inveterate drinker, so in order to help with that particular problem they established retreats and reformatories.

Both Evangelicals and High Churchmen were anxious to reform the prostitute. Although a few small societies were started by the Hon. and Rev. Baptist Noel, Theophilus Smith, Lieutenant J. Blackmore and others in the eighteen-thirties, it was not until the eighteen-fifties that Evangelicals made serious attempts to offer prostitutes a different sort of life. The Rescue Society (1853), the London Female Preventive and Reformatory Institute (1857) and the Homes of Hope (1860) were large societies. Also, from about 1860 onwards many small Evangelical rescue homes for women were opened. The majority of these had a friendly atmosphere where the social life was not regimented. As far as possible the residents were free to develop their own personalities. The larger societies also provided facilities for the confinement of unmarried mothers and the care of newly-born children. In addition they arranged for a number of the women to attend appropriate training homes in order to give them a viable alternative career.

In 1885 the National Vigilance Association was founded, with W. A. Coote, an Evangelical, as its secretary, in an effort to ensure that the provisions of the 1885 Criminal Law Amendment Act, especially in relation to prostitution, were effectively enacted. The association was concerned particularly with the suppression of houses of ill repute, the control of obscene and indecent literature and the registration of servants' agencies. It had limited success, and indeed despite the work of Evangelicals and others there was little reduction in the amount of prostitution in the later nineteenth century. But there was a great change in public attitudes. Sexual matters were discussed with greater freedom. 'The more understanding and kindly attitude towards the prostitute, which had been introduced by the Evangelicals, became a common approach'.[17]

Evangelicals also attempted to provide for the needs of prisoners and ex-prisoners. Susanna Meredith continued the work which Elizabeth Fry had started for female prisoners by caring for women in prisons, making adequate arrangements for after-care and rehabilitation, and helping to look after the other members of the family in the absence of the mother. The Royal Society for Discharged Prisoners, which was set up at Charing Cross in 1857 with the support of Lord Kinnaird, tried to help long-term prisoners either to return to their families and find local employment, or to emigrate.

The welfare of the physically and mentally handicapped was yet another cause which elicited Evangelical sympathy and response. It was an Evangelical, Dr Thomas Rhodes Armitage, who founded the British and Foreign Blind Association for Promoting the Education and Employment of the Blind (1868); it became the Royal National Institute for the Blind. The Christian Blind Relief Society of 1843 was one of a number of societies established to help the blind financially, and the first organization to grant pensions to blind people of all ages. In the eighteen-seventies homes for blind children were founded. By these and other means the Evangelicals were almost entirely responsible for the awakened interest in the blind in the second half of the nineteenth century.

It was two members of the Clapham Sect, Henry Thornton and William Wilberforce, who 'awoke the nation's conscience to the fact that the deaf were a group in the community in need of help, and that nothing was

[17] Heasman, op.cit., p.167.

being done to teach the deaf children of the poor'.[18] In 1792 Henry
Thornton was involved in the formation of a society to undertake the
education of the indigent deaf in Bermondsey. It was expanded in
response to demand and became the Royal School for Deaf and Dumb
Children. A number of Evangelicals were included among the education-
alists who continued to provide for the needs of the deaf in the late
nineteenth century, and missions for the deaf depended to a great extent on
Evangelical involvement.

In any account of the care of the sick by Evangelicals the work of the
Mildmay Institute deserves special mention. Medical work in connection
with the Mildmay mission was started at centres in Bethnal Green,
Walworth, Old Ford and Whitechapel. Full-time medical staff were ass-
isted by deaconesses who had taken the course in nursing started by the
Institution in 1866. The Mildmay mission hospital was opened in Bethnal
Green in 1877. It was rebuilt in 1892 with accommodation for 400 patients.
Connected with it were several convalescent homes and a home for the aged.
The hospital continued to meet the needs of the poor well into the twentieth
century, and represented home medical missionary work at its best.

Specialist medical work was undertaken by a variety of other Evangelical societies and organizations. The North Eastern Dispensary for
Women in Bethnal Green (1867) and the East London Dispensary for
Women (1868) concentrated upon the welfare and care of women. The
East London Nursing Association was started in 1868 and the Ranyard
nurses began their work in the same year, offering domiciliary nursing in
the homes of the poor. The introduction of an explicit religious emphasis
into nursing and other social work was criticized by some, including
Florence Nightingale, but the Evangelicals persisted in it.

In their philanthropic concern the Evangelicals did not neglect those
who encountered hardship or moral temptation in their places of employment. They provided institutions and homes for sailors and soldiers; care
for navvies by means of soup kitchens, nursing and general welfare centres
for railwaymen which offered food, reading and recreation facilities and
accommodation, and similar amenities for cabmen and policemen. The
Evangelicals tried to assist working women whose occupations were
reckoned to place them in exceptional moral danger – such as theatrical
workers, barmaids, city work-girls and needlewomen – or those who,
through lack of training, were forced to take unsuitable employment.

Assessment

'Most of the great philanthropic movements of the century have sprung

[18] *Ibid.*, p.200.

from the Evangelicals',[19] Lord Shaftesbury declared almost at the end of his life, in 1884: and he was right. What they attempted and what they achieved was massive and significant. The Evangelical voluntary organizations dealt in a practical way with many of the most blatant Victorian social problems. They also established principles and set the pattern for later developments of social welfare work. Nevertheless, they were not beyond criticism and reproach.

The Victorian Evangelicals have been accused of lacking social policy.[20] They have been censured for accepting the prevailing class structure, for being concerned with palliatives rather than radical social change.

There is some truth in this. The essential conservatism of Shaftesbury and other Evangelicals is undeniable. They largely accepted the *status quo* and performed their good works with little questioning of the social framework. They were pragmatists rather than theorists, and where they did theorize, as with Shaftesbury, they upheld and defended the existing order in its essentials, and deprecated any revolutionary change. They attacked particular social ills, such as aspects of the factory labour system, certain features in the administration of the lunacy system, and the neglect of various socially underprivileged groups in society. They were more anxious to do something about the immediate shortcomings and suffering of the needy than to analyze the underlying causes of the social problems confronting them.

The 'forward' movement within the churches in the eighteen–eighties, in which the conception of salvation was tentatively applied to society as well as to individuals, led to the formation of social unions whose members were often in favour of a modification of the class structure. But that movement found support among the more advanced nonconformist leaders rather than the Church of England Evangelicals. This was also the case with the ensuing Christian Labour movement.

Christian Socialism

From the middle of the nineteenth century until well into the twentieth century it was a small group of churchmen known as the Christian Socialists who most clearly understood the threat to the Christian faith of

---

[19] Hodder, *op.cit.*, Vol.II, p.3, quoted in Heasman, *op.cit.*, p.294.

[20] Of the various critiques, special mention should be made of Ian Bradley, *The Call to Seriousness: The Evangelical Impact on the Victorians* (1976), F.K. Brown, *Fathers of the Victorians* (1961), J.L. and B. Hammond, *Lord Shaftesbury* (1923), and E.R. Norman, *Church and Society in England 1770-1973: A Historical Study* (1976).

the secular spirit, and warned the church about it.[21] The theology of Christian Socialism was largely derived from F.D. Maurice. Maurice was repelled by what he regarded as Victorian attempts to restrict religion to a narrow moralism and pietism; an exclusive anxiety for personal moral behaviour and personal religion. He emphasized the concept of the Kingdom of God, which he considered must encompass nothing less than the whole of God's creation. Religion must concern itself intimately with the fate of all mankind and with the condition of the secular world in which men live. The economic philosophy of the movement was largely determined by certain French theories of the period 1830 to 1840, mediated directly and personally through J.M. Ludlow, who had been an eye witness to the French experimentation with co-operative associations. Mid-nineteenth century Christian Socialism stood for co-operation, profit-sharing and co-partnership. It expressed a Broad Church theology in which rationality and tolerance were highly regarded.

In the late Victorian decades the Christian Socialist mantle was assumed by the Anglo-Catholics, who adapted it to a new theological framework. There was first Stewart Headlam's Guild of St Matthew, established in 1877. This embodied a conviction that the best proof and witness of the socialism of Christ was to be found in the sacraments of the church and especially in baptism, and in what Headlam referred to as the mass. The Christian Social Union begun by H. Scott Holland, Charles Gore and B.F. Westcott in 1889 was sacramental, but much less socialist in outlook. In 1892 Charles Gore also founded a religious order, the Community of the Resurrection, which included several monks holding radical political and economic opinions. Throughout the last quarter of the century these bodies exercised an influence out of all proportion to their size. Many 'Christian Socialist' priests laboured energetically, and frequently with heroic devotion, in the slums of great cities, as an expression of the depth and extent of their distinctive beliefs.

Shaftesbury and many of his fellow Evangelicals disliked and distrusted the outlook of the Christian Socialists. They believed in hierarchy and rank and thought that these could not co-exist with what was seen as the Christian Socialist tendency towards liberty, equality and fraternity or brotherhood. The difference in churchmanship was also a major barrier at a time when ritualistic controversy was raging. So the two movements, both with at least the common concern for social action in the name of Christ, went ahead separately and often antagonistically.

---

[21] For accounts and critiques of Christian Socialism, see T. Christensen, *Origin and history of Christian Socialism 1848-54* (1962), Peter D'A. Jones, *The Christian Socialist Revival 1877-1914: Religion, Classes and Social Conscience in Late-Victorian England* (1968), Norman, *op.cit.*, and Maurice Reckitt, *Maurice to Temple: A Century of Social Movement in the Church of England* (1947).

Perhaps the social philosophy, of the Christian Socialists, had more in common with that of the Evangelicals than has often been assumed. Their socialism was more apparent than real. Maurice and his circle were in many respects classical bourgeois utopians. They accepted the existing social structures as satisfactory and necessary, and only sought, like the Evangelicals, to iron out by voluntary and co-operative enterprises what were perceived by them as unfortunate aspects of industrial society. For example, Christian Socialism opposed Chartism, which was a genuine working-class movement for parliamentary reform.

Maurice and his colleagues hated the middle-class manufacturers and the industrial society they had created, but they did not seek a revolutionary restructuring of society. Maurice espoused the co-operative ideal, but this did not make him a socialist in any radically political sense. Many of the Christian Socialists favoured the reform of individual social evils, but opposed the notion of systematic state power or state compulsion. The nearest approach to a genuinely socialist theory was that of Stewart Headlam, whose membership, as a Fabian Socialist, of the London County Council gave him a real knowledge of practical politics. He believed that society had to be recast, to allow for the redistribution of wealth by the state. He envisaged the church as doing on a large scale throughout the world the secular and socialistic works which he considered Christ had done on a small scale in Palestine.[22] Scott Holland, Gore, Westcott and most of the other Christian Socialists aimed at a far more vague creation of a sense of corporate mutual responsibility, not through state power, but by individual assent to the Christian ideals of brotherhood. A few Christian Socialist slum priests attracted working-class congregations for a time because they were sympathetic pastors, not because of their politics.

[22] See Stewart Headlam, *Christian Socialism* (Fabian Tract No.42).

14

World Mission

'It was the Evangelicals who taught the Church of England to be mission-ary'.[1] If this is so, and it is certainly a defensible assertion, a crucial and, in the view of Eugene Stock,[2] an historic year for missionary work was 1786. It was in that year that twelve, largely unconnected, events combined to produce a missionary awakening.

William Wilberforce dedicated himself, under the oak tree at Keston, to the task of abolishing the slave trade. Thomas Clarkson published his essay against the slave trade and in so doing greatly influenced public opinion. Granville Sharp formulated his plan for settling liberated slaves in Sierra Leone. David Brown, went to India as a chaplain. Charles Grant, while at Calcutta, conceived the idea of a great mission to India. William Carey proposed at a Baptist ministers' meeting the consideration of responsibility to the heathen, and was told by the chairman to sit down. The first ship-load of convicts was sent to Australia accompanied by a chaplain. The Eclectic Society discussed foreign missions for the first time. Christian Friedrich Schwartz, the SPCK Lutheran missionary in South India, visited Tinnevelley, and set in motion a series of actions which led over twenty years later to the establishment of the CMS

---

[1] S.C. Carpenter, *Church and People, 1789-1889* (London, 1933), p.428.
[2] Eugene Stock, *The History of the Church Missionary Society*, 3 vols. (London, 1899), Vol.I, p.57. The twelve events listed are those identified by Stock.

211

Tinnevelley Mission. Dr Coke, the great Wesleyan missionary leader, made the first of his eighteen voyages across the Atlantic, to the West Indies, and initiated a missionary enterprise in which the Church Missionary Society and other societies afterwards co-operated. An Act of Parliament was passed which enabled the Church of England to commence its colonial and missionary episcopate. And, finally, Dr Thurlow, the Bishop of Lincoln, in preaching the annual sermon of the SPG, advocated the evangelization of India, and appealed to the East India Company to build churches and support clergymen for them.

When the Eclectic Society had its discussion on the possibility of a Church of England mission to the 'heathen', only two or three out of the seventeen present – probably Charles Simeon, Thomas Scott and Basil Woodd – favoured any definite attempt being made. In the debate the majority expressed apprehension about the reaction of the bishops, shrank from seeming to interfere with the SPG and SPCK, doubted the possibility of obtaining men, or urged the claims of the church at home. Undaunted, the two or three persisted, and long afterwards Basil Woodd wrote across his MS notes of the discussion, 'This conversation proved the foundation of the Church Missionary Society'. It was on Friday, 12 April 1799 that the public meeting took place in a first-floor room in a hotel in Aldersgate, The Castle and Falcon, which established the CMS or rather the Society for Missions in Africa and the East, as it was originally called; a society which was to become the largest missionary organization in the world. It was the same hotel in which, four years earlier, the London Missionary Society had been founded.

As previously noted, the Evangelicals were willing to unite with others outside the Church of England in religious and philanthropic undertakings, as for instance with the Religious Tract Society, also founded in 1799, and the Bible Society, founded in 1804. Nevertheless they were *ex animo* loyal members of the Church of England, thoroughly believed in episcopacy and liturgical worship and set a high value on establishment. Several of the founder members of the CMS were subscribers to the SPCK and the SPG, but both societies were at a very low level of energy and efficiency, and the Evangelicals had no chance of being permitted to exercise any influence in the counsels of either. Also, the two existing Church of England societies confined their labours to the British plantations in America and to the West Indies. The Evangelicals decided that a new missionary initiative and a new Church of England missionary society were legitimate and needed.

The Church Missionary Society

In the first years of its life the Church Missionary Society faced many difficulties. There was no wave of missionary enthusiasm sweeping over English Christendom in the early nineteenth century as is often implied. Such a great event as the departure of William Carey for India in 1793 was only seen to be momentous many years later. At the time the 'consecrated cobbler' was mostly sneered at or ignored. The new society started with much discouragement; the glamour of it as a pioneer enterprise was only recognized in retrospect, after it had acquired great stature. For many years no bishop joined it and no British missionaries could be found. The one suitable candidate who offered, and who would have been joyfully accepted, Henry Martyn, went to India as an East India Company chaplain because of the difficulties and restrictions to which a professed missionary would have been subject.

The society had at first to be content, like the SPCK, with German Lutherans, who established a mission in West Africa. As an illustration of the early uphill struggle of the CMS it had, by the time it was ten years old, sent out five missionaries, all Germans, of whom one was dead, one had been dismissed and three were still at work. When Simeon called for chaplains for India the response was good. Clergy were ready to travel to the uttermost ends of the earth in order to work among white men, but to serve among peoples of other cultures and native religions was an unheard-of thing. As Balleine has observed, 'there was no missionary literature, no missionary tradition; the whole scheme seemed vague and nebulous, and not a man would come forward'.[3]

The committee was without experience and had no precedents from which to seek guidance. The whole undertaking was so new that many mistakes were made. When a mission was begun in Sierra Leone the untrained missionaries hung about the coast, appalled at the dangers of the country and the difficulties of the language. One of them caused a grievous scandal by engaging in the slave trade. When a mission was opened among the Maoris of New Zealand there were interminable delays, and some of the missionaries had to be dismissed for trading in liquor and guns. With great patience and much prayer the mistakes were rectified and strong churches were built up in both Sierra Leone and New Zealand.

The CMS was fortunate in its early leadership. Pre-eminent were John Venn, who showed remarkable wisdom in laying down the society's principles, drafting its rules and guiding its first proceedings from the chair of the committee; Thomas Scott, the Secretary; and the long-serving, industrious and able second Secretary, Josiah Pratt. From 1815 onwards Edward Bickersteth contributed his fervour, eloquence and

[3] G.R. Balleine, *The History of the Evangelical Party in the Church of England* (London, 1908), p.127.

reconciling influence as he undertook the home organization of the society. By that time leading clergymen were being sent to different counties and towns to deliver sermons and address meetings on behalf of the society. They were reminiscent of the eighteenth century itinerant preachers, and as such were highly suspect; but they became very important and drew large crowds. The impact of many of the missionary meetings was increased by the use of hymns, although these were also questioned by Evangelicals such as Simeon, who regarded them as quite unnecessary.

The founders of the CMS and their immediate successors pleaded that church people should not only support the new society, but continue to give full support to the SPG and the SPCK. They were supremely concerned to reach the unevangelized throughout the world, and the work of the two older societies was seen as part of such a global mission. When there was a sudden and marked expansion of the SPG in the second and third decades of the century and onwards, it was described by Pratt with unfeigned joy and unreserved sympathy. The CMS committee were also careful not to intrude into what might be SPG fields of labour.

The progress of the work of the CMS was uneven. From about 1812 to 1816, for example, the society experienced sudden and vigorous expansion: its influence at home grew as part of a general heightening of interest in missions among the Christian public; an Act of Parliament in 1813 placed the superintendence of the Anglican Church in India under a bishop, and thereby facilitated Christian work among the native population of the country; a mission was begun in New Zealand; and financial and other support for the society greatly increased so that it was able to send out a number of ordained Englishmen. At other times struggle, tragedy, hardship and loss were the dominant notes. Such was 1823: of seven new schoolmasters and five wives who landed at Sierra Leone in that year, ten died within eighteen months. Three missionaries and two chaplains and their wives also died in the same year.

Nevertheless, in spite of innumerable setbacks, the work of the society progressed in varying degrees in India, Sierra Leone and New Zealand. Also new mission fields were opened up, including Ceylon (1818), Egypt (1826), British Guiana (1827), Abyssinia (1830), Ibadan (1851), Lagos (1852), Mauritius (1856), Hong Kong (1862), Madagascar (1863), Japan (1868), Persia (1875), the Seychelles (1875), Uganda (1875) and Mombasa (1887). Missionary work was also undertaken in Palestine and China, and among the Zulus.

In this story of expanding missionary effort there were countless tales of heroism and sacrifice. One sphere of the work will suffice as a sample: Eastern Equatorial Africa. As Ludwig Krapf at the time of Victoria's accession, and then mid-century explorers, penetrated the interior of

Eastern Africa, there were reports of an inland kingdom called Buganda. It was finally reached by John Speke in 1861 and H.M. Stanley fourteen years later. In 1875, in a remarkable letter to the *Daily Telegraph*, Stanley, writing from Buganda, challenged Christendom to send a mission to the country. Two days later the CMS received an anonymous letter in which £5,000 was offered as an initial fund for such a project. The CMS made its plans with urgency and yet with great care. Special contributions poured in, and soon £15,000 had been donated. In deference to the political situation in Eastern Africa, the enteprise was called the Nyanza Mission, leaving its precise locale an open question.

The missionaries set sail in 1876, and journeyed inland. Two mechanics and Alexander Mackay had to be returned to England because of ill health; porters deserted, and Dr John Smith died of fever, thus creating the first missionary grave on the shores of the Nyanza. By then only, three of the party were left. Soon after arrival in Buganda two of them were murdered. In 1878 the one survivor, the Rev. C.T. Wilson, was joined by Mackay. By 1882 the first Protestant baptism took place. In 1884 James Hannington sailed for Buganda, as the first Bishop of Eastern Equatorial Africa. In the meantime, for a combination of reasons, the small Bugandan Christian church was facing persecution. Native Christians were banished and imprisoned. Three of them were put to death – cruelly cut about with long curved knives, and then thrown on a large fire. When Hannington and his group of fifty men arrived on the borders of the country they were held in a miserable hut, led out after eight days, surrounded, and all but four were slain. It was subsequently reported that the white man, before he fell, had given a message for the *kabaka* that he died for Buganda, and that he had purchased the road to Buganda with his life.

After this the church underwent great persecution. Some of the finest converts were burnt or tortured to death in horrific ways. A member of the church council was unmercifully clubbed and thrown into the flames. Another had his limbs cut off one by one and roasted before his eyes. Thirty-two others were burnt on one huge pyre. About 200 perished in all. The *kabaka*, Mwanga, was the first instigator of much of this suffering and death. In England voices were raised counselling despair and the abandonment of the mission, but the CMS resolutely continued on its course. A period of quiet succeeded the persecutions. Mwanga was plotting the destruction of all the leading Christians,. but he was deposed. Religious liberty was proclaimed and there was a rush of Ganda to receive Christian instruction. But the pendulum was to swing again. The Muslims expelled CMS and other missionaries in a determined effort to win the country for Islam, and once more the voices of despair were raised in England. Ironically, Mwanga was reinstated on the throne; and he then evicted the Muslims, and declared religious liberty. By the end of the century there were thousands of native Christians in Buganda with their own churches, clergy and teachers; an eloquent testimony to twenty-five years of quite epic endeavour. Many another tale could be told of other areas of the world to which missionaries were sent under the auspices of the CMS.

Henry Venn (1796–1873)

In the growth and consolidation of the work of the CMS, and in the evolution of the nineteenth century overseas missionary enterprise of the Church of England, a special place of significance and honour should be given to Henry Venn.[4] The events of his life were not dramatic, but he was arguably the greatest misionary statesman of the Victorian church; and as such he has suffered undeserved neglect from historians in the past.

Venn was born in 1796. His grandfather was the renowned vicar of Huddersfield whom we have already met as a key figure in eighteenth century Evangelicalism. His father John was the rector of Clapham, where he ministered among the great families of the Clapham Sect. It was in this unique and exceptional church circle, with the Wilberforces, the Thorntons, the Stephens and the Macaulays as neighbours or frequent visitors, that Venn was brought up. From Clapham rectory he went to Cambridge to prepare for the university; and in 1814 he entered Queens'. In 1819 he was ordained deacon and elected a Fellow of his college. After a curacy in London he returned to Queens' in 1824 as a tutor, acted as proctor of the university for a year, read towards a B.D. and gave evening lectures at Great St Mary's.

In 1827 Venn was appointed to St John's Drypool, Hull, and while there he married Martha Sykes in 1829. It was also during his time at Drypool, in 1834, that his biography of his grandfather appeared. In this same year he accepted the living of St John's, Holloway, and resumed his membership of the CMS committee which he had previously joined as a curate. In 1840 his wife died, and partly in reaction to this personal tragedy he resolved to give himself unreservedly to the work of the CMS. In 1841 he became Honorary Clerical Secretary, and in 1847 he resigned the living of St John's. From then on, except for service on two commissions, his public life was entirely devoted to the service of the CMS. He retired as Secretary in 1872, and died on 13 January 1873.

Throughout his Secretaryship Venn had to grapple with the often not easy relationship between the CMS as a voluntary body within the Church

---

[4] The following account rests heavily on Michael Hennell, *Sons of the Prophets: Evangelical Leaders of the Victorian Church* (London, 1979), pp.68-90; and T.E. Yates, *Venn and the Victorian Bishops Abroad* (London, 1978).

of England and the developing ecclesiastical structures abroad, as he and his society sought to promote evangelism and church development. As a missionary statesman he had one leading idea: 'the euthanasia of missions'. He was concerned that the non-departure of European missionaries would result in native churches becoming missionary-dominated. The foreign missionary should always be primarily an evangelist. Venn's aim was to plant indigenous churches, which would be self-supporting, self-governing and self-extending. The missionary society was to work in a country in such a way that the removal of the missionaries left the national church standing unassisted. The European and missionary presence should be interim only. Once brought into existence, the national church should be allowed to develop according to its own national character, with indigenous leadership and episcopate, and unencumbered by the continuing European presence. Perhaps inevitably Venn had to compromise his own principle in certain situations, and even when Samuel Crowther was consecrated bishop in 1864, he was not so much bishop of a developed indigenous church as a kind of pioneering evangelist in episcopal orders.

Throughout Venn's secretariat, Tractarian ideas on the church and the role of bishops found expression in the Universities' Mission to Central Africa and the heroic work of Bishop Mackenzie. A bishop was seen as essential to the church's being; the episcopate was viewed as of the *esse* of the church, and the church was not present without a bishop. Venn challenged such a view. He was concerned that bishops should be provided for the young churches, to confirm believers, to ordain and to exercise oversight, but he did not believe that they were indispensable for mission work and the establishment of a church. He expressed such views in the preface to his biographical study of *The Missionary Life and Labours of Francis Xavier*, which was published in 1862.

Venn was also concerned to initiate commercial enterprises in West Africa to make the inhabitants more self-supporting. He arranged for Africans to spend three months at Kew Gardens, where they learnt modern methods of cultivation. He established cotton gins at Abeokuta; he promoted the training of Africans in industrial employments and he helped them to establish themselves in profitable trade and commerce.

At home Venn avoided controversy, insisting on the essentially positive character of Evangelicalism. Matters of ecclesiastical dispute were not allowed to be mentioned at anniversary meetings and he seldom engaged in contentious issues. Evangelism was so imperative that time should not be squandered on fruitless disputes. At home and abroad the CMS of his day and the church at large owed him much; but the depth and profundity of his thinking, and his vision and broad sympathy, give him significance for the twentieth century also.

Fresh Enthusiasm for World Evangelization

Throughout the century the home support for missionary work overseas was subject to great fluctuation. In the period 1850 to 1875 income was not keeping pace with expanding activities.[5] But in the last quarter of the century there was a new surge of missionary enthusiasm. A period of strident imperialism gave a global perspective to many people and encouraged Evangelicals and other Christians to consider afresh the possibility of world evangelization. The Moody–Sankey mission in Cambridge, and the Keswick movement, resulted in new and zealous converts and stimulated missionary concern.

Extraordinary interest was aroused in the autumn of 1884 by the announcement that the captain of the Cambridge cricket eleven, C.T. Studd,[6] and the stroke of the Cambridge boat, Stanley Smith, were going out as missionaries with Hudson Taylor to China. Soon they were joined by the Rev. W.W. Cassels; Montagu Beauchamp, a nephew of Lord Radstock, and also well known as a rowing man; D.E. Hoste, an officer in the Royal Artillery; and the sons of a late M.P. for Bedford, C.H. and A.T. Polhill-Turner, the former an officer in the 6th Dragoon Guards, and both prominent Eton and Cambridge cricketers. A series of meetings, culminating in the valedictory gathering in Exeter Hall in 1885, generated wide-ranging and intense missionary ardour. Possibly 'no event in the century had done so much to arouse the minds of Christian men to the tremendous claims of the Field, and the nobility of the missionary vocation'.[7]

At the same time the death of General Gordon in Khartoum focused attention on Africa. Shortly afterwards, the murder of Bishop Hannington and the persecution of Christians in Buganda in 1886 caused an uproar in the British press, and sales of missionary literature soared. The extent to which the missionary cause came to life in the Christian world in the years covered by these various trends and activities can be seen, in England, in the creation of new Boards of Missions, and in the great interdenominational missionary conferences of 1878 and 1888. In 1886–7, thirty-five offers of service were accepted by CMS, of which eighteen were university graduates, twelve of them Cambridge men. Of the 514 men who passed through Ridley Hall during the time of Handley

---

[5] For example, see the *Record*, 13 January 1865, and Anne Bentley, 'The Transformation of the Evangelical Party in the Church of England in the later Nineteenth Century' (Durham University Ph.D., 1971), p.436.

[6] For the life and work of C.T. Studd, see Norman P. Grubb, *C.T. Studd: Cricketer and Pioneer* (London, 1933).

[7] Eugene Stock, *op.cit.*, Vol.III, p.284.

Moule (1881-99) 117 became foreign missionaries, while a further seventy-six served abroad in other capacities.[8]

In the eighteen-eighties the CMS played its part in promoting missionary interest by launching an all-out effort to reform and invigorate its local associations. Lantern slides were made available; missionary exhibitions were held in Cambridge in 1882, and in Norwich in 1883; and missionary speakers were sent to various towns to press the claims of the CMS. Deputation work was vigorously organized: 200 clergy and laymen held 800 meetings in 1886 in one week alone at over 150 different centres. In such gatherings the cause of mission in general, rather than the CMS in particular, was proclaimed, and this secured the sympathy of both High Churchmen and nonconformists. The society also established a Lay Workers' Union in 1882 in London, and in 1885 a Junior Clergy Union and Ladies' Union.

The CMS was not alone in such efforts. The need for world mission was declared by Hudson Taylor and Reginald Radcliffe at Mildmay and other similar conventions. This triggered off a spate of conferences specifically on the topic of missions. From 1886 missionary meetings were incorporated into the Keswick Convention, and soon the call to service became the climax of the convention. In 1890 about 300 people indicated their willingness to go out if the way was made open for them. In 1891 the *Record* claimed that in four years of the convention eighty candidates had offered themselves to the CMS, of whom at least fifty had eventually gone to the mission field.[9] Hudson Taylor reckoned that two-thirds of the missionaries in the China Inland Mission[10] had come via Keswick. From 1888 Keswick also provided the finances to send out and support its own missionaries. Of these the most famous was Amy Wilson Carmichael, who went to Japan in 1893, and later worked in Ceylon and South India. The link between the CMS and Keswick was strong, as instanced by the close involvement of Eugene Stock and the Rev. H.W. Webb-Peploe in both. The Student Volunteer Missionary Union of Great Britain and Ireland (founded in 1892) was a further agency for stimulating missionary interest and commitment. The greater acceptance of worldwide missionary responsibility is indicated by the fact that the average recruitment of the CMS, which had been less than eight a year in the first half of the century, rose in the period 1848 to 1880 to sixteen and a half, and from 1881 to 1894 to thirty a year.

[8] See C.M.S. *Annual Report 1886-7*, p.4, and Bentley, *op.cit.*, p.441.
[9] Ref. in Bentley, *op.cit.*
[10] For the history of the China Inland Mission, see A.J. Broomhall, *Hudson Taylor and China's Open Century*, 5 vols (London, 1981-).

The South American Missionary Society

Among the new Evangelical initiatives of the nineteenth century, the South American Missionary Society holds a distinguished place.[11] It probably had 'the most tragic birth in the history of modern missions'.[12] Allen Gardiner (1794-1850) reached the rank of Commander in the British Navy. He was converted during one of his voyages, and at the age of forty left the navy in order to devote himself to missionary work. His first efforts were in Natal. Arriving there in 1835, he visualized the possibility of a chain of mission stations stretching up the whole east coast of Africa as far as Zanzibar and beyond. But he was 'stronger in imagination than in execution'.[13] He had ideas of a mission to New Guinea, but then turned his attention to South America.

Having failed to undertake a work in Paraguay and Bolivia, he went in 1850, with six companions, to Tierra del Fuego, the desolate archipelago which forms the southernmost point of South America, one of the bleakest and most tempestuous regions in the world. The ship with their provisions failed to arrive; the natives would not feed them; the drifting ice broke their nets so that they could not fish; and during the severe winter on that inhospitable shore the whole party died of starvation. In his diary Gardiner had written: 'Poor and weak as we are, our boat is a very Bethel to our souls, for we feel and know that God is here. Asleep or awake, I am, beyond the power of expression, happy'.[14]

After seventeen years of hard and valiant missionary work, without having seen a single convert or any fruit from his labours, Gardiner's death was to achieve what his passionate appeals had failed to accomplish. When the bodies were found the words in his diary echoed around the world, and the church in England was stirred to take an interest in South America. A schooner named after Gardiner landed a party of missionaries. But the tragic saga continued. In 1859 the mission was almost wiped out when eight of its workers were murdered.

It only became evident many years later that the labours of Gardiner and the other pioneers had not been in vain. Before the mission began, Charles Darwin had described the inhabitants of the area as the most degraded beings in the world. In 1870 he wrote to the South American Missionary Society saying that 'the success of the Tierra del Fuego Mission is most wonderful, and charms me, as I always prophesied utter failure. It is a grand success. I shall feel proud if your committee think fit to elect me an

---

[11] For the early history of the South American Missionary Society, see Phyllis Thompson, *An Unquenchable Flame: The Story of Cpt Allen Gardiner* (London, 1983).

[12] Balleine, *op.cit.*, p.205.

[13] Stephen Neill, *A History of Christian Missions* (Harmondsworth, 1964), p.320.

[14] Quoted in Neill, *op.cit.*, p.321.

honorary member of your society'.[15] And he subscribed to the work from that day until his death. In 1872 the first group of Tierra del Fuegans was baptized. Gradually the society extended its work widely among Indian peoples never reached by the Roman Catholic Church. In Chile the society laboured among the Araucanian Indians; in Paraguay the mission concentrated on the violent Legua people; and in Brazil it was again the Indian tribes to which the missionaries were sent.

This Evangelical missionary zeal, of which only a few examples have been cited, undoubtedly had a considerable influence upon the whole process of colonization in the nineteenth century; and in turn it was affected by the onward march of Britain as an imperial power.[16] As Stephen Neill has pointed out, the great expansion of Christianity coincided in time with the worldwide and explosive expansion of Europe; the colonizing powers have been the Christian powers; and this has meant a whole variety of compromising relationships between missionaries and governments. In the main, Christianity was carried forward on the wave of western prestige and power.[17]

The cry of such Evangelicals as Charles Grant and Thomas Fowell Buxton was for Britain to assume a total civilizing role and to develop commerce in produce as an alternative to the slave trade. This inspired many to work not only for the conversion of the natives to Christianity, but also their conversion 'to animal husbandry, double-entry bookkeeping and all the other accomplishments of Western civilization'.[18]

For the Victorians,

the overwhelming purpose of empire was the conversion of the native inhabitants within it, whether to the doctrines of free trade, representative government or revealed religion. This was the enduring legacy of the missionary outlook which the Evangelicals had given to nineteenth-century Britain.[19]

Ecumenism

If the Evangelicals taught the Church of England to be missionary, it did

---

[15] See the *Daily News*, 25 April 1885, quoted in Balleine, *op.cit.*, p.207.
[16] See Ian Bradley, *op. cit.*, on which these comments are largely based.
[17] See Neill, *op.cit.*, p.450.
[18] Ian Bradley, *op.cit.*, pp.86, 87. It was in such a spirit that Buxton founded the Society for the Extinction of the Slave Trade and the Civilization of Africa, which held its first meeting under the chairmanship of the Prince Consort in 1840. A Niger Expedition was started in 1841. Treaties were made with chiefs to suppress the slave trade and engage in lawful commerce, and a model farm was started, but there were more than forty deaths among the Europeans, the government withdrew support and the Society was dissolved in 1843.
[19] Ian Bradley, *op.cit.*, pp.89, 90.

not fulfil such a role in regard to ecumenism.[20] The relatively low Evangelical regard for church distinctions and the oft-expressed high regard for nonconformists may seemingly have led to an enthusiastic involvement in the movement for Christian unity. In fact the Evangelical doctrine of the church militated against the pursuit of organic Christian unity. The Evangelicals made a clear distinction between the invisible church, which was the company of all true Christians, and the visible church as seen on earth, which includes many purely nominal Christians. They confined Christian unity to the sphere of the invisible church, and provided for its expression in conferences and conventions such as Mildmay and Keswick. The Evangelical Alliance to a great extent mirrored this Evangelical attitude. It sought to express an Evangelical, rather than a general Christian, union, based on a declared loyalty to the same essential truths.

Committed as they were to an exclusive and inorganic form of Christian unity, Evangelicals left the limited ecumenical initiatives to others; and it was High Churchmen who first, in the nineteenth century, looked outside the Church of England with a view to institutional reunion. The Tractarians regarded the English church as a branch in England of the Catholic church, and the hope was for a restoration of intercommunion with Rome. Since the eighteen-forties there had also been some churchmen who were interested in a *rapprochement* with the Eastern Church. Few Evangelicals co-operated in either of these movements.

Two ecumenical initiatives in the latter part of the century were especially significant. The Lambeth Conference of 1888 was largely concerned with ecumenism. The Quadrilateral which it issued declared that four Articles supplied the basis on which an approach to home reunion might be made:—

(a)   The Holy Scriptures of the Old and New Testaments, as 'containing all things necessary to salvation', and as being the rule and the ultimate standard of faith.

(b)   The Apostles' Creed, as the Baptismal Symbol; and the Nicene Creed, as the sufficient statement of the Christian faith.

(c)   The two Sacraments ordained by Christ Himself – Baptism and the Supper of the Lord – ministered with unfailing use of Christ's words of institution, and of the elements ordained by Him.

(d)   The Historic Episcopate, locally adapted in the methods of its administration to the varying needs of the nations and peoples called of God into the unity of His Church.

---

[20] The comments which follow owe much to Anne Bentley, *op.cit.*

Evangelicals generally did not take issue with the first three of these Articles, but a number regretted the fourth. The proposals were discussed at most of the denominational annual assemblies, and the general response was that the article on the historic episcopate presented an insuperable barrier.

The other initiative was the holding of a series of six conferences at Grindelwald on home reunion, the first of which took place in 1892. They were arranged chiefly at the instigation of Henry Lunn, a Methodist missionary. A wide range of denominations were represented, and every shade of theological belief. The Evangelical contingent consisted of Bishop J.J.S. Perowne of Worcester, William Hay Aitken and the Rev. A.R. Buckland. Among the leading Evangelicals who declined invitations to attend were Francis Chavasse, H.W. Webb-Peploe and Handley Moule, as well as the Baptist F.B. Meyer. The conference highlighted the problem of ministerial orders as being especially crucial to both church-men and nonconformists. It was also evident that one section of Evangelicalism, and that not the narrowest, was reluctant to admit nonconformists to full communion with the Church of England.

Part 4 1901-1945

15

Ritualism, Liturgy and the Prayer Book Controversy

At the dawning of the twentieth century the Evangelicals were wrestling with a crisis of confidence. After the invigorating years of the eighteenth century, the crusading era of the Clapham Sect, and the pioneering social involvement of the mid-Victorian decades, the latter part of the nineteenth century can justifiably be viewed as a period of decline.

Evangelicals had largely been preoccupied with a vigorous anti-ritualism campaign. They had vacillated between enthusiastic support for the militant tactics of the Church Association and painful questionings about the propriety of undertaking litigation and legislation against fellow Christians. As a group they had also been divided over issues such as the holiness movement, Christian Socialism, and the appropriate extent of participation in newly-emergent structures of church government.

There had been many, and very notable, achievements in evangelism, theological education, missionary work, and in ministry among students; and the Evangelicals were united by beliefs and practices held in common. But by the time Edward VII ascended the throne they were quite seriously dispirited, uncertain of their role within the church and in society, and without that cohesion, purposefulness and energy which had characterized them in the halcyon days of the past.

It is significant that the leaders among them were almost exclusively of the older generation. There was little evidence of new thinking or youthful initiative, although the new age demanded both from any group

227

which aspired to fullness of life and influence. It was to be half a century and more before they regained that remarkable degree of maturity, power, and effectiveness reminiscent of some former years.

Ritualism

Early in the century ritualism once again became an issue for the whole Church of England. In 1903, as his first public act as Archbishop, Randall Davidson received a deputation of over one hundred Unionist Members of Parliament who were concerned about ecclesiastical disorders. They urged upon him the need for effective action against ritualism in the Church of England, and he conceded that stern and drastic measures were required, especially in view of the widespead anxiety within the church about this state of affairs, and the contemporary agitation in the House of Commons. A Royal Commission on Ecclesiastical Discipline was appointed in 1904. It was composed of fourteen members, with Sir Michael Hicks Beach, late Chancellor of the Exchequer, in the chair, and was overwhelmingly lay. Of the membership, half were reckoned to be 'low' in ecclesiastical terminology,[1] and one of them, Sir Lewis Dibdin,[2] was largely responsible for the drafting of the final report, although the principal recommendations were of Archbishop Davidson's shaping.[3]

The Commission concluded that the law of public worship in the Church of England was too narrow for the religious life of that generation; it needlessly condemned much which a great section of church people, including many of the most devoted members, valued; and it did not take account of the quite remarkable changes in thought, care for ceremonial, and appreciation of liturgical continuity which had occurred since the law took its existing shape. In an age which had witnessed an extraordinary revival of spiritual life and activity there had not, said the Commission, been that power of self-adjustment in the matter of liturgical revision which is inherent in the conception of a living church. The Commission also asserted that the machinery for discipline had broken down. The means of enforcing the law in the ecclesiastical courts, even in matters which touched the church's faith and teaching, were defective and in some respects unsuitable.

[1] See G.K.A. Bell, *Randall Davidson: Archbishop of Canterbury*, 2 vols (London, 1935), Vol.I, p.462.

[2] Sir Lewis T. Dibdin, Born 1852. Chancellor of the Diocese of Rochester, 1886-1903; of Exeter, 1888-1903; of Durham, 1891-1903; Dean of the Arches, Auditor of the Chancery Court of York, Master of the Faculties, 1903-34; First Church Estates Commissioner, 1905-31; Member of the Royal Commission on Church Discipline, 1904-6; and on Divorce, 1909-12.

[3] For the terms of reference of the Commission, see Bell, *op.cit.*, pp.462, 471-473, 649-654, 799-815, 1325, 1326.

The report made two particularly significant recommendations, the first of which asked bishops to ensure that certain unacceptable liturgical practices should cease forthwith, if necessary by proceedings in the ecclesiastical courts. The second recommendation was that which inaugurated the whole legislative process of Prayer Book revision.

In 1908 an Historical Report on Ornaments was presented to the Upper House of Convocation by a subcommittee of five bishops, of whom Bishop John Wordsworth was the leader. It brought forward a great deal of evidence in favour of the legality of vestments. Even though it contained no recommendations relating to the policy to be adopted, it called forth a shower of memorials and protests.

Between 1908 and 1914 there was much discussion but no decision or action on Prayer Book revision; the policy was to do as little as possible. The movement in favour of revision grew, and an advisory committee of liturgical scholars was appointed in July 1912. The critical question continued to be that of eucharistic vestments, and by 1914 there appeared to be a fair prospect that it could be resolved.

During the war years the eucharist assumed greater importance in the worship of churchmen, and it became inreasingly prominent in the public discussions on the Prayer Book. There were important debates on reservation in the Upper House of Canterbury Convocation in 1915, 1917 and 1918, in the latter of which proposals from the Lower House were accepted for an alteration of the central part of the communion service. From 1918 onwards the public and private discussion of Prayer Book revision became increasingly animated. It culminated in the traumatic events of 1927 and 1928.

What were the attitudes and actions of Evangelicals in response to the ritualistic and liturgical developments during the years 1900 to 1918, and how did they react to the flow of official events in the Church of England in this sphere of its life which we have briefly outlined?[4]

In the early years of the twentieth century most Evangelicals did not align themselves with the more extreme opposition to ritualistic practices advocated by the Church Association, the National Protestant Church Union and other bodies. But there was a very explicit denunciation of what was regarded as abhorrent quasi-Roman Catholic conduct symbolic of totally unacceptable doctrine. Indeed, in their concern to defend the Reformation settlement, which they perceived as being under threat, some Evangelicals were prepared to co-operate with non-Evangelicals[5] in

---

[4] The description given owes much to Bell, *loc.cit.*

[5] As an example, many Evangelicals applauded the stance taken by the learned and much respected High Churchman F. Meyrick, who discerned an undesirable Romeward tendency in the Church of England ritualists. See F. Meyrick, 'Respice, Aspice, Prospice', *Churchman*, January 1904, pp.166, 167.

upholding what they thought to be true catholicity in the Church of England. They opposed ritualism on the grounds that it was not only counter to what they held dear, but was an attack upon the foundation beliefs of the Church of England. They could thus call upon those members of the Church of England who had a common concern with them to defend the faith of their fathers, even if they were not professed Evangelicals, to rally together and stand forth against the ritualistic innovators.

Opposition to ritualistic practices by Evangelicals as well as other churchmen was buttressed by an appeal to history. It was argued that the ecclesiastical vestments adopted by the ritualists were only introduced about 800 AD by the ecclesiastics and courtiers of the Emperor Charlemagne; the eastward position was unknown in France until the ninth century, and in Spain and North Italy until the eleventh century; the use of lights was a pagan custom; the use of incense was spoken of with contempt by the early Christians; the wafer bread, made with leaven, was first used in the West in the tenth century; and the mixed cup was not a ceremonial feature in the early church.[6]

In the Evangelical emphasis upon judgement at the bar of history, the greatest stress was laid upon the Reformation settlement: the Prayer Book and Articles of the Church of England were seen as enshrining the true catholic doctrines. Perhaps the most influential proponent of this view was W.H. Griffith Thomas. He and others acknowledged the Bible as the supreme authority, but sought corroborating and supporting evidence for their Evangelical view not only from the sixteenth century reformers, but from the early Fathers, and from such post-Reformation churchmen as Lancelot Andrewes, Jeremy Taylor, John Cosin and Edward Reynolds. Griffith Thomas said that fundamental disagreement on matters of doctrine and practice was only introduced into the Church of England by the Tractarians. He elaborated his arguments in his immensely popular book, *The Catholic Faith* (1904).[7]

Faced with the practical and pastoral problems of diocesan administration, the Evangelical bishops showed a reluctance to take or condone severe disciplinary action against ritualists; and yet they were resolved to remain faithful to what they thought was required of them. E.A. Knox[8] tried to rally all the clergy in loyal obedience to the Prayer

[6] See for example Henry Wace, 'What is Catholicity?', *Islington Clerical Meeting Report* (1904), pp.55, 56,

[7] W.H. Griffith Thomas, *The Catholic Faith* (London, 1904). See also W.H. Griffith Thomas, 'The Catholicity of the Church of England', *Islington Clerical Meeting Report* (1904), pp.64, 70, 71.

[8] See Edmund Arbuthnott Knox, *Reminiscences of an Octogenarian 1847-1934* (London, 1934), pp.301, 302.

Book. He determined to reason with them but, if that failed, he would not use the power given to bishops to veto prosecutions. Francis Chavasse set his face against intolerance and strove to be the bishop of the whole church rather than of a party. If, however, his clergy ignored the Lambeth judgements and the Archbishops' decisions on incense and reservation, he decided that he would neither preach for such clergy, confirm or license any assistant clergy nor support them in any way.[9] This moderate Evangelical approach, which sought to combine unwavering allegiance to Protestant doctrines and practice with a conciliatroy strategy, was adopted by many Evangelicals other than the bishops.[10]

But there was a more militant, aggressive and uncompromising strand in Evangelicalism which was evident from the beginning of the century, when it was spearheaded by John Kensit, and such organizations as the Church Association, the Protestant Truth Society, the Protestant Defence Brigade, and the Wickliffe Preachers. Two examples will indicate the tenor of the campaign conducted by these vehement enthusiasts. On Sunday, 14 January 1900 a visit was made by John Kensit, his son, and some of the Wickliffe Preachers to Christ Church, Belper, which was well known for its ritualism. The following is the text of a letter from John Kensit to the Bishop of Southwell:

Belper, January 15

My Lord Bishop – At the request of my own Diocesan, the Lord Bishop of London, I have in my crusade against the Mass and the confessional purposely abstained from any interference in the illegal services which have been, and are still being, conducted in our churches. His Lordship of London led me to believe that the Bishops intended to carry out their solemn promises made at their ordination to banish and drive away erroneous and strange doctrines. After waiting for sixteen months, being engaged with a band of my Wickliffe preachers in holding a Mission at Belper, I attended Christ Church being the district church where I am residing, and there to my disgust I witnessed the Mass performed by the curate holding your licence, the Rev. E.J. Scotcher. At the consecration of the bread a wafer was elevated high above his head. A server rang a bell, and all prostrated. The same illegality and idolatry were practised with the wine. I was compelled as a law-abiding Churchman to enter a protest and leave the building without partaking of the Holy Communion. The said curate, who holds your licence, is, I am informed, a member of the Confraternity of the Blessed Sacrament, an Association formed for restoring the Mass in our Church.

---

[9] See J.B. Lancelot, *Francis James Chavasse* (Oxford, 1929), pp.148, 149.

[10] This particular Evangelical view and practice is well expressed in Arthur Galton, '1904: Spectabilis Annus', *Churchman*, January 1905, pp.173, 174.

The new Vicar who has accepted the living is also a member of the same Society. On the Communion Table at Christ Church eight candles were burning, the curate several times kissed the table, and to all appearances ceremonially mixed the water with the wine. Now, my Lord Bishop, I call upon you to do your duty, and stop the Romanizing practices which have distinguished this and other churches in your diocese, especially at Derby, Sneinton, Buxton, and other places, and thus save me from the unpleasant duty of attending a service and entering in God's name a protest for my fellow-Churchmen, who are are being driven out of our Church by this abominable idolatry. – Awaiting your reply, yours for the truth,

(signed) John Kensit.[11]

The tactics adopted by the militants included similar disruption of services with consequent legal action against the disrupters in some cases; political action, as for example in Sheffield, where 12,000 signatures were obtained of voters promising not to cast their vote for any candidate who, as a Member of Parliament, would not fight against ritualism; and the widespread distribution of various forms of literature and publicity. Memories of past conflicts were stirred as the Church Asociation resurrected the slogan 'The Church in Danger'.

The more moderate of the Evangelicals openly expressed their distress. Typical of these was the speaker at the Islington meeting in 1907 who bemoaned the fact that 'extremists, really loving controversy for controversy's sake, often seem to lead us, in the Press or on the platform, without really representing us'.[12] For a certain hard-core section of Evangelicals it was in vain that Bishop Handley Moule of Durham issued his plea to his brethren to give the 1906 Report of the Royal Commission

> deliberate, patient, respectful, and prayerful attention, not hurrying into expressions of opinion, but first pondering facts and inferences, with hearts and minds set upon the highest and largest interests of the cause of God in and through the English Church.[13]

This polarization of views and policy within the ranks of the Evangelicals on the question of ritualism, and all the associated issues, together with every conceivable variant of opinion in between, continued unabated for the next few years after the report of the Commission. The fight against ritualism, and the tension caused by the strongly differing ideas on the subject, sapped the energies of Evangelicals. During the second decade of the century, however, a more tolerant attitude tended to prevail. There was a measure of weariness with the prolonged and somewhat fruitless controversy.

[11] Reported in 'The Kensit Crusade', Record, January 1900, p.68. See also Editorial, 'The Forces of Neo-Anglicanism', Record, 25 May 1900, p.505, and an advertisement, 'The Church in Danger', Islington Clerical Meeting Report (1907), p.6.

[12] F.S. Guy Warman, 'The practices respecting confession and prayers for the dead now existing, according to the commissioners, in the Church of England', Islington Clerical Meeting Report (1907), p.62.

[13] Handley C.G. Moule, 'Commission's Report: Some Messages', Record, 6 July 1906.

Indeed, not only was there much increased toleration, but some Evangelicals actually adopted a fairly elaborate ritualism themselves; a strange climax to the saga of conflict which extended well back into the previous century. Certain forms of ritualism were regarded by an influential body of Evangelicals as an aid to the beautification of churches, and the fuller, more meaningful worship of God; and so stately music, surpliced choirs and embroidered hangings were introduced by them. These Evangelicals resisted the ritualists in the Church of England with their 'medieval and sacerdotal pretensions', but claimed that Evangelicalism was not doctrinally compromised by the restricted use of certain forms of ritualism. The emergence of ritualistic Evangelicalism did not herald the end of the period of conflict; but one form and one phase of the strife was over.[14]

Prayer Book Revision

For the Church of England as a whole the next phase, the inter-war years, was to a large extent coloured by the feud over Prayer Book revision. In 1922 a committee of the new Church Assembly presented a report to the Assembly. The order of holy communion and the question of reservation were identified as areas of potential disagreement: five members, all Evangelicals, printed a note of objection to the proposals for reservation. In October 1922 the House of Bishops introduced the Revised Prayer Book (Permissive Use) Measure, which not only entailed three years of debates in the assembly, but produced a torrent of rival proposals, criticism, comment and protest. The revision stage began in October 1925, with a sitting in public; and for a year from January 1926, the House of Bishops (with between forty and fifty full days of sessions) met privately at Lambeth Palace. In June 1926 they approved the proposal for continuous reservation, and in February 1927 a draft Prayer Book was presented to the Convocations.

The Prayer Book Measure was passed by a large majority in all three Houses (Bishops 34 for and 4 against, clergy 53 for and 37 against, and laity 230 for and 92 against). Presented to the House of Lords, it was passed by 241 votes to 88, but it was then rejected by the House of Commons, with 238 against and 205 in favour. Re-presented in a slightly modified form the following year, it was again rejected by the House of Commons with a somewhat larger majority (266 to 220).

[14] For contemporary comments on the emergence of Ritualistic Evangelicalism, see W. Escott Bloss, 'The Relation of Modern Evangelicals to the Catholic Party', *Churchman*, August 1912, pp.596, 597; E.C. Dewick, Evangelicals and the Problem of Ritualism', *Churchman*, January 1913, pp.10, 11, 16, 17; J.R. Darbyshire, Vice-Principal of Ridley Hall, Cambridge, 'Evangelicals and the Problem of Ritualism', *Churchman*, March 1913, p.178; B. Herklots, 'Evangelicals and the Problem of Ritualism', *Churchman*, July 1914, p.486; and W.H. Griffith Thomas, 'Evangelicals in Transition', *Churchman*, March 1909, p.169.

Despite its repudiation by the House of Commons, the revised Prayer Book was published at the end of 1928. In July 1929 the Upper House of Canterbury Convocation, with the support of the Lower House, reckoned it impossible to bring back the conduct of public worship strictly within the limits of the Prayer Book of 1662. The Convocation therefore resolved that during the prevailing emergency bishops should not regard the use of additions and deviations from the book of 1662 which fell within the limits of the proposed book of 1928 as inconsistent with loyalty to the principles of the Church of England. The Convocation declared that other deviations from or additions to the forms and orders contained in the book of 1662 must be deemed as inconsistent with church order. In the exercise of their authority the bishops should not permit the ordinary use of any of the forms and orders contained in the book of 1928 unless they were satisfied that such use had the goodwill of the people as represented in the parochial church council.

The parliamentary rebuff especially raised the issue of the relationship between church and state. In 1930 the Archbishops appointed a commission on the subject. Indeed this was the most persistent and contentious topic within the domestic life of the church in the ten yeras prior to the outbreak of the war. The continuing resentment against Evangelicals which many felt as a result of the Prayer Book controversy, and the considerable post-mortem examination by Evangelicals themselves, was focused upon this church-state debate.[15]

Throughout these inter-war years there was no single, identifiable Evangelical mind on the question of revision. Although Evangelicals in the main were averse to revision, there were shades of opinion. Many were antagonistic to any revision, or at least nervous about it, thinking that the men who used the Prayer Book needed reforming rather than the book itself.[16] Others, while not resolutely resisting any changes whatsoever, only advocated limited modifications. Among such was Sir William Joynson-Hicks, who was to play such a crucial part in the decisive parliamentary debate.[17] A few Evangelicals more specifically recommended revision which would make the format and language of the Prayer Book more suitable for the twentieth century situation facing the church.[18] They were distressed by what they considered a widespread

---

[15] This summary of the events surrounding the attempted Prayer Book revision and its sequel is largely based on Bell, op.cit., pp.1325 f.

[16] See for example Albert Mitchell, 'The Public Worship of the Church', Churchman, March 1919, p.131.

[17] See for instance 'The Month', Churchman, December 1919, p.638.

[18] See for example H.A. Wilson, 'The Worship of the Church', Islington Clerical Meeting Report (1919), p.54.

combination of boredom and unreality in church services, and frustrated by what they regarded as an excessive delay in the introduction of drastic revision.

These divergent opinions did not represent any doctrinal disagreement. All Evangelicals were opposed to any revision which would entail a disturbance of the balance of doctrine contained in the existing Prayer Book.[19] Evangelicals as a whole were accused of adopting a purely negative position regarding the proposed changes in the Prayer Book. They were repeatedly depicted as mere obstructionists and obscurantists, with no desire to be helpful. In response, they claimed to be consistent and positive in upholding the basic requirements of doctrinal inviolability. They protested that the leaders of the majorities in the Church Assembly had wholly disregarded, and those in places of authority had made an inadequate attempt to maintain, the balance of doctrine in the Prayer Book. The strongly held views of Evangelicals had, they asserted, been ignored or discounted. They were responding to circumstances and pressures not of their own making. They had been forced to take a stand which might appear negative. In adopting this posture the Liberal and Conservative Evangelicals were at one. Thus, the Liberal Evangelical Canon Storr, speaking at the Islington meeting, was able to 'protest against any revision of the Prayer Book which shall ultimately destroy the balance of doctrine and the historical character of the Church of England'.[20] With this undivided and unyielding Evangelical alliance, a clash of major proportions at the final decision-making stages became more and more a probability.[21]

The setting aside of the eucharistic elements as in themselves representing the localized presence of God, and the adoration accorded to the elements, was especially abhorrent to Evangelicals.[22] The Liberal Evangelicals gave a cautious, qualified approval to the use of reserved elements in particular, well defined and circumscribed situations, but they quite clearly did not tolerate any setting aside for adoration. On the thorny question of the eastward position, the Liberal Evangelicals were not averse to flexibility. The mainstream Evangelicals had varying attitudes. Some were passionately against any compromise, while there were those who considered it a secondary matter.[23] Other issues under discussion in these

---

[19] For a contemporary expression of this unifying Evangelical concern, see H.W. Hinde, 'President's Introduction. The Present Position Concerning Prayer Book Revision', *Islington Clerical Meeting Report* (1925), pp.39, 40.

[20] V.F. Storr, *Islington Clerical Meeting Report* (1925), p.47.

[21] Some Evangelicals at the time were aware of this. See for example H.W. Hinde, 'The Conflict for the Truth. II. Prospective', *Islington Clerical Meeting Report* (1927), p.106.

[22] See for instance Dawson Walker, *Islington Clerical Meeting Report* (1925), pp.41, 42.

[23] *Ibid.*

years which were of vital concern to Evangelicals included prayers for the dead and vestments, and some ranked these with reservation as among the things of primary importance.[24]

The stage was set for a serious confrontation. There was a general mood of indignation among Evangelicals as they contemplated an assault upon those tenets of faith most cherished by them, and they were prepared to fight.[25] It was especially hurtful to them that the proposed changes seemed to be in a Romeward direction; and it was this fear, still dormant in even the most nominal churchmen, which particularly swayed opinion against the revisions.

Anti-revisionist Evangelicals communicated their views by means of a prolonged, persistent and intensive campaign using pamphlets and other means. Merely to list some of the booklets issued in the period before the parliamentary debates will indicate the extensiveness of the propaganda.

The Book Room publications numbered at least sixteen titles by such authors as Canon Girdlestone, Canon Barnes-Lawrence, Dean Henry Wace, Canon F. Meyrick and William Gillies; the Church Book Room produced at least three leaflets, two of which were by Bishop E.A. Knox; Longmans, Green and Co. contributed two pamphlets by Knox; and Chas J. Thynne and Jarvis, Ltd published twenty-four or more booklets, the authors of which included H.C.G. Moule, J.C. Ryle, Canon S. Garratt and W. Prescott Upton. Enormous numbers of these leaflets were distributed. For example, the sale of *Ritual and Ritualism* by F. Meyrick exceeded fourteen thousand, and the sale of *A Layman on Prayer Book revision* by Henry J. Guest was in excess of thirty thousand. The pamphlets were also supplemented by books. The most notable of those was by Sir William Joynson-Hicks, the Evangelical Home Secretary at the time of the parliamentary debate, which was published in May 1928 under the title *The Prayer Book Crisis*. It was particularly crucial in view of the prominence of its author and its timing.

The intense and sustained Evangelical campaign was reinforced by two submissions. In October 1918 a memorial was presented to the Archbishops signed by nine bishops, 3,000 clergy, and 100,000 laymen, protesting against any changes in the communion service, especially in so far as they would endorse reservation. The protesting bishops – Durham (Moule), Chester (Jayne), Liverpool (Chervasse), Manchester (Knox), Carlisle (Diggle), Sodor and Man (Denton Thompson), Bath and Wells (Kennion), and Chelmsford (Watts-Ditchfield) – were largely

---

[24] See for instance I. Siviter, *Islington Clerical Meeting Report* (1925), pp.45, 46,

[25] Evangelicals were summoned to unite in order to be more effective, as at the 1927 Islington meeting: see H.W. Hinde, 'The Conflict for the Truth. II. Prospective', *Islington Clerical Meeting Report*' (1927), p.111.

Evangelical, or in sympathy with the Evangelical view.[26]

In 1924, a memorial was presented to the House of Bishops which again objected to any alterations in the service of holy communion, and expressed resistance to any alternative communion service. It was signed by more than 304,500 communicants of the Church of England. In presenting it to the Archbishop of Canterbury, Bishop E.A. Knox appended an explanatory letter, and an influential representative deputation from among the signatories waited upon the Archbishop. The letter, and the comments of the delegation, not only clearly reflected the dominant concerns of Evangelicals, but also contained two specific warnings; first that the revisions would place limitations upon the comprehensiveness of the Church of England and, secondly, that there was danger in submitting to Parliament proposals on which there was such variance of opinion within the church.[27]

As the time of the parliamentary debate approached, the propagation of Evangelical opinion by means of leaflets, in newspapers and magazines, and through the spoken word was greatly intensified. The potency of their assertions was enhanced at a crucial juncture by the Malines Conversations, in which representatives of the Church of England discussed questions about unity with representatives of the Roman Catholic Church. The report on the Conversations, which was published early in 1928, raised the spectre of Romanism with added force, and caused widespread alarm.

Bishop Knox responded promptly in a pamphlet, *The Malines Conference and the Deposited Book*, in which he examined the significance of an apparent willingness to make major doctrinal concessions to the Romanists, and showed the bearing of this on the Prayer Book controversy. According to his interpretation of the conversations, the Anglican representatives unchurched all non-episcopalians; taught the presence of Christ in the elements; represented the sacrifice of the eucharist as the same as that of the cross, but offered in a mystical and sacramental manner; declared that the Church of England practised the sacrament of penance; required the church's interpretation of scripture; and were willing to give primacy of honour to the papacy.

---

[26] See Bell, *Randall Davidson*, Vol. II, p.1326.

[27] See E.A. Knox, 'A Letter to his grace the Lord Archbishop of Canterbury. On the occasion of the presentation of a Memorial against changes in the Communion office and Alternative Communion Service. Followed by a Verbatim Report of the Speeches made on that occasion (27 November, 1924)' (London, 1925), pp.5, 6.

Knox attempted to demonstrate that in the new Prayer Book 'many of the concessions and surrenders made at Malines are found to have been confirmed at Lambeth'. He warned that the new book would later be used to further reunion with Rome, and that that would mean submission.[28] 'None', said Hensley Henson, 'could doubt that the importance of the proceedings at Malines was very great. The immediate effect on the fortunes of the Prayer Book revision may, or may not, have been decisive; it was unquestionably large and unfavourable'.[29]

Despite the unremitting Evangelical pressure, it must not be concluded that opposition to the proposed new Prayer Book was an exclusive Evangelical concern. It was by no means so. The resistance was far-ranging; it was not the narrow preoccupation of a bigoted minority. Thus, within the church Hensley Henson was determined to guard the distinctive Reformed character of the Church of England. He was concerned about the temper and tendencies of the Anglo-Catholics. He considered that any other reservation than that for the sick should be resisted, both in the Church Assembly and in Parliament; and he carried a number of churchmen with him in these convictions.[30] The Modernists as represented by the *Modern Churchman* gave at most a qualified support to the proposed revisions.[31] There was even resistance to revision from within the Anglo-Catholic ranks.[32] In the population as a whole it seems that public opinion was to a marked extent sympathetic to the anti-revisionists.[33]

It is a sad commentary on the whole affair that the advocates of revision were themselves often lukewarm. J.G. Lockhart concluded that both Archbishops viewed revision as a question of expediency. 'The Prayer Book baby can hardly be said to have had very satisfactory godparents', he wrote, 'since one Archbishop did not really want it at all and the other Archbishop would have preferred something else'.[34] Perhaps the double rejection by Parliament was less of a blow liturgically to the church than it might superficially appear to have been; and perhaps a minority within the church was not dictating to a majority. The real issue at stake was not liturgical, or partisan: it was the question of the relationship of the Church of England to the state. The annulling by Parliament of such a major

---

[28] See *Churchman*, April 1928, pp.87, 88.

[29] Herbert Hensley Henson, *Retrospect of an Unimportant Life*, Vol.II, p.149.

[30] *Ibid.*, p.196.

[31] See for example E.W. Barnes, 'Evangelicals under the New Prayer Book', *Modern Churchman*, Vol.XVII, No.5, August 1927, p.265.

[32] See for instance G.L. Prestige, *The Life of Charles Gore* (London, 1935), pp.504, 505.

[33] See for example Notes and Comments, 'Press Opinion on the Debate', (*Churchman*, April 1928, p.84; and Editorial, *Modern Churchman*, Vol.XVII, Nos 11 and 12, February and March 1928, pp.612, 615.

[34] J.G. Lockhart, *Cosmo Gordon Lang*, (London, 1949), p.300.

decision, duly arrived at by the church through its own legislative process, was a shattering blow to many churchmen.

The Archbishops and other church leaders were not prepared to accept the decisions of Parliament as a *fait accompli*; so they authorized the publication of the revised Prayer Book, and stirred up a hornets nest. The National Church League[35] indignantly retorted that such an act was an encouragement to further lawlessness in public worship in the Church of England. On the suggestion of the House of Bishops, many bishops were encouraging the use of the communion office in the new book. Such action, the National Church League said, was plainly illegal, and showed a complete disregard for the solemn declaration made by every incumbent at his institution to the cure of souls, and by every archbishop and bishop at his consecration to 'use the form in the said Book prescribed and none other, except so far as shall be ordered by lawful authority'. The committee of the League thought that the publication of the revised Book would stimulate its use in cathedrals and churches, and that the decision of Parliament would thereby be ignored. This would, in their opinion, grievously damage the national church by identifying it with unconstitutional and irregular acts and policies.[36]

The Church Pastoral-Aid Society was generally careful to avoid comment on controversial matters of policy in the Church of England, and it shunned any undue partisanship, but it openly expressed its conviction that the church should accept and abide by the decision of Parliament.[37] The Church Association was more forthright and left no doubt about its reaction to the 'episcopal invasion of the rights of the laity'.[38] Various booklets commented critically on the action of the church.[39] The protestors included such eminent public figures and Evangelicals as Sir Thomas Inskip[40] and Sir Lewis Dibdin, the Dean of Arches.

[35] The National Church League was founded in 1906 by the amalgamation of the National Protestant Church Union (founded 1893) and the Church of England League (founded 1904, and formerly the Ladies' League, founded 1899). In 1950 the National Church League amalgamated with the Church Association to form the Church Society.

[36] See 'The New Prayer Book. N.C.L. Protest Against Publication', *Record*, 3 January 1929, p.3.

[37] See 'The Church Pastoral-Aid Society', *Churchman*, April 1935, p.116.

[38] For example see 'Lawful Authority'. Episcopal Invasion of the Rights of the Laity (London), last page.

[39] Examples include C.W. Hale Amos, *Behind the Anglican Smoke-Screen: The Coming Battle and the Call to Action: A Solemn Warning and Challenge to all who love the Established Church* (Eastbourne, 1933?) and Sir Lewis Dibdin, *A Christian State* (London, 1929).

[40] The Rt Hon. Sir Thomas Walker Hobart Inskip. Born 1876. Admiralty representative on War Crimes Committee, 1918-19; Chancellor of Truro Diocese, 1920-22; Solicitor General: 1922–January 1924, November 1924-1928, and 1931-32; Attorney General 1928-29 and 1932-36; Minister for the Co-ordination of Defence, 1936-39; Secretary for Dominion Affairs, 1939.

Although Evangelicals in general greeted the parliamentary rejection of the revised Prayer Book with euphoria, and were often vociferously resentful at the apparent defiance of the parliamentary decision, some sounded a note of caution. They pointed out that avid endorsement of the rule of Parliament had its dangers. What, they asked, would be the attitude of Evangelicals if, on another occasion, a Parliament possessed of a majority of members actively hostile to the Christian faith passed measures which were at variance with a particular Evangelical cause or interest? It was hazardous to look to Parliament as the last word in ecclesiastic and Christian matters.[41]

[41] See for example A.J.M. Macdonald, 'The Authority of the State', *Islington Clerical Meeting Report* (1935), pp.95, 96.

16

Biblical Criticism and the Emergence of Liberal Evangelicalism

Biblical criticism touched the nerve centre of Evangelicalism and under-standably produced very decided reactions. As with the protracted contention over ritualism, the issues raised probed deeply into the underlying presuppositions, as well as the more obvious declared beliefs of the Evangelicals, revealed basic inadequacies in their armoury, and caused grievous divisions among them. It was a battle in which some Evangelicals enthusiastically engaged the enemy, while others thought there was no enemy to engage; and almost all were ill-equipped to undertake any warfare at all on this particular front.

A number of Evangelicals viewed radical biblical criticism as a particu-larly virulent assertion of the supremacy of reason over faith, and their opposition to it was, in their estimation, a crusade against the misuse of reason, and an urgently needed defence of the faith once delivered to the saints. Others were sincerely of the opinion that biblical criticism should be welcomed as a new aid to the better understanding of the Bible. And there were those who persistently urged their fellow Evangelicals to remain calm: to accept that if the goal was 'truth', then ultimately there could be no incompatibility between the discoveries of biblical criticism and the sure facts of faith.

In the meantime these middlemen pleaded for the development of an Evangelical scholarship which would enable Evangelicals to engage in reasoned debate. They appealed for a sympathetic sifting of the evidence. They encouraged their fellow Evangelicals to examine what could be considered as of secondary importance, while vigorously holding fast to that which was basic and of primary importance; and they sought to promote among Evangelicals a deep faith which would commit the final outcome of the debate to God. There were many, often somewhat frenetic, responses to the varied forms and 'assured results' of biblical criticism, but this latter more rational approach was the one most frequently advocated by the Evangelical leadership. Although it was an attitude which demanded considerable restraint and patience, and despite the fact that it coexisted with the other less tolerant views, it asserted itself throughout this period.

Modernism

A number of theological developments particularly concerned and incensed the Evangelicals in the first decade and a half of the century. Of considerable importance among these was that movement collectively known as Anglican modernism. The attempt to win the 'modern cultivated man' back to practising Christianity had been energetically pursued since well into the preceding century. The Lux Mundi school had convinced many that critical study could be reconciled with orthodox faith. But although the marriage appeared for a while to escape undue strains, there remained those within the church who were radical and unappeased, and they were the parents of the twentieth century modernists. The modernists inherited the older Broad Church spirit. They wanted to separate inward religion from dogma, and to study the Bible like any other book. They opposed any rigid interpretation of subscription, and even questioned the necessity for subscription at all. Their concern was to keep the national church as comprehensive as the variety of religious outlook among the English people.[1] All those engaged in promoting these ideals were anxious that the Christian faith should be effectively communicated to the educated twentieth century man who rejected the orthodox formularies, but who was still willing, and indeed eager, to comprehend the essence of the faith in the light of modern thought.

At the beginning of the century modernism was greatly influenced by a powerful influx of continental thought: most notably the liberalism of

---

[1] See Arthur Michael Ramsey, *From Gore to Temple* (London, 1960), p.60.

Adolf von Harnack, and the eschatological teaching of Albert Schweitzer and Alfred Loisy. The eminence of Harnack in the field of theological interpretation at this time can hardly be overestimated. Some consider his dominance as great as Schleiermacher and Ritschl in a former generation, and Barth in a succeeding period. For forty years he bestrode the world of theological scholarship like a Colossus.[2] In a series of lectures in Berlin in 1901 he gave what came to be accepted as a classic exposition of liberal Protestantism; and this was subsequently translated into English under the title *What is Christianity?*[3]

The book helped to break down the normal isolation of English theology from continental thinking. Such was its impact, and the effect of similar teaching, that it must have seemed to many that the reign of liberal theology was permanent and assured. In England there was reproduced, amid the different conditions of English scholarship and piety, something akin to Harnack, both in critical method and religious attitude, which bore fruit in the work and lives of thinker as various and distinguished as T.R. Glover, W.R. Inge, William Sanday, B.H. Streeter, Hastings Rashdall and William Temple.

Albert Schweitzer introduced a very different interpretation of the life, death and significance of Jesus. He portrayed Christ as the apocalyptic teacher who proclaimed the imminence of the end, and died of a broken heart with the expectation unfulfilled. It was by means of such an evaluation of the gospel record that Alfred Loisy attempted to reconcile radical criticism of the gospels with loyalty to the Catholic faith, and by so doing brought Catholic modernism to birth. There were Anglicans who were sensitive to the religious outlook which this movement represented, and there was some affinity between it and its counterpart in the Church of England, although the kinship of English Anglican modernists was more with the liberal movement.

A definite stage in the advance of modernism was marked by the publication of *Foundations* in 1912. The purpose of this volume was to communicate a theology which was in harmony with modern science, philosophy and scholarship.[4] The contributors carefully re-examined and restated the foundations of their belief in the light of the knowledge and thought of the day. The appearance of the work immediately evoked a vigorous controversy, and generated a lively and widespread debate on the issues at stake. It gave a new boost to modernism, and in the following years the movement agitated the theological world in a more profound

---

[2] Stephen Neill, *The Interpretation of the New Testament 1861-1961* (Oxford, 1964), pp.130, 131.

[3] C.G.A. von Harnack, *What is Christianity?* (London, 1904).

[4] See the Introduction to B.H. Streeter (Ed.), *Foundations* (London, 1912), p.vii.

way than it had in the past. Indeed, *Foundations* was a formative influence for both Anglo-Catholicism and Evangelicalism.

In England the issues raised by the modernist movement found expression in controversy over subscription to two miraculous events mentioned in the Creed: 'born of the Virgin Mary', and 'on the third day he rose again from the dead'. In addition to those who held a doctrine which rigorously excluded the miraculous, there were those who believed in the incarnation as a supernatural event, but on grounds of historical criticism hesitated about the particular mode of the incarnation which the birth narratives in the gospels of Luke and Matthew describe. Others claimed that there was an apparent absence of reference in the earliest apostolic presentation of Christ either to the virgin birth or to the bodily resurrection of Christ from the tomb; and this made a suspension of judgement not only justified but obligatory for them. It was because of hesitancy concerning these two doctrines that William Temple was refused ordination in 1906. And it was largely because of his views on the incarnation that a storm of protest arose when it was proposed to appoint Hensley Henson to the see of Hereford in 1917.

From within the circles of nonconformity R.J. Campbell made his contribution to the theological turmoil of the early part of the century, and to the questioning of orthodox beliefs. He rejected the substitutionary or penal conception of the atonement but, with the publication in 1907 of *The New Theology*, he went beyond any restatement of one doctrine. Here was a reinterpretation of Christian theology under the influence of the idea of divine immanence. Campbell appeared especially to regard the incarnation as no more than the supreme example of God's indwelling: the distinction between God and man was blurred or, some even said, obliterated, through a comprehensive pantheism.

Underpinning all this new thinking was a vast amount of biblical criticism, in which the Bible was placed under a powerful scholarly microscope. The main conclusions of nineteenth century textual and literary criticism had become to a large extent a part of the stock-in-trade of many preachers and teachers. They were embodied in such influential works as S.R. Driver's *Introduction to the Literature of the Old Testament*[5], the writings of F.C. Burkitt, and the *Encyclopaedia Biblica*,[6] edited by T.K. Cheyne and J.S. Black. J.R.H. Moorman considers that by 1900 'all serious scholars had accepted without hesitation the main conclusions of biblical criticism'. He further asserts that fundamentalism was 'confined to a group of extreme Evangelicals and nonconformists, who clung to the

[5] S.R. Driver, *An Introduction to the Literature of the Old Testament* (eighth edition, revised 1891).
[6] T.K. Cheyne and J.S. Black (Eds), *Encyclopaedia Biblica* (London 1899-1903).

Bible in its literal sense as the final authority which could not be touched, and to the Roman Catholics'.[7] But the reaction of Evangelicals to biblical criticism, and to the kind of issues we have indicated, was not as uniform as Moorman seems to imply.

Evangelical Responses

Opposition to biblical criticism had characterized a large number of Evangelicals for two generations before the century began, and many of the grandchildren of the mid–nineteenth century controversialists maintained the assault. They were willing to concede little or nothing to the declared literary or historical discoveries and protested that any such analytical approach to the Bible was inappropriate and highly dangerous. The whole enterprise of applying 'modern thought' to the scriptures was dismissed as scandalous, or decried as totally unnecessary. The situation was presented with stark simplicity: no good thing could come out of higher criticism. The more extreme Evangelical opponents of higher criticism made no distinction between the various strands of biblical criticism. They were of the opinion that no investigation of the issues involved was necessary: all criticism was completely and unreservedly repudiated.[8]

Other Evangelicals drew a distinction between different types of biblical criticism. Thus, the octogenarian Canon A.M.W. Christopher of Oxford said that Evangelicals were not hostile to criticism which elucidated the history and meaning of scripture as long as it did not accept principles and adopt a standpoint which denied or minimized the supernatural. But no one who was truly Evangelical, he said, could be anything but uncompromisingly hostile to criticism of the Wellhausen type, and it was this school of thought which dominated the higher criticism of the day.[9]

[7] John R.H. Moorman, *A History of the Church of England* (London, 1953), p.395.
[8] There were frequent expressions of this view, of which the following are illustrative: Letter from Arthur W. Sutton, 'Evangelicalism and Modern Thought', *Record*, 21 June 1901, p.636; Letter from H.N. Watson, 'Evangelicalism and Modern Thought', *Record*, 28 June 1901, p.662; Letter from C.H. Waller, D.D., 'Evangelicalism and Modern Thought', *Record*, 19 July 1901, p.729; A.R. Buckland, 'Our Church: Her Faith and Catholicity: Summing-Up', *Islington Clerical Meeting Report* (1904), p.78; and W.T. Pilter, 'The attitude of Churchmen Towards I. Recent Criticism of the Old Testament; with special reference to Archaeological Discovery', *Islington Clerical Meeting Report* (1911), pp.16, 29.
[9] A.M.W. Christopher, 'Higher Criticism and Higher Criticism', *Churchman*, October 1907, p.690.

There was a still further body of Evangelicals who were even more conciliatory and more determined to seek after common ground with the higher critics. They were anxious to show that Evangelicals were not unenlightened and obtuse in their approach. Accepting the spirit and practice of criticism as inevitable, they thought it would be nothing less than disastrous for Evangelicals to place themselves out of sympathy with one of the ruling ideas of the age. They did not endorse all the results and conclusions of the criticism, but they were anxious to investigate the meaning of the movement before entering into condemnation; to see if there was anything in it which was acceptable to them, and compatible with fundamental Evangelical principles; and to use that which was good in their eyes for the promotion of the faith. They were anxious that Evangelicals should not find themselves stranded derelict on the shore, while the tide of progress flowed past and away from them, and they were alarmed at the attitude taken by some of their more inflexible Evangelical brethren.[10]

Indeed, it is a strange culmination to the relationship between Evangelicalism and higher criticism in the pre-First World War period that some of the more theologically 'liberal' Evangelicals became known as Evangelical Higher Critics. They made public their appreciation of the way the higher critical view had enlarged their understanding of the Bible. They were not ashamed to express opinions which were contrary to the more traditional Evangelicalism. They attracted the incredulous attention of conservative Evangelicals who suggested that they might more correctly call themselves Broad Churchmen, and that they had no right, in common honesty, to bear the name of Evangelical.

The differing Evangelical views were not held with a cold academic detachment, but with warm, and sometimes heated emotional earnestness. The issues at stake were too crucial, and too central to the heart of Evangelicalism for it to be otherwise. The combined effect of widespread Evangelical anti-ritualism and anti-higher criticism helped to produce rumblings of discontent, largely from those Evangelicals who sought a more reasoned and intellectually satisfying exposition of the faith than they said could be found in contemporary Evangelicalism. There was much frustration. Relationships were

---

[10] Examples of this approach are to be found in G.S. Streatfield, 'Questions that must be faced'; 'Evangelicals and Modern Thought', *Record*, 7 June 1901, pp.588, 589; Hay Aitken, The Annual Sermon of the Church Pastoral-Aid Society for 1911, in the Church Pastoral-Aid Society *Annual Report* (1911), p.35; Eugene Stock, 'A Plain Man's Thoughts on Biblical Criticism', *Record*, 10 March 1911, p.244; W.H. Griffith Thomas, 'Modernism', *Churchman*, December 1907, p.706; and J.A. Harris, 'Evangelical Doctrine and Modern Thought', *Churchman*, October 1907, pp.591, 592.

soured, and Evangelicalism was not infrequently depleted by the secession of those so alienated.[11]

The Group Brotherhood

This unease was most acutely felt by some of the younger generation. It was in 1905 that three of them, A.J. Tait,[12] C. Lisle Carr,[13] and Guy Warman,[14] decided to campaign for a more positive, thoughtful and relevant attitude among Evangelicals. They expressed themselves at various gatherings of the clergy, and after the Islington conference of 1906 they enlisted the support of J.E. Watts-Ditchfield,[15] J.C. Wright,[16] F.T Woods,[17] H.V. de Candole,[18] Dawson Walker,[19] and a number of others. It was decided to form groups of sympathetic friends up and down the country, to hold an annual conference in the summer, and a one-day conference on the day after the Islington meetings. The movement soon became known as the Group Brotherhood, although it remained for more than eighteen years a private, almost a secret organization. The first conference was held in 1907. Pamphlets were issued which expounded the views of the brotherhood. The movement became slightly more structured with the election of a committee. But the greatest importance was still given to informal group meetings throughout the country; small numbers gathered to pray and study together in an effort to 'think out afresh the doctrinal position of Evangelicals and to state in new terms the

---

[11] Evangelicals were aware of this disunity and concerned about it: see, for example, J.A. Harris, 'Evangelical Doctrine and Modern Thought', *Churchman*, op. cit., pp.586-588.

[12] Arthur James Tait. Born 1872. Principal of St Aidan's Theological College, Birkenhead 1901-7; Principal of Ridley Hall, Cambridge 1907-27; Canon Residentiary of Peterborough 1924-44. Died 1944.

[13] Charles Lisle Carr. Born 1871. Archdeacon of Norfolk 1916-18; Archdeacon of Norwich 1918-20; Vicar and Archdeacon of Sheffield 1920-22; Bishop of Coventry 1922-31; Bishop of Hereford 1931-41. Died 1942.

[14] F.S. Guy Warman. Born 1872. Bishop of Truro 1919-23; Bishop of Chelmsford 1923-29; Bishop of Manchester 1929-47.

[15] A brief biographical sketch of J.E. Watts-Ditchfield is given in a subsequent chapter.

[16] John Charles Wright. Born 1861. Canon Residentiary of Manchester 1904-9; Archdeacon of Manchester 1909; Archbishop of Sydney and Metropolitan of New South Wales 1909-33; Primate of Australia 1910-33. Died 1933.

[17] F. Theodore Woods. Born 1874. Bishop of Peterborough 1916-23; Bishop of Winchester 1924-32. Died 1932.

[18] Henry Lowe Corry Vully de Candole. Born 1868. Vicar of Holy Trinity, Cambridge 1902-18; Dean of Bristol 1926-33. Died 1933.

[19] Dawson Dawson-Walker. Born 1868. Professor of Biblical Exegesis in the University of Durham 1910-19; Co-Editor of the *Churchman* 1910-14; Principal of St John's College, Durham 1912-19; Canon Residentiary of Durham and Professor of Divinity and Ecclesiastical History, Durham University 1919-34. Died 1934.

contribution which they had to make to contemporary life and thought'.[20] This was felt to be a most urgent task. The movement reached the height of its influence in the inter-war years, when it emerged into the full light of day, and broadcast its findings more widely; but the foundations were laid in the pre-war years.

There was a certain identity of purpose between the Group Brotherhood and the attempt in 1911 by Canon J. Denton Thompson to present authentic Evangelicalism as the true Central Churchmanship; the key to the future of the Church of England.[21] The element common to both the Group Brotherhood and the Central Churchmanship concept was the search for openness and flexibility in things considered of secondary importance, combined with an unambiguous retention of those doctrines which were accepted as essential to the faith.[22]

The Modern Churchmen's Union

In the inter-war years both Anglican modernism and Liberal Evangelicalism became more coherent and distinguishable. There was great variety among the modernists, but they had certain common characteristics and objectives. Theirs was a rebellion and an ideal, rather than a system. It was a determined effort to protect the rights of free inquiry, to harmonize the findings of the modern sciences with Christian belief, and to insist that there is development in the understanding of the Christian faith. Although these common concerns were expressed in different ways, there was a unity of purpose sufficient to cement them as a party. And this identity of interest found expression in the Churchmen's Union for the Advancement of Religious Thought. Founded in 1898, in 1928 it was renamed the Modern Churchmen's Union. Between 1918 and 1939 it became more aggressive in its promotion of a more identifiable and self-conscious modernism. This was largely due to the exertions of men such as H.D.A. Major, for many years principal of Ripon Hall, and M.G. Glazebrook, first headmaster of Clifton and subsequently Canon of Ely.

In the immediate post-war years Christology provided the focus of modernist theological interest; and it was this subject which was debated at the notorious conference of the Modern Churchmen's Union at Girton College in 1921. The scene had been set by the appearance of the first

[20] Leonard Elliott-Binns, *The Evangelical Movement in the English Church* (London, 1928), p.71.
[21] The core of his thesis is identified in 'Central Churchmanship', *Record*, 13 October 1911, p.949.
[22] This enlargement of Evangelical sympathies is discussed in B. Herklots, *The Future of the Evangelical Party in the Church of England* (London, 1913), pp.29, 30.

volume of *The Beginnings of Christianity*, under the editorship of F.J. Foakes Jackson and Kirsopp Lake.[23] In it Jesus was depicted as the bearer of an ethical message, prophetic in a mild sense, but extraordinarily jejune. The Girton conference came to conclusions, as reported and commented upon by Major, which caused a considerable stir in the church, and indeed in the country. Newspaper articles, quoting phrases out of context, created the impression that Rashdall and others were denying the divinity of Christ.

In 1922, partly as a consequence of the Girton conference, the Archbishops appointed a commission to consider the nature and basis of Christian doctrine with a view to demonstrating the extent of existing agreement within the Church of England, and to investigating how far it was possible to remove or diminish differences. It did not report until 1938, by which time other issues were occupying the centre of the stage.

Liberal Catholicism

Charles Gore was foremost as a protagonist in the modernist controversy, and hammered them unmercifully. He was also the chief proponent of what he called 'Liberal Catholicism'. In the inter-war years, he set forth and popularized his presentation of the faith in a trilogy entitled *The Reconstruction of Belief*. The first volume, *Belief in God*, appeared in 1921, the second, *Belief in Christ*, a year later, and the final volume, *The Holy Spirit and the Church*, in 1925. By Catholicism Gore meant

> that way of regarding Christianity which would see in it not merely or primarily a doctrine of salvation to be apprehended by individuals, but the establishment of a visible society as the one divinely constituted home of the great salvation, held together not only by the inward Spirit but also by certain manifest and external institutions.[24]

By 'Liberal' he meant that the belief in the catholic church must go hand in hand with the constant appeal to scripture as the standard of doctrine and moral judgement, and with a continued concern for the intellectual integrity of the individual. He believed that Liberal Catholicism was precisely embodied in the Anglican appeal to scripture, antiquity and reason; for him it did not denote a party, or a type of religion, or peculiar dogmas. The greatest monument to Liberal Catholicism in the period

---

[23] F.J. Foakes Jackson and Kirsopp Lake (Eds), *The Beginnings of Christianity* (London, 1920).

[24] Charles Gore, *Catholicism and Roman Catholicism* (London, Oxford, 1923), p.1, quoted in Arthur Michael Ramsey, *From Gore to Temple*, p.100.

between the wars was *Essays Catholic and Critical*, published in 1926 under the editorship of E.G. Selwyn. The book was written in conscious succession to *Lux Mundi*. It was inspired by the belief that the catholic and the critical elements are necessary to one another. In this respect it, and the whole Liberal Catholic movement, reached out towards Liberal Evangelicalism.

Liberal Evangelicalism

In 1923 the members of the Group Brotherhood decided that it was appropriate and desirable for them to present a reasoned and comprehensive statement of their theological position, not as a challenge to fellow Evangelicals, but rather as an eirenicon; and they chose to do so by means of a volume of essays.[25] *Liberal Evangelicalism* was a plea that, in confident reliance on the basic Evangelical principles, Evangelicals, and Christians in general, should follow wherever the pursuit of truth led them. There should be no quarrel between science and religion and no divorce between religion and secular knowledge, which would assuredly happen if modern scholarship was rejected. Literary criticism, natural science and philosophy were not the enemies of Evangelicalism, but its three most powerful allies; its enemies were the forces of worldly indifference, superstition, ignorance, and fear. For too long, the writers said, Evangelicals had been afraid of the new learning. The right use of criticism, science, and philosophy, they asserted, would not disintegrate the Evangelical faith. So long as they remained true to the moral and religious teaching of Christ, Evangelicals were in no danger of becoming Unitarians. They could give stronger reasons than their spiritual ancestors for believing in God the Father, in the deity of Christ, in human immortality, and in the atonement. The future was with them.

Although no one person was preeminent in the Evangelical movement during this period, Vernon F. Storr was widely recognized as the foremost representative of Liberal Evangelicalism. As early as 1915 Archbishop Davidson indicated this by choosing him as one of twelve clergymen of different schools of thought charged with the task of recommending the most appropriate and effective ways whereby the church should respond to the peculiar challenges of the war years. The outstanding result of their deliberations was the National Mission. He was also consulted by Archbishop Davidson regarding the Malines Conversations, and Davidson took special note of Storr's views during the fraught time of Prayer Book revision.

[25] Their intentions were clear. See T. Guy Rogers, 'Introduction', *Liberal Evangelicalism* (pp. vii, viii).

Indeed, it was Storr who, in 1927, wrote to Davidson on behalf of Liberal Evangelicals, and drew from the Archbishop one of the strongest statements he made during the whole Prayer Book discussion, in which he reassured Storr that the bishops would require obedience to what was laid down in the new Book if the Measures introducing it received the Royal Assent. This was typical of the response of many non-Evangelical Churchmen to a man they respected for his unusual breadth of under-standing, knowledge and sympathy.

It was perhaps these qualities, together with his theological grasp, which resulted in his appointment as Archdeacon of Westminster (1931-1936), rector of St Margaret's, and examining chaplain to Archbishop Cosmo Gordon Lang. His outstanding theological acumen was exhibited in his book, *The Development of English Theology in the Nineteenth Century* (1913), which was highly regarded for decades. Dean Inge of St Paul's, when he declined consideration for appointment as Regius Professor of Divinity at Oxford, thought Storr would be the best man for the post: a further indication of the reputation of one of the most influential Evangelicals in the first half of the century.

Storr, and the other Liberal Evangelicals, emphasized that it was the mind of Christ and not the letter of holy scripture which was authoritative. They regarded the Bible as a literary product, in a class by itself among the national literatures of the world, but subject to the laws and principles which govern the growth of any literature. As a corollary to this, they considered some books and parts of the Bible as of more spiritual value than others. Most controversially, in the eyes of many Evangelicals, they also pronounced that the scriptures were not infallible.

The biblical authors were, they said, taught by God, but not so controlled by the Spirit that they were incapable of error, or lifted above the level of their contemporaries in their general knowledge of science and history. Revelation was progressive. The Bible did not claim infallibility for itself, and we should not do so either. Liberal Evangelicals gladly conceded that many of the books of the Bible were composite products, which had reached their present form by a process of gradual construction and revision. Even Christ, who was truly man as well as truly God, was subject to limitations of knowledge on such issues as the authorship of the Pentateuch and on scientific matters.

The Liberal Evangelicals were dissatisfied with some of the penal and substitutionary theories of the atonement, which they regarded as crude. They wanted to avoid a self-contained and closed twentieth century Evangelical theological system which was not open to change. Finally, some of them were fairly advanced in their liturgical views, being tolerant of the eastward position, and prepared to advocate elaborate vestments and the practice of reservation, as long as there was no worship of the consecrated elements. Predictably all this greatly aggravated many Evangelicals. They identified it as a sell-out to modernism, and a retreat from true Evangelicalism.

The Bible Churchmen's Missionary Society

The disunity of Evangelicals was perhaps most poignantly and publicly demonstrated by the dramatic split in that bastion of Evangelicalism, the Church Missionary Society, which culminated in 1922 in the establishment of the Bible Churchmen's Missionary Society. As early as 1912 a number of clergymen presented a memorial to the general committee of the CMS deprecating the occasional invitation to Tractarian sympathizers to speak at the society's meetings. The committee drew attention to the mood of co-operation between all churches and denominations since the 1910 Edinburgh Conference: the invitations to which objection was made were claimed to be consistent with the new, more harmonious climate, and with the principles upon which the society had been founded. A large number of letters and memorials followed during the next ten years. These can be divided broadly into two categories: those favouring a comprehensive approach, while maintaining loyalty to the traditional CMS evangelical stance, and those claiming that such loyalty did not permit comprehensiveness.

Many of those who advocated a broad approach were members of the Group Brotherhood. Prominent among their opponents was the Rev. D.H.C. Bartlett, a Liverpool incumbent. The critics of the CMS were mainly concerned that the absolute authority of the Bible, the finished work of Christ as the one and only Redeemer and the necessity of the work of the Holy Spirit in the regeneration and sanctification of the sinner should be unambiguously upheld.

It appeared to Bartlett and others that these beliefs were being compromised in four specific ways: by the teaching given to some CMS candidates; by the beliefs of certain candidates; by co-operation with societies which, it was alleged, did not hold basic CMS beliefs; and by some missionaries adopting the eastward position.

In reply the specially constituted CMS memorials subcommittee, under the chairmanship of F.J. Chavasse, Bishop of Liverpool, stated that there was no thought of swerving from the principles of the Reformation or those on which the CMS had been founded. The normal practice of the CMS officers was to take the north side for the celebration of the holy communion, but sometimes courtesy would lead some clergy to assume the eastward position on particular occasions. The committee recognized 'Holy Scripture as the Revelation of God mediated by inspired writers, and as holding a unique position as the supreme authority in matters of faith', but at the same time the committee resisted any attempt to 'lay down a formulated definition' of inspiration. The use and treatment of the Bible should, they said, be in harmony with that of Christ. Also, they added, 'it is the duty of the student of Holy Scripture, under the guidance of the Holy Spirit, to employ every faculty in its study, and to take into the fullest consideration every light that scholarship and saintliness can furnish'.

The committee were especially concerned about the selection of candidates as missionaries. They emphasized that 'personal devotion to Christ as Lord should be a primary condition of acceptance, and that such doctrinal definitions as are more appropriate to maturer years should not be required'. They were anxious that the appeal to the student world should be such as 'to show that the Society is neither out of date nor impervious to new ideas or new methods of working'. And, finally, the committee advocated openness without compromise in relationships with other societies. 'The growth of friendly intercourse in missionary work . . . is to be welcomed and fostered . . . provided that in all such intercourse the adherence of the Society to great Evangelical principles be maintained'.[26]

Much debate and correspondence ensued, both within the CMS and in the columns of Christian publications. It was conducted with intensity of conviction on both sides and generated considerable resentment. Not infrequently it was bitter and even personal, especially when it was directed at the CMS General Secretary, the Rev. Cyril Bardsley.

Events were now moving fast. Tension was heightened by a resolution from Bartlett on the authority of scripture, which was presented at the March 1922 meeting of the CMS general committee. The committee was divided in its response. The Bishop of Chelmsford called a conference in June at Coleshill, not in order to draw up any creed for evangelicals in general, or for the CMS in particular, but in an attempt to determine the limits of legitimate comprehensiveness acceptable to all the main factions concerned. No agreement was reached. At the August meeting of the general committee there was only a slight possibility of reconciliation. In desperation a subcommittee was set up in an effort to secure harmonious co-operation; but time had run out. Before the subcommittee report was published, a group of about thirty clergy and laity met on 27 October, at the Christian Alliance of Women and Girls, 24 Bedford Square, London and decided to found the Bible Churchmen's Missionary Society. Bartlett was appointed Secretary, and the new society launched out into independent life.

[26] CMS Archives ref: G/c13.

The force and intensity of emotion and conviction aroused by this whole debate was well demonstrated in the pages of the *Bible Churchmen's Missionary Messenger*, the monthly magazine produced from January 1923 onwards by the new society. By means of this periodical the infant missionary organization unequivocally declared its determination to abide by what it perceived as the distinctive Evangelical message. In bold type the cover of the magazine pronounced that the society was 'For the witness of Jesus and For the Word of God'. This was reinforced on the first page, where, under the title of the society, was written "Scriptural, Protestant, Evangelical – Hy Venn, 1842". Beneath that, again in bold type, St Luke ix. 26 was quoted: 'Whosoever shall be ashamed of *Me* and of *My words*, of him shall the Son of Man be ashamed, when He shall come in His own glory, and in His father's, and of the holy angels', with the annotation ' "Me" and "My Words" stand or fall together. The BCMS *knows* they stand'. In the editorial notes to the first edition the ambition of the society was left in no doubt: 'We hope the BCMS will become the rallying ground for true spiritual Scriptural Evangelicalism at Home and in the Mission Field'.[27]

The links with the CMS were plain from the outset. The Founders of the BCMS made it very clear that the new society was seen by them as the continuance of the original and traditional Evangelicalism of the CMS, which had been betrayed in recent years. Thus, as mentioned, Henry Venn, perhaps the most revered of the CMS Secretaries, was prominently quoted under the title of the society. And on the inside cover of the first edition of the magazine, under the heading 'From a Missionary-hearted Veteran', H.E. Fox warmly commended the magazine:

> One who all his life has been closely connected with Christian Missions desires to offer his hearty welcome to a new Missionary Magazine. He need not dwell on the circumstances which have called it into existence, but all the more he hopes and prays that it will deepen and widen the obedience of many to the parting command of Our Lord Jesus. Loyalty to Him, and to the Message, of which He has called us to be bearers, should be the motive of all who bear His name.

And the pathos of this eulogy is in the gloss at the end of his statement, where it recorded in heavy print that Mr Fox was the 'Hon Sec CMS 1895-1910'.[28] He was in fact the immediate predecessor in that post of the Rev. Cyril Bardsley. Also, the very name of the new society was

[27] Editorial Notes, *Bible Churchmen's Missionary Messenger*, Vol.I, No.I, January 1923, p.3.
[28] H.E.Fox, Hon.Sec. CMS 1895-1910, 'From a Missionary-hearted Veteran', *Bible Churchmen's Missionary Messenger*, Vol.I, No.I, January 1923, inside cover.

extremely suggestive. The initials only differed from those of the CMS by the prefixing of the letter B, and that stood for Bible.

The relationship between the two societies in the first few years of the life of the BCMS was at best tolerant, and at worst hostile. The dispute within the CMS and the eventual breakaway movement brought into the glare of public scrutiny the tensions and disagreements between the Liberal and the traditional, more conservative Evangelicals which had been festering since the early years of the century.

17

The Social Question

The strife over ritualism and higher criticism deeply divided Evangelicals. Their discomfort and disunity were, however, increased by the demands made upon them to face up to the equally searching questions raised by Socialism, the Labour Movement and the 'social question'. Ritualism and higher criticism sorely tested their mental and spiritual resources; social issues racked their social conscience, searched out their ability and willingness to indulge in social analysis, and examined the extent and depth of their social compassion.

The fervour of the Christian Socialist movement, which was subject to rapid variations, was kindled afresh in 1906 by the general election, and the subsequent Liberal programme of social legislation, and by the birth of the Church Socialist League. The Guild of St Matthew had become almost moribund by this time, and the Christian Social Union was ill prepared to take advantage of the newly aroused reforming zeal and social hope evident in various sectors of society.

The founding of the Church Socialist League helped to change this. At the time of its establishment there was a mood of almost unbounded confidence. At last, it was felt, a unifying principle had been found, and a slogan was coined by Lewis Donaldson to express this conviction: 'Christianity is the religion of which Socialism is the practice'. Many churchmen identified themselves with this sentiment, including the young William Temple. Conrad Noel, the League's first organizer, carried the message round the country. Priests, such as Donaldson at Leicester, Gobat at Darlington and Widdrington at Coventry, were fired by a new vision and enthusiasm. Demonstrations were held in Trafalgar Square. There was a great procession to Lambeth during the mining dispute in 1912, with George Lansbury bearing a scarlet cross at its head; and a number of Christian Socialists assumed posts of eminence and influence in the church. Nevertheless, by 1914 the movement was once again losing much of its momentum. To a marked extent it was infected by a too optimistic humanitarianism and had lost some of its former cutting edge. One of its leaders, Egerton Swann, writing just before the First World War, recognized this weakness:

> Too many Christian Socialists think of the Kingdom of God as merely a human society in which perfect justice rules and whose members are bound together by perfect human love. It is simply the apotheosis of humanitarianism . . . God for them remains quite in the background.[1]

The events of the next four years administered a severe blow to any such faith in the capacity for human progress and achievement.

Despite all its imperfections, and its decline around the time of the First World War, Christian Socialism in its different guises had accomplished much. During the first two decades of the twentieth century the permeation of the leadership of the Church of England by the ideals and attitudes previously confined largely to the enthusiasts of the Christian Social Union was truly remarkable, and the influence of social radicalism spread rapidly through the church. It was unusual, after 1900, to find a bishop who did not regard the declaration of social principles as a primary duty. The new analysis and criticism of the social order became especially articulate among the block of Christian Social Union bishops; and their social thought received its clearest expression in the persuasive oratory of William Temple. The official deliberations of the church were also coloured by the 1907 Canterbury Convocation report, 'The Moral Witness of the Church on Economic Subjects', the prominence given to social issues at the Pan-Anglican Congress in the same year, and the Lambeth Conference report of 1908 on the 'Moral Witness of the Church'. The importance of social issues was also acknowledged and placed more forthrightly before churchmen as a consequence of the Student Christian Movement conference held at Matlock in 1909 under the title of 'Christianity and Social Problems'. This was chaired by William Temple and reckoned by him as the precursor of the Conference on Christian Politics, Economics and Citizenship (COPEC) in 1924.[2]

[1] Quoted in Maurice B. Reckitt, *Maurice to Temple: A Century of the Social Movement in the Church of England* (London, 1947), p.154.

[2] This whole section owes much to E.R. Norman, *Church and Society in England 1770-1970: A Historical Study* (Oxford, 1960), pp.221-239.

As a consequence of the First World War, the church was more than ever thrown on the defensive and forced to re-examine a good many aspects of her apologetic and life. Conditions of war, and especially the experience of the three thousand Anglican chaplains, brought home to church leaders in a new and forceful way the extent of the alienation of the church from the people, and the widespread lack of Christian knowledge displayed by ordinary Englishmen. The war provided a stimulus for a more thorough examination of those areas of concern to the 'average man' which so materially affected the life styles of millions of ordinary citizens, but on which the church had so little to say.

The first major initiative by the church in response to this renewed awareness was taken during the war itself. The Archbishops appointed five committees as part of the National Mission in 1916. The one most directly concerned with social policy produced a report on *Christianity and Industrial Problems*, which was something of a summary of recent radical thought. In 1920 yet another committee appointed by the Archbishop of Canterbury examined *The Church and Social Service*, and showed both in its terms of reference and its report the degree to which the church had accepted collectivist principles. The Lambeth Conference in the same year echoed current criticism of existing social relationships. It declared that nothing less was required than a fundamental change in the spirit and working of contemporary economic life. This change could only be effected by accepting as the basis of industrial relations the principle of co-operation in service for the common good in place of unrestricted competition for private or sectional advantage. All Christian people ought to take an active part in bringing about this change, by which alone there was any hope of removing class dissensions and resolving industrial discords.[3] The Lambeth principles were popularized in the church by the work of the Industrial Christian Fellowship, which was founded in 1919.

Of central importance in the social thinking of the church in the inter-war years was the 1924 assembly in Birmingham of the Conference on Christian Politics, Economics and Citizenship (COPEC). It was a watershed in that it provided a more systematic and co-ordinated statement than previously achieved of the Christian social radicalism of the preceding decade. It also prepared the ground for the criticism and social writing known as Christian Sociology, which did so much in the years between the wars to condition the future attitudes of the church. The span of subjects covered at the conference is shown by the titles of its reports: *The Nature of God and His Purpose for the World, Education, The Home, The Relation of the Sexes, Leisure, The Treatment of Crime,*

---

[3] See Norman, *op.cit.*, p.245.

International Relations, Christianity and War, Industry and Property, Politics and Citizenship, The Social Function of the Church, and *Historical Illustrations of the Social Effects of Christianity*. The COPEC philosophy that 'the Gospel provides the Christian with the solution of all the problems involved in our earthly life' was, however, rejected by many. The most distinguished of its critics, Hensley Henson, asserted that this assumption was false, and the true position was the exact reverse. For, he said, 'it is fundamental in Christ's religion that the redemption of the world must be effected through the redemption of individuals'.[4]

Another important contribution to the reinforcement of the principles of social radicalism in these years was the publication in 1926 of R.H. Tawney's *Religion and the Rise of Capitalism*.[5] It was a historical explanation of the transition from the medieval practice of Christian economic teaching to modern competitive individualism. Economics and religion had, according to Tawney, become separated. The unhappy result reported by every Christian Socialist, and many others not of that school, was:

> a dualism which regards the secular and religious aspects of life, not as successive stages within a large unity, but as parallel and independent provinces, governed by different laws, judged by different standards, and amenable to different authorities.[6]

Tawney's other books, notably *The Acquisitive Society* (1921), and *Equality* (1931), became essential reading for those interested in social criticism.

The leading socialist movement in the Church of England in the years between the wars was the 'Christendom Group'. It arose out of a gathering of Anglo-Catholics at Coggeshall in Essex in 1920; the findings of which were published in 1922 under the title *The Return of Christendom*. In 1931 a quarterly was started entitled *Christendom: A Journal of Christian Sociology*; and the following year an annual conference was instituted. The 'Christian Sociology' which they did so much to foster was not sociology in the technical, scientific sense, for it was normative and propagandist; but it was a serious attempt to define distinctly Christian principles of society derived from Christian doctrine. It acquired an interdenominational dimension, and drew upon various Protestant bodies. V.A. Demant was especially active; and by his prolific writings he furthered the ideals at the core of Christian Sociology. He said that the prophetic duty of the church justified it in intervening in political affairs.

---

[4] Hensley Henson, *Quo Tendimus?*, the Primary Charge delivered at his Visitation (London, 1924), pp.84, 86, quoted in Norman, *op.cit.*, pp.310, 311.

[5] R.H. Tawney, *Religion and the Rise of Capitalism: A Historical Study*, revised edition (London, 1944).

[6] Tawney, *op.cit.*, p.279, quoted in Norman, *op.cit.*, p.31.

To some extent Christian Sociology filled the gap left by the Christian Social Union in acting as an expression of Christian social radicalism; but it was the ascendancy of William Temple in the years after COPEC which most contributed to this. He continued for many years to symbolise the church leaderships general acceptance of a respectable version of social radicalism. Even if the church as a whole lacked the social commitment which the radicals would have wished, there was in the inter-war years a growing social consciousness in church circles. But what of the Evangelicals?

Evangelical Response

Evangelicals were aware of the serious social issues which confronted them,[7] but they were somewhat tardy and ineffectual in their response. They had a magnificent tradition of social and philanthropic service, as has been previously indicated, but this merely served to throw into stark relief their rather meagre and inadequate efforts in the first four decades of the twentieth century.[8] Leading Evangelicals such as J.E. Watts-Ditchfield, vicar of St James the Less, Bethnal Green, were intimately involved in practical work to help meet major social problems in deprived areas. They urged their fellow Evangelicals to address themselves to issues such as poor housing, malnutrition, unemployment, poor employment, and intemperance,[9] but few responded sympathetically. Some stoutly resisted such appeals, claiming that no special attention should be given by Evangelicals to social problems.[10]

There was very little concentrated Evangelical thought given to the root causes of social problems. It was too easy for the explanation to be given in terms of a simplistic reference to individual sin, and the pervasive effect of original sin.

The social thinking of the church as a whole had, for about forty years, been dominated by High Church incarnational theology, and the concept of the Kingdom of God.[11] In the light of this particular theological focus,

---

[7] See for example H. Barlow, 'Introduction', *Islington Clerical Meeting Report* (1908), pp. 10–12.

[8] These shortcomings were acknowledged by most Evangelicals. See for example Canon Lewis, 'Evangelical Churchmen and Social Problems', *Churchman*, September 1907, pp.544, 545.

[9] See for instance J.E. Watts-Ditchfield, 'The Church and Social Problems: The Church and the Solution', *Islington Clerical Meeting Report* (1908), pp.82, 84.

[10] See for example Canon Lewis, 'Housing in Town and Country', *Islington Clerical Meeting Report* (1908), p.26.

[11] See Arthur Michael Ramsey, *From Gore to Temple: The Development of Anglican Theology between Lux Mundi and the Second World War 1889-1939* (London, 1960), p.16.

the fact that God was incarnate in Christ, and thereby fully identified with the affairs of this world, gave special significance to social problems, and Christian social work. The immanence of God, manifested supremely in the incarnation, gave a framework for the consideration of specific social issues. Likewise, the biblical teaching on the Kingdom of God was used as a blueprint or ideal for social relationships, and for society as a whole.

The Evangelicals, with their focus on the atonement, did not produce a similar conceptual framework for the analysis of social matters. They were not able to develop a Christian social or ethical philosophy based on the 'extention of the atonement'. Their primary doctrinal emphasis equipped them well for coping with individual spiritual matters, and even individual behavioural problems, but it was less helpful in the theological understanding of such questions as bad housing and sweated industries. Evangelicals were engaged in social work in an unheralded way, but theirs was a pragmatic approach. They did not think profoundly about social issues or develop their own distinctive philosophy and theology for social action.

Most Evangelicals rejected the Socialist interpretation of society. Socialism appeared to them to be a menace which must be resolutely resisted.[12] Others at least seriously questioned it.[13] A mere handful of Evangelicals were tentatively enthusiastic about the movement, perhaps with certain qualifications, or were themselves active Socialists. Among the clear sympathizers, at least with Socialism in its more moderate form, as seen in the British Labour movement, were J.E. Watts-Ditchfield, A.J. Carlyle and the Labour leader George Lansbury.[14]

Evangelical comments on social issues assumed that the Bible was the source for Christian principles. Some Evangelicals, as with many Christian Socialists, looked primarily to the biblical teaching on the Kingdom of God for a vision of the ideal society.[15] When contemporary society was considered, concern was especially expressed at the high level of competitiveness. Competition was recognized as an element in

---

[12] For some contemporary expressions of this view see Richard Glover, Letter to the Editor, *Record*, December 1911; A.E. Barnes-Lawrence, 'The Unseen and the Seen', *The Annual Address to the Church Pastoral-Aid Society* (1911), p.34; and Canon Lewis, 'Evangelical Churchmen and Social Problems', *Churchman*, September 1907, p.547.

[13] See for instance W. Edward Chadwick, 'The Clergy and Social reform', *Churchman*, February 1908, pp.86, 87.

[14] An indication of their opinions is given in J.E. Watts-Ditchfield, 'The Church and the Labour Movement', *Churchman*, January 1908, p.35; A.J. Carlyle, 'The Church and the Solution', *Islington Clerical Meeting Report* (1908), p.74; and George Lansbury, 'The Unemployed', *Islington Clerical Meeting Report* (1908), pp.45, 46.

[15] See for example W. Edward Chadwick, 'Children and Sweating', *Islington Clerical Meeting Report* (1908), p.12.

capitalism but, with varying degrees of emphasis, Evangelicals pointed to the ill effects of its overdevelopment: the exploitation of cheap labour, pressures to outdo rather than love competitors, and the tendency for employers and employees to be set in opposing camps rather than working for the common good.

Some thought that the existing social and economic system in England was clearly unsuccessful in distributing wealth. The competition inherent in capitalism produced luxury without abolishing poverty. It had split society into two great classes with conflicting ideals and it was the most important contributory factor in unemployment. Nonetheless, most Evangelicals appear to have accepted capitalism as a system; they sought for a reform of the more blatant evils in it.[16] Only a few advocated a total replacement of the existing order by some form of socialistic system.[17] A few showed an openness to any social structure which would promote social conditions most in conformity with the Christian ideal, but even these tended to repudiate socialism.

Although only a very small minority of Evangelicals gave serious consideration to the current social malaise, they did try to face the realities of specific social problems. Poverty was seen as a root cause of much social evil, and some Evangelicals called for a fundamental redistribution of wealth by means of personal philanthropy, local rates or state taxes. Bad housing could, they believed, be eradicated by a similar combination of radical private and public action. The churches should confront bad landlords with their responsibilities, and stir up Christians to their social obligations.

In the inter-war years, with their frequent and often catastrophic slumps, sustained and sometimes alarmingly high level of unemployment, and serious industrial unrest, it is understandable that industrial relations attracted comment from Evangelicals. In attempting to apply distinctly Christian principles to the complex industrial scene, they drew attention to the infinite value of all men as children of God, the consecration of labour by Christ, who earned his living as a carpenter, and the Christian duty to promote the ideals of the Kingdom of God.

As with other social issues, the majority of Evangelicals who made such pronouncements did not advocate a revolutionary, root-and-branch solution; they favoured reform, laid stress on gradualism, and

[16] Comments on this include C.J. Proctor, 'Chairman's Address', *Islington Clerical Meeting Report* (1908), p.12; and T. Guy Rogers, 'National Religion in Relation to Social Problems. (A) Masters and Men II', *Islington Clerical Meeting Report* (1908), pp.78, 79.

[17] For a graphic description of the dominant Evangelical response to a possible fundamental reordering of society, see A.J. Carlyle, 'The Church and the Solution', *Islington Clerical Meeting Report* (1908), pp.78, 79.

upheld the essentials of the capitalist system.[18] In as much as they gave any thought to the problems of industry, Evangelicals mostly saw hope in the promotion of greater co-operation between employer and employee based on a growing sense of brotherhood and identity of interest.

Despite the dire social problems of the period 1918 to 1939, there was less discussion of social issues by Evangelicals than in the pre-war years, and the debate was conducted with less intensity. This was probably due to their preoccupation with Prayer Book revision and the CMS controversy.

Again, as in the earlier part of the century, even those who most enthusiastically advocated Evangelical social concern and social involvement clearly declared what were their cardinal beliefs and priorities.[19] Behind most if not all the Evangelical attempts to understand social matters there was the assumption that, however serious might be the socio-economic situation, either for any particular individual or for society as a whole, the spiritual dimension was of paramount importance. For the Evangelical the final answer to the enigma surrounding such complicated issues was to be found in the person of Christ. He alone was the provider of individual and corporate regeneration, and he also was the clue to the unravelling of social mysteries.

[18] See for example G.E. Ford, 'The Message of Christ concerning Labour', *Churchman*, July 1919, pp.393-395, 400, 401, 403; E.A. Dunn, 'Fellowship in Industry', *Islington Clerical Meeting Report* (1921), p.47; and Sir George B. Hunter, 'The Church and Industrial Problems, *Churchman*, October 1919, pp.544, 545, 552, 553.

[19] See for example Dunn, *op.cit.*, p.307; Hunter, *op.cit.*, pp.553, 554; and Henry Edwards, 'Organised Religion and Labour', *Churchman*, August 1919, pp.455-7.

18

Evangelism, Teaching and Mission

In approaching the task of evangelism in the period 1900 to 1918 Evangelicals were agreed that indifference rather than aggressive infidelity or hostility was the prevailing characteristic of the age. The so-called working classes were in the main alienated from any form of worship, and the hold of the church upon the middle classes was lessening.[1] In the Church of England as a whole, and not least among Evangelicals, prolonged preoccupation with controversy over ritualism and the issues associated with modernism and 'liberalism' detracted from any major and sustained evangelistic effort, in the same way that it diverted attention from an effective social involvement.

Not that Evangelicals were inactive. In the parishes there were many examples of persevering evangelistic work by Evangelical parochial clergy. Evangelicals were convinced churchmen not least in the value they placed on the parochial system and the opportunity it gave for evangelism in every part of the country. The Church Pastoral-Aid Society was the main evangelistic organization with the clear purpose

---

[1] For an indication of the Evangelical assessment of the contemporary situation, see *The Sixty-seventh Report of the Church Pastoral-Aid Society*, May 1902, pp.39, 40; and J. Denton Thompson, 'A Divine Remedy for Human Ills', A Foreword to the *CPAS Annual Report* (1914), pp.32, 33.

of maintaining, strengthening and extending the work of the parish clergymen. In addition there were such bodies as the Church of England Scripture Readers Association, the Church Army, the Church Parochial Mission Society, the London City Mission, and the Evangelisation Society, all of which were founded and sustained entirely or largely by Evangelicals. Also, closely allied to the more specifically evangelistic work, so closely indeed in some cases as to be indistinguishable from it, were the many social and philanthropic efforts maintained or supported by Evangelical churchmen. Examples of these were the Ragged School Union, the Field Lane Institution, the National Refuges, Doctor Barnardo's Homes, the Waifs and Strays Society, rescue work among 'fallen women' carried out by organizations such as the London Female Guardian Society and various clergy charities, the Church Lads' Brigade, the YMCA, and the Girls' Friendly Society.

At the national level, the most outstanding evangelistic event of these years, from the point of view of the Evangelicals, was the Torrey-Alexander Mission of 1903 to 1905. Although it was non-denominational, and was widely supported by nonconformists, Church of England Evangelicals co-operated, and it had a powerful effect in many parishes. R.A. Torrey was the successor to D.L. Moody. Assisted by C.M. Alexander as singer, Torrey concentrated on major cities; and in Edinburgh, Aberdeen, Glasgow, Dundee, Belfast, Dublin, Birmingham, Liverpool, Manchester, London and other places he attracted capacity crowds to auditoriums seating many thousands. This surge of evangelism coincided with the Welsh revival in which Evan Roberts took a prominent part. Gipsy Smith was also active in itinerant evangelism, but he did not achieve his remarkable impact until after the Torrey-Alexander Mission.

Although they were somewhat sluggish about domestic evangelism, Evangelicals were thoroughly committed to overseas mission. The May meetings of the Evangelical missionary societies were well attended and marked by zeal and enthusiasm. Some Evangelicals thought that foreign missions were experiencing golden years of support.[2] For example in 1912 the income of the CMS was the largest ever received, except for certain years in which there had been a special appeal.[3] Neither were Evangelical churchmen confined in their liberality. In their concern for worldwide evangelization, they also supported the Society for the Propagation of the Gospel, which was not specifically Evangelical, as well as the Church of

[2] See for example W.H.M.H. Aitken, 'Spiritual Progress in the New Century', *Record*, 28 June 1901, p.659; unsigned article, 'Wanted: A Revival', *Record*, 3 October 1902, p.924; and unsigned article 'Past and Present', *Record*, 4 May 1906, p.382.
[3] See 'CMS Finance (Official)', *Record*, 26 April 1912, p.387.

England Zenana Missionary Society (for the conversion of women in India and the Far East), the Zenana Bible and Medical mission, the South American Missionary Society, the South Africa General Mission, the Colonial and Continental Church Society and the Industrial Missions Aid Society. The global expansion of the church has been greater numerically in the twentieth century than in any previous period in history. The Evangelicals played an invaluable part in promoting this in the years before the First World War.

With the advent of peace in 1919, Evangelicals faced the task of evangelism with a renewed sense of urgency. The initiative was taken with alacrity by the Church Pastoral-Aid Society, in an effort to mobilize resources for 'the spread of the Gospel at home and abroad'. Its conference on the evangelization of England was held within weeks of the cessation of war; and from it was issued not only a clear call to evangelism, but a suggested course of action.

In order that evangelistic work might be effective, the conference recommended that careful attention should be given to raising the level of spiritual life in the parishes by means of personal, family and corporate prayer and Bible study. High ideals should be set. More attention should be given to evangelistic preaching. A salaried missioner should be appointed to organize conventions and home mission training schools. The CPAS should encourage the production and distribution of devotional literature to meet the needs of communicants in Evangelical parishes; and incumbents of CPAS grantee parishes should consider introducing special additional simple and attractive services in churches or mission-rooms, both on Sundays and weekdays, to suit the majority of the people, and especially the men.[4]

Some of these proposals were tried with varying degrees of success, but the note of disappointed hope, disillusionment and failure was repeatedly, and perhaps increasingly, sounded by Evangelicals throughout the inter-war period.[5]

Parochial or district missions were tried in many areas with some success,[6] but they were not conspicuously or universally effective, and they were soon somewhat discredited among Evangelicals.[7] A major

---

[4] Reported in 'Notes of the Week', *Record*, 28 November 1918, p.745.

[5] See for instance J.T. Inskip, 'The Present Phase in the Movement for Evangelisation', *Churchman*, April 1919, pp.184, 185; Francis James Chavasse, 'Centenary Sermon. A Hundred Years of Evangelicalism', *Islington Clerical Meeting Report* (1927), p.10; Leading Article, 'Evangelicalism and Evangelism', *Record*, 30 August 1928, p.594; Letter to the Editor, from Geo. W. Coultas, 'Evangelistic Campaigns', *Record*, 14 November 1930, p.733; Colin C. Kerr, 'Protestantism: Our Endorsement', *Islington Clerical Meeting Report* (1932), p.108; and Leader 'Looking Forward', *Record*, 7 January 1938, p.8.

[6] See Leading Article, 'Review of the Year', *Record*, 28 December 1923, p.846.

[7] See for example T.J. Pulvertaft, 'Evangelism', *Churchman*, January 1927.

hindrance to such a campaign was the absence of any suitable missioner. Some of the larger missions which were undertaken seem to have suffered from diversity and conflict in the doctrines preached, as there were typically a number of missioners involved, and they were not always united in the content of their preaching.

There were some wistful recollections of the Moody campaigns, and it was realized that the effectiveness of these had largely been due to the simple and unmistakable evangelical message which was proclaimed. As we have seen, the force of Moody's preaching had derived to a great extent from his uncomplicated, intense, direct, challenging and uncompromisingly evangelical message. 'Moody has had no successor', T.J. Pulvertaft lamented, 'and our home Evangelists have not been more successful whether they worked on denominational or undenominational lines'.[8]

Some special evangelistic missions were conducted, as at the 1924 British Empire Exhibition, in which there was co-operation between such disparate bodies as the London Diocesan Evangelistic Committee, the National Council of the Evangelical Free Churches, the Salvation Army, and the Evangelical Alliance, with a programme of meetings at which the speakers included the Bishop of London (Winnington-Ingram) and Gipsy Smith. These special missions were, however, infrequent, and seemingly not very successful.

Theological Education

Evangelism at home and abroad was a priority for Evangelicals; but theological teaching, training for the ministry, and the exposition and defence of the faith were also very precious to them. This was demonstrated by the establishment of new theological colleges. St John's Hall, Durham was founded in 1909, largely by Evangelicals. It was, however, in the inter-war years that the greatest expansion took place: five new colleges were inaugurated within the space of seven years, approximately doubling the Evangelical college provision.

The first was the Bible Churchmen's Missionary Society College for men in Bristol.[9] A house was purchased in 1925, and further adjacent properties were added in 1926, 1928 and 1936. The college was opened in 1925, with Dr Sydney Carter as principal. Recognition as a theological college of the Church of England was granted in 1927, and the first

---

[8] T.J. Pulvertaft, *op.cit.*, p.24.

[9] The following account is based on W.S Hooton and J. Stafford Wright, *The First Twenty-Five years of the Bible Churchmen's Missionary Society*, (1922-47), (London, 1947), pp.45-52.

ordinations of its students for both home and overseas work took place in 1928. The aim of the college was to give a training which was true to the recognized formularies of the Church of England. Non-Evangelical theological training and liturgical studies were not ignored, and could not be, since all candidates for ordination had to take the General Ordination Examination, but the Evangelical view and interpretation was given priority. From 1928 the college was associated with Durham University in an arrangement whereby students could proceed to an L.Th. degree during their college course or, if preferred, and if suitable, to a B.A. by means of a further year at Durham. In addition to academic studies, stress was laid on practical work, with ample opportunity for helping at church and mission services, Bible classes and Sunday schools. Visits were also made to hospitals and men's lodging-houses.

Early in its career the college experienced a devastating disruption. In 1931, there was strong disagreement between the principal and the executive committee of the BCMS regarding their respective rights to dismiss students for one cause or another, or to receive them back. The upshot was the resignation of the principal and the staff in 1932; with the subsequent withdrawal of the Bishop of Rochester, Linton Smith, from his position as college Visitor. This meant that the college was no longer recognized by the bishops. Dr Carter and the staff established a new college nearby. A number of students went with them. J. Stafford Wright, a former student of the original college, returned as tutor in the same year, and a new principal, W. Dodgson Sykes, was installed. In 1934 recognition was regained, and the Bishop of Bristol, Dr Woodward, accepted the post of Visitor. Under its new principal, the college again increased its numbers, until it reached its capacity of about fifty students in residence.

In 1930 the BCMS opened a college in Bristol for women, named Dalton House, with Marjorie Nevin as principal. It started with eleven students, and by the second term there were eighteen. The curriculum was simpler than that of the men's college, since there was no necessity to undertake the General Ordination Examination: it concentrated upon a more detailed knowledge of the Bible and Christian doctrine. In 1933 the students also began to work for the Bible Diploma, which had first been introduced in the men's college. Practical work was incorporated, which included help in Bristol parishes, conducting services and visiting in the men's and women's wards in the Eastville Institute.

St Peter's Hall, Oxford, was a more academically sophisticated institution than any of the colleges so far mentioned. The idea for such a college had been put forward initially at the 1926 Islington Clerical Meeting by Bishop Chavasse. The project was set in motion with an appeal for £150,000 to which there was a very prompt and generous response. A strategically placed site was acquired in 1928 and work began for the construction of a college which, according to its Trust Deed, would exist 'to promote religion and education generally and especially to assist students of limited means, to encourage candidates for Holy Orders and missionary work abroad, and to maintain the principles of the Church of England as set forth in the Book of Common Prayer'. In the 1929-30 academic year forty men were in residence, half of whom were preparing for ordination. The project proved financially viable, and a new wing was added to the building to house twenty more students during the following university year. The successful launching of the scheme, and its evident advance, was a cause of great rejoicing for Evangelicals.[10]

Oak Hill College owes its existence to the liberality of Charles Baring-Young.[11] He was concerned about the serious shortage of clergy in the post-war years. He was most anxious that the right type of men should be assisted, and that those candidates who were unfitted should not proceed to ordination. He believed that standards should not be lowered in order to meet the demand for men. He envisaged a kind of test school where candidates who were seeking to qualify for entrance to a theological college could receive sound tuition for the preliminary examinations; and if at the end of this early stage a student failed or felt unable to continue his studies, he could give up, free of all obligations. To carry out this scheme he purchased the fifty-acre estate, Bohun Lodge, adjoining his old home, Oak Hill in Southgate, and started a school, with A.W. Habershon as the first principal.

Baring-Young died in 1928, and in 1932, under an order of the Court of Chancery, power was given to the Trustees for his estate to 'found, endow and carry on Theological Schools or colleges for the purpose of training persons who are desirous of obtaining ordination in the Church of England and are without adequate means'. This extension of the work was in full accord with the founder's wishes. The first principal was H.W. Hinde. As with the BCMS College, Oak Hill was, until the outbreak of war, linked with Durham University for the L.Th. and B.A. degrees. In 1947, the pre-matriculation test school at Bohun Lodge was sold, and the work was concentrated under one roof. From its inception until the war in 1939, thirty-seven of its students were ordained.

When Dr Carter ceased to be principal of the BCMS College in 1932, he immediately founded Clifton Theological College. Starting with twenty-eight students, in one term it outgrew its accommodation. At the end of the first year forty-two students were in residence, and in the following

[10] See the report 'St Peter's Hall, Oxford: Second Year. A Story of Remarkable Progress. A call to Evangelicals', *Record*, 24 October 1930, pp.685, 686.
[11] See Alfred F. Jarvis, *Charles Baring-Young of Daylesford 1850-1928: His Life and Work* (London, 1950).

years the numbers ranged between forty-five and fifty. The college was threatened by financial difficulties in its early life, but the efforts of Sir Thomas Inskip, Bishop Knox and others ensured its survival.

Despite this expansion of theological education, Evangelicals did not engage in theological debate to any significant extent. It was perhaps the writings of Karl Barth which most attracted Evangelical attention, but realization of the importance of Barth did not extend beyond a very confined Evangelical academic circle in England until the fourth decade of the century. Individual Evangelicals welcomed his teaching, and the Oxford Conference of Evangelical Churchmen in 1932 gave a warm, if somewhat muted assent to it. Evangelicals especially appreciated the Barthian emphasis on the sovereignty of God, the merits of Reformation theology and the distinctiveness of Protestantism.[12]

The influence of Barth was part of a remarkable Christian intellectual revival in the period 1930 to 1945, of which the Evangelicals at the time did not seem to be aware. There was a rediscovery of biblical orthodoxy, in which Reinhold Niebuhr was perhaps even more influential than Barth. C.H. Dodd did much to convince lay Christians, and scholars too, that modern biblical scholarship could be reconciled with and indeed support, a traditional belief in Christ, and Sir Edwyn Hoskins did some seminal work in biblical studies. C.S. Lewis, T.S. Eliot, W.H. Auden, C.E.M. Joad and other laymen contributed to what amounted to a reassertion of doctrinal orthodoxy.

Although they did not play much of a part in this theological movement, Evangelicals continued to be involved in the wider sphere of education. Independent schools founded by Evangelicals, or in which subsequent Evangelical influence has been outstanding, include Monkton Coombe, Bath; St Lawrence College, Ramsgate; Trent College, Long Eaton, Nottingham; Weymouth College; Wadhurst College, Kent; and Clarendon School, Bedford. The Allied Schools (Felixstowe College, Harrogate College, Westonbirt School, Riddlesworth Hall, Wrekin College, Stowe and Canford) originated in 1923 when a remarkable Protestant clergyman, the Rev. P.E. Warrington, a vicar of Monkton Coombe, founded both Canford and Stowe. In state schools, and in universities and colleges, Evangelicals were increasingly to exercise influence through the Scripture Union and Inter-Varsity Fellowship groups and, in the case of some universities and colleges, as chaplains.

---

[12] For a sample of Evangelical comments see R. Birch Hoyle, 'Karl Barth and the Protestant Revival', *Churchman*, April 1931, pp.122, 123; A.J. Macdonald, 'Professor Karl Barth and the Theology of Crisis', *Churchman*, July 1932, p.201; and 'Findings of the Oxford Conference of Evangelical Churchmen', *Churchman*, July 1932, p.158.

Evangelical Ministry

The priority given by Evangelicals to evangelism, and pastoral responsibility, is shown in the lives of the leading Evangelicals of the period.

Handley Carr Glyn Moule (1841-1920)

Handley Moule, whom we have previously met in various connections, took up his episcopal duties in 1901 as Bishop of Durham with a sincere and awesome sense of responsibility. Not only was he assuming a very considerable spiritual burden at the age of sixty, and at the end of a long and demanding succession of prominent appointments, but he was acutely conscious that he was the immediate successor in the see to those two outstanding bishops, Lightfoot and Westcott. He applied himself with diligence to his task, and by his scholarly frame of mind, his evident personal piety and his breadth of view, he largely gained the confidence of all shades of churchmanship in the diocese. His strength lay chiefly in his character, and in his spiritual sensitivity. He was a great pastor and encourager, with the heart of an evangelist and teacher; but he was not great as a diocesan. He often failed to give a lead in such issues as educational policy. He was not at times a good chairman. He found diocesan finance distasteful, took less and less part in it, and in the process rather lost touch with the laity. To some extent he neither understood nor appreciated the realities of the secular world of the north-east. It was, however, his saintliness which carried him through and won the day.[13]

Francis James Chavasse (1846-1928)

Francis Chavasse, whom we have also formerly encountered, assumed responsibility as Bishop of Liverpool in 1900. There followed twenty-three years filled with dedicated labour in the service of the city and diocese. If anything, it appears that he was over-busy with meetings and other varied functions, which not infrequently meant that he had little time for the personal problems of individuals. Again, as with Handley Moule, it was his sanctity of character which was most telling. This is

---

[13] For the life of Moule, see especially John Battersby Harford and Frederick Charles Macdonald, *Handley Carr Glyn Moule, Bishop of Durham: A Biography* (London, 1922).

indicated in the preamble to the presentation by the University of Liverpool to him of the degree of Doctor of Laws. In the somewhat flamboyant language typical of such oratory, and of the age in which it was delivered, he is described as 'Reverend, beloved, rich in the mellowed wisdom of age, and holding in his heart the happy secret of youth; a man of courage undaunted and of hope undimmed', and one who kept alive in his days 'the august tradition which unites piety and letters, religion and sound learning'.[14] As these words were uttered after the completion of almost a quarter of a century of unremitting, much appreciated civic and ecclesiastical toil, they can be taken not as mere felicitous phrases required by the occasion, but as a genuine expression of gratitude for a remarkable Christian.[15]

Edmund Arbuthnott Knox (1847-1937)

By the beginning of the twentieth century E.A. Knox had a weight of experience behind him as Fellow, Tutor and then Dean of Merton College, Oxford, and subsequently as rector successively of Kibworth, Ashton under the Peakes, Birmingham and St Philip's, Birmingham.[16] He was consecrated Bishop of Manchester in 1903. What was most apparent was his energy, application to work, and love for people in the many-sided facets of their lives. He was immersed in the life first of his parish, and then of his diocese. He identified with the joys and sorrows, the hopes, aspirations and disappointments of the people committed to him, and this showed in his public actions.

Knox was intensely concerned about education and, as chairman of the Birmingham school board, and later chairman of the Convocation education committee, he applied himself with great ability, earnestness, tenacity of purpose, and imperturbable good humour to the difficult work of guiding the Birmingham Board and the Lower House of Convocation in their attitudes to the Balfour Education Bill, and other proposed legislation. So passionately did he believe in the upholding of distinctive elementary school religious education that he organized and led a gigantic demonstration in London in 1906, in opposition to the projected Birrell Education Bill, which seems to have greatly influenced the climate of opinion on the issue. He engaged in forthright debate in the various relevant municipal bodies in both Birmingham and Manchester, and at the Church Congress in Manchester he spoke with forceful directness on the duty of the church to concern itself with the social and moral problems

---

[14] J.B. Lancelot, *Francis James Chavasse, Bishop of Liverpool* (Oxford, 1929), p.227.
[15] For the life of Chavasse, see Lancelot, *op.cit.*
[16] For a full account of the life of Knox, see Edmund Arbuthnott Knox, *Reminiscences of an Octogenarian (1847-1934)* (London, 1934).

created by industrial and commercial life.

In more specifically ecclesiastical matters Knox was in many ways an innovator. He was a pioneer in establishing what was later called the diocesan quota scheme, which was introduced in order to safeguard the financial welfare of all the clergy. He opened Egerton Hall as a post-graduate college for the training of ordinands. He encouraged support for overseas missions as an essential element in the life of the diocese by forming a board of missions, and by establishing regular diocesan missionary days. He founded the Blackpool mission, whereby annually 'the Church bore witness for her Lord on the shores of Blackpool'[17] to thousands of holidaymakers. He developed the diocesan conference in such a way that it greatly strengthened diocesan life. He also anticipated Church Assembly reforms when he provided an ordination candidates fund, and a dilapidation fund. With all this, he did not neglect his duties in the national deliberations of the church.

When Knox was translated to Manchester, Bishop Charles Gore said, 'The work awaiting Bishop Knox at Manchester is tremendous; there is, perhaps, no single diocese in the Church of England where the work is so arduous'.[18] By his single-minded application to the charge laid upon him, he met the challenge and fully justified the confidence placed in him.

Henry Wace (1836–1924)

Henry Wace was Dean of Canterbury from 1903 until the year of his death.[19] Prior to this he had served in various London churches until 1875, when he was appointed Professor of Ecclesiastical History at King's College, London, and subsequently principal. He was Boyle Lecturer in 1874 and 1875, and Bampton Lecturer in 1879, and he also engaged in a well-publicized controversy with Professor Huxley in 1889. As Dean he made a substantial contribution to the civic life of Canterbury, which was recognised by the conferring upon him of the freedom of the city.

During the whole of his ministry Wace was an avowed Evangelical, but it was during the last thirty years of his life that he exercised the most profound and widespread influence. For some years he edited the *Church-man* and he made frequent contributions to it, and to the *Record*. His activities included work on behalf of King's College Hospital, the chairmanship for many years of the Clergy Mutual Insurance Society, of St John's Hall, Highbury, and of the National Church League, and countless addresses at conferences and meetings throughout the land. In

[17] Quoted in Knox, *op.cit.*, p.237.
[18] Quoted in Knox, *op.cit.*, p.209.
[19] The brief account of the life of Henry Wace owes much to Guy Johnson, 'Dean Wace', *Churchman*, April 1924, pp.95–101.

1900 he acted as chairman of a round table conference, initiated by Bishop Creighton, on the doctrine of the holy communion and its expression in ritual, and the following year he chaired a second conference of the same kind on the subject of confession and absolution. During the whole period of his deanery he took a strong stand against what he viewed as a revival of medievalism and what he regarded as dangerous tendencies in the modernist movement. He was hailed by many Evangelicals as a champion of their cause, and he was one of the most potent and respected voices within Evangelicalism for three decades and more.

William Henry Griffith Thomas (1861-1924)

William Henry Griffith Thomas was noted for his immense hard work, and determination.[20] Over a period of many years he studied incessantly in the spare time afforded first by a curacy in London, and then by a senior curacy at St Aldate's Oxford; an effort which was crowned in 1895, at the age of thirty-four, with a first class degree.

In his subsequent studies, writings, and academic leadership he showed a fine grasp of complicated matters and was foremost among his Evangelical contemporaries in his ability to grapple with the issues of the day. As the first vicar of St Paul's, Portman Square in London, with its distinguished congregation, and as principal of Wycliffe Hall, Oxford, as well as through his Bible commentaries, pastoralia, apologetics, theological works and biographical studies, Griffith Thomas exerted a great influence among Evangelical churchmen, and in the wider church. This was reinforced by his years as editor of the *Churchman*, and by his addresses at the Islington clerical meetings, Keswick Conventions, the Pan-Anglican Congress, the Church Congress and other lesser gatherings.

Griffith Thomas maintained his dedication to academic study, and was awarded an Oxford D.D. He developed a capacity for carefully considering all the evidence bearing upon any subject, but he remained unequivocal in his submission to the authority of the scriptures, and in his loyalty to the Evangelical faith. He was one of the most intellectually competent Evangelicals of his generation, presenting his views with a balance of reason and appeal to faith which was acceptable to churchmen of all theological shades, as well as to many outside the church. His most influential book was *The Catholic Faith* (1904). Although he retained his connections with England after he went to Canada in 1910 as a professor at

---

[20] The brief biographical sketch of Griffith Thomas relies heavily on M. Guthrie Clark, *William Henry Griffith Thomas 1861-1924: Minister, Scholar, Teacher, Great Churchman* (London, 1949).

Wycliffe College, Toronto, his loss was felt acutely by a very wide circle. He had established himself as a distinguished representative of Evangelicalism.

John Edwin Watts-Ditchfield (1861-1923)

Of those Evangelicals who demonstrated the depth and genuineness of their faith in both parochial and diocesan ministries, none was more conspicuous for his devotion, and more worthy of notice, than John Edwin Watts-Ditchfield.[21] Perhaps his greatest work was done in establishing a ministry among men both at St Peter's, Holloway, where he was a curate, and then, with very marked success when he was vicar of St James, Bethnal Green. He was concerned at the general failure of the church to attract and to hold the allegiance of men. He succeeded in raising funds, drawing together workers, and sustaining a flourishing work among men in a way which few others have ever done. After seventeen years of such strenuous labour he was chosen to be the first bishop of the new diocese of Chelmsford, and there he continued to work with equal energy and enthusiasm, always willing to try unconventional methods in his unflagging and vigorous evangelistic and pastoral efforts.

Other leading Evangelicals in this period included Canon A.M.W. Christopher and Dean William Hagar Barlow, who have previously been considered; Bishop Taylor Smith (1860-1937), who will demand attention when the war years are discussed; Bishop Arthur Burroughs (1882-1934); Bishop F. Theodore Woods; and such varied personalities as A.J. Tait, Charles Lisle Carr, Herbert William Hinde, A.R. Buckland, Stuart Holden, F.S. Guy Warman, H.V. Storr, Sir Lewis Dibdin, Sir Thomas Inskip and Sir William Joynson-Hicks. A number of these were identified with liberal rather than mainline Evangelicalism, but with such an array of talent it is evident that the broad spectrum of Evangelicalism in these years was not devoid of leaders of quality.

---

[21] See Leonard Elliott-Binns, *The Evangelical Movement in the English Church*, pp.74, 75.

19

Facing Two World Wars

The First World War

Evangelicals in general unhesitatingly and confidently asserted that Britain had no option but to take up arms against Germany in 1914; it was a just and holy war.[1]

These were the sentiments held by the population as a whole and by many, but by no means all, church leaders. Germany had set Europe ablaze for no other reason than that she might become a world power. In her mad lust her armies were guilty of atrocities. Such aggression must be resisted or it would mean the triumph of evil over righteousness. Great Britain and her allies were defending the cause of right against might. Not to have done so would have been a betrayal of friendship and the breaking of a solemn pledge. Non-action would have meant dishonouring the name of Britain: it would have ensured that henceforth the country was held in righteous contempt, and the British would have been dubbed a timorous, time-serving people, terrorized by the dominance of German militarism. The blatant wickedness and ungodliness of the German nation was

[1] See for instance Editorial, 'A Righteous Cause', *Churchman*, September 1914, p.641; Editorial, 'The Great War', *Churchman*, October 1914, p.721; C.J. Proctor, 'Opening Address', *Islington Clerical Meeting Report* (1915), pp.10, 11; Henry Wace, 'Christianity and War', *Islington Clerical Meeting Report* (1915), pp.21, 22; and W. Edward Chadwick, 'German Christianity (?) and the Great War', *Churchman*, November 1914, pp.811, 812.

proclaimed with passion and indignation. The whole German philosophy and behaviour was declared to be a violent rejection of the Christian standard of righteousness and justice: it was a repudiation of the Sermon on the Mount and of the meekness and gentleness of Christ. Britain was launched on a godly crusade.

Opposition to this dominant preaching of a holy war was weak, unorganized, and late in developing. In the midst of an apathetic or hostile espiscopate, Bishop Gore was outstanding in his denunciation of what, to his mind, represented a shameful, unchristian upsurge of fanaticism. He chided the enthusiasts for resorting to language traditionally associated with the Crusades, not the most glorious period in church history. While acknowledging the duty of Britain to join the struggle against Germany, he deplored the spirit of national self-righteousness. Since the history of Britain was hardly immaculate, national repentance was more appropriate to the needs of the hour. Any such utterance suggestive of a wider, supra-national view was, however, most commonly met with suspicion, and even hostility, particularly in the early part of the war, or at times of special anti-German feeling. Hensley Henson, who made very evident in his speeches that he was completely loyal to the national war effort, nevertheless aroused a storm of protest and animosity when he quite casually made reference in a sermon to his pre-war experience of the kindness of the Kaiser.

Belief in the guilt of Germany was generally accepted as unquestionable, to be conceded even by the German people themselves. Even Archbishop Davidson was incredulous when he received the German Christian view on the causes of the war, and when his overtures to the German church were rejected because of their premise of German guilt.[2] Among the Evangelicals these dominant themes persisted throughout the war and beyond.

But this sustained proclamation of the war as a crusade, and the tendency to identify the purposes of Britain in it with the purposes of God, did not go unchallenged in Evangelical circles. For instance, at the Islington gathering of 1915, Dr Simpson, Canon of St Paul's, forcefully and boldly questioned such an interpretation of the national role.[3] Before confidently declaring that the call to the British people was to co-operate with God in castigating another nation, he said, those so assured should consider what would have been their reaction to events if they had been placed in the German situation. Evangelicals and others should shun sanctimoniousness. How much theological validity could be given to the stand taken by the ultra-patriotic Christians? The call of God could well

[2] See G.K.A. Bell, *Randall Davidson*, Vol.2, pp.740–744.
[3] Canon Simpson, 'God's Call to the Nation', *Islington Clerical Meeting Report* (1915), pp.25–28.

appear little different from the call of king and country. The Christian pulpit could become nothing more than a second best to a jingoistic press. Such critics of the holy war were pilloried as over-intellectual prigs by every Anglican newspaper except the *Challenge*; and this included the High Church *Guardian* at the one extreme, and the *Record* at the other. The Evangelicals, often a very small minority voice in the community, were, in this matter, part of an extremely vociferous majority public opinion.

Bearing in mind these strong and widely held opinions, it is of little surprise that only a very few Evangelicals were pacifists. It was generally taken for granted that war was valid as a defence against evil, and no justification was considered necessary. The biblical evidence against pacifism was reckoned to be overwhelming. The views of conscientious objectors were therefore regarded with incomprehension by the great majority of Evangelicals, and little sympathy was accorded to them.[4]

In the entire columns of the *Record*, the *Churchman*, the *Church Pastoral-Aid Society Reports*, or the official *Reports of the Islington Clerical Meetings* for the whole of the war period, it is difficult to find any presentation by a conscientious objector of their case. In one rare example, when a correspondent to the *Record* suggested that conscientious objectors should be respected for their sincere principles, another replied with extreme aggression that sincerity was not a mark of truth or acceptability. Pacifist opinions were no more worthy of consideration than those of other perpetrators of deviant behaviour. These strictures abruptly terminated the correspondence on the subject.

Whether through fear of publicly declaring themselves, or because of editorial censorship, the absence of even a debate over the issues involved is a remarkable feature in the Evangelical response to the war. No doubt discussion took place, but it was kept well in check by an apparent conspiracy of silence in the Evangelical media, and in the preaching and speaking of Evangelical leaders. Nothing was allowed to detract from the main thrust of the war effort. No opinion was countenanced, which even hinted at the possibility of non-participation in the war as a consequence of conscientious objection.[5]

But if few Evangelicals believed, or gave voice to the belief, that conscientious objection was a valid Christian conviction, and worthy of respect, there was much more explicit division of opinion over the question of clergy enlistment.

---

[4] See for example C.J. Proctor, 'Opening Address', *Islington Clerical Meeting Report* (1915), p.9.

[5] For instance see M.W. 'To Conscientious Objectors. An Open Letter', *Record*, 13 July 1916, p.577.

Were the clergy to be treated as an exceptional category, exempt from military service by virtue of their special calling, or were they subject to the same criteria as any other sincerely committed Christian person? The leaders of the church mostly regarded ordination as a setting apart for a distinctive ministry within the church; it was not compatible with military service. Nevertheless, they also generally favoured a maximum freedom of choice for individual clergy. The *Record* and the *Churchman* were unqualified and dogmatic in their opposition to clergy enlistment, at least in the early stages of the war.[6]

Although the church as a whole concurred with this, there was a minority opinion which saw no impropriety in the military involvement of the clergy, and this was reflected in Evangelical opinion.[7] There is also some evidence that the dogmatism of those opposed to clergy enlistment was somewhat moderated towards the end of the war.[8]

Another agonizing ethical and moral question arising out of the war was that of reprisals. The zeppelin and aeroplane raids by Germany on British cities, the shelling of coastal towns, and the menacing U-boats intensified popular hysteria, and resulted in a demand for reprisals against German civilians. There was an immediate and resolute response from many Evangelicals. Despite their typically unreserved and outspoken patriotism, a number of them unambiguously condemned any retaliatory acts.[9] It is to the abiding credit of such Evangelicals that on this, as well as on other issues, they were not swept along by a strong wave of public opinion, but were able to penetrate through the immediate very emotive circumstances to the underlying principles, as they understood them. They then had the courage to declare what they believed with an unmistakable clarity.

There were some topics, however, which did not lend themselves to such perspicuity; which defied any lucid and neat pronouncement. Of these the most pertinent in the war years was that of suffering. Evangelicals generally did not explore the profound theological problems associated with the causes of suffering. They approached the subject with a strong faith in the sovereignty of God, belief in the Satanic origin of all evil, and an assurance that good would ultimately triumph. In so doing they were able to integrate suffering into their cosmic view, and reconcile

---

[6] See for example Editorial, 'Exemption of the Clergy', *Churchman*, February 1916 p.84.

[7] Such a view was vehemently expressed by Albert Mitchell in a 'Letter to the Editor', *Record*, 11 November 1915.

[8] See for instance *Churchman*, May 1918, p.257.

[9] Representative of their stance is the forthright statement of the Leading Article, 'Reprisals?', *Record*, 21 October 1915, p.920.

it with their faith in a God of love. To most Evangelicals, suffering was the inevitable consequence of engagement in a holy war.[10]

No Evangelical was more aware of the anguish, torment and tribulation of the war than Bishop Taylor Smith, the Chaplain-General of the armed forces. He was subject to much criticism, but his response was to maintain almost total silence. He did not think it right to jump to his own defence. A number of subsequent historians and commentators on the war have expressed varying degrees of regret that Taylor Smith occupied such a post at such a time. Sir John Smyth considered it regrettable.[11] Alan Wilkinson thought it was tragic, as Taylor Smith had no university theological training and lacked theological insight and sophistication. He was, said Wilkinson, too apolitical, and his view of faith too atomistic for him to appreciate that conversion to a pietistic religion was an inadequate answer to the issues raised by the war both for faith and for society.[12]

Such criticism is difficult to assess for it came from men who had an almost totally different theological view from Taylor Smith, and it would possibly have been levelled at most traditional Evangelicals of the time if they had undertaken the same duties. The criticism focused on what were seen by non-Evangelicals as some of the most salient weaknesses of Evangelicals; but these very characteristics could as well be presented as strengths rather than shortcomings. The conclusion reached depended, and depends, so much on the theological presuppositions of the one making the judgement.

On the home front, Evangelicals were concerned about the state of the nation. It was probably Evangelicals who proposed one of the foremost church initiatives in the war years, the National Mission.[13] Far from concentrating on individuals to the exclusion of the nation, the Evangelicals viewed the moral condition of the country with the utmost gravity and alarm. Where they most differed from others of a contrary theological outlook was in their conviction that much of the national malaise was attributable to the sins of individuals in the aggregate, and that even for those failures which were distinctly national there was still a final and ultimate necessity for personal repentance. They could not so focus on the national sins as to think lightly of individual sins, or be so absorbed in social issues as to lose sight of the personal religious need. They sought a balance between the two. Their enthusiastic participation in the National Mission expressed this dual concern.[14]

[10] An illustration of this is Henry Wace, 'The Holy War', *Record*, 18 December 1914, p.1153.

[11] John Smyth, *In this Sign Conquer: The Story of the Army Chaplains* (London, 1968).

[12] Alan Wilkinson, *The Church of England and the First World War* (London, 1978), pp.295, 2'

[13] See Leading Article, 'A National Mission', *Record*, 11 November 1915.

[14] For example, see 'The Bishop of Liverpool's Pastoral', *Record*, 11 September 1914, p.861; and 'The Month', *Churchman*, March 1916, pp.165, 166.

The Second World War

The reaction of the Church of England in general and of Evangelicals in particular to the Second World war was restricted, restrained and reasoned in comparison with the responses to the First World War. The dramatic and emotive appeals which typified the 1914–18 period were replaced by more moderate and cerebral comments during the years 1939 to 1945. National propaganda in general was more subdued, and venomous remarks were exceptional. Evangelical patriotism was as strong as in the First World War, but Evangelical attitudes were more subtle, and the language in which they were expressed was decidedly less nationalistic.[15]

Belief in the righteousness of the national cause was widespread and intense. William Temple typified the Church of England attitude in this respect, and indeed largely helped to mould it. He determined from the outset of the war that he could and would only speak for the Christian conscience. He proclaimed the war to be a 'divine judgement', and he upheld the national cause. In his first broadcast after the outbreak of war, on 3 October 1939, he declared that the country entered 'the war as a dedicated nation'. He went on to say that 'the prevailing conviction is that Nazi tyranny and oppression are destroying the traditional excellences of European civilization and must be eliminated for the good of mankind'.[16]

Temple's attitude was reinforced by others. To cite but one; Hensley Henson regarded Hitlerism as self-evidently standing for all that was evil. The country could make no terms with it. The issue was not merely political, or solely national, but essentially moral and spiritual. Two conceptions of human nature, two ideals of human destiny were in conflict, and no man could serve two masters. Henson and others even described the war effort of the nation as a crusade and a holy war, but they did so in more measured tones than their parents had done twenty-five years earlier.[17]

---

[15] As an indication of the mood and tone of the Church of England in general, and Evangelicals in particular, see Angus Calder, *The People's War: Britain 1939-1945* (London, 1969), pp.38, 60, 65, 555, 558, 562, 564, 599; Trevor Lloyd, *The Church of England 1900-1965* (London, 1966), p.457; John Barnes, *Ahead of his Age: Bishop Barnes of Birmingham* (London, 1979), pp.353-363; F.A. Iremonger, *William Temple: His Life and Letters* (Oxford, 1948), pp.540-542; Ronald C.D. Jasper, *George Bell, Bishop of Chichester* (Oxford, 1967), pp.86, 87, 146, 256-285; *Churchman*, July-September 1942, pp.452, 453, January-March 1943, p.1; *Record*, 25 August 1939, p.525, 1 September 1939, pp.538, 539, 15 September 1939, p.561.

[16] Iremonger, *op.cit.*, p.540.

[17] See Herbert Hensley Henson, *Retrospect of an Unimportant Life*, (Oxford, 1942, 1950), Vol.3, pp.47, 48, 57, 59, 68, 69, 77, 142, 143; and Iremonger, *op.cit.*, pp.540-542.

Of all the bishops it was perhaps George Bell of Chichester who spoke most penetratingly and with most effect on the issues raised by the war.[18] He said that it was impossible for the church to speak of any earthly war as a crusade. The supreme concern of the church was not the victory of the national cause. Links should be fostered between Christians of all nations, and they should be strengthened between the churches of warring countries. Bell distinguished between Germany and National Socialism; the allies could never make terms with National Socialist ideology, but could with Germany, under certain conditions. Bell was outstanding in his Christian perceptions and in his fearless utterances in the war years. He also personified, albeit in a more refined and clearly enunciated way than perhaps any other contemporary Christian spokesman, the change of attitude in the church compared with the First World War era.

Evangelicals in general were as convinced as Temple and Henson of the righteousness of the cause.[19] They even identified the national as coinciding with the divine purpose. In the main the conflict was seen as between two different and opposing ideological systems: it was the Nazi ideology which had to be overthrown. Remarkably, however, there was very little comment on the war at all by Evangelicals; a vivid contrast to their fulsome and impassioned language during the First World War.

In the columns of the *Churchman* throughout the entire war period there was almost no space given to any issue connected with the war. When Evangelicals did comment, in the religious press or elsewhere, reason and balance, and a peacable tone, were characteristic. The Evangelical mood is conveyed in the exhortation of Guy Warman at a service of intercession on the eve of the war. He appealed to all present to hold fast to their faith and their courage, and let all things be done in love. Let those present see to it that, come what may, they maintained the Christian spirit. The present crisis, he said, was being faced in a calmer and quieter spirit than had been the case with the last war or the Boer war. Nothing was to be heard of jingoism and nothing of enmity. He encouraged his hearers to keep out of their hearts and lives the very spirit that made war, the spirit of hate and fear.

As in the First World War, pacifism was rejected by most Evangelicals.[20] The Christian duty was to fight for a righteous cause when no other course of action remained. The limits of permissible action were open to debate. Thus, on the question of bombing civilian targets, the editor of the *Record* accepted the military argument. If raids on Cologne

---

[18] See Jasper, *op.cit.*

[19] See for example *Islington Clerical Meeting Report* (1939); *Record*, 8 September 1939, pp. 549, 550, 5 January 1940, p.1, 9 February 1940, p.62, 11 May 1945, p.229.

[20] See for instance *Record*, 22 September 1939, p.573, Letters to the Editor, 21, 29 March 1940, 10 May 1940, p.229.

and Essen were necessary from a tactical point of view as part of an obligation to our allies, so be it; Germany had been the cruel initiator of town and factory bombing as a weapon of warfare, and Rotterdam alone cried to heaven for divine retribution. Other Evangelicals condemned such a view. It is, however, indicative of the more temperate tone of Evangelicals that only one week after endorsing the bombing of German civilian targets, the editor of the *Record* was at pains to stress that hatred must be avoided, in attitude, language and action.

Part 5 1945-1984

20

Renaissance

In recent years there has been a clearly identifiable Evangelical resurgence in the Church of England. When it began is open to debate, but it appears to have had its roots in the immediate post-Second World War period. It was then that the Evangelicals started in a significant way to emerge from the 'ghetto in which they had incarcerated themselves'[1] since the turn of the century, or even earlier.

Indications of such a renaissance were at first somewhat faint and dispersed. In 1944 Tyndale House was opened in Cambridge as an Evangelical centre for biblical and theological study and research, and its undramatic influence was to be of increasing importance. Linked with this was the inauguration of the Tyndale Fellowship as an attempt to encourage Evangelical postgraduate students to think more seriously about biblical and theological matters, and to undertake research in these fields. Its objectives were to some extent achieved in the promotion of a far more theologically sophisticated Evangelicalism, and in the emergence of Evangelical academics of considerable standing. In 1945 the Church of England Commission on Evangelism, chaired by the Evangelical Bishop of Rochester, Christopher Chavasse, produced its widely circulated and influential report *Towards the Conversion of England*. It reads like an Evangelical treatise and it helped to give prominence and official Church

[1] Christopher Catherwood, *Five Evangelical Leaders* (London, 1984), p.9.

287

of England endorsement to the particular Evangelical emphasis which pervaded it. Three years later, in the year of the Lambeth Conference, there was a gathering representative of the varying shades of the Evangelical tradition which issued a book of papers entitled *Evangelicals Affirm*. For all its omissions and deficiencies it at least showed a degree of Evangelical concern for effectiveness in the era of post-war reconstruction.

During the nineteen-fifties a gradual further change took place. In 1950, in response to an invitation from Geoffrey Fisher, the Archbishop of Canterbury, a group of Evangelicals published a report under the title *The Fulness of Christ: The Church's Growth into Catholicity*. It was indicative of the importance accorded to Evangelicals as a component of the Church of England that they were asked for such a report. Despite its shortcomings, the document they produced demonstrated their willingness and ability to make a contribution to the life and thought of the church as a whole.

In the same year, 1950, John Stott began his twenty-five-year tenure as rector of All Souls Langham Place, London. He, more than any one other person, was to be at the heart of the impending Evangelical renaissance.

Four years later, in 1954, the 'first major co-operative evangelical effort in the biblical field for many years'[2] resulted in the publication by the Inter-Varsity Fellowship of the *New Bible Commentary*.

It was also in 1954 that the little-known American evangelist Billy Graham conducted a remarkable three-month crusade in Harringay arena in London. Overnight it gave a national focus not only to Billy Graham, but to evangelism, and to the Evangelicals who sponsored and mainly supported the venture. Thousands were influenced, and many future candidates for the Church of England ministry attributed their conversions to the crusade. In the succeeding months and years certain church leaders and others spoke disparagingly of the menace of fundamentalism. John Stott and Jim Packer promptly produced reasoned and biblically based responses, the one in a booklet entitled *Fundamentalism and Evangelism*, and the other in a book under the title *'Fundamentalism' and the Word of God*.

Other developments followed which were specific to the Church of England Evangelicals. In 1955 Stott founded the Eclectic Society as a forum for Evangelical clergy under forty years of age, in which uninhibited discussion of important issues could take place. It helped to unite the younger Evangelicals and gave them a sense of corporate importance, strength and purpose. In 1959 two leading Evangelical laymen purchased the *Church of England Newspaper* which, under the

---

[2] John Capon, *Evangelicals Tomorrow: A Popular Report of Nottingham 77, the National Evangelical Anglican Congress* (London, 1977), p.14.

editorship of John King, rapidly developed into a vigorous organ for the promotion of an outward-looking Evangelicalism. In the following year Latimer House began its life as an Evangelical research centre in Oxford.

It was also in the nineteen-fifties that Gervase Duffield took a leading part in organizing Evangelicals into a cohesive group in the House of Laity of the Church Assembly.[3] During these years Evangelicals were increasingly appointed to official Church of England commissions.

In 1960 the Church of England Evangelical Council (CEEC) was established as the English group member of the newly-formed Evangelical Fellowship in the Anglican Communion. It was a means whereby Evangelical leaders from the various strands of the movement and from different parts of the country could confer and plan strategically. It also encouraged an international awareness among Evangelicals. Over the years it spoke with authority on a wide range of matters. It commented on the Anglican-Methodist unity proposals, and the Anglican-Roman Catholic International Commission deliberations and reports; contributed to the discussions on many aspects of mission and ministry; declared its mind in various theological debates; and made its voice heard on a variety of matters arising out of the ever-changing agenda of the General Synod.

By the mid-sixties Evangelical theological colleges, Cranmer Hall (St John's College), Durham, Oak Hill, London, St John's College, Nottingham, Trinity College, Bristol (previously Clifton and Tyndale); Ridley Hall, Cambridge and Wycliffe Hall, Oxford – the latter two having varied somewhat theologically throughout their histories, were full. An

---

[3] The Enabling Act of 1919 inaugurated the Church Assembly. The Assembly comprised the two Convocations of Canterbury and York, forming the House of Bishops and the House of Clergy, plus a House of Laity, the members of which were elected by the laity of the diocese. The Convocations continued to meet separately to deal with matters of doctrine and worship and to debate about moral, social and international issues. The Church Assembly dealt mainly with administrative and financial matters. It had power to legislate through Measures which, when approved by Parliament and having received the Royal Assent, had the force of statute law. The system had various shortcomings, most notably the lack of full participation by the laity in discussions and decisions on the church's doctrine and worship.

After much debate the Assembly passed the Synodical Government Measure, which received the Royal Assent in 1969. Th Measure provided for a General Synod and a pattern of synodical government throughout the Church of England at diocesan and deanery level. The General Synod consists of three houses: bishops, clergy and laity. It has power to make canons and to pass Measures, and it also has wide-ranging responsibilities relating to the national and international life of the Church of England. It allows for full participation by the laity, and the diocesan and deanery synods give the laity the opportunity for a fuller involvement in the life of the diocese and deanery than they ever had before.

For a detailed description of both the Church Assembly and the synodical government system, see Paul A. Welsby, *A History of the Church of England 1945-1980* (Oxford, 1984), pp.146-150, on which the account above is based.

active and fruitful work by the Inter-Varsity Fellowship in the universities and colleges helped to produce a steady stream of ordinands.

In the Evangelical parishes rigid adherence to the 1662 Prayer Book and a Sunday pattern of eight o'clock communion, eleven o'clock morning prayer and six-thirty pm evening prayer started to give way to a wide use of the various alternative services and to the holding of parish communions or family services as the main Sunday morning worship gathering.[4]

It was likewise during the mid-sixties that Evangelicals were in the forefront of the charismatic movement in Britain. Evangelicalism was also invigorated and strengthened by the 1966 Billy Graham crusade.

Keele and after

The Evangelicals were beginning to discover something of the maturity, power and effectiveness reminiscent of former years long ago. This new confidence found expression in the National Evangelical Anglican Congress at Keele University in 1967, attended by a thousand delegates. The distinctive marks of this gathering were a willingness to give greater consideration to the views of non-Evangelicals; a concern to relate the Christian faith to contemporary political, social and economic issues; and a desire to take the ecumenical movement seriously.

The most far-reaching and controversial effect, however, was that Keele set Church of England Evangelicals squarely in the historic church. Loyalty to the historic church for some Evangelicals assumed a new importance.[5] The participants may not have been aware of this particular re-orientation at the time, but non-Anglicans as well as Anglican Evangelicals subsequently identified such a new alignment. Passions were aroused. The debate within Church of England and nonconformist evangelicalism on this issue continued for many years. On the one side were those who claimed that membership of doctrinally 'mixed' churches like the Church of England was incompatible with evangelicalism, and that it compromised those Evangelicals concerned, or even removed their right to be called evangelical. On the other hand were the Evangelicals who thought that continued membership of the Church of England was not only allowable, but desirable. Even within this latter group there increasingly developed a difference of emphasis. Some found their deepest identity in their evangelical faith while some stressed their Church of England membership. It was an Anglican Evangelical identity problem.

[4] Capon, *op.cit.*, p.15. The summary in the foregoing paragraph is also largely based on Capon, *op.cit.*, p.15.
[5] See comments in John C. King, *The Evangelicals* (London, 1969), p.12.

Keele was a watershed for Evangelicalism. 'The Church of England now had to take the evangelicals seriously, with the result that they have played a full part in the life of the Church at both diocesan and national level'.[6] 'Keele . . . was in many ways a turning-point for our evangelical constituency in the Church of England', wrote John Stott ten years later, but, he went on,

> most of us would also have to agree that the promise of Keele was not fulfilled. The follow-on was disappointing. We failed to maintain and extend the kind of fruitful dialogue which began at the Congress itself.

Stott particularly hoped for 'a simple structure for continuing debate and action at the diocesan, regional and national levels'. He also wished that all the evangelical theological colleges would become the centres of study, stimulus and renewal which one or two already were, not only for staff and students but for the whole region; that the envisaged Latimer Fellowship of Anglican Evangelical Theology would carry Latimer House's vision of research and writing on the issues of the day to Evangelical scholars throughout the Anglican Communion; that Anglican Evangelicals would take a full and responsible part, particularly through the Evangelical Alliance, the Graduates' Fellowship and the Tyndale Fellowship, in joint study with Free Church evangelicals; and, finally, that Evangelicals would gladly study with others who, while not necessarily calling themselves 'evangelical', were 'none the less anxious to give their minds to contemporary questions in a spirit of humble submission to the Lord Christ who addresses his people through Scripture'.[7]

Although the aspirations of many Evangelicals were unfulfilled in the post-Keele decade, there is little doubt that this period witnessed a further considerable Evangelical advance. Evangelical theological colleges continued to flourish. The number of Evangelical clergy so increased that by the late nineteen-seventies there were not enough benefices with Evangelical patronage to accommodate them all, and some went into parishes with other traditions. Evangelical parishes became some of the most vigorous in the country with large congregations and a wide range of thriving activities. Evangelicals became Archbishops of Canterbury and York and were increasingly appointed to the episcopal bench. Some, such as Colin Buchanan and Professor Sir Norman Anderson, played a full part in the central councils of the church, Sir Norman being lay chairman of the General Synod. Some competently participated in the Methodist-Anglican unity discussions, and others, such as the Rev. Julian Charley, were active in ecumenical consultations. Evangelicals took a full and

---

[6] Paul A. Welsby, *A History of the Church of England 1945-1980* (Oxford, 1984), p.214.

[7] John Stott, 'Obeying Christ in a Changing World', in John Stott (Ed.), *Obeying Christ in a Changing World* (London, 1977), Vol.I, pp.22, 23.

distinctive part in the debates engendered by the publication of James Barr's *Fundamentalism* (1977) and John Hick (Ed.), *The Myth of God Incarnate* (1977). They were also in the forefront of liturgical debate and change, and in the blossoming of hymnology. The Grove booklets and other more extended works provided an Evangelical comment on a wide spectrum of ecclesiastical, social and ethical issues. The charismatic movement in its various manifestations brought widespread renewal. Non-denominational developments such as the lively, varied and imaginative forms of evangelism undertaken by Youth for Christ, and the well-supported National Festival of Light, also helped to stimulate Evangelical life. On the international stage, John Stott in particular helped to spearhead a movement for evangelical unity, co-operation and reinvigoration, which found its focus in the Lausanne Congress on World Evangelisation in 1974.

Such new life and growth were not achieved without tensions. The stresses over Anglican Evangelical identity, previously noted, persisted. The charismatic movement produced divisions as well as renewal. Evangelicalism in the late nineteen-seventies was even more diffuse and the Evangelical base less sharply defined than it had been in the late sixties.

Many of the developments, shortcomings and differences of opinion were evident in the programme, agenda and deliberations of the second National Evangelical Anglican Congress held in Nottingham in 1977. In very broad terms there were two themes running through the Congress: the need to present the gospel to every citizen of the country in such a way that they could understand it, and the steps to be taken to help make the country 'more just, more righteous, more responsibly free, more compassionate, and so more pleasing to God'.[8] It is perhaps too soon after the event to comment on the results of this gathering of two thousand Evangelicals, and it will never be possible to determine exactly how much it reshaped the character of Evangelicalism. There appears to have been less commitment to pan-evangelical co-operation among the younger generation of the Evangelical leadership and Evangelical academics than among their counterparts at Keele. Some expressed a 'high' doctrine of the church and declared their primary loyalty to be to the Church of England.

The Evangelical identity problem became more acute. Non-Anglican evangelicals sometimes thought that their brethren in the Church of England gave less attention to them than they did to discussion and dialogue with Roman Catholics and charismatics. Non-denominational activities such as Spring Harvest and Greenbelt, the Luis Palau Mission to

---

[8] Stott, *op.cit*, Vol.I, p.15.

London, and the Billy Graham Mission England did much to encourage pan-evangelicalism, but for ordinary evangelicals, and indeed among the evangelical leadership, the major concern appeared to be with evangelicalism within the Church of England. It was a dilemma. It seemed that as Anglican Evangelicalism prospered, so the felt need among its members for pan-evangelical involvement declined.

Evangelicalism was strengthened, and its acceptance and influence in the wider church enhanced by the Evangelical Anglican Assemblies of 1983 and 1984. Their institution meant that:

> for the first time in its long and varied history the evangelical movement in the Church of England had brought into being a representative structure in which its various constituent parts could find a voice through delegates responsible to the movement at its grass-roots level.[9]

It is too early to gauge whether the new Assembly will be a means whereby the distinctive Evangelical voice will be heard with clarity by the wider church, and indeed beyond that by society as a whole. For this to happen the significance of the Assembly, and for that matter the importance of the Church of England Evangelical Council which gave birth to it, needs to be recognized by a larger number and more comprehensive range of Evangelicals, among whom are many who are shy, and even cynical or suspicious, of such structures. It remains to be seen whether such recognition is forthcoming, and whether the Assembly and the Council realize the potential which their advocates claim for them.

The present chapter has given a cursory look at the Evangelical scene in the post-Second World War period. In order to delve into this in a more detailed and analytical way it is useful to adopt a thematic approach.

---

[9] Foreword, *Anglican Evangelicals and Their New Assembly: A Forum for United Thought and Action in the Church of England* (1983).

21

Contending for the Faith

Before the Second World War had ended 'lay apologetics of a quite new, even an original, kind began to appear from the press, and did much to redress the scandal of the mass apostasy of the intellectual world from the Christianity which had served all their forefathers'.[1] C.S. Lewis brilliantly communicated Christian truth in such works as *The Problem of Pain* (1941), *Christian Behaviour* (1943), *The Screwtape Letters* (1943) and *Beyond Personality* (1944). T.S. Eliot, who became a convinced Anglo-Catholic, conveyed something of his faith in his apologia, *The Idea of a Christian Society* (1939) and indirectly in his plays and poetry, as in *Four Quartets* (1944). Robert Bridges, the Poet Laureate, also made his contribution through the new, wartime editions of his long epic, *The Testament of Beauty* (1929), and Dorothy Sayers was beginning to gain a wide readership. All of these 'found new and challenging ways of presenting the truths of the Gospel, and the philosophy underlying the Christian Faith'. They made 'Christian theology exciting again', and did much 'to restore to the church, which had long lost it, the reputation of intellectual respectability'.[2]

Biblical studies had received a great stimulus in Anglican circles from the work of Sir Edwyn Hoskins, who died in 1937. 'His constant theme

---

[1] Roger Lloyd, *The Church of England 1900-1965*, p.458.
[2] Lloyd, *op.cit.*, pp.458, 459.

was that there was the closest possible connection between history and theology in the New Testament and, while he insisted on a rigorous use of critical methods, he maintained that questions about the New Testament are all ultimately questions of theology and history'.[3] His mantle fell upon Alan Richardson, who popularized Biblical theology in his widely read book *Preface to Bible Study* (1943). Biblical theology brought about a rediscovery of the unity of the Bible, and it reasserted the principle that the primary commentary on particular texts was the theological themes running through the whole Bible. It also attempted to demonstrate that what might be regarded as historical, textual or critical questions were in fact theological matters: the Bible was more than a source book for historians; it had its own authority as the word of God.

In 1947 there was published a book of a very different genre from those mentioned so far: *The Rise of Christianity* by E.W. Barnes, the Bishop of Birmingham. It rapidly created a furore in the Church of England. Barnes's admiration for modern science was much in evidence in the book. The 'orderly universe of modern science' was 'contrasted sharply with the, by inference, disorderly and therefore unacceptable miraculous elements in the Gospels'.[4] Barnes identified himself with modern man, whose thoughts were shaped by scientific activities, and who is certain that miracles, in the sense of finite–scale activities contrary to the normal ordering of nature, do not happen. Despite the disturbing of the ecclesiastical waters by Barnes, the Lambeth Conference in the following year gave the impression of a church 'thinking aloud before the era of that theological 'shaking of the foundations' . . . had begun. Problems enough indeed there were. But, for the most part, attempts to deal with them seem to have been approached from positions of certitudes not now as easy to assume as then'.[5]

Evangelical Theological Scholarship

In Evangelical circles there was an attempt to revive theological scholarship. After the traumatic rift in Evangelicalism in the nineteen-twenties over 'liberal' views, there was danger in the following decade of a drift 'into the sands of indefiniteness on the one hand, or pietistic insignificance on the other'.[6] A resurgence of genuine evangelical thought and churchmanship was needed at a time when the growing strength of

[3] Paul A. Welsby, *A History of the Church of England 1945-1980*, pp.56, 57.
[4] William Purcell, *Fisher of Lambeth: A Portrait From Life* (London, 1969), p.165.
[5] Purcell, *op.cit.*, p.182.
[6] G.J.C. Marchant, 'Through Fire and Water . . . to a Place of Liberty', *Churchman*, 1979-I, p.13.

Karl Barth's influence, biblical theology and developments in reformed theology on the continent were providing new theological insights. There were various Evangelical responses. A rekindled concern for Evangelical theology was fostered by the Inter-Varsity Fellowship, and in turn this nurtured the newly-founded Fellowship of Evangelical Students. T.C. Hammond wrote his widely read and long-to-be-used trilogy: *In Understanding Be Men* (1937), a handbook of Christian doctrine; *Perfect Freedom* (1938), a much-needed book on Christian ethics; and an introduction to Christian apologetics entitled *Reasoning Faith* (1943). Other Evangelicals published books on biblical and controversial issues.

A further response was the formation in 1942 of the Evangelical Fellowship for Theological Literature, which was initiated by Max Warren, then General Secretary of the CMS, and the staffs of Wycliffe and Ridley Halls. Warren made its purpose clear:

> It had a strictly limited theological purpose, that of producing articles and books which represented an Evangelical contribution to the contemporary debate. It was in no sense a 'pressure group'. It was not interested in church politics. Anyone who was interested in this kind of writing and was willing to accept the name 'Evangelical', with or without a prefix, was welcome.[7]

At the time of its establishment Evangelicals were making little contribution to serious scholarship. By 1972, when its work was done, the membership of the EFTL included such distinguished academics as the Regius Professors of Divinity at Oxford and Cambridge, the Regius Professor of Ecclesiastical History at Oxford, the Lady Margaret Professor at Cambridge, and the Lightfoot Professor and the Van Mildert Professor at Durham. The Fellowship encouraged both younger men and senior scholars. It produced from its membership authors who built up the St Paul's Library of popular books that were to help a new generation after the war 'to think in creative terms about evangelical truth and churchmanship, preaching, sacraments, liturgy and devotion'.[8] Hitherto Evangelicals had depended largely on older works such as Griffith Thomas's *Principles of Theology*. Now they were given new tools for the job, and an incentive to use them.

Throughout its life, the EFTL owed much to Warren, and it was coloured to a remarkable extent by his views and theological perspective. He was convinced that Evangelicals either neglected theology or concentrated their attention upon too narrow a range of theological principles. His theological sympathies were comprehensive. He stressed the danger of over-simplification, and 'such a concentration upon one

---

[7] Max Warren, *Crowded Canvas: Some Experiences of a life-time* (London, 1974), p.223.
[8] Marchant, *op.cit.*, p.14.

form of experience that the manifold work and wisdom of God revealed in other ways came to be forgotten'.[9] Although 'he distrusted all qualifications of the term evangelical, there could be no doubt that the direction of his thought and action was liberal rather than conservative'.[10] This theological and philosophical approach was characteristic of the EFTL.

One element in such Evangelical thinking was a fresh and deeper grasp of the doctrine of the church. The contributors to the 1950 report, *The Fulness of Christ*, were drawn mainly from the membership of the EFTL. The Fellowship enabled some Evangelicals to think theologically about the church and churchmanship, as well as about Evangelical doctrine and Christian living in modern society. It has been asserted that in so doing it encouraged a breach between the more sophisticated and discerning Evangelicals and others who were unable or disinclined to apply themselves seriously to the discipline of thinking theologically. It has been claimed that the latter were, for example, glad to avail themselves of any work of intellectual merit that said what they wished to hear, such as *Fundamentalism and the Word of God*, (IVF, 1958), but were not disposed to follow other modes of thinking through current issues. They were content to think, speak and act in pre-established patterns of traditional outlook that could be affirmed easily in simplistic slogans.

There is an element of truth in this. Certainly many Evangelicals had withdrawn into a pietistic, non-intellectual world of their own. The Church of England was about to face a prolonged period in which radical theology challenged foundation Christian doctrines, and the Evangelicals responded to such an assault upon their cherished basic beliefs with varying degrees of profundity. Many were distinctly relieved to discover that in their midst there were those who so effectively combined theological acumen with communicative skill that they were able to provide an authentic response to the radicals. As the years passed, and the radicalism continued, an increasing number of the 'new-Evangelicals' grew in their awareness of the issues at stake and demonstrated greater ability to grapple with the theological implications. As a whole Evangelicals appear to have gained in maturity as a result of the process: there was less obscurantism and plain theological ignorance among them in 1984 than there had been forty years before.

Debate on Fundamentalism

The major theological debate for Evangelicals in the nineteen-fifties was

[9] F.W. Dillistone, *Into All the World: A Biography of Max Warren* (London, 1980), p.158.
[10] Dillistone, *op.cit.*, p.154.

on 'fundamentalism'. It was mainly aroused by the growing influence and membership of the IVF Christian Unions, the Billy Graham crusade of 1954–55, which included an invitation to conduct a mission in the University of Cambridge, and the increase in the number of Evangelical candidates for the ministry. In a letter to *The Times* Canon H.K. Luce, headmaster of Durham School, said that the Billy Graham invitation raised an issue which did not seem to have been squarely faced in this country. Universities exist for the advancement of learning: on what basis, therefore, he asked, could fundamentalism claim a hearing at Cambridge?[11] A considerable correspondence followed, which was later published. One bishop sharply disagreed with another, and all kinds of views were expressed. In the ensuing months Dr Michael Ramsey, then Bishop of Durham, was trenchant in his criticism. He was concerned that the act of decision and conversion in the Billy Graham meetings, for all its value, might involve 'the stifling of the mind instead of its liberation into a new service of God and man'.[12] In an article in *The Bishoprick* in February 1956 under the title 'The Menace of Fundamentalism', he went even further, and described the fundamentalism of Billy Graham as heretical and sectarian.

The attack on 'fundamentalism' was most comprehensively elaborated in Gabriel Hebert's *Fundamentalism and the Church of God* (1957). He made it plain which particular 'fundamentalists' he had chiefly in mind:

> It is with the conservative evangelicals in the Church of England and other churches, and with the Inter-Varsity Fellowship of Evangelical Unions, that this book is to be specially concerned . . . I believe that Fundamentalism (in the evil sense) is a grave menace to the Church of God.[13]

He regarded 'any rigid doctrine of the Bible' as 'too narrow to fit the facts'.[14] He accepted that the evangelicals to whom he was addressing himself repudiated a 'mechanical', 'dictation-theory' of inspiration; but he objected to the assertion that the Bible was literally true, and he denounced evangelicals for their condemnation of those who disagreed with them. Such rigidity, he said, was dangerous. When Christians who were nurtured on such teaching were confronted with proof that the biblical account of the creation was unscientific, or when they were faced with biblical discrepancies, they might then suspect that they were not being told the whole truth about the Bible. Having been told that they must believe everything, they might end by believing nothing. This could and did happen. The evangelical view, said Hebert, was unconsciously

---

[11] *The Times*, 15 August 1955.
[12] Welsby, *op.cit.*, p.60.
[13] Gabriel Hebert, *Fundamentalism and the Church of God* (London, 1957), pp.10, 13.
[14] *Ibid.*, p.55.

dominated by the materialistic, intellectualistic presuppositions of a scientific age. It was a style of thinking which was alien to the Bible. It was the reason, said Hebert, why the man in the street thought that if Balaam's ass did not speak, then the Bible was not true.

Hebert was offended by what he saw as the fundamentalist sectarian party spirit: the tendency of fundamentalists to be self-sufficient, to consider they possessed all the truth, and to regard themselves as wholly right and others wrong. Fundamentalists treated the ground of unity not as the gospel but as the gospel plus the inerrancy of the Bible and the necessity for a particular kind of conversion. Hebert was fearful of minds which were firmly closed: it was too reminiscent of Fascism and Nazism. He endorsed the judgement of Dr Ramsey that, in responding to the message proclaimed by the fundamentalists, 'the mind of the hearer has either to be stifled or ignored on account of the crudity of the doctrine presented, and the appeal is made to *less than the whole man*'. Ramsey maintained that:

> the act of decision and conversion, instead of being related to man's place and duty in society, abstracts a man from his place and duty in society, and society becomes the mere stage and scenery alongside which the moral decisions are made. The moral will is separated from its context, because the appeal is made to less than the whole man as a reasoning being and a social being.[15]

Hebert thought that 'conservative evangelicals and Fundamentalists' should not resent such criticisms but take them seriously. This is just what some Evangelicals did.

In April 1956, before the publication of Hebert's book, John Stott had issued a leaflet entitled *Fundamentalism and Evangelism*. In it he succinctly examined the term 'fundamentalist'; identified what he discerned as the authentic conservative evangelical view of the Bible; discussed the relative places of the mind and the emotions in evangelism and what doctrines should be included in the proclamation of the gospel; and considered the rightness of urging immediate decisions with the expectation of sudden conversion.

Stott denounced such extremes and extravagances as the total rejection of all biblical criticism, an excessively literalist interpretation of the Bible and the definition of biblical inspiration in very mechanical terms. Conservative evangelicals should, and mostly did, regard the investigation of literary sources and historical circumstances of the books of the Bible as indispensable to a right understanding of the Bible. The arbitrary use of isolated proof texts was recognized by Stott and, he

[15] *Ibid.*, p.146.

claimed, by evangelicals in general, as a practice to be avoided; evangelicals normally gave full weight to the context, and interpreted each scripture in the light of the whole. Further, God's revelation was progressive, 'culminating in Jesus Christ and in the apostolic testimony to Him in the New Testament'.[16] Some of the Bible is metaphorical and symbolic, and there are anthropomorphic descriptions of God which are not intended to be literally understood.

As far as Biblical inspiration was concerned, conservative evangelicals believed that 'the Holy Spirit spoke through the human authors so directly that their words were in a very real sense his words'.[17] But the process was not mechanical. The human personalities of the biblical authors 'were not violated or transformed into machines: they were fashioned, enriched and fully employed'.[18]

On the matter of evangelism, Stott acknowledged the importance of the mind in preaching to the unconverted:

> We shall not seek to murder their intellect (since it was given to them by God), but neither shall we flatter it (since it is finite and fallen). We shall endeavour to reason with them, but only from revelation, the while admitting our need and theirs for the enlightenment of the Holy Spirit.[19]

The cross must be central in evangelism even if, in an attempt to simplify its unfathomable mystery for the benefit of the outsider who is neither familiar with biblical categories nor versed in theological terms, 'the evangelist is sometimes guilty of crudity or distortion'.[20] Conversion may be sudden or gradual, but it is right for an evangelist to ask for an immediate decision.

A more extended exposition of the conservative evangelical view was published two years later, after the appearance of Hebert's work. In 'Fundamentalism' and the Word of God (1958), J.I. Packer offered 'a constructive re-statement of evangelical principles in the light of the current 'Fundamentalism controversy''.[21] He concluded that, because of its prejudicial character, and associations, fundamentalism was not a useful alternative title for contemporary evangelicalism. The belief and behaviour of Christians must, said Packer, be controlled and directed throughout by the teaching of scripture. Having examined the biblical concept of scripture he declared that:

[16] John R.W. Stott, *Fundamentalism and Evangelism* (London, 1956), p.3.
[17] *Ibid.*, p.5.
[18] *Ibid.*, p.6.
[19] *Ibid.*, p.25.
[20] *Ibid*, p.35.
[21] J.I. Packer, 'Fundamentalism' and the Word of God: Some Evangelical Principles (London, 1958), Foreword, p.7.

the Bible asks to be regarded as a God-given, error-free, self-interpreting unity, true and trustworthy in all that it teaches . . . Faith and reason only come into conflict when reason defies God's authority, refuses to be a servant of faith, and reverts to some sort of unbelief.[22]

The real choice according to Packer was between accepting the authority of Christ and the biblical doctrine of scripture, or bowing to modern subjectivism and hankering after the spirit of the age. Either the intellect must be submitted to the rule of God and the whole of the Bible accepted as authoritative, or the thought-life freed from the rule of God and the bible circumscribed and delimited by biblical criticism and the decisions of historians. Evangelicals were being asked to enter into a marriage of convenience with subjectivism; but they could not in conscience consent

> If the human mind is set up as the measure and test of truth, it will quickly substitute for man's incomprehensible Creator a comprehensible idol fashioned in man's own image; man wants a god he can manage and feel comfortable with, and will inevitably invent one if allowed.[23]

When subjectivism stops short of destroying Christianity altogether it perverts the nature of it as a religion of grace. The temptation is to find a way in which man can contribute something to his salvation. Evangelicals must be wary of any form of Gnosticism which detracts from salvation as the free gift of God. Evangelicalism, far from being sectarian, schismatic and un-catholic in its outlook, is in fact the truest catholicism:

> The catholicity of evangelicalism appears, first, in its uncompromising submission to the teaching of Christ and of Scripture on authority, as on all other matters, and, second, in its oneness with all those who down the ages have taken this same position, bowing to the authority of Scripture, glorying in the biblical gospel of free grace, and contending earnestly for the apostolic faith.[24]

Packer was not oblivious to the lessons to be deduced by Evangelicals in the face of the contemporary criticism. First, they should live more under the authority of scripture. Then it should be admitted that much evangelical worship was slipshod, and sometimes even downright irreverent. As far as the actual debate was concerned, Packer urged Evangelicals to discern and keep before them the real issues, not to react to the various polemical terminology used by their critics. They should always request a reasoned statement of the accusations against them,

[22] *Ibid.*, pp.169, 170.
[23] *Ibid.*, p.171.
[24] *Ibid.*, p.174.

which should then be answered by a reasoned defence in terms of their own first principles. Evangelicals should take courage. When evangelicalism was weak it was ignored. The prevailing controversy was a testimony to renewed vitality in evangelical circles. It is 'the nature of the gospel to create controversy; and the vigour with which the gospel is spoken against is an index of the faithfulness and power with which it is being preached'.[25]

'Soundings' and 'Honest to God'

The next theological debate to command the widespread attention of Evangelicals was far more public, and had far greater long-term significance for the church as a whole, than that which has just been discussed. In fact, so dramatic and disturbing was it that it could perhaps best be described as a storm. The book of theological essays called *Soundings*, published in 1962, provided the first rather vague rumblings. In the next year John Robinson's *Honest to God* 'set all the fireworks and thunderings of the long-pent storm free to rage in fury'.[26]

Soundings was a collection of essays by ten theologians.[27] Their task was not to provide confident answers, but rather identify pertinent questions needing to be explored. It seemed to them that:

> the great problem of the Church (and therefore of its theologians) is to establish or re-establish some kind of vital contact with that enormous majority of human beings for whom Christian faith is not so much unlikely as irrelevant and uninteresting. The greatest intellectual challenge to faith is simply that thoroughly secularized intelligence which is now the rule rather than the exception, whether it expresses itself in science or philosophy or politics or the arts. It is by no means clear that anything like Christian faith in the form we know it will ever again be able to come alive for people of our own time or of such future time as we can imagine. It is just as uncertain that Christian ideals and ways of thought, as we know them, will be able to re-engage an intelligence and imagination now so far separated from them.[28]

Except for the fact that the book gave the first public airing to what has been christened the New Morality, it produced little reaction. It was a very scholarly work by a group of academics who always wrote with caution and restraint; but it heralded a revolution. It at least implied a radical

[25] *Ibid.*, p.177.
[26] Lloyd, *op.cit.*, p.597.
[27] A.R. Vidler (Ed.), *Soundings: Essays Concerning Christian Understanding* (Cambridge University Press, 1962).
[28] Vidler, *op.cit.*, pp.6, 7.

questioning of traditional theology. It was a foretaste of what was to come in a more controversial, sensational and popular (but not necessarily easy to understand) form in the following year.

When John A.T. Robinson wrote *Honest to God* [29] he made publishing history. 'The book appears to have sold more quickly than any new book of serious theology in the history of the world'. [30] In the first three months of the book's life its author received over a thousand letters of response. In television programmes and on the radio, by means of cartoons and satirical jokes, newspaper articles and reviews, sermons and letters to editors, the debate it provoked was perpetuated for a long time.

Honest to God was inspired by three German theologians: Rudolf Bultmann, Dietrich Bonhoeffer and Paul Tillich. Bultmann with his concern to 'demythologize' the gospel, was a challenge to the 'biblical' theologians. Bonhoeffer, with his vision of a 'religionless' Christianity, was a challenge to Christian escapism and undue pietism. Tillich with his philosophy based on faith as 'ultimate concern' with the 'ground of our being', was a reminder of the call of the church to embrace all mankind in its concern.

In order to communicate Christian doctrine, Robinson believed that the church was being called not merely to a restatement of traditional orthodoxy in modern terms, but to a much more radical recasting 'in the process of which the most fundamental categories of our theology – of God, the supernatural, and of religion itself – must go into the melting'. [31] The lay world, said Robinson, found the traditional orthodox supernaturalism largely meaningless.

Indeed, Robinson himself identified with this incomprehension. His concern was that those, like him, who radically questioned the established religious frame, should be accepted as no less genuine, or in the long run necessary as defenders of the faith, than the orthodox; but he was not sanguine. He anticipated increasing alienation 'both within the ranks of the Church and outside it, between those whose basic recipe is the mixture as before (however revitalised) and those who feel compelled above all to be honest wherever it may lead them'. [32]

Man, said Robinson, had come of age, and the old images of God were no longer adequate. The pictures of God 'up there' or 'out there' were unhelpful. More appropriate was the terminology of depth psychology, in which God was thought of as 'the ground of our being'. Jesus was the 'man

---

[29] John A.T. Robinson, Bishop of Woolwich, *Honest to God* (London, 1963).
[30] David L. Edwards, *The Honest to God Debate: Some reactions to the book 'Honest to God'* (London, 1963), Preface, p.7.
[31] Robinson, *op.cit.*, Preface, p.7.
[32] *Ibid.*

for others', who is united with 'the ground of his being' because of his utter concern for other people. Worship should not be an act of withdrawing. The test of worship is how far it makes us more sensitive to the beyond in our midst, to the Christ in the hungry, the naked, the homeless and the prisoner. In the sphere of morals the radical 'ethic of the situation' was advocated, in which nothing was prescribed except love.

It was once again J.I. Packer who provided the most widely-read Evangelical response to *Honest to God*, in the form of a booklet entitled *Keep Yourselves from Idols* (1963). Its argument is representative of the many points which were reiterated by Evangelicals, and it expressed the essence of the conservative Evangelical view. Packer paid tribute to *Honest to God* as a most frank and, for that reason, most engaging book.[33] Nonetheless, in common with Evangelicals at large, he wished it had not come from a bishop. 'No doubt the church needs its gadflies and even its heretics . . . But it is not to the office and ministry of a gadfly that a bishop is consecrated'.[34] Packer accepted that *Honest to God* legitimately raised questions which needed to be answered. He also recognized that it was not a definitive answer to profound theological and philosophical questions: it was a tentative exploration. Indeed, considering the originality of Dr Robinson's mind, Packer thought the book was 'just a plateful of mashed up Tillich fried in Bultmann and garnished with Bonhoeffer'. It bore 'the marks of unfinished thinking on page after page'.[35]

Packer was critical of Robinson's proposal that we should stop thinking of God as a person separate from ourselves, and should give the name 'God' to the 'ground of our being'. Such a 'God', Packer declared, could not meaningfully be called 'Father'. Robinson's real message was not that God is love, but that love is God, and the bishop's Jesus (whose pre-existence and virgin birth he certainly denied, and apparently his bodily resurrection, present dominion and future return also) could not really be called either Saviour or Lord.

'No wonder', exclaimed Packer, 'that the Moslems of Woking acclaimed this book!'[36] All the distinctive features of the Christian faith in God, as opposed to the Moslem or Hindu, had been eliminated from the bishop's theology. Also, if the God of Tillich-Robinson was the true God, the biblical heroes of the faith and those who had lived by faith in the living Lord in subsequent centuries had been deluded. There was, additionally, the inconvenience that the impersonal God of Dr Robinson could not speak and therefore could not give laws or promises. Belief in such a God made evangelism a nonsense. For, according to Robinson, one must agree

[33] J.I. Packer, *Keep Yourselves from Idols* (1963), p.4.
[34] *Ibid.*, p.4.
[35] *Ibid.*, p.5
[36] *Ibid.*, p.7.

with modern man that historic Christianity is irrelevant to him, but at the same time tell him that he is not, and cannot be, an atheist since his 'ultimate concern' (whatever that may be) is 'God'. Packer sarcastically commented that a non–Tillichite might be forgiven for feeling that this was more of a policy for calling worldlings Christians than for making them such.[37]

Packer considered that the saddest thing about *Honest to God* was its genuine pastoral and evangelistic intent, but its unhelpful and inept attempt to meet such pastoral and evangelistic needs. The cure was far worse than the disease. The God offered by Robinson was no less, but no more than the deepest thing within us. The God of creation, providence, and revelation, the God in whose image we were made, the Lord of history, self-existent and tri–personal, vanished from the scene. Nor was there any place in the picture for the incarnation, the atoning sacrifice of Christ, the resurrection, the second coming, the law and the promises.

A gospel for intellectuals (or anyone else) that was bought at the price of such a loss was not worth having. By mutilating the Christian message in this fashion, Packer continued, the bishop had not, as he thought, rescued the perishing, he was 'merely sinking the lifeboat'.[38] The choice was not 'between two images of the same God, but between two Gods, two Christs, two histories, and ultimately two religions'. The God portrayed by Robinson was, said Packer, no longer recognizable as 'the God and Father of our Lord Jesus Christ', and when that point is reached one has 'changed the truth of God into a lie and started to worship a false God'.[39] The admonition of the Apostle John to 'keep yourselves from idols',[40] applied in the case of *Honest to God*, and the warning should be heeded.

In his concluding remarks Packer identified the true radicals in the post-Christian world. They were not those who changed the gospel under the shallow delusion that man had changed, but those who were bold enough to face 'modern man', and maintain that the Bible was still right, that God was still on the throne, that the risen Christ was still mighty to save. Man remained the sinner he had always been. The apostolic gospel was still 'the power of God unto salvation', and not even such great mistakes as those Packer had been examining could finally 'stop its course, or thwart its triumph'.[41]

Some liberal Evangelicals were less critical. Max Warren, to whom inflexibility was anathema, had been a reader of the original manuscript of *Honest to God*, and had encouraged Robinson to publish it. After

[37] *Ibid.*, p.10.
[38] *Ibid.*, pp.10, 11.
[39] *Ibid.*, p.14.
[40] 1 John, ch.5 v.21.
[41] Packer, *op.cit.*, pp.19,20.

publication he defended the book as an honest attempt to re-examine the Christian vocabulary, and see if it could be used to commend Jesus Christ to those who did not know the kind of religious shorthand of orthodox Christianity. It was, said Warren, not a dogmatic book. The author was gentle and sensitive, and was asking himself questions: he was an explorer. It was not an easy book to read, but 'honest to goodness', said Warren, it was worth reading.[42] And in 1968, despite all the trauma it had caused, Warren joined with others in celebrating the fifth anniversary of its publication.

The Myth of God Incarnate

The next major theological agitation occurred fourteen years later with the appearance of John Hick (Ed.), *The Myth of God Incarnate* (1977). The book was part of an extended debate on Christology. In 1973 John Robinson issued *The Human Face of God*, in which the historical Jesus was frankly presented as 'an entirely human personality through which divinity was manifested . . . Jesus', Robinson wrote, was 'different from other men, not in kind, but in degree'.[43] Even more radically, in 1974 Maurice Wiles published *The Re-Making of Christian Doctrine*, in which he maintained that incarnational theology was difficult if not impossible; we must either discard traditional Christology or accept incoherence. In 1975 Don Cupitt, the Dean of Emmanuel College, Cambridge, declared that 'the Eternal God, and a historical man, are two beings of quite different ontological status'. It was, Cupitt asserted, 'simply unintelligible to declare them identical'.[44]

The debate was further fuelled by Professor G.W.H. Lampe in his 1976 Bampton Lectures, *God as Spirit*. God as Spirit was always and everywhere at work, said Lampe. The only exceptional thing about Jesus was that he provided 'the focal instance and key to God's dealings with the world and with men and women. God acted as Spirit in Jesus decisively and in unparalleled fashion, but this activity was in a totally human Jesus'.[45] The Commission on Doctrine, under the chairmanship of Maurice Wiles, caused much concern when, in 1976, it produced a document entitled *Christian Believing*. The Christian faith and life for all believers was depicted as 'a voyage of discovery', rather than an assurance, and, in the opinion of many, the Commission pushed the limits of comprehensiveness to such an extent that it downgraded the standards of orthodoxy.

[42] Edwards, *op.cit.*, p.91.
[43] Welsby, *op.cit.*, p.235.
[44] *Ibid.*, p.236.
[45] *Ibid.*, p.237.

The Myth of God Incarnate was launched amid great publicity, and 30,000 copies were sold in the first eight months. It consisted of a series of essays in which the New Testament and the development of Christian doctrine were declared to be culturally conditioned. The conception of Jesus as God incarnate, the second person of the Trinity, living a human life, was declared to be a mythological or poetic way of expressing his significance for us. The Chalcedonian definition of Christology was rejected as incomprehensible to modern man. The whole matter of the incarnation and 'orthodox' Christology was brought into question.

There were many emotional and often somewhat ill-informed responses to the book. A reasoned and theologically sophisticated reply was promptly provided within a few months in the form of a volume of essays entitled *The Truth of God Incarnate* (1977). The authors were from a variety of theological and cultural backgrounds. The editor was an Evangelical, Michael Green, and Evangelicals fully identified with almost if not all the opinions expressed. The essayists had in mind 'the man in the street' who, after reading *The Myth of God Incarnate*, or seeing on television that a number of theologians had written a book on such a subject, would ask basic questions. 'Were the early Christians mistaken in ascribing deity to Jesus? Had the Church been guilty of idolatry ever since? What actually is the New Testament evidence? Is it reliable? Can the contentions of historic Christianity confidently be jettisoned after two thousand years?'[46]

Although the issues raised by *The Myth of God Incarnate* were thoroughly and sensitively discussed, the conclusions reached were severly critical. Stephen Neill wished that he could be more certain as to what exactly *was* being offered in exchange for the Nicene faith:

> It seems that we are being offered a God who loved us a little, but not enough to wish to become one of us; a Jesus who did not rise from the dead, and therefore offers no answer to the great and bitter problems of humanity; and a gospel which is just one of many forms of salvation, and perhaps not that which is most suitable to modern Western man. If that is so, we may perhaps be excused if we say respectfully to our friends that it looks to us remarkably like the diet which the younger son enjoyed in the far country.[47]

Michael Green addressed himself to the treatment of the incarnation given by reductionist theologians. He accepted the validity of questioning the literalness of the Chalcedonian definition of the two natures of Christ, and seeking to reinterpret Christology in a philosophical framework which would ring true in the modern world. 'All right and proper', he continued.

[46] Michael Green (Ed.), *The Truth of God Incarnate* (London, 1977), p.16.
[47] *Ibid.*, p.68.

'But what in fact they seemed to be doing, at least in the recent symposium, was to evacuate the divine element from Jesus' just as surely as they had done it with scripture. 'They were denying not merely the Nicene and Chalcedonian definitions of Christ but the basic truth which these definitions sought, in the cultural heritage of their own day, to express, that Jesus shared the nature of God as well as our nature'. They were not reinterpreting traditional Christology but abandoning it.[48]

John Macquarrie also observed that the contributors to *The Myth of God Incarnate* were united in their dissatisfaction with traditional doctrines of the incarnation but had no common reconstruction of belief to offer. The impression was of a negative reductionism. Maurice Wiles had claimed that the discarding of the doctrine of the incarnation would not involve the discarding of all the religious claims associated with it. But what doctrine, asked Macquarrie, would be thrown out next, and how do the other doctrines surrounding the person of Christ survive if the incarnation is discarded? Creeds and liturgies, prayer books and hymn books and the scriptures would need to be rewritten. Finally, Macquarrie questioned 'whether such a reduced Christianity would move us either to acceptance or rejection'. He concluded that it would hardly survive 'as a living religious faith'.[49]

The concluding statement of the second National Evangelical Anglican Congress in 1977 made the view of the delegates on this whole issue abundantly clear. Under the sub-heading 'The Incarnation is no myth', it stated:

The widespread present-day view that the New Testament confession of Jesus Christ as God incarnate is a myth concerning a mere man is a real, if unintended, denial of Christianity. It does not see the problem of sin or the need of mediation, is Unitarian rather than Trinitarian and is destructive of true faith. We therefore call upon the bishops of the Church of England as guardians of its doctrine to confirm the Church's historic faith concerning the person of Jesus Christ the Lord, as reliably witnessed to in Scripture and by the Creeds.[50]

Barr on 'Fundamentalism'

In this same year, 1977, James Barr, 'one of the most penetrating minds at work in biblical study in Britain',[51] issued his controversial book

[48] *Ibid.*, p.109.
[49] *Ibid.*, p.144.
[50] *The Nottingham Statement*, p.11.
[51] John Goldingay, 'James Barr on Fundamentalism', *Churchman*, October 1977, p.295.

Fundamentalism. Professor Barr identified the most pronounced characteristics of fundamentalist belief as:

(a) a very strong emphasis on the inerrancy of the Bible, the absence from it of any sort of error;

(b) a strong hostility to modern theology and to the methods, results and implications of modern critical study of the Bible; and

(c) an assurance that those who do not share an identical religious viewpoint are not really 'true Christians' at all.

He found the clearest embodiment of fundamentalism in Britain to be the Universities and Colleges Christian Fellowship (UCCF, formerly the IVF), and his critique was based largely on its publications. He drew heavily on the writings of J.N.D. Anderson, C. Brown, F.F. Bruce, H.F.R. Catherwood, D. Guthrie, D. Kidner, G.T. Manley, R.E Nixon, J.I. Packer and J.W. Wenham. Although Barr wrote his book with the declared goal of understanding, he unhesitatingly expressed his disagreement with fundamentalism. 'Its doctrinal position . . . especially in regard to the place of the Bible, and its entire intellectual apologetic' seemed to him 'to be completely wrong'.[52]

In general, evangelicals appreciated the recognition by Barr of the importance of the conservative evangelical movement and his attempt to understand and evaluate it. But they regretted the polemical tone of his book, the use of the term 'fundamentalist' with all its negative connotations, rather than the term 'evangelical', and an apparent unawareness of developments in evangelicalism during the previous decade and more. Although he had worked through a large amount of British conservative evangelical literature, he had ignored or misrepresented the works of such prominent Evangelicals as Michael Green and John Stott. David Edwards, a former editor of the CMS Press, noted that Barr never discussed 'the teaching of Mr Stott, the most influential Conservative Evangelical in the Church of England'. And he commented that Barr's research into what Evangelicals were actually saying had not been sufficiently comprehensive.[53]

Evangelicals acknowledged that they were often severely critical of non-evangelical views. But this was not the same as unchurching non-evangelicals, nor was it incompatible with the recognition that at some points Evangelicals themselves were possibly wrong and had things to learn as well as teach. Barr's analysis and critique of the fundamentalist cast of mind was frequently compelling, but evangelicals criticized it as sometimes mistaken and often overstated. Also, Evangelical exclusivism and hostility to modern theology and biblical study, which Barr

[52] James Barr, *Fundamentalism* (London, 1977), p.8.
[53] *Church Times*, 15 July 1977.

castigated, although present, was not normative, or probably even dominant, among those who subscribed to the IVF basis of faith. The acceptance of biblical criticism by conservative evangelicals had probably gone much further than Professor Barr thought possible.[54]

Radical theology continued to provoke an evangelical response in the nineteen-eighties. Christology remained at the centre of much of the debate, and resulted in various evangelical defences of the orthodox, traditional doctrine. The issues under discussion were highly publicized in 1984 with the controversial appointment of Dr David Jenkins as Bishop of Durham. Dr Jenkins gave a 'liberal' interpretation of the virgin birth and the resurrection. In the post-Second World War years there had been a growth of liberalism, and it was accepted by Evangelicals as well as other churchmen as part of the theological scene; but an appointment to the episcopal bench of one who publicly expressed such views as Dr Jenkins was a contentious and provocative matter.

It persuaded many Evangelicals to reconsider Anglican doctrine, reappraise the whole concept of comprehensiveness, and re-examine the question of subscription. Some pressed hard for an official, unambiguous declaration by the Church of England, that the faith and doctrine it taught presupposed a firm historical basis. Speculation on the authenticity of the fundamentals of the faith by bishops or clergy was unacceptable. If the Church of England would not affirm clearly through its constituted bodies, and through its leaders, that its faith was biblically-based and deviation from the core beliefs enshrined in the Bible was not allowable for its ordained clergy, then some Evangelicals questioned whether they could remain in such a church. It was not the first time that Evangelicals had faced this particular dilemma.

---

[54] See Goldingay, *op.cit.*, p.307.

22

Breaking New Frontiers in Evangelism and Social Involvement

Evangelism

The Commission on Evangelism, appointed by the Archbishops of Canterbury and York, which delivered its report in 1945 under the title, *Towards the Conversion of England*, pointed to the 'wide and deep gulf between the Church and the people'. [1] The statistical information was limited, but there was ample evidence of a 'wholesale drift from organised religion'. [2]

One source had estimated that only ten to fifteen per cent of the population were already linked to some Christian church; that twenty-five to thirty per cent were sufficiently interested to attend a place of worship upon great occasions; that forty-five to fifty per cent were indifferent to religion though more or less well disposed towards it; while ten to twenty per cent were hostile.

Commenting on the figures, the report remarked that it was 'open to question which was the more alarming feature, the failure of the Church to attract or its failure to repel'. [3] A survey by Mass Observation entitled

[1] *Towards the Conversion of England* (London, 1945), p.2
[2] *Ibid.*, p.3.
[3] *Ibid.*, p.3 and n.

311

Puzzled People showed that only one in ten of the population belonged to a church or a church organization, and two thirds said that they never went to church. In a disturbing book, *How Pagan is Britain?* (1946), B.G. Sandhurst exposed widespread appalling ignorance about Christianity. It was clear that the evangelistic task facing the church in the immediate post-war years was gigantic and daunting.

Evangelicals were concerned to respond to the evangelistic challenge. A congress was called in 1948 and the participants earnestly sought ways of promoting evangelism with 'a definite emphasis on the imperative need for conversion'.[4] A copy of the book of papers which resulted from the congress was sent to each bishop attending the 1948 Lambeth Conference with the hope that it might 'serve to emphasise the necessity for conversion, and the intense concern with which Evangelicals view the cause of Evangelism'.[5]

Yet, despite these exhortations and protestations, not much was done by the church at large, or by the Evangelicals, to work towards the conversion of the nation. The Tom Rees rallies at the Central Hall, Westminster and then at the Royal Albert Hall, which began just at the end of the war, attracted thousands and resulted in innumerable converts. Rees also extended his evangelistic outreach into the provinces and, in 1945, opened Hildenborough Hall as a Christian conference centre.[6] Certain organizations such as the Crusaders were active; others, such as Pathfinders, were soon to be started, and Christian fellowships were established in factories, hospitals and business houses of all kinds. No doubt there were also parishes where evangelism was to the fore, but there was no major evangelistic thrust within the Church of England, with the notable exception of the ambitious Mission to London in 1949.[7]

Nevertheless, despite the poor evangelistic effort in the nineteen-forties, a quiet, unobtrusive yet highly strategic enterprise was being undertaken by the Rev. E.J.H. Nash. He organized camps at Clayesmore School, Iwerne Minster, Dorset. Attendance was limited to boys at major public schools, and was by invitation only. Simple Bible teaching was accompanied by personal friendship and pastoral care. The 'Bash Camps' had a profound impact upon such 'campers', and future Evangelical leaders as Michael Green (subsequently Principal of St John's College, Nottingham and rector of St Aldate's, Oxford), Dick Lucas (subsequently rector of St Helen's Bishopsgate, London) and John Stott.

---

[4] *Evangelicals Affirm in the year of the Lambeth Conference: The Proceedings of the Congress held in London, April 13th-14th, 1948* (London, 1948), Foreword, p. vii.

[5] *Ibid.*, pp. vii, viii.

[6] For a life of Tom Rees, see Jean A. Rees, *His Name was Tom: The Biography of Tom Rees* (London, 1971).

[7] See J.W.C. Wand (Ed.), *Recovery Starts Within: The Book of the Mission to London* (London, 1949).

It was also in the nineteen-forties that Billy Graham first appeared on the British scene.[8] He made a visit in the Spring of 1946 and addressed a number of public meetings. When he returned in October of the same year he was accompanied by Cliff Barrows, and the two of them spoke in twenty-seven cities and towns at 360 meetings in the ensuing five months, almost entirely to young people. At the conclusion of the tour a conference of two hundred and fifty leaders in youth work gathered on Graham's initiative at Birmingham. Torrey Johnson flew over especially to be present. Several of the British representatives at the meeting began to wonder if Billy Graham should some time return for a campaign not limited to youth. 'They had caught a gleam which could pierce war weariness and the defeatism, the littlemindedness which had settled on much of British religion'.[9]

The year of Graham's return was 1954, and the results were extra-ordinary. The crusade was based on Harringay arena in London, but extended to various other centres by the novel means of Post Office landline relays, and concluded at Wembley stadium with what John Pollock has described as 'the greatest religious congregation, 120,000, ever seen until then in the British Isles'.[10] It captured the popular imagination and drew enormous crowds. More than thirty-eight thous-and people went forward at the meetings in response to the appeals by the evangelist.[11] For the Evangelicals there was not only the direct benefit of increased converts, but the stimulus and opening up of new possibilities for evangelism after long years in the wilderness.

It is difficult to assess to what extent Evangelicals grasped this opportunity. While acknowledging notable exceptions it does appear that the following decade and more produced no radical change in Church of England evangelism; and the Evangelicals as part of that church must take a share of the blame. Writing in 1967 Philip E. Hughes and Frank Colquhoun perceived much confusion, hesitation and weakness:

> In a day when the Church's evangelistic mission was never more urgent, it
> would seem that the Church's evangelistic enterprise was never more lack-
> ing or ineffectual. One might almost say that the contemporary Church is
> better equipped for every other task than for its primary responsibility of
> making known the gospel of Christ and winning others to Him. It is cert-
> ainly true that the Church as a whole displays more enterprise in other fields
> (for example, in theological debate, liturgical reform and social service) than
> in the realm of evangelism.

[8] For the life of Billy Graham, see John Pollock, *Billy Graham: The Authorised Biography* (London, 1966).

[9] *Ibid.*, p.65.

[10] *Ibid.*, p.175 and n.

[11] *Ibid.*, p.178.

For many the very word evangelism seemed to have almost dropped out of currency, except in a debased form: in certain quarters it appeared to be looked upon with ill-disguised scepticism and suspicion. Some questioned the necessity for conversion, or denied that it was the church's job to convert anyone. Others substituted 'some form of humanitarianism for positive and aggressive Christian witness'.[12] Writing in the same year, John Stott ruefully considered the meagre response of the church to the report *Towards the Conversion of England* and to its urgent call to mobilize for evangelism. 'We do not seem to have moved any further 'towards the conversion of England", he commented, 'rather the reverse'.[13]

In the task of evangelism most Evangelicals continued to rely mainly on the continuous and consistent witness of the local church and individual Christians. Despite the somewhat gloomy picture for the Church of England as a whole, there is some evidence of a certain, albeit slight, improvement in the evangelistic effort in many Evangelical parishes and organizations during the late nineteen-fifties and the sixties. There was a sharp rise in the number of ordinands and recruits to missionary societies. Evangelism became an important part of many church programmes. Christian Unions continued to multiply in business establishments and elsewhere. For the Inter-Varsity Fellowship, the period 'was one of almost uninterrupted expansion',[14] and Evangelicals in the country generally were increasing in numbers and influence.

In 1966 Billy Graham revisited England for a crusade. This time some eighteen hundred ministers involved their churches, and Anglicans were fully represented, not only by Evangelicals. Again, the effect of the campaign was dramatic. The preparation and the follow-up were more thorough than in 1954-55 and the results achieved, whether as a consequence of this or for other reasons, appeared to be more profound. Graham gave a solemn warning to the church at large and to the Church of England in particular. 'The Holy Spirit is moving in the Church today', he declared, 'and if you do not contain this movement of evangelism and Bible study within the Church, in twenty-five years it will find its way out, as had the Wesleyan movement'.[15] He thought that the time had come for the church to take the offensive.

There are indications that in the late nineteen-sixties, and increasingly in the seventies, Evangelicals did take evangelism more seriously. There was a healthy questioning of an overdependence on crusade evangelism,

---

[12] John R.W. Stott, *Our Guilty Silence: The Church, the Gospel and the World* (London, 1967), Introduction, p.5.
[13] Stott, *op.cit.*, p.13.
[14] Douglas Johnson, *Contending for the Faith: A History of the Evangelical Movement in the Universities and Colleges* (Leicester, 1979), p.238.
[15] John Pollock, *Crusade 66: Britain Hears Billy Graham* (London, 1966), p.96.

accompanied by a widespread renewed determination that the local church should be the basis for effective and continuous evangelism. The task was accepted as hard, needing patience and persistence. Nonetheless, if there was to be sustained evangelism, there was no effective alternative to the age-old concept of the whole Christian *laos* witnessing to Christ through personal contacts.

At the same time there was new thinking and there were new initiatives. In 1960 the College of Preachers had been inaugurated with the Rev. D.W. Cleverley Ford as its director. Its purpose was to promote good preaching by conducting training courses for clergy and lay readers. The Evangelical Alliance report *On the Other Side* (1968), which helped to demonstrate the extent of the evangelistic failure of the church in Britain, was an added spur to greater efforts. Liturgical renewal in the church and the charismatic movement brought a new sense of Christian commitment and new vitality to much local church life, and this overflowed into new and more imaginative forms of evangelism. The remarkable and transforming effect of evangelism in the ministry of David Watson, especially in the parish of St Michael-Le-Belfry in York, was an example and an inspiration to Evangelicals;[16] and the church-based evangelistic ministry of All Souls Langham Place, London, was a stimulus to parochial evangelism.

The 1973 'Call to the North', by the Archbishop of York, with its emphasis on local initiative, and the 1975 'Call to the Nation' by the two Archbishops, were further means of encouraging evangelism. After the 'Call to the Nation' letters arrived at Lambeth Palace by the sackful; 27,000 in about ten weeks. Making the normal estimate applied in broadcasting circles for non-respondents who failed to write merely because they never 'got round to it', the volume of replies indicated a positive response from between two and three million British people. If the letters received by the Archbishop of York are included, then the indicated response is increased to about four million. It exposed something of the hidden needs and yearnings of people from all strata of society.[17]

Donald Coggan was also one of the driving forces behind the National Initiative in Evangelism.[18] A group of representatives from bodies involved in evangelism were brought together in 1976. They were in agreement that priority should be given to evangelism through the local congregation. A National Assembly on Evangelism was held at Nottingham in 1980. The attendance was below expectation and the

---

[16] See David Watson, *You are my God* (London, 1983).

[17] See John Poulton, *Dear Archbishop* (London, 1976).

[18] See Paul A. Welsby, *A History of the Church of England 1945-1980*, pp.261-263.
'National' was later changed to 'Nationwide' in order to indicate that the emphasis was on local initiative.

debates also revealed differences of emphasis. The majority preferred local and regional enterprises, but strong voices were raised in favour of a national mission. There was some theological convergence in the Assembly between Evangelicals and others, but little hard dialogue.

Those Evangelicals who favoured a mission to the nation tended to think of Dr Billy Graham as the evangelist most likely to have the desired impact and produce the longed-for response. A special committee of 100 invited him to visit Britain. He declined the invitation, but later agreed to take part in a special evangelistic effort in 1984. Under the title 'Mission England' Dr Graham preached in a series of meetings in provincial towns. In the same year the Argentinian evangelist Luis Palau undertook an extended mission based on the Queen's Park Football Stadium in London.

In both crusades great care was taken to enlist the support of churches willing to co-operate, and an immense effort was made to ensure as far as possible that those who responded at the meetings were integrated into a local church. There were Evangelicals who did not participate, and others who did so with a measure of reluctance because of reservations about mass evangelism, but the level of involvement was high. There are good indications that many respondents at the meetings were already attached to or preferred the Church of England to any other denomination.

As an aside, it is interesting to note how radio and television helped to promote the campaigns of both Billy Graham and Luis Palau by introducing the evangelists to a wide range of the non-church-going public. Indeed, a number of Evangelicals were increasingly becoming aware of the opportunity presented by radio and television for conveying the Christian message and its implications to those who might not otherwise hear it. Some of them, such as David Winter, entered broadcasting professionally, and others, such as John Stott and David Watson, acquired an ability for effective radio and television communication. Mary Whitehouse rapidly achieved a considerable influence as the driving force behind the Viewers and Listeners Association. The greater involvement of Evangelicals in this and other aspects of the media, was indicative of their concern to use modern means for the proclamation of the faith, and to touch the whole life of the nation.

Social Involvement

The Billy Graham and Luis Palau missions were in keeping with the Evangelical tradition of evangelism, which was conceived as the verbal proclamation of the gospel to individuals and groups. Increasingly, however, both nationally and internationally, Evangelicals interrelated evangelism in this traditional sense with social activity. The two began to be seen as inextricably interconnected: the one should not be undertaken by Christians in complete isolation from or unawareness of the need for the other. This understanding was slow to appear, and by 1984 it still needed much further exposition, clarification and elaboration.

In adopting this new perception Evangelicals were catching up on many decades during which they had temporarily mislaid their social conscience.[19] For much of the first half of the century they had been known within the church, and publicly, more for what they affirmed and proclaimed. They attracted attention more for their internal divisions, their contentiousness and their aggression, than for their unity, poise and positive contributions to the church and the nation. They were identified with anti–ritualism, anti–Biblical criticism, anti–modernism, anti–Prayer Book revision, resistance to the Liberals in their midst, and controversy in their missionary stronghold, the Church Missionary Society.

It is arguable that they were justified in this predominantly defensive posture, but it did entail a neglect of social and ethical thinking and social action. Although a few tried to forge a Christian social critique and to apply it, there was no major Evangelical contribution. Perhaps there was excessive fear about the dangers of liberalism and a drift towards a 'social gospel'. Christian social radicalism was associated with Christian Liberalism and Anglo–Catholicism; the two prime targets for Evangelical attack. Evangelicals largely upheld the *status quo*. They tended to accept conventional social and ethical thinking which might at some time, possibly in the near past, have been radical and non–conformist. Their supreme concern for preservation in theological matters may, even unconsciously, have spilled over and made them reluctant to question the prevailing political, social and ethical systems. In the social as well as in the theological arena they were overshadowed by others in the Church of England. They were largely ignored.

In the post–Second World War era in academic circles, and in society as a whole, there was an accelerating process of social and ethical rethinking. There was a dislocation of inherited ideas. Increasingly the received Christian social and ethical teaching, in as far as it was coherently articulated, was debunked and rejected. Belief in absolutes of right and wrong in matters of religion and ethics was derided; relativism became the order of the day.

It was a period which demanded clear and hard thinking if traditional Christian values were to be upheld and if biblically–based principles and practices were to be commended. But for twenty years after the Second

---

[19] See John Stott, *Issues Facing Christians Today* (London, 1984), p.xi.

World War, in the midst of this general departure from Christian perspectives, Evangelicals in England did not engage in much serious thinking on social and ethical issues.

The Keele Congress statement of 1967 recognized this Evangelical shortcoming:

> We believe that our evangelical doctrines have important ethical implications. But we confess to our shame that we have not thought sufficiently deeply or radically about the problems of our society. We are therefore resolved to give ourselves to more study of these critical issues in future.

The statement expressed the determination of Evangelicals to 'work not only for the redemption of individuals, but also for the reformation of society'.[20] And these resolves were taken seriously. In the nineteen-seventies there was a surge forward. The Evangelical Race Relations Group was established, the Shaftesbury Project was started, the National Festival of Light was launched, Third Way was inaugurated, and the Grove booklets on ethics began to be published.

The Lausanne Congress on World Evangelisation, held in July 1974, gave a fresh impetus to these efforts. It introduced an international dimension and encouraged Christians to link social responsibility with evangelism.[21] This was particularly appropriate in view of the worldwide consideration given to liberation theology. The Lausanne Covenant juxtaposed the section on 'The nature of Evangelism' with that on 'Christian Social Responsibility', and clearly enunciated the new emphasis. Affirming that God was both creator and judge of all men, it elaborated on the need for Christians to 'share his concern for justice and reconciliation throughout human society and for the liberation of men from every kind of oppression'. Mankind is made in the image of God, and therefore 'every person, regardless of race, religion, colour, culture, class, sex or age, has an intrinsic dignity because of which he should be respected and served, not exploited'.

The Covenant expressed penitence 'for having sometimes regarded evangelism and social concern as mutually exclusive'. Although 'reconciliation with man is not reconciliation with God, nor is social action evangelism, nor is political liberation salvation', the Covenant affirmed that 'evangelism and socio-political involvement are both part of our Christian duty. For both are necessary expressions of our doctrines of God and man, our love for our neighbour and our obedience to Jesus Christ'.[22]

---

[20] Philip Crowe (Ed.), *Keele '67: The National Evangelical Anglican Congress Statement* (London, 1967), p.26.
[21] John R.W. Stott, *Obeying Christ in a Changing World*, Vol.3, p.12.
[22] Lausanne Covenant, quoted *Ibid.*, p.13.

The relationship between evangelism and social action was a matter of continued discussion among Evangelicals in the years after 1974. Much was written on the subject, especially by John Stott.[23] The issue was debated at the Islington Conference in 1975 and at the Second National Evangelical Anglican Congress in 1977. In 1982 the Lausanne committee and the World Evangelical Fellowship jointly sponsored the 'Consultation on the Relationship between Evangelism and Social Responsibility' (CRESR), held in Grand Rapids. The participants reached a remarkable degree of consensus. Social activity was said to be both a consequence of and a bridge to evangelism, and indeed the two were declared to be partners.[24]

David Sheppard was notable among those who adopted this new approach. He had a varied and rich experience of inner city life as curate of St Mary's Church, Islington, Warden of the Mayflower Family Centre in the East End of London, Bishop of Woolwich and Bishop of Liverpool. This gave a solid foundation for his analysis and interpretation of the urban situation.

In *Built as a City* (1974) he drew particular attention to the powerless ess of the socially and educationally disadvantaged inner city dwellers. In *Bias to the Poor* (1983) he examined the plight of the urban poor, black people and the unemployed, and considered the relevance of the gospel to the situation and lives of such deprived people. In the 1984 Richard Dimbleby Lecture, entitled 'The Poverty that Imprisons the Spirit',[25] he took up the same theme of the poor and underprivileged. With indignation and even anger he reflected on 'the alienation, imprisonment of spirit, sick human relationships and waste of God-given talents represented by such groups and individuals'.

The life, work and writings of David Sheppard exemplified a new breadth and profundity in Evangelical social involvement and thinking. Others made their contributions. Professor Sir Norman Anderson expanded his Keele Congress paper into a book which was published as *Into the World : The Need and Limits of Christian Involvement* (1968). Four years later he provided a perceptive examination of ethical issues in *Morality, Law and Grace* (1972); and other works by him clearly show his social concern.[26] Bishop John V. Taylor adopted a global perspective as he reflected on poverty in *Enough is Enough* (1975), and made a plea for

---

[23] See for example John R.W. Stott, *Christian Mission in the Modern World* (London, 1975).

[24] See John Stott, *Issues Facing Christians Today* (1984), p.10.

[25] Published in *The Listener*, 19 April 1984.

[26] Other works by Norman Anderson include *Evidence for the Resurrection* (London, 1950), *A Lawyer among the Theologians* (London, 1973), *Issues of Life and Death* (London, 1976), *The Mystery of the Incarnation* (London, 1977), *The Teaching of Jesus* (London, 1983), and *Jesus Christ: The Witness of History* (London, 1985).

Christian simplicity of life style. The writers of the Grove booklets on ethics covered a wide range of topics, and a host of Evangelicals wrote articles and books on a variety of social matters.

There was a distinct widening of concern beyond the traditional Evangelical focus upon problems of personal morality. Oliver O'Donovan gave careful consideration to such diverse and sensitive subjects as the unborn child, marriage, a Christian view of war, the question of justice and the moral implications of the death penalty. John Gladwin explored some biblical motives for social involvement by Christians; and this catalogue of Evangelicals who examined social issues from a Christian point of view could be greatly extended.

John Stott was foremost in demonstrating the Evangelical concern to remain loyal to the revelation of God and yet relevant to the needs and demands of the modern world. The London Institute for Contemporary Christianity came into being in 1982 largely as a result of his vision. It was dedicated to the task of thinking biblically about contemporary issues. Accepting the Bible as 'God's Word written', John Stott sought through his writings and through the London Institute to apply biblical principles to the world of space probes and micro-processors. He crystallized much of his own thought in his book *Issues Facing Christians Today* (1984). This was a significant contribution to the revitalized social thinking of Evangelicals. In it he struggled to think Christianly about the nuclear threat, the human environment and its conservation, North-South economic inequality, human rights, work and unemployment, industrial relations, the questions of race, poverty, wealth and simplicity of life style, the status and ministry of women, marriage and divorce, abortion, and homosexuality. To each topic he brought an impressive social awareness, breadth of knowledge, and the ability to apply biblical principles.

23

Liturgy, Hymnology and the Ministry of Women

Liturgy

Between 1928 and 1947 no significant steps were taken to enable the Church of England to revise its forms of worship. Nonetheless, there was a quiet but effective and widespread recovery and renewal within the church of 'its worship and the understanding of that worship as central to its life and work'.[1] This was accomplished largely by means of what is known as the Liturgical Movement, and as a consequence of four published works.

In 1935 A.G. Hebert's *Liturgy and Society* examined the whole movement of contemporary society away from God, and demonstrated how the eucharist could be the source and centre of power by means of which the social order might be redeemed. Also of considerable influence was Evelyn Underhill's book on *Worship*, which was published in 1936. In 1937 Hebert edited a series of essays on *The Parish Communion* which brought together the various strands of liturgical thinking, and so helped to propagate the movement in the parishes which aimed at making the holy communion the central act of worship. The authority of these seminal works was reinforced in 1945 by the appearance of a scholarly

---

[1] Paul A. Welsby, *A History of the Church of England 1945-1980*, p.68.

321

study which was to have a profound effect upon the course of liturgical reform: Dom Gregory Dix, *The Shape of the Liturgy*. 'It transformed Anglican liturgiology almost overnight from a remote and academic branch of scholarship into a study whose immediate relevance became evident to multitudes of parish priests'.[2] In his book Dix discerned a fourfold pattern in the institution by Christ of the eucharist which was reproduced in the rites of the early church. Jesus took bread and wine, gave thanks, broke the bread and shared the bread and wine with the disciples. This was to form the basis of future Prayer Book revision. Dix convincingly portrayed the potential power of the eucharist, which turned the individual worshipper into 'a fit member of the redeeming and redeemed social order'.[3] These various insights of liturgical and theological scholarship found organizational expression in 1950 in the *Parish and People* movement.

In 1947 the Canon Law Commission proposed a new Canon which 'gave power to the Convocations of Canterbury and York to authorise additions, omissions and alternative uses for the Prayer Book services in their respective provinces'.[4] Five years later the Moberly Commission considerably widened the scope of the proposed canon. It provided for entire alternative services to those in the Prayer Book and gave the House of Laity legislative rights in their authorization. The resulting Measure, which initiated a process for authorizing revised texts without recourse to Parliament, was approved by the Church Assembly on 7 July 1964 and came into force on 1 May 1966.

In 1954, in response to a request from both Convocations, the Archbishops established a Standing Liturgical Commission which first met in 1955. It was initially chaired by Bishop Colin Dunlop; he was succeeded in 1960 by Dr Donald Coggan and by Canon R.C.D. Jasper in 1964. Other groups and commissions were involved directly or indirectly in the succeeding years of liturgical revision, but the Standing Liturgical Commission was central to the innovative process.

The various services proposed to the Convocations and House of Laity up to 1970, and subsequently to the General Synod, were classified under three 'Series'. It was perhaps to Canon Jasper more than any other person that the movement of revision was most indebted. The culmination of this whole period of liturgical revision was the publication in 1980 of the Alternative Service Book.

In the post-Second World War era it was twenty years before Evangelicals took an active part in this process of liturgical revision. In 1967 the

---

[2] *Ibid* p.68.

[3] Roger Lloyd, *The Church of England 1900-1965*, p.538.

[4] Colin Buchanan, *Recent Liturgical Revision in the Church of England* (Grove Books, Bramcote, 1973), p.6. The summary which follows is based on Buchanan.

Keele statement was able to declare that liturgical revision was long overdue; Evangelicals, it was admitted, had been fearful of change, and somewhat hidebound by their individualism. They had been slow to learn from other parts of the church. They greatly valued the doctrinal basis of the 1662 services, but by the late nineteen sixties they were not 'so wedded to their structures, contents or language as not to see the need for new forms'.

Indeed, the necessity for change was increasingly conceded by Evangelicals, although there was not unanimity regarding how far this should go and what form it should take. Some looked for a conservative revision of the Prayer Book services, while others looked for 'something much more radical, though retaining the same doctrinal position as 1662'. Almost all welcomed the period of experimentation. There was a widespread Evangelical persuasion that although the ideal of common prayer should not be forgotten, there should not be alarm at the loosening of legal uniformity. Incumbents and parochial church councils should carefully study the proposed services in order to discharge their biblical and legal responsibilities. No unlawful innovations should be introduced. The law should be honoured even if at times it seemed irksome. Reform should be sought by lawful means. The proper basis of liturgical revision was 'not the practice of the second and third centuries, but the teaching of the Bible applied with reference to contemporary needs and in the light of existing services.' All proposed changes should be assessed accordingly.[5]

The general tenor of this approach is in many respects in marked contrast to the somewhat negative and strongly critical Evangelical campaigning which had characterized the inter-war years, with its post-Second World War legacy of suspicion and defensiveness. The new attitude called for a biblical and reasoned appraisal of the suggested revisions. Thus, the Keele statement of 1967 paid tribute to the many excellent structural features in the services presented by the Liturgical Commission, and the considerable merit of much of the new baptism and confirmation services, but questioned certain doctrinal points in some of the proposed services. The assembled Evangelicals in expressing their longing for liturgy which would be 'consistently biblical and consequently unifying', affirmed their 'readiness to enter into dialogue' with those from whom they differed, 'with a view to finding the best way of securing such liturgy'.[6]

A number of Evangelicals devoted themselves unstintingly and with immense patience and perseverance to such dialogue and to the demanding task of liturgical revision. Of these none was more informed and

[5] See Philip Crowe (Ed.), *Keele '67: The National Evangelical Anglican Congress Statement*, p.33.

[6] Crowe, *op.cit.*, p.34.

influential than Colin Buchanan (appointed Bishop of Aston, Birmingham in 1985). He joined the Liturgical Commission in 1964 and the
General Synod in 1970, and was also on the 1971-72 Liturgical Steering
Committee of Synod. He frequently commented on issues of liturgical
revision, and during the nineteen-seventies was a key figure in the Group
for the Renewal of Worship (GROW). This consisted of youngish authors
who wrote and commissioned Grove booklets on ministry and worship.
They tried 'to give the right information and stimulus to the Church of
England for its worship to be truly contemporary whilst true to New
Testament principles'.[7] Robert Runcie, the Archbishop of Canterbury,
testified to the success of their endeavours. 'When seeking lively and
informed contemporary reflection on matters liturgical', he wrote, 'I, like
many others, have developed a habit of reaching for a Grove booklet'.[8]

By the late nineteen-seventies the Series 3 services were widely
welcomed among Evangelicals, particularly because of their emphasis on
joy, freedom, flexibility and congregational participation. Experimentation 'with drama, dance, music, movement, colour, furnishings
and setting to heighten the awareness and involvement of God's people in
true worship' was commended by the second National Evangelical Congress in 1977, and Evangelicals were foremost in such developments.

When we turn to a consideration of particular services we find that
throughout the post-1945 period there was a measure of continuity in the
Evangelical view on the central principles underlying the rites of baptism,
confirmation and holy communion.

The blessings of baptism were seen as conditional upon right reception.
It was asserted by Evangelicals that the Bible, the Book of Common
Prayer and the Articles did not teach a mechanical *ex opere operatio* view of
the sacraments, but a 'receptionist' view. Both the outward sign and the
inward work of grace were necessary. Evangelicals remained loyal to the
church's practice of baptizing the infant children of professing Christian
parents, although they recognized that some Anglicans would prefer adult
believers' baptism to be the norm. Indiscriminate baptism was invariably
denounced as a scandal.[9]

It was consistent with their view of baptism that the Evangelicals at
Keele in 1967 should declare adult Christian initiation to be sacramentally
complete in baptism: 'The confirmation of those baptized as adults should
be combined with their baptism, as proposed by the Liturgical

[7] Colin Buchanan, Trevor Lloyd and Harold Miller (Eds), *Anglican Worship Today: Collins Illustrated Guide to the Alternative Service Book 1980* (London, 1980), Introduction, p.7.
[8] *Ibid.*, Foreword, p.6.
[9] For examples of such Evangelical teaching, see T.C. Hammond, *What is an Evangelical?* (London, 1959), p.13 f, and *The Nottingham Statement: The official statement of the second National Evangelical Anglican Congress held in April 1977*, p.25.

Commission'.[10] The declaration of repentance and faith made in infant baptism needed to be ratified by the child at the age of discretion.

The Nottingham delegates in 1977 were divided over the advisability of admitting children to communion. Some welcomed the possible admission of younger children to confirmation when this was requested, but they urged that such discretion should be exercised with the utmost caution and with carefully controlled safeguards. They were also not convinced that it was wise to make confirmation available to children below secondary-school age. Others advocated the admission to holy communion of 'baptised children of communicant parents after due preparation'.[11] They thought that confirmation was best left as an act of commitment to adult discipleship.

In the post-Second World War period Evangelicals frequently pronounced holy communion to be of prime importance, but in practice they often devalued it. Prior to this period, in 1930, V.F. Storr detected a new feeling for sacramentalism in the Evangelical wing of the church.[12] He claimed that the trend was towards dynamic receptionism and away from memorialism. At the 1945 Congress of Evangelicals one speaker declared that the instinct of Evangelicals was 'to set an immensely high value upon the Holy Communion'.[13] Yet, looking back twenty-one years later, the Keele delegates confessed that Evangelicals had failed to do justice 'to the twin Evangelical truths that the Lord's Supper is the main service of the people of God, and that the local church as such, is the unit within which it is properly administered'. They had rather 'let the sacrament be pushed to the outer fringes of church life, and the ministry of the Word be divorced from it'. Somewhat controversially the Keele statement expressed a resolve 'to work towards the practice of a weekly celebration of the sacrament as the central corporate service of the church'.[14] The Nottingham Assembly ten years later was undecided about reaffirming this call.

In the proposed revisions of the holy communion service three doctrinal issues especially caused concern among Evangelicals: petitions for the dead, what was regarded as a misconceived concept of eucharistic sacrifice and permanent reservation of the elements. They were anxious that there should be no intentional verbal ambiguity in an effort to bring together mutually contradictory doctrinal positions. The main focus of the service of holy communion should be the once-for-all sacrifice of Christ upon the cross, and nothing should be allowed to detract from it.

---

[10] Crowe, op.cit., p.35.

[11] Ibid., p.29.

[12] A.J. Macdonald (Ed.), The Evangelical Doctrine of the Holy Communion (1930), p.312.

[13] Evangelicals Affirm in the year of the Lambeth Conference: The Proceedings of the Congress held in London, April 13th-14th, 1948, p.160.

[14] Crowe, op.cit., p.35.

In all these doctrinal and liturgical matters Evangelicals appealed to the Bible as the supreme authority; likewise Bible readings and Bible exposition were central to Evangelical worship. It is therefore worthy of note that both prior to and during the period of liturgical revision there was a quite remarkable increase in the number of new versions of the Bible.

In 1946 a committee of thirty-two American scholars produced the *Revised Standard Version* of the New Testament, and the whole Bible appeared in 1952. On the whole it avoided 'Americanisms', and its modern but dignified language made it popular, not least of all among Evangelicals. In 1949 Ronald Knox's translation of the Bible appeared. It was intended for private use only.

In the meantime J.B. Phillips had caused much excitement with his *Letters to Young Churches* (1947), followed by *The Gospels in Modern English* (1952), *The Young Church in Action* (1955), covering the Acts of the Apostles, and *The Book of Revelation* (1957). The whole *New Testament in Modern English* appeared in 1958.

Dr E.V. Rieu produced a translation of *The Four Gospels* (1952), and his son C.H. Rieu followed this by the *Acts of the Apostles* (1957). A 'major event in the world of scholarship, of printing and of ecumenical co-operation'[15] came to fruition in 1970 with the publication of the *New English Bible*. It was well received, and many millions of copies were sold.

Of immense popularity was *The Bible in Today's English Version* (1976), usually known as 'The Good News Bible'. This version aimed to provide a faithful translation of the original text expressed in standard, everyday English, avoiding words and forms not in current and widespread use.[16] An English edition of *The Living Bible* appeared in the early nineteen-seventies. It was more a paraphrase than a translation. Finally, a group of English-speaking Roman Catholics produced *The Jerusalem Bible* (1966). It was an annotated version of the whole Bible based on the work of French biblical scholars. It was appreciated by many Anglicans who used it in public worship. It was revised in 1985.

Hymnody

The new versions of the Bible and the period of liturgical revision helped to produce an upsurge of hymnology.[17] Up to about 1950 most Church of England churches used one of a small range of hymn books, all of which were probably at least fifty years old, with their roots set deeply in

---

[15] Donald Coggan, *Word and World* (London, 1971), p.75.

[16] See Welsby, *op.cit.*, pp.158, 159.

[17] The following comments owe much to Robin Leaver, *A Hymn Book Survey 1962-80* (Grove Books, Bramcote, 1980), pp.3, 4; and Welsby, *op.cit.*, pp.159-161.

Victorian soil. The post-war period had seen composers of the eminence of Sir Arthur Bliss and Benjamin Britten composing church music. Contributions were also made by Edmund Rubbra, Michael Tippett, Malcolm Williamson, Geoffrey Bush, William Matthias and Peter Anson. The Royal School of Church Music, founded in 1927, was particularly effective in promoting high standards of teaching for church musicians, enthusing choirs and stimulating church music generally. Its influence became both worldwide and ecumenical. Credit for this must go largely to Dr Gerald Knight, the Director from 1952 to 1973, and his successor, Dr Lionel Dakers.

It was in the nineteen-fifties that the major hymn books of the immediate post-war years were published. *Hymns Ancient and Modern Revised* (1950), *Congregational Praise* (1951) and *The BBC Hymn Book* (1951) soon established their place in the worship of English churches. The same decade also saw the first serious questioning of accepted axioms about church music, and the appearance of a radically new and freer type of music. In 1956 Geoffrey Beaumont produced his *Folk Mass* as a means 'whereby those unfamiliar with traditional forms might enter into the worship of the Church'.[18] It attracted considerable attention, and it led to the formation of the Twentieth Century Church Light Music Group which produced its own books and a number of popular hymns. Sydney Carter was prominent in writing and popularizing new songs for church worship, among which were 'The Lord of the Dance', 'When I needed a Neighbour', and 'No use knocking on the window'. It was also during these years that vocal and instrumental (usually guitar) groups were introduced to lead worship.

The 'explosion of modern hymn writing',[19] accompanied by new hymn books, supplements to standard hymn books and a multiplicity of home-grown parish booklets can be traced to the early nineteen-sixties. The innovations were not confined to the Church of England. New Roman Catholic hymn books appeared, and there were various denominational and non-denominational productions. A landmark for Evangelicals was the publication in 1965 of the *Anglican Hymn Book*.[20] The critics were probably justified in their assertion that the title was misleading. The book tended to serve the needs of the Evangelicals rather than the needs of Anglicans as a whole. The collection was condemned by some for omitting such hymns as 'Lead, kindly Light' and 'Nearer, my God, to

---

[18] Welsby, *op.cit.*, p.160.

[19] Leaver, *op.cit.*, p.4. As discussed elsewhere, the development of Evangelical hymnody during the nineteen-sixties and seventies and up to the end of our period was part of a greater Evangelical interest in spirituality. This was exemplified at the end of the period by the introduction in 1982 of the Grove booklets on spirituality.

[20] For some comments on the *Anglican Hymn Book*, see Leaver, *op.cit.*, pp.7, 8.

Thee', and it was berated for being too traditional in not including contemporary material by such writers as Albert Bayly and Timothy Rees. It was certainly open to criticism, but it did have its merits. The collection included about forty new tunes, twenty or so new texts and many alternative musical settings; it also introduced Timothy Dudley-Smith as a hymn writer and gave to the Christian public his 'Tell out, my soul, the greatness of the Lord'. Supplementary hymns were added in 1975 and 1978.

Meanwhile a group under the chairmanship of Michael Baughen produced *Youth Praise* (Vol I, 1966; Vol 2, 1969) and *Psalm Praise* (1973). Both contained a great amount of new material. Hymn writing was gaining momentum among Evangelicals. In 1973 another group, also chaired by Michael Baughen, met with the aim of producing 'the first major new hymn book of the new era',[21] to harmonise with the new Bible translations and revised liturgy. A number of traditional hymns, revised into more contemporary language, were combined with a wide selection of post-1950 hymns and a variety of previously unpublished works. Three kinds of revision were incorporated: a change in usage from 'thee' to 'you', which had become a liturgical commonplace, and was therefore not very controversial; the replacement of archaic endings such as '-est' and '-eth' which, in verse, frequently entailed changing whole lines; and, the most difficult to achieve, a judicious rewriting of the more sentimental sections of certain, especially nineteenth century, hymns, which demanded a new and appropriate twentieth century style. There was an explicit attempt to draw upon various Christian traditions. Although many of the group, which became known as the *Jubilate Hymns* team, were Evangelicals, there were members with Free Church backgrounds, and material was culled from Roman Catholic, Free Church and Orthodox as well as Anglican sources; the only conscious exclusion being hymns in the Marian tradition. In the area of eucharistic doctrine certain linguistic modifications were introduced in an attempt to make some traditionally divisive hymns more widely acceptable and useful.

In this corporate enterprise Evangelical hymn writers and musicians of considerable ability were brought together. In addition to Michael Baughen they included Richard Bewes, Christopher Idle, Michael Parry, James Seddon and Noel Tredinnick. The most outstanding contributor to the collection was perhaps Timothy Dudley-Smith, the Bishop of Thetford. Forty-six of his hymns were included, and some of them had a quality of greatness about them. The work of this gifted team culminated in 1982 with the publication of *Hymns for Today's Church*.

An important part was played in the cultivation of a freer and more invigorating atmosphere for creative hymnology by a collection entitled

---

[21] Michael A. Baughen, *Hymns for Today's Church* (1982), Consultant Editor's Preface.

With One Voice. It was produced in 1979 by an editorial committee on which Evangelicals were strongly represented. It contained hymns and musical styles which ranged from plainsong and eighteenth century productions to post-nineteen-fifties works in the style of the Twentieth Century Light Music Group.

The introduction of new hymns in modern language and style, and the adaptation of familiar well-established hymns, was not accomplished without much protest. This was especially so with *Hymns for Today's Church*. In such hymn books as the *New Catholic Hymnal* (1971) and *With One Voice* there was modernization of some of the texts into a 'you' form, but *Hymns for Today's Church* broke new ground by consistently applying the principle to all hymns. And it was not just a matter of language, for the new approach entailed questions about theology, sexism, syntax, thought-form and imagery. The whole subject had many ramifications, and by 1984 the issues were far from being resolved.

The Ministry of Women

While all these liturgical revisions and developments in hymnology were taking place and were being hotly discussed, the question of the ministry of women was assuming an increasingly important part in Church of England deliberations. In 1947 Convocation discussed the possibility of authorizing qualified women to 'take special services in church and to speak at them'. It was, however, not until the nineteen-sixties that the Church Assembly opened up the debate on the ordination of women, and women began to participate more fully in services – conducting them, reading the scriptures, preaching and assisting with the holy communion. The Lambeth Conference of 1968 declared that the theological arguments as then presented for and against the ordination of women to the priesthood were inconclusive. In 1975 the General Synod expressed the view that there were 'no fundamental objections to the ordination of women to the priesthood', but it did not proceed to any consequent action. The bishops at the 1978 Lambeth Conference, recognizing that some Anglican provinces had women clergy, agreed to respect each other's discipline in that matter. In 1984 the General Synod resolved that legislation for the ordination of women should be prepared. Meanwhile, in the Anglican Communion worldwide changes were taking place. The diocese of Hong Kong ordained women in 1971 and was followed by the Church of the Province of New Zealand in 1974, the Anglican Church in Canada (1975) and the Episcopal Church of the USA (1976).

During these forty post-Second World War years Evangelical concern about the ministry of women reflected the growing concern of the Church of England as a whole. At first Evangelicals gave the subject little attention. Gradually more comments were made. They were mostly cautious and moderate in tone, with a general tendency at least to question if not to openly reject the concept of the ordination of women.[22] By degrees, and in keeping with the changing mood within the Church of England in the nineteen-seventies, more Evangelicals declared themselves in favour. By the eighties some were prepared to expound their views in works which advocated, and indeed forthrightly championed, the cause of women's ordination.[23] As Evangelical opinion became more explicit, so the variety of their views became apparent. It is to the credit of nearly all involved that the case for and against was almost consistently presented in a non-combative, reasoned and biblically based way, in what for many was a highly emotive matter.

It does scant justice to the arguments employed by Evangelicals to give a terse summary of the opposing cases, but the main drift of the debate can be indicated. Unlike many others in the Church of England who thought the ordination of women was inadmissible, the Evangelical opponents generally did not place much emphasis on the ecumenical implications. They did not stress the damage that the ordination of women could do to Anglican relationships with the Roman Catholic and Orthodox Churches. They rather pointed to biblical evidence: that all the apostles and the presbyters in New Testament times were men, and there were specific New Testament instructions that women must 'not teach or have authority over a man'. The biblical prohibition on women's ordination was seen to be grounded in creation, in the divinely intended relationship between men and women. Evangelicals of this persuasion identified a biblical embargo on any kind of teaching by women which infringed the principle of male headship. The Bible allowed for a full and satisfying ministry of women other than what was implied in ordination.

Evangelical advocates of the ordination of women pointed to Old and New Testament examples of women who were active leaders: prophetesses like Miriam, Huldah, and Deborah, who also 'judged' Israel, and New Testament women who exercised various gifts. They also went back to creation. In origin man and woman were two sexes sharing the generic name Adam. Both were made in the image of God. The biblical emphasis was upon their equality and complementarity. Their relationship was marred by the fall, but Christ had swept away all social, sexual, religious and cultural barriers. As there is in Christ 'neither Jew nor Greek', and 'there is neither slave nor free', so 'there is neither male nor female'. If the

---

[22] See for example Gervase E. Duffield, 'Feminism and the Church', *Churchman*, Winter 1971, pp.246-262.

[23] For instance, see George Carey, 'Women and Authority in the Scriptures', in Monica Furlong (Ed.), *Feminine in the Church* (London, 1984), pp.44-55.

Spirit of God is bestowed on all the church, what right has the church got to suppress genuine gifts solely on the basis that they are being exercised by gentiles, slaves or women? The Pauline writings which appear to limit the ministry of women could be otherwise interpreted.

Already, by 1984, it was clear that many people both within and outside the church were determined that the matter should not be shelved. Women had for some time played a crucial role in overseas missionary work and as lay workers or deaconesses in the home church, but it was evident that a substantial number of them, and others on their behalf, were not prepared for the continuance of what they perceived as unacceptable restrictions on the scope of ministry open to them. Both the ordination of women and the wider question of the place of women in the life, worship and work of the church were becoming increasingly emotive and potentially divisive, issues. Evangelicals continued their discussions among themselves and with Christians of other traditions. They searched the scriptures to find the right way ahead. By 1984 they had not reached a common mind.

24

The Charismatic Movement

The beginning of modern Pentecostalism may be traced to the first few years of the twentieth century, to Topeka and Los Angeles in the United States.[1] The first attested example of the contemporary charismatic movement within the Anglican communion occurred in 1959-60 in the parish of St Mark's, Van Nuys, California under the ministry of Dennis Bennett.

Between 1962 and 1964 members of the Church of England became vaguely aware that something new and extraordinary was happening in parishes like St Mark's, Gillingham, St Mark's, Cheltenham, and St Paul's, Beckenham, where there were reports of speaking in 'tongues'. In

---

[1] For a history of modern Pentecostalism, see Michael Harper, *As at the beginning: The Twentieth Century Pentecostal Revival* (London, 1965); and Walter Hollenweger, *The Pentecostals* (London, 1972). For a description and commentary on various aspects of Pentecostalism and of the Charismatic Movement, see Dennis Bennett, *Nine O'clock in the Morning* (USA, 1970); C.O. Buchanan, *Encountering Charismatic Worship* (Grove, Nottingham, 1977); J.D.G. Dunn, *Baptism in the Spirit* (London, 1970); Edward England, *The Spirit of Renewal* (Eastbourne, 1982); Fountain Trust/Church of England Evangelical Council report, *Gospel and Spirit*, published in the *Churchman* (April 1977); John Gunstone, *Pentecostal Anglicans* (London, 1982); Michael Harper, *A New Canterbury Tale* (Grove, Nottingham, 1978); Michael Harper, *Bishop's Move* (London, 1979); Lesslie Newbigin, *The Household of God* (London, 1953); John Root, *Encountering West Indian Pentecostalism* (Grove, Nottingham, 1979); Colin Urquhart, *When the Spirit Comes* (London, 1974); David Watson, *One in the Spirit* (London, 1973); and *The Charismatic Movement in the Church of England* (CIO Publishing, London, 1981).

1964 Michael Harper resigned as curate of All Souls, Langham Place, London and founded the Fountain Trust to help Christians in all the denominations who had been 'baptized in the Spirit' to be taught more about the individual and corporate experience of renewal. Perhaps the Trust did more than anything else to keep the renewal within the bounds of the traditional church.

The charismatic movement continued to grow among Evangelicals. Between 1964 and 1970 leaders such as John Collins, David Watson, David McInnes and Tom Walker became associated with it. Visits by some of the foremost American charismatic figures, including David du Plessis, Larry Christensen, Dennis Bennett and David Wilkerson, gave encouragement to the movement. Books by some of the British charismatic leaders began to be published. Journals appeared and parishes received a new vitality and sense of purpose as they 'overflowed with the distinctive marks of Pentecostalism'.[2] The first international conference was held under the auspices of the Fountain Trust at Guildford in 1971 when, for the first time ever, Roman Catholics, traditional Protestants and members of designated Pentecostal churches shared the same platform. It was a milestone. 'After Guildford it was easier to talk about Pentecostal renewal in Anglican circles'.[3]

During the nineteen-seventies the movement manifested itself publicly in prayer meetings and conferences in various centres, as well as in the life of a growing number of parishes.[4] Music and drama assumed a more central part in the worship of charismatic churches. Overtly charismatic collections of songs and hymns such as *Sound of Living Waters* (1974) and *Fresh Sounds* (1976) became popular in Evangelical circles beyond those recognized as committed to renewal. There was an increasing awareness of the pan-Anglican character of the movement. This was expressed in a pre-Lambeth Conference for Spiritual Renewal at Canterbury in July 1978, from which arose the trust Sharing of Ministries Abroad (SOMA); and a further conference in Singapore in February 1981. There was also a development of the international, ecumenical power and significance of the movement. In the late seventies the trustees of the Fountain Trust decided that the distinctive role of the Trust was coming to an end. It therefore ceased operations on 31 December 1980 and handed some of its functions to other agencies.[5] It was a bold move, which emphasized that renewal was as much the continuous task of the local church as the specialist responsibility of an organisation.

[2] *The Charismatic Movement in the Church of England, op.cit.*, p.8.
[3] Gunstone, *op.cit.*, p.12.
[4] For examples, see *ibid.*, p.18.
[5] For a list of these, see *The Charismatic Movement in the Church of England, op.cit.*, pp.49, 50, (n.19).

A mere recital, like this, of the main events in the history of the charismatic movement is in certain respects somewhat banal and pedestrian; it does not capture the essence of what was a life-transforming experience for individuals, groups and churches. Any detached description or analysis of the movement can perhaps be likened to 'digging up the potatoes to see if they are growing'.[6] Behind the outward events which marked its progress there was all the vitality of what has been described as 'perhaps the most important single post-war movement to cut across every denominational boundary'.[7]

From its early years the modern charismatic movement in the Church of England created debate, painful differences of opinion and even schism. Three of the curates at All Souls, Langham Place in 1962-64 were convinced of the biblical and experiential validity of the 'baptism in the Spirit'. The rector, John Stott, and some other members of the staff, were not convinced. They thought that such teaching did not conform to scripture, and would in practice be highly divisive. To Evangelicals at large the phenomenon was viewed as somewhat bizarre, unwelcome or even incredible, and it was given scant attention. The Keele Congress in 1967 only made a passing reference to the movement. Then, with its increasing influence, there were severe divisions at local and national levels. There was a serious questioning of the biblical justification for pentecostal views. Evangelicals sought from the charismatics a systematic theology of the Holy Spirit drawn from scripture, for they appeared to many Evangelicals as 'unsystematic, untheological, and in the last resort unbiblical'. The fear was that they based 'their doctrine ultimately on experience (flavoured with some scriptural-sounding theological terminology)'.[8] They were called upon to 'set up a case for their distinctive teaching confidently argued from the New Testament'. Evangelical charismatics co-operated with charismatic Roman Catholics, and this only reinforced the concern of their critics that doctrinal differences were being disregarded or underplayed in the euphoria of shared experience.

Of all the issues on which there was division of biblical and experiential interpretation, none was more vexed than the matter of how far baptism in the Spirit could be considered as a second stage in the initiation into Christ. In the face of claims to a second blessing which completed the experience of conversion, many Evangelicals stressed the unitary work of God in Christian initiation. At conversion, they declared, forgiveness, justification, adoption, regeneration, new creation, death, burial and resurrection with Christ, and the giving and receiving of the Holy Spirit,

---

[6] Ibid, p.50.
[7] Paul A. Welsby, A History of the Church of England 1945-1980 (Oxford, 1984), p.242.
[8] Colin Buchanan, 'Baptism in the Holy Spirit', Churchman (Spring 1972), p.41.

were all entailed in an act of repentance and faith in Jesus Christ as Lord and Saviour. There were subsequent real and enriching experiences of the grace of God, but these should not be thought of as a receiving of the Holy Spirit for the first time.

There were also strong and often agonizing differences of opinion over the question of speaking in tongues. There was concern that in certain circumstances the phenomenon appeared to be provoked and learned in a predictable way, and there were frequent cases where the interpretations of the same tongue differed. There was also resistance to the claim that speaking in tongues was necessary for the completion of Christian experience or Christian maturity, or for the apprehension of Christian truth. Furthermore, it was not acceptable to many Evangelicals to equate glossolalia with Spirit-baptism. Most importantly, many Evangelicals were anxious that the New Testament examples and teaching on the subject should be examined with the utmost care to determine the function, significance and meaning of speaking with tongues within the total life of the early church. Then, there should be an evaluation of the contemporary importance of tongues against the background of nineteen hundred years of its nearly complete absence.

The charismatic movement raised other issues which, in varying degrees, caused consternation among so-called non-charismatic Evangelicals. Concern was expressed about what was regarded as the disorderly conduct of some charismatic worship; the often divisive effect of renewal upon local congregations; the apparent disregard for the structures and organizations of the church; the unsatisfactory relationship in some churches between charismatic lay leadership and the incumbent; unwarranted claims to apostleship, prophetic gifts, and powers of healing and exorcism; and an over-concentration upon the miraculous.

From 1970 onwards, after having reached somewhat polarized positions, a genuine attempt was made by charismatic and non-charismatic Evangelicals to reach a fuller, more satisfactory understanding and appreciation of each other's views. A group nominated by the Church of England Evangelical Council met with the Fountain Trust for four separate day conferences over a period of eighteen months. The report, *Gospel and Spirit*, which they published in 1977, was a clarification of their respective views, and it clearly showed a search after unity, harmony and a common purpose. The Bible was accepted as the source of authority and the standard by which all views and practices were to be tested. Some of the differences of opinion did not coincide with the charismatic and non-charismatic divide. There was thankful recognition that what united the charismatics and non-charismatics was far greater than the matters on which they disagreed.

Nonetheless, despite this drawing together there were, by 1979, several hundred 'churches' with over 50,000 members, in what came to be known as the House Church Movement. This was largely a result of charismatics deserting the historic churches in order to meet together to enjoy their newly-discovered experience of the Holy Spirit and the accompanying new forms of worship. Some met in such groups but retained their denominational allegiance.

For all its weaknesses and excesses, and the disruption it caused, the charismatic movement had great and beneficial effect, not only upon the Evangelicals but upon the whole Church of England and most other churches. Wherever charismatic revival occurred there was almost invariably a deepening of faith, fellowship and prayer, an enhanced evangelistic concern, growth in the number of communicants and greater giving to the church at home and overseas. The movement introduced forms of praying, praising, singing and sharing which were novel to most Anglicans. The worship was distinguished by chorus singing, the use of gesture and dance, ministries of healing and deliverance, gifts of tongues and interpretation, prophecies and singing in the Spirit. The general 'loosening' of Church of England public worship with the flexibility of the authorized period of liturgical experimentation and the surge in hymnology was influenced by the charismatic movement. Liturgical revision also helped to ensure that charismatic worship in the Church of England, with its new awareness of the liberty, power, joy and trans-forming effect of the Spirit of God, did not detach itself from the official services of mainstream Anglicanism.

25

Ecumenism and World Mission

The Search for Unity at Home

When the Archbishop of Canterbury, Geoffrey Fisher, delivered his sermon in the university church in Cambridge on 3 November 1946, he reopened the whole question of union with the Free Churches in England, and gave a much-needed impetus to the ecumenical movement. He did not believe that the English churches were ready for constitutional revision, but thought that they should grow towards full communion with one another. In particular, since the Free Churches had often accepted that any future united church would be episcopal, Fisher suggested that they could 'take episcopacy into their system' and explore its nature and value.

It was a new, imaginative and hopeful concept and received a positive response. The Free Churches agreed to send delegates to a joint conference with Church of England representatives to assess the implications of the Cambridge sermon. The conference published *Church Relations in England* (1950). It concluded that 'negotiations for the establishment of intercommunion would have to be conducted in a parallel series between the Church of England on the one hand and the individual Free Churches on the other'.[1]

---

[1] Quoted in Paul A. Welsby, *A History of the Church of England 1945-1980*, p.80.

The Methodist Church was alone in its willingness to proceed further, and in 1955 official 'Conversations' were initiated. An *Interim Report* was published in 1958. Both churches accepted it, and organic unity thus became the official goal. In 1963 the report *Conversations between the Church of England and the Methodist Church* proposed a plan for uniting the two churches, and asked for decisions on this in 1965. For the first time since discussion on home reunion started, following the Lambeth *Appeal to all Christian People* of 1920, a definite scheme was proposed for reintegrating the national episcopal church with one, and that the largest, of the non-episcopal Free Churches.

Most Evangelicals wanted organic unity, but they attached varying degrees of importance to episcopacy. As early as 1948 some of them, while upholding and commending episcopal ministry in the Church of England and, incidentally, in the Church of South India, urged their fellow Anglicans 'not to deny the fact of His grace given through others, lest they "be found even to fight against God" '.[2] Evangelicals believed that they, and the Church of England in general, were free to recognize non-episcopal churches as true churches, albeit defective in order, provided they preached the pure word of God and administered the sacraments in accordance with the requirements of Article XIX.[3]

The Evangelicals who wrote *The Fulness of Christ* (1950) gave somewhat greater importance to episcopacy. Although it was not said to be an essential part of the visible church in the same way as the word and sacraments are, it was accorded major significance as a feature in any scheme of organic union:

> We can and must say that episcopacy and episcopal succession is the way in which the Church learnt, under the Spirit's guidance, to express and preserve the principle of a ministry which is one throughout the ages and one throughout all areas of the Church, and that therefore in a reunited Church it will be an important element in that outward unity which both expresses and conveys the inward unity of Christ's people in him.

But the authors were careful not to make episcopacy a *sine qua non* for unity. They acknowledged that God raises up and uses 'other forms of ministry for the effectual ministration of his word and sacraments'.[4]

Episcopacy and the mutual recognition of ministries continued to be central issues in the Anglican-Methodist Conversations in the nineteen-

---

[2] *Evangelicals Affirm in the year of the Lambeth Conference: The Proceedings of the Congress held in London, April 13th-14th, 1948*, p.107.

[3] Article XIX of the Church of England. 'The visible Church of Christ is a congregation of faithful men, in the which the pure Word of God is preached, and the Sacraments be duly ministered according to Christ's ordinance in all those things that of necessity are requisite to the same'.

[4] *The Fulness of Christ* (1950), p.65.

sixties. They were clearly recognized as such by Evangelicals. Three key statements expressed the Evangelical view: *The Church of England and the Methodist Church* (1963), edited by J.I. Packer, the Open Letter of 1964 to the episcopate, signed by thirty-nine leading Evangelicals, and the 1965 collection of ten Anglican essays with Free Church comments, edited again by J.I. Packer and entitled *All in Each Place: Towards Reunion in England*.

The Service of Reconciliation, which was pivotal to the whole proposed scheme of union, was declared in the Open Letter to be unacceptable because it implied 'the ordination to a priesthood not hitherto exercised of Methodist ministers' who were 'already true ministers of God's word and sacraments'. The signatories of the letter were 'whole-hearted' in their 'desire for the unity of the visible church' and they warmly welcomed the report of the Conversations, but they could not accept any service which failed to declare the unambiguous and unqualified acceptance of the validity of the existing Methodist ministry. They were 'convinced that the right way to unite ministries' was by 'mutual recognition, with episcopal ordination thereafter, as in the Church of South India'.

They therefore requested full communion with the Church of South India, 'so eliminating discrimination against ministers of an episcopal Church who have not themselves been episcopally ordained'. They did not oppose a provision, corresponding to the Church of South India 'Pledge', whereby no congregation would be compelled to accept a ministry about which its members objected on grounds of conscience. The Faith and Order conference at Nottingham in 1964 was strongly convinced that justice had not been done to the South India pattern. They thought that it required and deserved fuller consideration.[5] So did many Evangelicals.

A large proportion of Evangelicals also found the theological statements in the majority report arising out of the Methodist Conversations to be unsatisfactory. They were particularly concerned about the sections on scripture and tradition, episcopacy, priesthood and the sacraments. In addition, the wisdom of piecemeal reconciliation with one church at a time was questioned. Lastly, such Evangelicals could not agree to a two-stage process in which acceptance of stage one was expected without clari-fication of the implications of stage two 'with regard to such matters as doctrinal standards, the Establishment, the Parochial system and Prayer Book revision'.[6]

As these Evangelicals dissented from what was officially proposed, and yet earnestly sought after organic union, they felt bound to enunciate

---

[5] See J.I. Packer (Ed.), *All in Each Place: Towards Reunion in England. Ten Anglican Essays with some Free Church comments* (1965), pp.9-16.

[6] *Ibid.*, p.16.

clearly what was their ecumenical ideal, and what kind of action they envisaged for attaining it. They did so in a comprehensive and coherent manner in a number of publications.[7] They sought a way into union which did not compromise anybody's convictions, which precipitated no new separations and did not attack any body of sincerely-held opinion. Many of them advocated the initial realization of unity at the local level and thought that denominational mergers in advance of local unity were premature. They asked for a frank facing of theological differences, and an avoidance of ambiguity as a shortcut to unity.

Their goal was a reintegrated English church which would embrace diversity but at the same time be genuinely national and comprehensive within the limits set by biblical essentials. Such a united church would be fully committed to maintaining the faith which the existing formularies of the Anglican and Free Churches expressed. They looked for a united church in which diocesan episcopacy operated within a synodical framework.

In 1970 two Anglo-Catholic opponents of the scheme for Anglican-Methodist union, the Bishop of Willesden, the Rt Rev. Graham Leonard, and Dr E.L. Mascall, and two Evangelicals, Dr J.I. Packer and the Rev. Colin Buchanan, published a book entitled *Growing into Union*, in which an alternative scheme was presented in some detail. It was essentially in line with the goals and principles just outlined. It was generally not received with enthusiasm in the Church of England and the Methodist Church. The tone of the book was considered by some as somewhat 'arrogant, polemical, and even abusive',[8] and the authors were seen by the unsympathetic to be self-satisfied with the rightness of their views. Many Anglo-Catholics were as unhappy with the suggested method of dealing with non-episcopally ordained ministers as they were about the original scheme. The implementation of the proposals was also seen as possibly leading to administrative, legal and financial chaos. More fundamentally, the entire 'piece by piece' approach was regarded by certain of its opponents as untheological, highly divisive, and productive of little more than a form of congregationalism.

During this whole period of debate there was a small, albeit less influential strand of Evangelical thinking which fully accepted Methodist orders, but was in favour of the scheme, including the service of reconciliation.

Meanwhile the Church of England-Methodist search for unity went on. Twenty years of negotiation ended in May 1972 with the rejection of the

---

[7] *Ibid.*, pp.11-14.
[8] Welsby, *op.cit.*, p.171.

proposed scheme by the General Synod of the Church of England. The defeat was undoubtedly the consequence of no one simple factor. An underlying fear of change, concern about the possibility of fragmenting the Church of England, an increasing weariness with the debate and the proposals, and the attraction of counter pleas for a multilateral approach to church unity in England were all important influences. Nevertheless, it was the unlikely but powerful alliance of a formidable body of Evangelicals and Anglo-Catholics, largely over their dissatisfaction, for almost entirely different reasons, with the Service of Reconciliation, which was the crushing blow to the scheme. Few gloated over the agonizing failure. There had been a common concern for union; the disagreements were over the terms on which it was acceptable, and the means best suited to its achievement.

In the same year, 1972, which saw the final defeat of the Anglican-Methodist scheme for union, the Presbyterian Church of England and the Congregational Church came together to form the United Reformed Church. It was this newly inaugurated church which took the initiative in opening discussions between all the major churches in Britain, including the Roman Catholic and Orthodox Churches, on how unity might be accomplished. In 1974, at the conclusion of the talks, the Churches Unity Commission was formed, charged with the task of working for union between the churches. In 1976 it issued a report, *Visible Unity in Life and Mission*, which contained 'Ten Propositions' as an acceptable basis for the continued search for unity. The propositions called upon the churches to join in a covenant to seek visible unity. In accepting such a covenant, participating churches would recognize each other's members as 'true members of the Body of Christ and welcome them to Holy Communion without conditions'. They would also recognize each other's ministries as 'true ministries of word and sacraments in the Holy Catholic Church'.[9] Non-episcopal churches would take episcopacy into their systems. When the proposals for a covenant came to the General Synod in July 1980 they received a very qualified response.

Evangelicals generally welcomed the ten propositions, and especially the concept of multilateral talks from which they had sprung. The National Evangelical Anglican Congress in 1977, in keeping with the constantly reiterated theme of Evangelicals, stressed first that no rite should be contemplated which would imply that other ministers were not truly ordained and, secondly, that visible unity should involve a common acceptance of the authority of scripture. The value of episcopacy was once again underlined, and the wish expressed that it would be retained in any union of churches, but the Congress statement did not declare it to be

[9] Quotations from Welsby, *op.cit.*, p.265.

'essential for the existence of the church'. Neither was it declared to be 'in all cases the means by which ordination should be conducted'. Indeed, the statement asked for the existing Anglican practice of episcopacy to be reformed.

Relations with Roman Catholicism

During the post-war era up to the late nineteen-fifties the Roman Catholic Church did not allow any discussions on theological matters with non-Roman Catholics, or any sharing of prayer or worship.[10] The Encyclical *Mystici Corporis Christi* (in 1943) reaffirmed that the Roman Catholic Church and the Church of Christ were identical; and seven years later there was the dogmatic definition of the Assumption of the Blessed Virgin Mary. In the same year, 1950, the Encyclical *Humani Generis* condemned any attempt to deny the identification of the Mystical Body of Christ and the Roman Catholic Church. The following year these exclusive claims were reinforced by another Encyclical, *Sempiternus Dei*, which asked rhetorically if it was not 'holy and salutary and according to the will of God that all at long last return to the one fold of Christ'.

At that stage the possibilities for fruitful dialogue between the Church of England and the Roman Catholic Church looked bleak. But a drastic change in Anglican-Roman Catholic relations and within the Roman Catholic Church itself was about to take place. It was heralded when the seventy-seven year old Giuseppe Roncalli was elected Pope in 1958 as John XXIII. Within the first year of his pontificate he announced the calling of an 'Ecumenical Council of the Universal Church', and established a new Secretariat for the Promoting of Unity among Christians as part of the preparation for this.

Geoffrey Fisher took advantage of the new openness, and became the first Archbishop of Canterbury to visit the Pope in Rome since 1397. The meeting was most amicable, and the Pope, after referring to 'the time when our separated brethren should return to the Mother Church', humbly accepted the Archbishop's alternative portrayal of two churches running on parallel paths 'until, in God's good time, our courses approximate and meet'. Fisher commented that from that moment, so far as he knew, the Pope and the Vatican never talked about returning to past situations or looked backwards for their objective.[11] With the agreement of the Vatican a Church of England representative, Canon Bernard Pawley, was appointed in 1961 to live in Rome in order to act as a

---

[10] The following comments are based on Welsby, *op.cit.*, pp.85, 86.
[11] William Purcell, *Fisher of Lambeth: A Portrait from Life* (London, 1969), p.283, quoted in Welsby, *op.cit.*, pp.177, 178.

two-way link between the Archbishops and the Pope and to promote mutual understanding.

The Second Vatican Council opened in October 1962 and came to an end in December 1965. During the Council Pope John died and was succeeded by the liberal and open-minded Cardinal Montini as Paul VI. In March 1966, Michael Ramsey, the new Archbishop of Canterbury, accepted an invitation to visit the Pope. In contrast to Geoffrey Fisher's courtesy call, this was an official and public event. Dr Ramsey was received formally by the Pope in the Sistine Chapel as head of the Anglican Communion. The Pope and Archbishop issued a joint declaration in which they expressed their intention 'to inaugurate between the Roman Catholic Church and the Anglican Communion serious dialogue which . . . may lead to that unity in truth for which Christ prayed'.[12] Within a month of this visit the Anglican Institute was established in Rome as a meeting-place for members of the Anglican Communion and other churches, particularly the Roman Catholic Church. Also, the Archbishop and the Pope set up an Anglican-Roman Catholic Joint Preparatory Council out of which came the Anglican-Roman Catholic International Commission (ARCIC). Various official and unofficial contacts and dialogue ensued over the next twenty years.

The Second Vatican Council was perhaps the most important ecclesiastical event of this century.[13] It expressed a determination to decentralize the administrative power of the Roman Catholic Church which was so concentrated on Rome, to reduce the hierarchical autocracy of the clergy and the bishops and to guard more carefully against the potentially corrupting effects of accumulated wealth and secular power. Scripture was reinstated to a more central role in the church. A redressing of the balance between the authority of the Bible and that of tradition was to be achieved by the introduction of the vernacular or new versions into the liturgy, by giving greater importance to the Bible in the interpretation of doctrine, and by granting more freedom to biblical scholars. The Council proposed a new strategy for the training and redeployment of clergy and laity to make them more effective in meeting the needs of the contemporary world. The 'Liturgical revival' was to be implemented as an enrichment of the life of the church. The theology of the church was reviewed and the escalation of Marian doctrines halted. A declaration on religious liberty was issued. Greater freedom was granted to take up 'dialogue with the contemporary world'. Lastly, a new ecumenical spirit was made explicit.

Evangelicals welcomed all these changes. Although some retained a

[12] Quoted in Welsby, op.cit., pp.179, 180.
[13] The following brief summary is based on Bernard C. Pawley (Ed.), The Second Vatican Council. Studies by Eight Anglican Observers (London, 1967), pp.13-27.

deeply ingrained suspicion, in general it was acknowledged that the Roman Catholic Church held many of the fundamental Christian doctrines so dear to Evangelicals, and the evidence of biblical reformation was greeted with gladness. In the immediate post-Vatican Council situation, although no form of reunion with the Roman Catholic Church was seen to be even worthy of consideration as a present possibility, dialogue on the basis of scripture was welcomed, and a team of Evangelical theologians was appointed to confer with Roman Catholic theologians. The drawing together of Evangelicals and Roman Catholics was also facilitated by the charismatic movement which cut across barriers of tradition and denomination.

The 1977 National Evangelical Anglican Congress rejoiced in the movement for renewal in the Roman Catholic Church. It supported and wanted to encourage opportunities for dialogue at all levels. In declaring that they believed 'that agreement on fundamental doctrines must precede any formal act of reunion', the assembled Evangelicals made it clear that such organic union was seen as at least a possibility. Indeed they resolved to 'encourage every kind of co-operation that may bring the goal of full communion nearer'. It was asserted that 'some would welcome inter-communion as a step in this direction'.[14]

Such statements as these disturbed many Evangelicals. They were also viewed by a number of non-Anglican evangelicals as highly dangerous and even heretical. Dr Martyn Lloyd-Jones, the Minister of Westminster Chapel, London was the most eloquent and influential of those who, as early as the mid-nineteen-sixties, publicly denounced the contemporary Evangelical overtures to the Roman Catholic Church. Evangelicals appeared to such critics to be caught up in the prevailing attempts to achieve an Anglican-Roman Catholic entente at the expense of their relationship to Free Church evangelicals. The Nottingham statement reflected the Evangelical awareness of this. 'In restating our attitude to the Roman Catholic church', it declared, 'we want simultaneously to affirm our close doctrinal and spiritual ties with non-Anglican evangelicals, which we are most anxious not to jeopardise'.[15]

Relations with the World Council of Churches

Martyn Lloyd-Jones and other non-Anglicans of a like mind were apprehensive about the whole ecumenical movement.[16] Indeed, by the

[14] For these quotations and an indication of the views described, see Philip Crowe (Ed.), *Keele '67: The National Evangelical Anglican Congress Statement*, pp.39, 44, 45.

[15] *The Nottingham Statement: The Official statement of the second National Evangelical Anglican Congress held in April 1977*, p.45.

[16] For this account, see Christopher Catherwood, *Five Evangelical Leaders* (London, 1984), pp.83-94.

mid-sixties they considered the World Council of Churches to be such a threat to the evangelical faith that evangelicals could not in good conscience remain in denominations affiliated to it. In a dramatic speech at the National Evangelical Assembly on 18 October, 1966, Dr Lloyd-Jones made his position clear. He called upon evangelicals in what he termed doctrinally mixed denominations to separate themselves from their denomination and join their fellow evangelicals in a new, doctrinally pure fellowship.

Lloyd-Jones had largely based his analysis and proposed action on the biblical concept of the remnant. John Stott, who was chairing the meeting, could not accept the opinions expressed and was fearful of the consequences of such a powerful appeal. So, after giving thanks for the speech, 'with much nervousness and diffidence' he added that, in his opinion, Dr Lloyd-Jones had 'both history and Scripture against him' in his view of the remnant.

The effect of this open declaration of differing views by two of the foremost evangelicals in the country was immediate and long-lasting. It focused Evangelical attention on their own identity problem and their doctrine of the church. It also made them think afresh about their involvement in the ecumenical movement.

The first British Faith and Order Conference was held at Nottingham in September 1964. In an attempt to reach out beyond the circle of committed ecumenists a number of non-ecumenists were invited. The participation of Evangelicals was encouraged. Those few who attended were convinced that Evangelicals could not, and should not, ignore the ecumenical discussions of the day, but should in some sense be involved in them. They were sure that the way forward was through the meeting of Christians on the basis provided by the WCC. Nevertheless, they were aware that their willingness to participate in ecumenical discussions was a major change of Evangelical attitude, and that there was much hostility towards such an innovation.[17]

Their critics[18] argued that even if the ecumenical movement was formally orthodox it had in practice over-concentrated on social concerns, blurred theological distinctions and tended to compromise with the unreformed Roman Catholic Church. The Evangelical ecumenists countered by asserting that these trends were more apparent than real, and that where they were a reality they were actively opposed within the movement. Some Evangelicals thought that the movement was of little consequence in comparison with the urgent and continuing imperative to preach the gospel to a desperately needy world. Ecumenical talk hardly helped in that task; it was indeed a distraction. Those Evangelicals

[17] See for example J.D. Douglas (Ed.), *Evangelicals and Unity* (1964).
[18] See for example Leith Samuel, *Evangelicals and the Ecumenical Movement* (1962).

committed to the movement saw no incompatibility between evangelism and the search for unity.

The Rev. Julian Charley, speaking at the Anglican Evangelical Assembly in January 1984, articulated this conviction, declaring:

> The prayer of Jesus in John 17, 20-23 clearly indicates some link between the church's unity and its effectiveness in evangelism. Our divisions are a crying scandal and they grieve the heart of Christ. To see the restoration of a genuine unity in love and truth, visibly expressed, should be the concern of all of us, not just a specialised interest for the few.

He acknowledged that there was an understandable fear of a mammoth world church which stifled healthy diversity in unity, but said that reunion between separated communions need not result in this. Unity should be 'a strength for apostolic mission and a safeguard for apostolic truth'. Realistically, he warned that such a vision might require a readiness for dcnominational *hara-kiri*, and a sacrifice of the vested interests of clergy.[19]

Those Evangelicals who resisted Evangelical involvement in the ecumenical movement were not necessarily unenthusiastic about organic unity. Some were, but perhaps most Evangelicals combined a realization of the rightness of the search for unity with grave doubts about the contemporary means and structures entailed for achieving it. The variety of views remained, and the debate was still unresolved by 1984.

Whatever their views on ecumenism, Evangelicals were at one in their concern for world mission; but it was a concern which intensified and changed in emphasis during the forty years under review. In the immediate post-war years mission was understood largely in terms of evangelism. Education and medical work were in the main seen as adjuncts to evangelistic work, and even as 'platforms' or 'springboards' for evangelism. By the nineteen-sixties this concept was being challenged. There was also an increasing consciousness of the emergence, and the vigorous growth of indigenous churches throughout the world.

The strong sense of national identity, especially in former colonial countries which were achieving independence, and in others striving for such independence, was reflected in the expectations of local church autonomy. The role and function of 'missions' was brought into question, as was that of 'missionaries'. Short-term missionary work, Voluntary Service Overseas and Christian service through 'secular' employment in Third World countries were increasingly seen as part of the changing world mission scene. The visit of overseas Christian leaders to this

---

[19] Julian Charley, 'Mission Today and Tomorrow – A Fresh Look', in David D. Sceats (Ed.), *Anglican Evangelical Assembly: Proceedings*, No.2, 1984, p.19.

country, and the help they gave to the work and life of the church in England, brought home the smallness of the world, and the reality of mutual interdependence. Partnership and not paternalism was called for. A new willingness for service was demanded, and a new relationship to the overseas local church.

The Contribution of Max Warren (1904-77)

For over twenty years Max Warren was the foremost Evangelical missionary thinker and leader.[20] He openly declared himself to be an Evangelical, but one with broad 'liberal' sympathies.[21] From 1942 to 1963 he was Secretary of the Church Missionary Society, and his influence in the church worldwide and in ecumenical circles was incalculable. He was dedicated to the task of communicating the gospel effectively 'in a world where its personal values and corporate insights were increasingly under attack or contemptuously ignored'. He judged that this would mean 'giving the missionary movement a different image from its traditional one, without, if possible, losing its traditional bases of support'.[22] He worked for world evangelism, and at the same time encouraged Evangelicals to continue to play a vital part within the comprehensiveness of the Church of England.

For Warren ecumenism and evangelism were interconnected. He was almost unrivalled in his enthusiasm for the ecumenical movement. He sought to lower barriers to intercommunion, delighted in his associations with leaders of non-Anglican missionary societies, was one of the leading voices in the Church of England to welcome the coming into being of the united Church of South India, and played a notable part in the International Missionary Council's conferences at Whitby, Canada in 1947 and at Willingen, Germany in 1952. In all such involvement he retained a clear vision of the ultimate evangelistic goal. When the incorporation of the International Missionary Council into the World Council of Churches was being enthusiastically advocated, he warned against any premature merger. This was illustrative of his concern that no bureaucratic structure or organization should replace the spirit of expectant evangelism characteristic of a relatively autonomous body. In the view of many, the actual incorporation of the IMC at New Delhi in 1961 had the consequences which Warren feared.

Committed as he was to responsible action, Max Warren stressed the

---

[20] For the life and work of Max Warren, see Max Warren, *Crowded Canvas: some experiences of a life-time* (London, 1974); and F.W. Dillistone, *Into all the World: A biography of Max Warren* (London, 1980).

[21] See Warren, *op.cit.*, pp.214, 215; and Dillistone, *op.cit.*, p.154.

[22] Warren, *op.cit.*, p.116.

obligation laid upon Christians to think hard. 'Missionary action must be inspired by and checked by missionary theology'. Much as he admired those who went out as missionaries in the nineteenth century, he was convinced that 'the compelling urge to evangelise had led evangelicals, in particular, either to neglect theology or to concentrate their attention upon too narrow a range of theological principles'.[23] He was acutely aware of the dangers of oversimplification. For example, although he appreciated the spontaneity and evident work of the Spirit of God in the East African revival, he warned that unless the movement grew in stature it would be bogged down in emotionalism and infantilism out of which would come breakaway sects. It was with reluctance and humility that he uttered such strictures, and solely with the concern that the genuine work of God should be promoted. 'God forgive me for a miserable sinner', he wrote. 'Who am I to judge other men? Yet even a miserable sinner has to make decisions and that means passing judgements. Browning was right: "How hard it is to be a Christian!" '[24] It is not surprising that a man with such a spirit was highly regarded and trusted by liberals and conservatives alike.

World Mission

'Mutual responsibility and interdependence in the body of Christ' was a concept which dominated Anglican thinking during the decade after its conception in 1963. It was an attempt to communicate to both clergy and lay people the awareness that mission should be central in the life of the church and not viewed as something done in far-off lands. John Taylor, who succeeded Max Warren as General Secretary of the CMS, was a fervent advocate and able interpreter of such a global perspective. In 1973 the Anglican Consultative Council launched 'Partners in Mission' to promote the principle that there is one mission in the world, shared by the worldwide Christian family. Simon Barrington-Ward, who replaced Taylor as General Secretary of the CMS in 1975 (and who was to become Bishop of Coventry in 1985) shared the same vision, and clarified the aims of the Society within the overall framework of 'interchange'. He emphasized that sharing was to be expressed in evangelism, in renewal and in the search for social justice. It was not a matter of 'spirituality and renewal or social action, but spirituality and renewal and social action, with the Cross central to all'.[25] Such a view was shared by many Evangelicals.[26]

[23] Dillistone, *op.cit.*, p.145.

[24] *Ibid*, p.160.

[25] Jocelyn Murray, *Proclaim the Good News: A Short History of the Church Missionary Society* (London, 1985), p.269.

[26] See for example Julian Charley, 'Mission Today and Tomorrow – A Fresh Look', in Sceats, *op.cit.*

The Lausanne International Congress on World Evangelisation in July 1974 was a landmark. Half of those present, including fifty per cent of the key planning committee and of the speakers, were from Third World countries. The Congress put the Third World on the map of Evangelical Christianity in a new way. It was another acknowledgment that Western domination of the church was over. As previously mentioned, it contributed new insights into the nature and purpose of Christian mission in the modern world, which was seen as including both evangelism and socio-political action, but with priority being given to evangelism.[27] Evangelicals showed a new concern for human rights, and for such matters as government aid to developing countries. The escalating support for The Evangelical Alliance Relief Fund (TEAR Fund) amply demonstrated this enlarged concept of world mission. TEAR Fund was one of the many non-denominational world mission and relief societies which commanded Evangelical support. Indeed, Evangelical enthusiasm was often greater for such pan-evangelical as opposed to specifically Anglican-based missionary enterprises.

The post-Second World War era also witnessed a greater concern for co-operation between the various Anglican missionary societies. In some cases this resulted in amalgamation, as between the CMS and the Church of England Zenana Missionary Society in 1957, and between the Universities Mission to Central Africa and the Society for the Propagation of the Gospel in 1965. The societies also worked together in Partnership for World Mission and the Board for Mission and Unity; and discussions were still continuing in 1984 about the possibility of various societies being located within one building. Such planning envisaged the continued separate identity of each society; but there would be shared resources and closer contact in order to improve effectiveness and eliminate some of the problems experienced in the past.

By 1984 many Evangelical parishes had become more outward looking and conscious of their membership of a universal church than in former years. There was widespread Evangelical commitment to the task of world mission. The function and purpose of missionary societies, their relationship to one another in the light of their different churchmanship and historic connections, their integration into the network of worldwide inter-church activities, and their role within independent, self-governing nations and churches, had become matters of intense debate. Churches and missionary societies were also confronted by frequently fierce

---

[27] For an exposition of this approach, see John R.W. Stott, *Christian Mission in the Modern World* (London, 1975).

opposition from non-Christian religions, or by local strife and civil war. Evangelicals have taken their full share in the pain and suffering entailed. They have continued to be intimately involved in the search for appropriate responses to such traumatic situations, and to the rapidly changing world mission scene.

26

Epilogue

The Other Side of 1984

How stands Evangelicalism the other side of 1984? It is not only very different from its counterpart in the early eighteenth century, it has undergone notable changes even in the short post-Second World War period of upsurge. How equipped is it to serve society in the late twentieth century? What part will it, and should it play within the Church of England? And how are its own character and internal dynamics likely to change in the last decade or so?

It would probably be widely accepted among Evangelicals that there is a need for a 'genuinely missionary encounter between a scriptural faith and modern culture'.[1] Evangelicals are both peculiarly well suited to meet such a demand and yet, in certain respects, frustratingly ill-equipped or prepared to do so. They have a faith which focuses on the Bible and is established upon the foundation truths of the Christian faith. As we have seen in scanning the past two-and-a-half centuries, no Christian tradition glories more than Evangelicalism in the supremacy of the Bible and the truths it contains. Nevertheless, much contemporary Evangelicalism is 'light-weight, even flimsy, compared with its antecedents'.[2] There is a

[1] Lesslie Newbigin, *The Other Side of 1984: Questions for the churches* (Geneva, 1983), p.47. See also Lesslie Newbigin, *Foolishness to the Greeks* (London, 1986).
[2] John King, 'Evangelicals going up Church ladder', in the *Church Times*, 2 November, 1984, p.5. The present analysis of Evangelicalism is indebted to this article by King.

widespread lack of seriousness, and a paucity of concern for searching the scriptures and applying biblical teaching to individual, church and community life. Aspects of the Christian life are frequently trivialised. Rock music, choruses and drama can make valuable contributions to the life of the local church, and neat, rather simplistic religious formulae have their place in encapsulating Christian truth, but they can be substitutes for more demanding spiritual exercises, and more stringent attempts to think biblically. Yet the option is not between a somewhat sombre and inert cerebral faith, and a scintillating, imaginative, vibrant but shallow spiritual life. Intellectual profundity and integrity can co-exist with spiritual depth and vitality.

Too often Evangelicals display either an unhealthy, perhaps rather introverted, pietism, or an enthusiastic involvement in socio-political affairs with little regard for distinctive Christian values. The former can be unpleasantly bigoted, narrow and intolerant, while the latter can devalue or dilute Evangelical theology. There is an urgent need for Evangelicals to demonstrate a 'balanced concern for personal faith, a pure Church and a godly society'.[3] Evangelicals are not in the majority in the church, but neither are they a beleaguered minority. They have found a new liberty, but they must use it for growth into maturity. They need to cultivate a faith which harmonises full, unfettered individual development, responsible membership of the church and compassionate, informed social thinking and action. For all their 'success', there has been little evangelistic impact on the nation as a whole. Evangelicals have the potential for an effective missionary encounter with the post-Christian culture and society of late twentieth-century England, but it waits to be fully realised.

Viewed more narrowly in the context of the Church of England, Evangelicalism has blossomed during the second half of this century. There are many signs of strength, as we have seen. Evangelical theological colleges are training about fifty per cent of ordinands. A large number of Evangelical clergy and congregations are to be found throughout the land, and the standard of parish ministry is high. Although the number of Evangelical bishops is disproportionately small compared with the number of Evangelical ordinands, they do have a strong voice on the bench, and Evangelical leaders are prominent in various areas of church life locally and nationally. But growth and influence has brought change. Evangelicalism has become 'a large amorphous minority shading off into other groups'.[4] This metamorphosis has been facilitated by the

---

[3]   J.I. Packer, *A Kind of Noah's Ark? : The Anglican commitment to Comprehensiveness* (Oxford, 1981), p.7. Some of the comments in this epilogue on the dynamics of Evangelicalsm owe much to Packer.

[4]   King, *op.cit.*

charismatic movement, and by the responsible participation of Evangelicals in liturgical innovations, urban evangelism, synodical government, socio-political and other debates and action, and pastoral strategy. No longer are Evangelicals a small group, united in opposition to a common, clearly definable, threat such as Prayer Book revision. Contemporary arguments are about issues which are of wide concern – such as the ordination of women, the remarriage in church of divorced people, nuclear war and embryology – in which opinions cut across divisions of churchmanship. The matters under debate are intricate and new subjects proliferate. On some the teaching of the Bible is not clear, or Evangelicals appear little concerned about the appropriate biblical principles. As far as Evangelicalism is concerned, 'the result is a questioning disarray instead of implacable phalanxes'.[5]

The life of Evangelicals within a comprehensive church has been made more complicated and painful because some ordained Church of England leaders openly deny the supreme authority of the Bible and claim 'unlimited freedom to reconceive the Christian fundamentals'.[6] When such accredited custodians of Church of England doctrine can no longer conscientiously teach what is central to that doctrine, and indeed when they sometimes openly deny such teaching, Evangelicals are agreed that those concerned should resign. This is not to disallow full and honest debate and vigorous criticism. It is a matter of church discipline. The thorny question comes when any perpetrator of what Evangelicals regard as heretical or sub-Christian views, refuses to resign. What action should the Church take? On this Evangelicals are not agreed. When the problem becomes especially acute the siren calls to withdraw from the Church of England become particularly alluring to some of them. Certain prominent nonconformist evangelicals have not hesitated to urge Church of England Evangelicals to flee from such a 'doctrinally mixed' church into 'a tighter fellowship where the pre-critical, pre-liberal view of Scripture is rigorously upheld and sceptical revisionism in theology is debarred'.[7] But very few have actually departed the fold. Nonetheless, for Evangelicals as a whole, there is a need to maintain Church of England allegiance, and at the same time cope with what they may consider to be Anglican doctrinal disorder; all the while retaining a healthy, constructive relationship with nonconformists. To achieve a balance between these various, often competing, demands is not easy: it requires much resolution and wisdom.

Finally, Evangelicals have their own identity problem. Late twentieth-century Evangelicalism is complex. There are still fundamentals of the faith which Evangelicals hold in common, which bind them together and

[5] *Ibid.*
[6] Packer, *op.cit.*, p.9.
[7] *Ibid.*, p.10.

give them distinctiveness within the Church of England. Yet, as we have seen, there are wide differences of emphasis: from the most enthusiastic charismatics to the most diehard traditionalists; from the rigid Puritan or ultra-Protestant dogmatists to the most unintellectual dependents on experience; from those with an all-consuming passion for Third World improvement, to the most extreme pietists; and from the ardent advocates of pan-evangelicalism to the ultra-loyal Anglicans. Some rest content with their parochial commitments, while others earnestly seek for national, and indeed international, Evangelical influence. Some stress the need for personal evangelism and personal pastoral care, while others search for a more effective Christian penetration of secular society. Some see the Church in local terms; others urgently look for an Evangelical impact upon every aspect of the Church's life – its theology and liturgy, its training and ministry, and its fellowship and ecumenical relationships. There are also new alignments: there has been a shrinking of the previously felt gap between the more conservative Evangelicals and the more conservative Anglo-Catholics, but also a widening of the gap between Evangelicals and Anglo-Catholics on the one side, and liberals and radicals on the other.

The situation Evangelicals face in society, in the church as a whole and in the Church of England in particular is likewise complicated, even confused. They have to grapple with intricate, and sometimes seemingly insoluble problems. But history shows that they have trod such paths before, and have found a way through. They have been most true to themselves and the distinctive task which is laid upon them, when they have remained faithful to their biblical foundations, and concerned to make a positive contribution to the needs of their generation; and when they have exercised boldness yet humility in their service. Authentic Evangelicalism has two distinctive hallmarks: humble submission to the authority of scripture and acceptance of the Lordship of Christ, with all that flows from belief in him as pre-eminent. In an age of relativism, pluralism and syncretism, Evangelicals still have their essential part to play in the life of the church and of the world.

Bibliography

Because of lack of space this bibliography does not include 'background' works, but is restricted to selected books, theses and articles more directly relevant to the history of the Evangelicals. The place of publication is London (or unknown) unless otherwise stated.

Abbey, Charles J. and Overton, John H., *The English Church in the Eighteenth Century*, 2 vols (1878).

Acheson, A.R., 'The Evangelicals in the Church of Ireland, 1784-1859' (The Queen's University, Belfast, Ph.D., 1967).

Adair, John, *The Becoming Church* (1977).

Anderson, J.N.D., *Into the World: The Need and Limits of Christian Involvement* (1968).

Anglican Evangelicals and their new Assembly: A Forum for United Thought and Action in the Church of England (1983).

Atkinson, James, *Rome and Reformation Today* (Oxford, 1982).

Baker, Frank, *John Wesley and the Church of England* (1970).

Baker, W.J., 'The Attitudes of English Churchmen, 1800-1850, towards the Reformation' (Cambridge University Ph.D., 1966).

Balleine, G.R., *A History of the Evangelical Party in the Church of England* (1908).

Barnes, John, *Ahead of his Age: Bishop Barnes of Birmingham* (1979).

Barr, James, *Fundamentalism* (1977).

Bateman, Josiah, *The Life of the Right Rev. Daniel Wilson* (1860).

Beckwith, R.T., *Rome and Canterbury* (Oxford).

Beeson, Trevor, *The Church of England in Crisis* (1973).

Bell, G.K.A., *Randall Davidson: Archbishop of Canterbury*, 2 vols (1935).

Benson, F.J. *The Life of Rev. John William de la Fléchière* (1817).

Bentley, A., 'The Transformation of the Evangelical Party in the Church of England in the later Nineteenth Century' (Durham University Ph.D., 1971).

Best, G., *Shaftesbury* (1964).

Bradley, Ian, *The Call to Seriousness: The Evangelical Impact on the Victorians* (1976).

Bradley, I.C., 'The Politics of Godliness: Evangelicals in Parliament, 1784-1832' (Oxford University D.Phil., 1974).

Braithwaite, Robert, *The Life and Letters of Rev. William Pennefather*

Bready, J. Wesley, *Doctor Barnardo : Physician, Pioneer, Prophet* (1930).

Bready, J. Wesley, *England Before and After Wesley: The Evangelical Revival and Social Reform* (1939).

Brierly, Peter, *Mission to London: Phase 1 Who responded?* (1984).

Brilioth, Y., *Evangelicalism and the Oxford Movement* (1934).

Brown, Ford K., *Fathers of the Victorians: The Age of Wilberforce* (Cambridge, 1961).

Bromiley, Geoffrey W., *Introduction to the Theology of Karl Barth* (Edinburgh, 1979).

Browning, W.R.F. (Ed.), *The Anglican Synthesis: Essays by Catholics and Evangelicals* (Derby, 1964).

Bruce, Steve, 'The Student Christian Movement and the Inter-Varsity Fellowship: a sociological study of two student movements' (Stirling University Ph.D., 1980).

Bruce, Steve, *Firm in the Faith* (Aldershot, 1984).

Buchanan, Colin O., *Evangelical Anglicans and Liturgy* (Nottingham, 1984).

Buchanan, Colin O., *Recent Liturgical Revision in the Church of England* (Nottingham, 1973).

Buchanan, Colin, Lloyd, Trevor and Miller, Harold (Eds), *Anglican Worship Today: Collins Illustrated Guide to the Alternative Service Book 1980* (1980).

Buchanan, C.O., Mascall, E.L., Packer, J.I., The Bishop of Willesden, *Growing Into Union: Proposals for Forming a United Church* (1970).

Bullock, F.W.B., *The History of Ridley Hall, Cambridge*, 3 vols (1941).

Cadogan, W.B., *The Life of William Romaine* (1821).

Calder, Angus, *The People's War: Britain 1939-1945* (1971).

Capon, John, *Evangelicals Tomorrow: A Popular Report of Nottingham 77, the National Evangelical Anglican Congress* (1977).

Carpenter, Humphrey, *The Inklings: C.S. Lewis, J.R.R. Tolkien, Charles Williams and their friends* (1978).

Carpenter, S.C., *Winnington-Ingram: The Biography of Arthur Foley Winnington-Ingram Bishop of London 1901-1939* (1948).

Carpenter, S.C., *Eighteenth Century Church and People* (1959).

Carpenter, S.C., *Church and People, 1789-1889: A History of the Church of England from William Wilberforce to 'Lux Mundi'* (1933).

Carus, William, *Memoirs of the Life of the Rev. Charles Simeon with a Selection from his Writings and Correspondence* (1847).

Catherwood, Christopher, *Five Evangelical Leaders* (1984).

Cecil, David, *The Stricken Deer: Life of William Cowper* (1929).

Chadwick, Owen, *The Victorian Church*, 2 vols (1966, 1970).

The Charismatic Movement in the Church of England (CIO Publishing, 1981).

Christensen, T., *Origin and History of Christian Socialism 1848-1854* (1962).

Church, R.W., *The Oxford Movement 1833-45* (1891).

Clark, M. Guthrie, *William Henry Griffith Thomas 1861-1924: Minister, Scholar, Teacher* (1949).

Clarke, W.K. Lowther, *Eighteenth Century Piety* (1944).

Clegg, H., 'Evangelicals and Tractarians. An investigation of the connecting links between the two movements in the Church of England in the earlier part of the last century and a consideration of how, and how far, these links came to be broken' (Bristol University M.A., 1965).

Coggan, F.D. (Ed.), *Christ and the Colleges: A History of the IFEU* (1934).

Coggan, Donald, *Word and World* (1971).

Coggan, Donald, *Convictions* (1975).

Cohn, Norman, *The Pursuit of the Millennium* (1970).

Conversations between the Church of England and the Methodist Church: A Report (1963).

Coombs, P.B., 'A History of the Church Pastoral-Aid Society, 1836-1861' (Bristol University M.A., 1960).

Cornish, F. Warre, *The English Church in the Nineteenth Century*, 2 vols (1910).

Coupland, R., *Wilberforce: A Narrative* (1923).

Cragg, George G. *Grimshaw of Haworth* (1947).

Craston, Colin (Chairman, Working Group), *The Charismatic Movement in the Church of England* (1981).

Crowe, Philip (Ed.), Keele '67: The National Evangelical Anglican Congress Statement (1967).

Daniel-Rops, H., *The Church in the Eighteenth Century* (1960).

Dark, Sydney, *Wilson Carlisle* (1945).

Davies, G.C.B., *The Early Cornish Evangelicals 1735-1760* (1951).

Davies, G.C.B., *The First Evangelical Bishop* (1958).

Davies, G.C.B., *Men for the Ministry: The History of the London College of Divinity* (1963).

Davies, Horton, *Worship and Theology in England: The Ecumenical Century: 1900-1965* (1965).

Davies, Rupert E., *The Testing of the Churches 1932-1982: A Symposium* (1982).

Davies, Rupert E., *The Church of England Observed* (1984).

Davies, Rupert E. and Rupp, Gordon (Eds), *A History of the Methodist Church in Great Britain*, 3 vols (1965-83).

Dawson, E.C., *James Hannington First Bishop of Eastern Equatorial Africa: A History of his Life and Work 1847-1885* (1893).

Dictionary of National Biography.

Dillistone, F.W., *Into All the World: A Biography of Max Warren* (1980).

Douglas, J.D. (Ed.), *Evangelicals and Unity: Six Essays* (1964).

The Easter People, A Message from the Roman Catholic Bishops of England and Wales In light of the National Pastoral Congress Liverpool 1980 (1980).

Edwards, David L. (Ed.), *The Honest to God Debate* (1963).

Edwards, David L., *Religion and Change* (1969).

Edwards, David L., *Leaders of the Church of England, 1828-1978* (1978).

Edwards, David L.. *Christian England*. 3 vols (1981, 1983, 1984).

Elliott-Binns, L.E., *The Evangelical Movement in the Church of England* (1928).

Elliott-Binns, L.E., *Religion in the Victorian Era* (1936).

Elliott-Binns, L.E., *The Early Evangelicals: A Religious and Social Study* (1953).

England, Edward, *The Spirit of Renewal* (1982).

Erickson, Millard, *The New Evangelical Theology* (1968).

Ervine, W.J.C., 'Doctrine and Diplomacy: Some aspects of the life and thought of Anglican Evangelical Clergy 1797-1837' (Cambridge University Ph.D., 1979).

Evangelicals Affirm in the Year of the Lambeth Conference: The Proceedings of the Conference held in London 13-14 April 1945.

Ewing, John W., *Goodly Fellowship: A Century Tribute to the Life and Work of the World's Evangelical Alliance 1846-1946* (1946).

The Final Report: Anglican-Roman Catholic International Commission (1982).

Finlayson, Geoffrey B.A.M., *The Seventh Earl of Shaftesbury 1801-1885* (1981).

Flew, R. Newton and Davies, Rupert E. (Eds.), *The Catholicity of Protestantism* (1950).

Flindall, R.P. (Ed.), *The Church of England 1815-1948. A Documentary History* (1972).

Forrester, D.W.R., 'The Intellectual Development of E.B. Pusey, 1800-1850' (Oxford University D.Phil., 1967).

Fox, Adam, *Dean Inge* (1960).

Fox, L.P., 'The work of the Rev. Thomas T. Biddulph, with special reference to his influence on the Evangelical Movement in the West of England' (Cambridge University Ph.D., 1953).

Furlong, Monica (Ed.), *Feminine in the Church* (1984).

Furneaux, Robin, *William Wilberforce* (1974).

Garbett, Cyril, *In an Age of Revolution* (1952).

Gibb, Jocelyn (Ed.), *Light on C.S. Lewis* (1965).

Gibson, William, *The Year of Grace: A History of the Ulster Revival of 1859* (Edinburgh, 1860).

Gilbert, Alan D., *The Making of Post-Christian Britain: A History of the Secularization of Modern Society* (1980).

Gilbert, A.D., *Religion and Society in Industrial England: Church, Chapel and Social Change 1740-1914* (1976).

Gilley, S.W., 'Evangelical and Roman Catholic Missions to the Irish in London, 1830-1870' (Cambridge University Ph.D., 1970).

Gladstone, William Ewart, *Letters on Church and Religion*, 2 vols (1910).

Gladwin, John, *God's People in God's World: Biblical Motives for Social Involvement* (Leicester, 1979).

Gore, Charles (Ed.), *Lux Mundi: A Series of Studies in the Religion of the Incarnation* (1889).

Gosse, Edmund, *Father and Son: A Study of Two Temperaments* (1907).

Green, Michael (Ed.), *The Truth of God Incarnate* (1977).

Green, Roger Lancelyn and Hooper, Walter, *C.S. Lewis: A Biography* (Glasgow, 1974).

Grisewood, H. (Ed.), *The Ideas of the Victorians* (1966).

Grubb, Kenneth, *Crypts of Power: An Autobiography* (1971).

Grubb, Norman P., *C.T. Studd: Cricketer and Pioneer* (1933).

Gunstone, John, *Pentecostal Anglicans* (1982).

Halévy, E, *A History of the English People in the Nineteenth Century* 6 vols.

Hammond, T.C., *What is an Evangelical?* (1956).

Hardman, B.E., 'The Evangelical Party in the Church of England, 1855-1865' (Cambridge University Ph.D., 1964).

Hardy, R. Spence, *Life of Grimshaw* (1860).

Harford, John Battersby and Macdonald, Frederick Charles, *Handley Carr Glyn Moule Bishop of Durham* (1922).

Harper, Michael, *As at the Beginning: The Twentieth Century Pentecostal Revival* (1965).

Harrison, G. Elsie, *Son to Susanna: The Private Life of John Wesley* (1937).

Harvey, G.L.H. (Ed.), *The Church and the Twentieth Century* (1936).

Hastings, Adrian, *A History of English Christianity* 1920-1985 (1986).

Haweis, T., *The Life of William Romaine* (1797).

Heasman, Kathleen, *Evangelicals in Action: An Appraisal of their Social Work in the Victorian Era* (1962).

Hebert, Gabriel, *Fundamentalism and the Church of God* (1957).

Hennell, M. *John Venn and the Clapham Sect* (1958).

Hennell, M., *Sons of the Prophets: Evangelical Leaders of the Victorian Church* (1979).

Hobsbawm, E.J., *The Age of Revolution* (1962).

Hodder, E., *The Life and Work of the Seventh Earl of Shaftesbury, K.G.*, 3 vols (1886).

Henson, Herbert Hensley, *Retrospect of an Unimportant Life*, 3 vols (Oxford, 1942, 1950).

Hewitt, Gordon, *The Problems of Success: A History of the Church Missionary Society 1910-1942*, 2 vols (1971).

Hole, Charles, *The Early History of the Church Missionary Society* (1896).

Hollenweger, Walter, *The Pentecostals* (1972).

Hopkins, Hugh Evan, *Charles Simeon of Cambridge* (1977).

Howden, J. Russell (Ed.), *Evangelicalism: By Members of the Fellowship of Evangelical Churchmen* (1925).

Howse, Ernest Marshall, *Saints in Politics: The 'Clapham Sect' and the Growth of Freedom* (1953).

Ideas and Beliefs of the Victorians: An Historic Revaluation of the Victorian Age (1950).

Idle, Christopher, *Hymns in Today's Language* (Nottingham, 1982).

Iremonger, F.A., *Men and Movements in the Church: A Series of Interviews* (1928).

Iremonger, F.A., *William Temple Archbishop of Canterbury: His Life and Letters* (1948).

Isaac, Robert and Wilberforce, Samuel, *The Life of William Wilberforce*, 5 vols (1838).

Jasper, Ronald C.D., *George Bell: Bishop of Chichester* (Oxford, 1967).

Jay, E., 'Anglican Evangelicalism and the Nineteenth-Century Novel' (Oxford University D.Phil., 1975).

Johnson, Douglas, *Contending for the Faith: A History of the Evangelical Movement in the Universities and Colleges* (Leicester, 1979).

Kent, John, *Holding the Fort: Studies in Victorian Revivalism* (1978).

Kent, John H.S., *The End of the Line? The Development of Christian Theology in the Last Two Centuries* (1978).

King, John C., *The Evangelicals* (1969).

Kirby, Gilbert W., *Ernest Kevan: Pastor and Principal* (1968).

Knox, Edmund Arbuthnott, *Reminiscences of an Octogenarian, 1847-1934* (1934).

Lancelot, J.B., *Francis James Chavasse, Bishop of Liverpool* (1929).

Langston, E.L., *Bishop Taylor Smith: A Biogpaphy of the Rt Rev. John Taylor Smith, Bishop of Sierra Leone, 1897-1901* (1938).

Laycock, J.W. (Memorials compiled by), *Methodist Heroes in the Great Haworth Round 1734-1784* (Keighley, 1909).

Leaver, Robin, *A Hymn Book Survey 1962-80* (Nottingham, 1980).

Lecky, William Edward Hartpole, *A History of England in the Eighteenth Century*, 7 vols (1892).

Lewis, C.S., *Surprised by Joy* (1960).

Lewis, Donald Munro, 'The Evangelical Mission to the British Working Classes: A Study of the growth of Anglican support for a pan-evangelical approach to evangelism with special reference to London 1828-1860' (University of Oxford D.Phil., 1981).

Liddon, H.P., *Life of E.B. Pusey*, 3 vols (1894).

Linnan, J.E., 'The Evangelical Background of J.H. Newman, 1816-1826' (Louvain University D.Th., 1965).

Lloyd, Trevor, *The Church of England 1900-1965* (1966).

Loane, Marcus L., *Oxford and the Evangelical Succession* (1951).

Loane, Marcus L., *Cambridge and the Evangelical Succession* (1952).

Lockhart, J.G., *Cosmo Gordon Lang* (1949).

Macdonald, A.J. (Ed.), *The Evangelical Doctrine of the Holy Communion* (1930).

Mainwaring, Randle, *From Controversy to Co-Existence: Evangelicals in the Church of England 1914-1980* (Cambridge, 1985).

Marrin, Albert, *The Last Crusade: The Church of England in the First World War* (Durham, North Carolina, 1974).

Marsh, P.T., *The Victorian Church in Decline: Archbishop Tait and the Church of England 1868-1882* (1969).

Martin, R.H., 'The Pan-Evangelical Impulse in Britain 1798-1830; with special reference to Four London Societies' (Oxford University D.Phil., 1974).

Mascall, E.L., *The Secularisation of Christianity: An Analysis and a Critique* (1965).

McLoughlin, William G., *Modern Revivalism* (New York, 1955).

Meacham, S., *Henry Thornton of Clapham 1760-1815* (1964).

Member of the House of Shirley and Hastings, *Life and Times of Selina, Countess of Huntingdon*, 2 vols (1839).

Members of the Church of England, *The Inner Life: Essays in Liberal Evangelicalism* (London, undated).

Middleton, Erasmus, *Biographia Ecclesiastica*, Vol.IV (1816).

Moody, W.R., *The Life of Dwight L. Moody* (New York, 1900).

Moore, E.R., 'John Bird Sumner, Bishop of Chester, 1828-48' (Manchester University M.A., 1976).

Moorman, John R.H., *A History of the Church of England* (1953).

Moorman, John, *Vatican Observed: An Anglican View of Vatican II* (1967).

Moule, Handley C.G., *Charles Simeon* (1892).

Moule, Handley C.G., *The Evangelical School in the Church of England* (1901).

Mulliner, H.G., *Arthur Burroughs: A Memoir* (1936).

Murray, Jocelyn, *Proclaim the Good News: A Short History of the Church Missionary Society* (1985).

Murray, Nancy, 'The Influence of the French Revolution on the Church of England and its Rivals 1789-1802' (Oxford University D.Phil., 1975).

Neill, Stephen, *Anglicanism* (Harmondsworth, 1958).

Neill, Stephen, *A History of Christian Missions* (Harmondsworth, 1964).

Neill, Stephen, *The Interpretation of the New Testament 1861-1961* (Oxford, 1964).

Newbigin, Lesslie, *The Other Side of 1984* (Geneva, 1983).

Newbigin, Lesslie, *Foolishness to the Greeks* (1986).

A New Canterbury Tale: The Reports of the Anglican International Conference on Spiritual Renewal held at Canterbury, July 1978 (Nottingham, 1978).

Newell, A.G., 'Studies in Evangelical Prose Literature: Its rise and decline' (Liverpool University Ph.D., 1976).

Newman, John Henry, *Apologia Pro Vita Sua: Being a History of his Religious Opinions* (New edition, 1893).

Newsome, D., *The Parting of Friends* (1966).

Newton, John, *An Authentic Narrative* (1764).

Newton, John, *Cardiphonia* (1780).

Norman, E.R., *Church and State in England, 1770-1970: A Historical Study* (1976).

The Nottingham Statement: The Official Statement of the second National Evangelical Anglican Congress held in April 1977 (1977).

Orchard, S.C., 'English Evangelical Eschatology, 1790-1850' (Cambridge University Ph.D., 1968).

Orr, J. Edwin, *The Second Evangelical Awakening in Britain* (1949).

Orr, J. Edwin, *The Light of the Nations: Progress and Achievement in the Nineteenth Century* (1965).

Overton, John H., *The English Church in the Nineteenth Century 1800-1833)* (1894).

Packer, J.I., *'Fundamentalism' and the Word of God* (1958).

Packer, J.I., *Keep Yourselves from Idols* (1963).

Packer, J.I. (Ed.), *The Church of England and the Methodist Church* (1963).

Packer, J.I. (Ed.), *All in Each Place: Towards Reunion in England: Ten Anglican Essays with some Free Church Comments* (1965).

Packer, J.I. (Ed.), *Guidelines: Anglican Evangelicals Face the Future* (1967).

Packer, J.I., *A Kind of Noah's Ark? The Anglican Commitment to Comprehensiveness* (Oxford, 1981).

Padilla, C. Rene (Ed.), *The New Face of Evangelicalism: An International Symposium on the Lausanne Covenant* (1976).

Patten, John A., *These Remarkable Men: The Beginning of a World Enterprise* (1945).

Pawley, Bernard C., *The Second Vatican Council: Studies by Eight Anglican Observers* (1967).

Perkin, Harold, *The Origins of Modern English Society 1780-1880* (1969).

Pollock, John, *The Cambridge Movement* (1953).

Pollock, John, *The Cambridge Seven: A Call to Christian Service* (1955).

Pollock, John, *Moody without Sankey: A New Biographical Portrait* (1963).

Pollock, John, *Crusade 66: Britain Hears Billy Graham* (1966).

Pollock, John, *The Keswick Story: The Authorised History of the Keswick Convention* (1964).

Pollock, John, *Billy Graham: The Authorised Biography* (1966).

Pollock, John, *Wilberforce* (1977).

Poole-Connor, E.J., *Evangelicalism in England* (1951).

Poulton, John, *Dear Archbishop* (1976).

Pratt, John H., *The Thought of the Evangelical Leaders: Notes on the Discussions of the Eclectic Society London during the Years 1798 to 1814* (1956).

Prestige, G.L., *The Life of Charles Gore: A Great Englishman* (1935).

Purcell, William, *Fisher of Lambeth: A Portrait from Life* (1969).

Ramsey, Arthur Micheal, *From Gore to Temple, The Development of Anglican Theology between Lux Mundi and the Second World War, 1889-1939* (London, 1960).

Ramsey, Michael, *Image Old and New* (1963).

Reardon, Bernard M.G., *Religious Thought in the Victorian Age: A Survey from Coleridge to Gore* (1971).

Reckitt, Maurice, *Maurice to Temple: A Century of the Social Movement in the Church of England* (1947).

Rees, Jean, *His Name was Tom: The Biography of Tom Rees* (1971).

Rennie, I.S., 'Evangelicalism and English Public Life, 1823-1850' (University of Toronto Ph.D., 1962).

Reynolds, J.S. *The Evangelicals at Oxford 1735-1871* (Oxford, 1953).

Reynolds, J.S., *Canon Christopher of St Aldate's Oxford* (1967).

Roberts, R. Ellis, *H.R.L. Sheppard: Life and Letters* (1942).

Robinson, John A.T., *Honest to God* (1963).

Robinson, John A.T., *The New Reformation?* (1965).

Robinson, John A.T. and Edwards, David L., *The Honest to God Debate* (1963).

Rogers, T. Guy (Ed.), *Liberal Evangelicalism: An Interpretation: By Members of the Church of England* (1923).

Rosman, Doreen M., 'Evangelicals and Culture in England, 1790-1833' (Keele University Ph.D., 1978).

Routley, Erik, *Hymns and Human Life* (1952).

Rowdon, H.H., *The Origins of the Brethren 1825 to 1850* (1967).

Russell, G.W.E., *A Short History of the Evangelical Movement* (1962).

Ryle, J.C., *Christian Leaders in the Eighteenth Century* (1885).

Samuel, D.N., *The Evangelical Succession in the Church of England* (1979).

Samuel, Leith, *Evangelicals and the Ecumenical Movement* (1962).

Sandhurst, B.G., *How Heathen is Britain?* (1946).

Saward, Michael, *Evangelicals on the Move* (London and Oxford, 1987).

Sceats, David D., *Anglican Evangelical Assembly: Proceedings 1984.*

Scott, Thomas, *The Force of Truth* (1835).

Seeley, M., *The Later Evangelical Fathers* (1879).

Semmel, Bernard, *The Methodist Revolution* (1973).

Sheppard, David, *Built as a City: God and the Urban World Today* (1974).

Sheppard, David, *Bias to the Poor* (1983).

Sheridan, T.L., 'Newman and Justification: A Study in the Development of a Theology' (Institut Catholique de Paris Th.D., 1965).

Smith, A.G., *Henry Martyn* (1892).

Smith, Stanley A.C., *Road to Revival: The Story of the Ruanda Mission* (1946).

Smyth, C.H., *Simeon and Church Order* (Cambridge, 1940).

Smyth, C.H., *Cyril Foster Garbett: Archbishop of York* (1959).

Southey, Robert, *The Life and Works of William Cowper*, 8 vols (1854)

Spring, D., 'The Clapham Sect', *Victorian Studies* 5(1), 1963.

Stephen, James, *Essays in Ecclesiastical Biography* (1860).

Stillingfleet, James, *Life of Thomas Adam* prefaced to his *Posthumous Works.*

Stock, Eugene, *The English Church in the Nineteenth Century* (1910).

Stock, Eugene, *History of the Church Missionary Society*, 4 vols (1899-1916).

Stott, John R.W., *Fundamentalism and Evangelism* (1956).

Stott, John R.W, *Our Guilty Silence: The Church, the Gospel and the World* (1967).

Stott John R.W., *Christian Mission in the Modern World* (1975).

Stott, John R.W., *What is an Evangelical?* (1977).

Stott, John (Ed.), *Obeying Christ in a Changing World*, 3 vols (1977).

Stott, John, *Issues Facing Christians Today* (1984).

Stott, John, *Evangelical Anglicans and the ARCIC Final Report* (Nottingham, 1982).

Stoughton, J., *Religion in England 1800-1850*, 2 vols (1884).

Streeter, B.H. (Ed.), *Foundations: A Statement of Christian Belief in Terms of Modern Thought: By Seven Oxford Men* (1912).

Sydney, Edwin, *Life and Ministry of Samuel Walker* (1838).

Sykes, Norman, *Church and State in England in the Eighteenth Century* (Cambridge, 1934).

Symondson, A. (Ed.), *The Victorian Crisis of Faith* (1970).

Tatlow, Tissington, *The Story of the Student Christian Movement of Great Britain and Ireland* (1933).

Taylor, H.A., *Jix Viscount Brentford: Being the Authoritative and Official Biography of the Rt Hon. William Joynson-Hicks, First Viscount Brentford of Newick* (1933).

Thompson, E.P., *The Making of the English Working Class* (Harmondsworth, 1968).

Thompson, K.A., *Bureaucracy and Church Reform: The Organizational Response of the Church of England to Social Change 1800-1965* (Oxford, 1970).

Toon, Peter, *Evangelical Theology 1833-1856: A Response to Tractarianism* (1979).

Toon, Peter and Smout, Michael, *John Charles Ryle, Evangelical Bishop* (1976).

Towards the Conversion of England (London, 1945).

Trevelyan, G.O., *The Life and Letters of Lord Macaulay* (1876).

Tyerman, L., *The Oxford Methodists* (London, 1873).

Tyerman, L., *Wesley's Designated Successor* (London, 1882).

Venn, John, *Memoir of Henry Venn* (1834).

Vidler, A.R. (Ed.), *Soundings* (Cambridge, 1962).

Voll, D., *Catholic Evangelicalism* (1963).

Vulliamy, C.E., *John Wesley* (Third edition, 1954).

Wallis, Arthur, *The Radical Christian* (1981).

Walsh, J.D., 'The Yorkshire Evangelicals in the Eighteenth Century, with special reference to Methodism' (Cambridge University Ph.D., 1956).

Walsh, J., 'Origins of the Evangelical Revival' in Bennet, G.D. and Walsh, J.D. (Eds), *Essays in Modern Church History* (1966).

Wand, J.W.C. (Ed.), *Recovery Starts Within: The Book of the Mission to London 1949* (1949).

Ward, Maisie, *Young Mr Newman* (1948).

Ward, W.R., *Religion and Society in England 1790-1850* (1972).

Wardle, J.A., 'The Life and Times of the Rev. Dr Hugh McNeile, 1795-1879' (Manchester University M.A.).

Warren, Max, *Crowded Canvas: Some experiences of a life-time* (1974).

Watson, David, *You are my God: An Autobiography* (1983).

Watts, Michael R. *The Dissenters from the Reformation to the French Revolution* (Oxford, 1978).

Wearmouth, Robert F., *Methodism and the Common People of the Eighteenth Century* (1945).

Weber, Max, *The Protestant Ethic and the Spirit of Capitalism* (2nd ed., 1976).

Welsby, Paul A., *A History of the Church of England 1945-1980* (Oxford, 1984).

White, J.W., 'The influence of North American evangelism in Great Britain between 1830 and 1914 on the origin and development of the ecumenical movement' (Oxford University D.Phil., 1963).

Whitehouse, Mary, *A Most Dangerous Woman?* (1982).

Whittingham, Richard, *The Works of the Rev. John Berridge A.M.* (1833).

Wilkinson, Alan, *The Church of England and the First World War* (1978).

Wilson, Bryan, *Contemporary Transformations of Religion* (1976).

Wirt, Sherwood Eliot, *The Social Conscience of the Evangelical* (1968).

Wood, A. Skevington, *The Inextinguishable Blaze* (Exeter, 1960).

Woods, Edward and MacNutt, Frederick, B., *Theodore, Bishop of Winchester: Pastor, Prophet, Pilgrim: A Memoir of Frank Theodore Woods, D.D., 1874-1932* (1933).

Wright, J. Stafford, *The First Twenty-Five Years of the Bible Churchmen's Missionary Society (1922-47)* (1947).

Yates, T.E., *Venn and the Victorian Bishops Abroad* (1978).

Index of Authors

Abbey, C. J. 5, 351
Acheson, A. R. 351
Adair, John 351
Adam, Thomas 30
Aitken, W. Hay 246, 265
Amos, C. W. Hale 239
Anderson, J. N. D. (Sir Norman)
    309, 319, 351
Ashton, T. S. 3
Atkinson, James 351

Baker, Frank 19, 351
Baker, W. J. 351
Balleine, G. R. 19, 25, 32, 34, 102,
    120, 145, 147-9, 152f., 155-8,
    164-6, 178, 213, 220f., 351
Barclay, Oliver R. 193
Barlow, H. 260
Barlow, Margaret 168f.
Barnes, E. W. 238, 295
Barnes, John 281, 352
Barnes-Lawrence, A. E. 261
Barr, James 292, 308f., 352
Bateman, Josiah 54, 106, 352
Battiscombe, G. 196
Baughen, Michael A. 328
Bayley, Mrs 202
Beckwith, Roger T. 352
Beeson, Trevor 352
Bell, G. K. A. 228f., 237, 277, 352
Bennet, G. D. 5, 363
Bennett, Dennis 332
Bennett, G. V. 34
Bennett, W. J. E. 129
Benson, Frank J. 44, 352
Bentley, Anne 128, 142, 173, 176f.,
    180f., 185f., 190, 195, 218f., 222,
    352
Berkeley, George 5
Berridge, John 43n.8, 52
Best, G. 352
Bickersteth, E. H. 132
Birks, T. R. 139
Black, J. S. 244
Bloss, W. Escott 233

Bonney, T. G. 141
Bradley, Ian C. 79f., 89f., 96, 103,
    208, 221, 352
Braithwaite, Robert 150f., 352
Bready, J. Wesley 3, 5, 103, 352
Bridges, Robert 294
Brierly, Peter 352
Briggs, Asa 63f.
Brilioth, Y. 352
Bromiley, Geoffrey W. 352
Broomhall, A. J. 219
Brown, Colin 309
Brown, Ford K. 79, 90, 103, 105,
    208, 352
Browning, W. R. F. 352
Bruce, F. F. 309
Bruce, Steve 352
Buchanan, Colin O. 322, 324, 332,
    334, 340, 352f.
Buckland, A. R. 245
Bullock, Charles 148
Bullock, F. W. B. 184, 353
Butler, Joseph 6f.
Buxton, Charles 86

Cadogan, W. B. 28, 353
Calder, Angus 281, 353
Capon, John 288, 290, 353
Carey, George 330
Carlyle, A. J. 261f.
Carpenter, Humphrey 353
Carpenter, S. C. 5, 65-7, 77, 112,
    123, 133, 136, 164-6, 211, 353
Carus, William 70f., 76, 97, 353
Catherwood, Christopher 287, 344,
    353
Catherwood, H. F. R. 309
Cecil, David 41f., 57, 353
Chadwick, Owen 111, 123, 131,
    133, 142, 148, 353
Chadwick, W. Edward 261, 276
Charley, Julian 346, 349
Chavasse, F. J. 266
Cheyne, T. K. 244
Christensen, T. 209, 353

Index of Persons

Unless otherwise indicated, tenure of last post mentioned lasted until death.

Garbett, James (1802-79); Bampton
Lecturer, 1842; Archdeacon of
Chichester, 1851) 139
Gardiner, Allen (1794-1850) 220
Garratt, Samuel (1817-1906) 190,
236
Garrick, David (1717-79) 100
George I (1660-1727) 1f., 8
George II (1683-1760) 1, 8
George III (1738-1820) 69, 83
George IV (1762-1830) 154
Gibson, Edmund (1669-1748; Bishop
of Lincoln, 1716; of London, 1720)
115
Gilbert, John (1693-1761; Archbishop
of York, 1757) 39
Gillies, William 236
Girdlestone, R. B. (Principal of
Wycliffe Hall, Oxford, 1877-89)
184, 236
Gisborne, Thomas (1758-1846) 84
Gladstone, William Ewart (1809-98)
51, 67, 105, 119f., 125, 140, 159
Gladwin, John 320, 356
Glazebrook, Michael George
(1853-1926; Headmaster of
Clifton, 1891-1905) 248
Glenelg, Lord (1778-1866) 105
Gloucester, Bishop of 50, 70 (Ryder)
Gloucester & Bristol, Bishop of 158
(W. Thomson), 159 (Ellicott)
Glover, Terrot Reaveley (1869-1943)
243
Glyn, Edward Carr (Vicar of St Mary
Abbots, Kensington, fl. 1880)
180
Gobat (of Darlington) 257
Golightly, Charles Pourtales
(1807-85) 115
Goode, William (1801-68) 116f., 139
Goodwin, Charles Wycliffe (1817-78)
136
Gordon, General Charles George
(1833-85) 202, 218
Gore, Charles (1853-1932; Principal
of Pusey House, 1884; Bishop of
Worcester, 1901; of Birmingham,
1904; of Oxford, 1911-19;
Bampton Lecturer, 1891) 141f.,
209f., 249, 273, 277, 360f.,

Gorham, George Cornelius
(1787-1857) 123-5, 156, 161
Graham, Billy (William George) (b.
1918) 288, 290, 293, 298, 313f.,
316, 360
Grant, Charles (1746-1823) 79, 83f.,
87, 211, 221
Green, John (1706-79; Dean of
Lincoln, 1756; Bishop of Lincoln,
1761) 39
Green, Michael (E. M. B.) (b.1930);
Principal of St John's College,
Nottingham, 1969; Rector of St
Aldate's, Oxford, 1975) 307, 309,
312
Green, S. F. (fl. 1880) 130f.
Greer, William Derrick Lindsay
(Bishop of Manchester, 1947-70)
126
Grenville, Thomas (1750-1842) 51
Grimshaw, William (1708-63; Vicar
of Haworth, 1742) 11, 20, 24-7,
29f., 39, 44, 47, 56, 354
Grosvenor family 69
Guest, Henry J. 236
Guthrie, Donald 309

Habershon, A. W. (Principal of Oak
Hill College) 269
Haldane, Alexander 96, 102, 183
Haldane, Robert (1764-1842) 96
Hamilton, Walter Kerr (1808-60;
Bishop of Salisbury, 1854) 119
Hammond, John (fl. 1782) 72
Hammond, Thomas Chatterton (b.
1908) 296
Hampden, Renn Dickson (1793-1868;
Bishop of Hereford, 1848;
Bampton Lecturer, 1832) 114
Hannington, James (1847-85; Bishop
of Eastern Equatorial Africa, 1884)
215, 218, 354
Harford-Battersby, T. D. (1822-83)
138, 192
Hargreaves, James (d. 1778) 4
Harnack, Adolf von (1851-1930) 243
Harper, Michael Claude (b. 1931)
333
Harris, Howel (1714-73) 9, 188
Harrowby, Dudley, 1st Earl of
(1762-1847) 69f., 159

Index of Places

In general, pre-1972 County names are used. But for ease of reference, 'London' includes districts now in the Metropolis, though formerly in the Home Counties of Essex, Kent, Middlesex, or Surrey.

Abeokuta, Nigeria 217
Aberdeen 188, 265
Abyssinia 214
Ahoghill, Co. Antrim 187
Aldwinckle, Northants 48, 57, 97
Alstone, Glos 146
Alton, Hants 156
Armagh 188
Aston (Birimingham) 272, 324
Aston Sandford, Bucks 39n.5
Australia 88, 211

Ballymena, Co. Antrim 187
Barnet, Herts 150f., 190
Bath, Somerset 47. 147
Bedford 270
Bedfordshire 43
Belfast 175, 194, 265
Belper, Derbyshire 231
Berkhamsted, Herts 40
Bermondsey, London 203, 207
Bethnal Green, London 207
Bexley, Kent 31
Bideford, Devon 20
Bierley, Yorks 35
Birkenhead, Cheshire 83
Birmingham 3, 70, 147, 150n.15, 171, 175, 258, 265, 272
Blackpool, Lancs 273
Blackwall, London 203
Bolivia 220
Boston, Mass. 187
Botany Bay, Australia 88
Bow, London 175
Bradford, Yorks 32, 35, 76, 147
Brazil 221
Brecknock (Brecon) 9
Brighton, Sussex 47, 127, 150n.15 162, 191
Bristol 18, 31, 34, 36, 56, 180, 267f.

British Guiana 214
Buganda, East Africa 215f., 218
Buxton, Derbyshire 232

Camberwell, London 203
Cambridge 47f., 71, 74, 98, 111, 175, 193f., 219; *see also* Cambridge churches; Cambridge University; theological colleges (*all in* General Index)
Cambridgeshire 43
Canada 274, 329
Cardiff 202
Cardiganshire 188
Ceylon 214, 219
Channel Islands 155f.
Charing Cross, London 206
Cheltenham, Glos 47, 76, 145-7, 149, 191
Cheshire 25, 157
Chichester, Sussex 76
Chile 221
China 176, 194, 214, 218
Christchurch, Hants 156
Clapham, London 46, 49, 79-81, 83, 93, 105, 216
Claybrook, Leics 69
Clerkenwell, London 203
Clifton, Glos 76, 147
Coggeshall, Essex 259
Colchester, Essex 76
Coleraine, Co. Derry 188
Colne, Lancs 26
Cologne, Germany 282
Connor, Co. Antrim 187
Cornwall 4, 18, 20-3, 32, 67
Cornwood, Cornwall 32
Coventry, Warwickshire 3, 257
Creaton, Northants 34
Croydon, Surrey 162

General Index

Dates when societies, journals, etc, were founded have been added.

abolitionists 58, 76-8, 82, 84-7, 90-3, 211, 221n.18
academic study and Evangelicals
  appointments, university 104f., 159, 167, 274, 289, 296
  and doctrinal issues 297, 304-8
  obscurantism 142, 297
  research 287f., 295
  theological studies 184, 267-70, 289, 291
  (*see also* biblical criticism; fundamentalism; publications, Evangelical)
African Association (1788) 88
African Institution (1807) 88
All Saints, Lewes, Sussex 127
Alternative Services Book (1980) 322f.
Anglican Consultative Council (1969) 348
Anglican Evangelicals, early
  acceptability, social 68, 201f.
  achievements 50-60
  development 10-13, 19-32, 37, 66
  distinctiveness 11-13, 19, 33, 35, 37
  identity 33f.
  intolerance, shown by some 106; but not all 156
  leaders, national 49, 202
  maligned 50, 67, 69
  minority 19, 50, 67, 103
  mutual support 33f., 48, 75, 84
  opposition to 20, 26f., 47, 57, 72f.
Anglican Evangelicals and Methodists
  co-operation 26, 31, 45-7
  differences 11-13, 19, 36f.
  influence 11, 30

  union, attempts at 11, 35f., 289, 291, 338-41
Anglican-Rome Catholic International Commission (ARCIC) 289, 343
Annals of the Poor (Legh Richmond, 1809-10) 100f.
Anti-Maynooth Committee (1845) 115
apologetics, lay-written 294
apostasy, national 111, 121, 294
apostolic succession, doctrine of 112f.
Arethusa training ship (1874) 199
Arminian-Calvinistic divide 10-13, 35, 52, 74f., 97
Articles, Thirty-Nine
  biblically based 52, 68
  subscription to 114, 120, 136, 242
  doctrinal standard 129, 131, 230
  Calvinism, moderate 164
  and sacraments 324, 338
Assize Sermon, Keble's (1833) 111
atonement 244, 251, 261
authority
  of bible 138f., 230, 252f., 301, 320, 330, 335, 341
  of Fathers 116f.
  Tractarian view 116f.

Bampton Lectures 139, 273, 306
Band of Hope movement (1847) 205
baptism
  and Christian Socialists 209
  doctrine 97, 101n.8, 324
  Gorham case 123-5, 156, 161
  numbers for, increase under Evangelicals 51
  practice 324f.